THE GLOBAL
ENVIRONMENT

THE GLOBAL ENVIRONMENT

INSTITUTIONS, LAW, AND POLICY

Second Edition

Edited by

Regina S. Axelrod
Adelphi University

David Leonard Downie
Columbia University

Norman J. Vig
Carleton College

CQ PRESS

A Division of Congressional Quarterly Inc.
Washington, D.C.

CQ Press
2300 N Street, N.W., Suite 800
Washington, D.C. 20037

Phone: 202-729-1900; toll-free, 1-866-4CQ-PRESS (1-866-427-7737)

Web: www.cqpress.com

Printed and bound in the United States of America

11   10   09   08   07   2   3   4   5   6

⊗ The paper used in this publication exceeds the requirements of the American National Standard for Information Sciences—Permanence of Paper for Printed Library Materials, ANSI Z39.48-1992.

Library of Congress Cataloging-in-Publication Data

The global environment : institutions, law, and policy / edited by Regina S. Axelrod, David Leonard Downie, Norman J. Vig -- 2nd ed.
    p. cm.
  Includes bibliographical references and index.
  ISBN 1-56802-827-X (alk. paper).
  1. Environmental law, International. 2. Environmental policy. I. Axelrod, Regina S. II.
    Downie, David Leonard. III. Vig, Norman J. IV. Title

K3585.4.G58 2005
344.04'6--dc22   2004013762

For
Lenny and Gregg
Laura, William, and Lindsay
Carol

Contents

III. Implementing Global Policy: Cases and Controversies in Sustainable Development

Preface

This volume is designed to meet the need for an authoritative collection of readings on international environmental institutions, laws, and policies at the beginning of the twenty-first century. Although there are numerous texts in individual disciplinary fields, we have brought together original essays by distinguished American and European scholars who span the traditional boundaries between political science, international relations, international law, policy studies, and comparative politics. We believe that only by integrating the perspectives of diverse fields can we begin to address the enormous complexities of global environmental problems.

The introductory chapter explains some of the most important concepts derived from these fields for the study of international environmental law and policy. These include basic perspectives on international cooperation drawn from international relations theory, the nature of international institutions and policy regimes, and the concept of sustainable development. The first two sections of the book focus on the development of global environmental institutions, laws, regimes, and policies. The third section presents case studies of national and regional implementation of international environmental and sustainable development policies. Linkages between national and international actors, as well as between official institutions and nongovernmental organizations, are discussed throughout the book.

In one sense, all serious environmental threats are now international in scope, given that nearly all forms of pollution, use of resources, and destabilization of natural ecosystems have implications for the sustainability of life as we know it. Global biogeochemical cycles circulate materials and energy throughout the planetary biosphere, and losses of Earth's inherited biodiversity and mineral resources are irreversible. The consumption of resources by one country or group of people ultimately affects the life chances of other— and much larger—segments of the human population, including all those in future generations.

The nations of the world have begun to deal with many of the most obvious environmental threats over the past century, particularly since the twin imperatives of ecological sustainability and development of the world's poorest economies were put on the global agenda at the United Nations Conference on the Human Environment, held in Stockholm in 1972. The concept of sustainable development, articulated in the 1987 report of the World Commission on Environment and Development and in the United Nations Conference on Environment and Development, held in Rio de Janeiro in 1992, established a broad intellectual framework and agenda for action by the international community. Commitments to the implementation of this agenda were discussed by representatives of 191 nations at the World Summit on Sustainable Development, held in Johannesburg in 2002.

Despite this hopeful progress, the prospects for attaining the levels of international cooperation necessary to manage the impact of humans on the natural life-support systems of the planet remain grim. The authors of this book have all been asked to evaluate initial steps toward strengthening international policies and institutions to achieve the goals of sustainable development set out in 1992. Although some advances are documented, the record to date is not encouraging. The political will to make substantial economic and political changes appears to be lacking in most parts of the world. The declining leadership of the United States in international environmental policymaking is sadly even more striking than it was when the first edition of this book was published in 1999.

Disagreements over the meaning of sustainable development as well as problems in implementing environmental policies are evident throughout this book. Several contributors note the persistence of deep cleavages among "developed," "developing," and "transitional" states in various regions of the world. Political differences among the United States, Europe, and the developing world have widened rather than narrowed in recent years (chapters 10–12). Projects such as the Three Gorges Dam in China (chapter 13) and expansion of nuclear power in the Czech Republic (chapter 14) raise profound questions about the trade-offs that may be required to achieve sustainable development and about the role of international financial interests in promoting incompatible forms of development.

We hope this second edition will be even more useful as a text in college and university courses than the first edition was and that it will also be of interest to a broad range of scholars, professionals, and citizens who are concerned about the state of the global environment. It is a companion volume to *Environmental Policy: New Directions for the Twenty-first Century,* edited by Norman J. Vig and Michael E. Kraft, also published by CQ Press and now in its fifth edition. Attentive readers will notice that our publisher follows style guidelines set forth in the fifteenth edition of *The Chicago Manual of Style* in capitalizing the names of legislative, administrative, and judicial entities only upon mention of the full name of such entities.

We wish to acknowledge the support of our colleagues and staff at Adelphi University, Columbia University, and Carleton College, without whom we would not have been able to complete the project. Regina S. Axelrod owes thanks to the National Science Foundation for a grant (SBR-9708180) that allowed her to study nuclear power development in the Czech Republic; to colleagues at Charles University, Prague; and to many anonymous officials there and at the Environment Directorate of the European Commission, who facilitated her research. She also extends special gratitude to her long-suffering secretary, Pat Koslowski. Finally, all of the editors express their appreciation to Brenda Carter and Charisse Kiino of CQ Press for their encouragement and assistance throughout this project. They also extend their gratitude to manuscript editor Janet Wilson and production editor Joan Gossett, also of CQ Press. Any remaining errors are, of course, the authors' responsibility.

Regina S. Axelrod
David Leonard Downie
Norman J. Vig

Selected Acronyms in Global Environmental Policy

AMAP	Arctic Monitoring and Assessment Programme[1]
AOSIS	Alliance of Small Island States
ASEAN	Association of South East Asian Nations[2]
BAT	Best Available Technology
BEP	Best Environmental Practices
CBD	Convention on Biological Diversity[3]
CDM	Clean Development Mechanism under the Kyoto Protocol
CDR	Common but Differentiated Responsibilities
CEC	Commission for Environmental Cooperation (North America)[4]
CEE	Central and Eastern Europe
CEIT	Countries with Economies in Transition
CFCs	Chlorofluorocarbons
CITES	Convention on International Trade in Endangered Species[5]
CLRTAP	Convention on Long-range Transboundary Air Pollution[6]
COP	Conference of the Parties
CSD	Commission on Sustainable Development[7]
EC	European Community
ECOSOC	United Nations Economic and Social Council[8]
EIA	Environmental Impact Assessment
EPA	Environmental Protection Agency (USA)[9]
EU	European Union[10]
FAO	Food and Agriculture Organization of the United Nations[11]
G-77	Group of 77 (developing country negotiating block)[12]
GATT	General Agreement on Tariffs and Trade
GEF	Global Environment Facility[13]
GEMS	Global Environmental Monitoring Systems
GHGs	Greenhouse Gases
GIS	Geographic Information Systems
GPA	Global Programme of Action for the Protection of the Marine Environment from Land-Based Activities
GRID	Global Resource Information Database
HABITAT	United Nations Centre for Human Settlements[14]
IAEA	International Atomic Energy Agency[15]
IDA	International Development Agency
IFCS	Intergovernmental Forum on Chemical Safety[16]
IGO	Intergovernmental Organization
ILO	International Labor Organization[17]
IMF	International Monetary Fund[18]

IMO	International Maritime Organization[19]
INC	Intergovernmental Negotiating Committee
IOMC	Inter-Organization Programme for the Sound Management of Chemicals[20]
IPCC	Intergovernmental Panel on Climate Change[21]
IPCS	International Programme on Chemical Safety[22]
IRTC	International Registry of Toxic Chemicals
IUCN	World Conservation Union[23]
MARPOL	International Convention for the Prevention of Pollution from Ships[24]
MEA	Multilateral Environmental Agreement
NAFTA	North American Free Trade Agreement
NAM	Non-Aligned Movement
NGO	Nongovernmental Organization
NIEO	New International Economic Order
NIP	National Implementation Plan
ODS	Ozone Depleting Substance(s)
OECD	Organization for Economic Cooperation and Development[25]
PIC	Prior Informed Consent[26]
POPs	Persistent Organic Pollutants[27]
REIO	Regional Economic Integration Organization
SAICM	Strategic Approach to International Chemicals Management[28]
UN	United Nations[29]
UNCCD	United Nations Convention to Combat Desertification[30]
UNCED	United Nations Conference on Environment and Development, 1992
UNCHE	United Nations Conference on the Human Environment, 1972
UNCTAD	United Nations Conference on Trade and Development[31]
UNDP	United Nations Development Programme[32]
UNEP	United Nations Environment Programme[33]
UNEP GC	UNEP Governing Council
UNESCO	United Nations Educational, Scientific and Cultural Organization[34]
UNFCCC	United Nations Framework Convention on Climate Change[35]
UNFPA	United Nations Population Fund[36]
UNICEF	United Nations Children's Fund[37]
UNIDO	United Nations Industrial Development Organization[38]
UNITAR	United Nations Institute for Training and Research[39]
WCO	World Customs Organization[40]
WHO	World Health Organization[41]
WMO	World Meteorological Organization[42]
WSSD	World Summit on Sustainable Development, 2002[43]
WTO	World Trade Organization[44]
WWF	World Wide Fund for Nature[45]

Notes

1. www.amap.no
2. www.aseansec.org/home.htm
3. www.biodiv.org
4. www.cec.org
5. www.cites.org
6. www.unece.org/env/lrtap
7. www.un.org/esa/sustdev/csd/csd12/csd12.htm
8. www.un.org/esa/coordination/ecosoc
9. www.epa.gov
10. www.europa.eu.int
11. www.fao.org
12. www.g77.org
13. www.gefweb.org
14. www.unhabitat.org
15. www.iaea.org
16. www.who.int/ifcs
17. www.ilo.org
18. www.imf.org
19. www.imo.org
20. www.who.int/iomc/en
21. www.ipcc.ch
22. www.who.int/pcs
23. www.iucn.org
24. www.imo.org/home.asp
25. www.oecd.org
26. www.pic.int
27. www.pops.int
28. www.chem.unep.ch/saicm
29. www.un.org
30. www.unccd.int/main.php
31. www.unctad.org
32. www.undp.org
33. www.unep.org
34. www.unesco.org
35. http://unfccc.int
36. www.unfpa.org
37. www.unicef.org
38. www.unido.org
39. www.unitar.org
40. www.wcoomd.org
41. www.who.org
42. www.wmo.ch/index-en.html
43. www.johannesburgsummit.org
44. www.wto.org
45. www.panda.org

Global Environmental Policy
A Brief Chronology

1900   First multinational treaty to protect endangered species signed

1909   Treaty between the United States and Great Britain Respecting Boundary Waters; International Joint Commission formed

1911   Treaty for the Preservation and Protection of Fur Seals

1933   London Convention on the Preservation of Fauna and Flora in Their Natural State

1940   Convention on Nature Protection and Wildlife Preservation in the Western Hemisphere

1941   Final decision of Trail Smelter arbitration

1944   United States and Mexico adopt Treaty on Colorado and Tijuana Rivers

1945   United Nations created

1946   International Bank for Reconstruction and Development (World Bank) created
International Convention on the Regulation of Whaling

1948   International Maritime Organization (IMO) created
International Union for Conservation of Nature (IUCN) founded

1949   International Convention for the North-West Atlantic Fisheries
United Nations Conference on Conservation and Utilization of Resources

1950   World Meteorological Organization (WMO) created
International Convention for the Protection of Birds

1952   Four thousand people die in the worst of the London "killer fogs"

1954   International Convention for the Prevention of Pollution of Sea by Oil

1957   International Atomic Energy Agency (IAEA) created
Treaty of Rome establishing European Economic Community

1961   World Wildlife Fund established

1963   Agreement for the Protection of the Rhine against Pollution
Nuclear Test Ban Treaty

1965   United Nations Development Program (UNDP) created

1971   UNESCO's Man and the Biosphere program launched
        Ramsar Convention on Wetlands of International Importance
        Greenpeace established

1972   Conference on the Human Environment (often referred to as
            the Stockholm Conference), the first global environmental
            conference
        United Nations Environment Programme (UNEP) created
        UNESCO Convention Concerning the Protection of the World
            Cultural and Natural Heritage (World Heritage Convention)

1973   Convention on International Trade in Endangered Species of Wild
            Fauna and Flora (CITES)
        International Convention for the Prevention of Pollution from
            Ships (MARPOL)

1974   World Population Conference, Bucharest
        M. J. Molina and F. S. Rowland publish their theory that CFCs
            threaten the ozone layer

1976   Convention for the Protection of the Mediterranean Sea Against
            Pollution
        United Nations Conference on Human Settlements, Vancouver

1977   UNEP International Register of Potentially Toxic Chemicals
            (IRPTC)
        UN Conference on Desertification

1978   CFCs in spray cans banned in the United States

1979   Convention on the Conservation of Migratory Species (CMS)
        Convention on Long-Range Transboundary Air Pollution
            (CLRTAP)

1980   Convention on the Conservation of Antarctic Marine Living
            Resources

1982   United Nations Convention on the Law of the Sea (UNCLOS)

1983   International Tropical Timber Agreement

1985   Vienna Convention for Protection of the Ozone Layer
        Discovery of the Antarctic ozone hole

1987   Montreal Protocol on Substances That Deplete the Ozone Layer
        World Commission on Environment and Development publishes
            "Our Common Future" (Bruntland Commission Report)

1989   Basel Convention on the Control of Transboundary Movements of
            Hazardous Wastes and Their Disposal
        Oil spilled in the Gulf of Alaska by the *Exxon Valdez*

1991   Global Environment Facility (GEF) created
       Convention on the Ban of the Import into Africa and the Control
          of Transboundary Movement and Management of Hazardous
          Wastes within Africa

1992   United Nations Conference on Environment and Development
          (UNCED), also known as the Earth Summit, Rio de Janeiro
       United Nations Framework Convention on Climate Change
          (UNFCCC)
       Convention on Biological Diversity (CBD)
       Rio Declaration
       Agenda 21
       Maastricht Treaty establishing the European Union
       Commission on Sustainable Development created
       Construction of Three Gorges Dam approved by Chinese
          parliament

1993   North American Free Trade Agreement (NAFTA) signed

1994   United Nations Convention to Combat Desertification (UNCCD)
       United Nations Conference on Population and Development,
          Cairo
       World Trade Organization (WTO) established

1997   Kyoto Protocol to the FCCC

1998   Rotterdam Convention on the Prior Informed Consent (PIC)
          Procedure for Certain Hazardous Chemicals and Pesticides in
          International Trade

2001   Stockholm Convention on Persistent Organic Pollutants
       United States rejects Kyoto Protocol

2002   UN World Summit on Sustainable Development (Johannesburg
          Summit)

Contributors

Regina S. Axelrod is professor of political science and chair of the political science department at Adelphi University. She has published numerous articles and books on environmental and energy policy in the United States, the European Union, and Central Europe, including *Conflict between Energy and Urban Environment: Consolidated Edison versus the City of New York* (1982) and *Environment, Energy, Public Policy: Toward a Rational Future* (1981). She has lectured at Charles University in Prague and the University of Budapest on nuclear power and the transition to democracy. She is an academic associate of the Atlantic Council and past president of the New York Political Science Association.

Michele M. Betsill is assistant professor of political science at Colorado State University, where she specializes in international relations and global environmental politics. She has published several articles and book chapters on the governance of global climate change and is coauthor with Harriet Bulkeley of *Cities and Climate Change: Urban Sustainability and Global Environmental Governance* (2003).

Elizabeth R. DeSombre is Frost Associate Professor of Environmental Studies and associate professor of political science at Wellesley College. Her first book, *Domestic Sources of International Environmental Policy: Industry, Environmentalists, and U.S. Power* (2000) won two book prizes. She has also published *The Global Environment and World Politics* (2002).

David Leonard Downie is director of the Earth Institute Fellows Program at Columbia University. He has written extensively on global environmental politics and international relations, including *Northern Lights against POPs: Combatting Toxic Threats in the Arctic* (2003), coedited with Terry Fenge. He has taught courses in international environmental politics at Columbia University since 1994 and served as Director of Environmental Policy Studies at Columbia's School of International and Public Affairs from 1994 to 1999.

Daniel C. Esty is director of the Yale Center for Environmental Law and Policy and a professor at the Yale School of Forestry and Environmental Studies. He also holds an appointment at the Yale Law School and is director of the Yale World Fellows Program. He formerly served at the Environmental Protection Agency as special assistant to administrator William Reilly, as deputy chief of staff, and as deputy assistant administrator for policy. He is the author or editor of a number of articles and five books on trade and the environment, including *Greening the Americas: NAFTA's lessons for Hemispheric Trade* (2002), *Regulatory Competition and Economic Integration: Comparative Perspectives* (2001), *Sustaining the Asia Pacific Miracle: Environmental Protection and Economic Integration* (1997), and *Greening the GATT: Trade, Environment, and the Future* (1994).

Michael Faure is professor of comparative and international environmental law at Maastricht University, the Netherlands. He is academic director of the Maastricht Institute for Transnational Legal Research (METRO). He has published widely in the area of environmental criminal law. With Jürgen Lefevere, he has written articles on the issue of environmental federalism within the European Union.

Jonathan Krueger works with the Chemicals and Waste Management Programme of the United Nations Institute for Training and Research (UNITAR). He holds a PhD from the London School of Economics and Political Science and has previously published on international chemicals and waste management issues.

Jürgen Lefevere is administrator at the Climate Change and Energy Unit of the Environment Directorate General of the European Commission in Brussels, Belgium. From October 1998 until August 2003 he worked at the London-based Foundation for International Environmental Law and Development (FIELD), where he was programme director of the Climate Change and Energy Programme. He is a former legal adviser of the Alliance of Small Island States (AOSIS) and from 1998 until 2003 participated in the international climate change negotiations as a representative of Samoa. Lefevere has a degree in administrative and European community law from the University of Maastricht (the Netherlands). He has also lectured on EU environmental law at the Universities of Amsterdam, the University of Maastricht, the University of Lomé (Togo), the London School of Economics and Political Science, and the School of Oriental and African Studies (London), and is currently a guest lecturer at the University of Leuven (Belgium) and University College London.

John McCormick is professor and chair of the Department of Political Science at the Indianapolis campus of Indiana University, where he specializes in comparative politics, environmental policy, and the politics of the European Union. During the 1980s he worked for two London-based environmental NGOs, the World Wildlife Fund, and the International Institute for Environment and Development. He is author of *Environmental Policy in the European Union* (2001) and *The Global Environmental Movement*, 2nd edition (1995).

Adil Najam is an associate professor at the Fletcher School of Law and Diplomacy, Tufts University. He serves on the board of the Pakistan Institute for Environment–Development Action Research and is a fellow at the International Institute for Sustainable Development. His recent books include *Environment, Development and Human Security: Perspectives from South Asia* (2003) and *Civic Entrepreneurship: A Civil Society Perspective on Sustainable Development* (2002).

Jacqueline Peel is currently a lecturer with the Law Faculty, University of Melbourne. She holds an LLM from New York University, where she studied as a Fulbright scholar. During 2003–2004 she was a research fellow with the Jean Monnet Center at NYU. Her research focuses on international environmental law, with recent research projects including a book on the precautionary principle.

Philippe Sands is professor of laws and director of the Centre for International Courts and Tribunals at University College London. He is also a practicing barrister with Matrix Chambers. He served as legal adviser on the delegation of St. Lucia during the negotiations on the climate change convention and at the United Nations Conference on Environment and Development and as legal counsel in several of the cases mentioned in his chapter.

Miranda A. Schreurs is an associate professor in the Department of Government and Politics at the University of Maryland. Her research focuses on comparative environmental and energy politics. Her many publications include *Ecological Security in Northeast Asia* (1998), coedited with Dennis Pirages, and *The Internationalization of Environmental Protection* (1997), coedited with Elizabeth Economy.

Henrik Selin is assistant professor of international relations at Boston University, where he conducts research and teaches classes on international cooperation and policymaking on environment and sustainability issues. He has published several articles and book chapters on international chemicals management.

Marvin S. Soroos is professor of political science and public administration at North Carolina State University, where he teaches courses on global environmental politics, law, and policy. During the spring semester of 2003 he was the class of 1946 visiting professor of international environmental studies at Williams College. His research has focused on the management of global commons, in particular the atmosphere, oceans, and outer space. Among his books are *The Endangered Atmosphere: Managing a Global Commons* (1997) and *Beyond Sovereignty: The Challenge of Global Policy* (1986).

Lawrence R. Sullivan is associate professor of political science at Adelphi University and a research associate at the East Asian Institute, Columbia University. He has also taught at Wellesley College, Miami University, and the University of Michigan, Ann Arbor. He is coeditor and cotranslator with Dai Qing of *The River Dragon Has Come! The Three Gorges Dam and the Fate of the Yangtze River and Its People* (1997); coauthor of *Historical Dictionary of the People's Republic of China, 1949–1997* (1997); and editor and translator of numerous other books and articles on China.

Norman J. Vig is Winifred and Atherton Bean Professor of Science, Technology, and Society, Emeritus, at Carleton College. He has written extensively on environmental policy, science and technology policy, and comparative politics and is coeditor with Michael E. Kraft of *Environmental Policy: New Directions for the Twenty-first Century*, 5th edition (CQ Press, 2003). His most recent book is *Green Giants? Environmental Policies of the United States and the European Union* (2004), coedited with Michael Faure.

1

Introduction: Governing the International Environment

Norman J. Vig

At the dawn of the twenty-first century, the Earth's physical and biological systems are under unprecedented strain. The human population reached 6.3 billion in 2003 and is projected to increase to about 9 billion in the next half century. The United Nations estimates that one-third of the world's people live in countries with moderate to high shortages of fresh water and that this percentage could double by 2025. Many of the world's largest cities are increasingly choked by pollution. As carbon dioxide and other greenhouse gases build in the atmosphere, the average surface temperature of the Earth has reached the highest level ever measured on an annual basis. The biological diversity of the planet is also under heavy stress. Scientists believe that a mass extinction of plants and animals is under way and predict that a quarter of all species could be pushed to extinction by 2050 as a consequence of global warming alone. Without question, the human impact on the biosphere will be one of the most critical issues of the century.[1]

Threats to the Earth's flora and fauna, water systems, and atmosphere have been recognized by scientists and conservationists for more than a century, but it is only in the past three decades that nations have begun to address these issues on a global scale. The 1972 United Nations Conference on the Human Environment in Stockholm, Sweden, attended by 113 states, marked the beginning of organized international efforts to devise a comprehensive agenda to safeguard the environment while also promoting economic development.[2] Although no binding treaties were adopted at Stockholm, the United Nations Environment Programme (UNEP) was established, creating a permanent forum for monitoring global environmental trends, convening international meetings and conferences, and negotiating international agreements. Among its most important achievements were the Vienna Convention for the Protection of the Ozone Layer in 1985 and the binding Montreal Protocol on Substances That Deplete the Ozone Layer in 1987.[3] In 1987 the World Commission on Environment and Development (known as the Brundtland Commission, after its chair, the former Norwegian prime minister Gro Harlem Brundtland) issued its historic report, *Our Common Future,* calling for a new era of "sustainable development."[4] To begin implementing this strategy, the UN Conference on Environment and Development (UNCED), known as the Earth Summit, was convened in Rio de Janeiro, Brazil, in June 1992. The conference produced major international treaties on climate change and biodiversity, as well as two declarations of principle and a lengthy action program (Agenda 21) for implementing sustainable development throughout the world. Ten years later, in August 2002, 191 nations attended the World Summit on Sustainable Development (WSSD) in Johannesburg, South Africa, to reassess and renew commitments to sustainable development.[5]

As a result of these and other diplomatic achievements, a system for global environmental governance now exists. This system consists of three main elements:[6]

- intergovernmental organizations (IGOs) such as UNEP, the UN Development Programme, the Commission on Sustainable Development, the World Meteorological Organization, and dozens of specific treaty organizations (see Chapter 2)
- a framework of international environmental law based on several hundred multilateral treaties and agreements (see Chapter 3)
- financing institutions and mechanisms to carry out treaty commitments and build capacity in developing countries, including the World Bank and specialized lending agencies such as the Multilateral Fund and the Global Environment Facility

In addition, there are hundreds of bilateral and regional treaties and organizations such as those involving the United Nations Regional Seas Programme and the European Union (see Chapter 11) that deal with more limited transboundary and shared resource issues. By one count, there are more than 900 international agreements with some environmental provisions.[7]

Especially in the past decade, a host of nongovernmental organizations (NGOs), including international environmental interest groups, scientific bodies, business and trade associations, women's groups, and indigenous peoples' organizations, have also come to play an important role in international environmental governance (see Chapter 5). These organizations participate in international negotiations, help to monitor treaty compliance, and often play a leading role in implementing policies. At the Johannesburg summit, more than 20,000 individuals registered as participants and countless others attended a parallel Global People's Forum and summit of indigenous peoples.[8] The increased access to and transparency of international environmental governance is one of the most remarkable achievements of the past decade.

Despite these strides, there is a growing perception that the current international governance system remains weak and ineffective.[9] Many of the international environmental institutions lack adequate funding and effective enforcement mechanisms. Because there is no world government or sovereign political authority, international agencies often work at cross purposes and must rely on individual states to carry out their policies. States are reluctant to relinquish their sovereignty and right to pursue their own national interests. Consequently, it appears that many patterns of global environmental degradation have not been reversed and may result in devastating ecological crises unless global institutions are strengthened and many other actors (including private organizations and citizens) take on far more responsibility for environmental governance.[10]

The role of the United States in international environmental diplomacy has been especially disappointing in recent years. Although the Clinton administration signed the 1997 Kyoto Protocol, which set targets and timetables for reducing greenhouse gas emissions that may cause global warming, neither this treaty nor others such as the Convention on Biological Diversity were ratified by the U.S. Senate. President George W. Bush repudiated the Kyoto Protocol in 2001 and has shown little interest in other multilateral environmental agreements and institutions. U.S. support for international environmental programs has declined. This indifference has resulted in deepening divisions between the United States and both the European Union and the developing nations of the "South" (see Chapters 10–12).[11]

This book presents an overview of the development of international environmental institutions, law, and policies and attempts to assess their adequacy. The authors analyze developments since World War II, with special emphasis on trends since the Earth Summit of 1992. They share some of the current pessimism about trends in global environmental governance in the past decade, but take a longer view in evaluating the new environmental regimes that are emerging.

The next two sections of this chapter provide a brief overview of the theoretical context for studying international environmental governance. The first of these summarizes the most important perspectives from international relations theory relevant to the emergence of international environmental institutions and law. The second section discusses the concept of "sustainable development," which became the dominant ideological framework for global environmental policies in the 1990s. The third section of the chapter outlines the organization and contents of the book, briefly discussing each of the three parts: (I) international environmental law, institutions, and regimes, (II) global environmental policies and policy implementation, and (III) national and regional case studies and controversies in sustainable development. A short conclusion summarizes some of the themes of the book.

International Relations, Regimes, and Governance

A large body of international relations theory is applicable to the development of international environmental institutions and agreements (see Chapter 4).[12] The study of international relations has traditionally been dominated by two broad theoretical schools: realism and liberalism. "Realists" view the world as an anarchic collection of sovereign nation-states, each of which is a unitary actor in pursuing its unique national interests. These interests are largely defined in terms of relative power and security as compared with other states. In this perspective, nation-states do not cooperate with one another unless it is clearly in their self-interest to do so, and cooperative behavior will continue only so long as the parties perceive this condition to be met. International laws and institutions are thus essentially instruments for promoting or defending national interests and have little or no independent effect on the behavior of nations. Indeed, they can usually function only if strong or "hegemonic" states maintain them and enforce their decisions against weaker members or other states. The potential for international cooperation is therefore quite limited, and international laws and institutions are likely to be fragile and impermanent.[13]

This anarchic, state-centered perspective has been increasingly challenged in recent decades by a variety of "liberals," "neoliberals," and "liberal institutionalists." While most of these theorists concede that states are the primary actors on the international level, they hold that the traditional view of state sovereignty and unitary interest cannot explain the steady growth of international cooperation or the persistence of many specialized international institutions in the contemporary world. Although there are many strands of thinking, most liberal theorists hold that states are interdependent and, in fact, have many common interests that lead them to cooperate; moreover, they believe that international institutions not only serve these common interests but create further incentives for cooperation.[14] In other words, institutions matter, and they influence the preferences and behavior of states by allowing them to improve collective welfare outcomes by cooperating. Whereas realists focus on *relative* status gains (especially regarding military security), liberals tend to emphasize *absolute* benefits (especially mutual economic gains) made possible by international agreements and institutions that solve collective action problems.

Over the past two decades many environmental policy scholars have turned to the more neutral concept of policy "regimes." International environmental regimes are composed of the international treaties and agreements, intergovernmental organizations, binding and nonbinding norms and principles, relevant national and local government institutions, and associated nongovernmental and private institutions that define and implement policies in different issue areas such as climate change, maritime oil pollution, or endangered species protection. In Chapter 4, David Downie explains regime theory in more detail and discusses a dozen prominent examples of such regimes. Drawing on many other strands of international relations theory and systems theory, he also analyzes the obstacles to effective international cooperation. His chapter thus brings out the real difficulties of achieving effective international environmental policies.

Some theorists are more optimistic about potentials for a global governance system comprising an increasingly dense and interactive network of international regimes.[15] "Governance" in this sense does not presuppose a central "government"; rather, that coordination of action can occur through many different institutions, including private social and economic systems and nongovernmental organizations, as well as a variety of governmental institutions at different levels. This concept often presupposes some kind of global "civil society" or decentralized network of autonomous social institutions that represent citizens and organized interests and engage in cooperative actions to achieve broad goals such as sustainable development. Increased communication and exchange of information among individuals and groups around the world through the Internet and other means can magnify the impact of such civic action to the point where common ideas and values begin to influence the actions of governments from the bottom up.[16]

This brief discussion should highlight the fact that whatever one's basic theoretical perspective, the development of international environmental cooperation has become one of the most fruitful and dynamic fields of international relations. Although there is no consensus among scholars as to the nature of the world system or the autonomy and durability of current international environmental institutions, laws, and policies, it is undeniable that the global environment has become a principal concern of political actors as well as scholars throughout the world. From this broader vantage point, the halting and confused human response to gathering evidence of potential ecological catastrophe may be less discouraging than short-term observations suggest.

Sustainable Development

Cutting across theoretical disputes are the realities of world economic and social development. Environmental threats are the product not only of population growth and ignorant or careless individual actions; they are deeply embedded in our religious, cultural, economic, and social systems. Perhaps the most obvious realities are that these systems are highly fragmented and differentiated and that global economic development is grossly uneven. The gap between the rich and the poor nations of the world is enormous and continues to grow. This difference among nations at various stages and levels of development has profound implications for the global environment. As has been recognized at least since the Stockholm conference, the needs and agendas of developed nations (the "North") and developing countries (the "South") are fundamentally different, making it difficult to reach consensus on international policies that benefit all parties (see Chapter 12). Essentially, while the North gives substantial attention to "environmental" issues that threaten ecological stability, the South has placed greater emphasis on immediate needs for economic growth to raise standards of living. Indeed, developing countries at the Stockholm conference feared that environmental protection was a plot by the North to limit their development—a concern that still echoes through all international negotiations.[17]

The North-South division raises fundamental issues of international equity.[18] Developing countries rightly argue that the developed countries have benefited from environmental exploitation in the past and are responsible for most of the world's pollution and resource depletion, including that leading to ozone depletion and climate change; therefore it is primarily their responsibility to deal with these problems. Furthermore, they are not willing to foreclose opportunities for economic growth that would permanently lock them into poverty and dependency while the peoples of the North engage in profligate consumption. Representatives of developing countries (organized as the Group of 77 in the United Nations since 1964 but now actually including more than 130 states) thus usually condition their willingness to participate in international environmental treaties and agreements on concessions from the North, such as guarantees of special funding and transfer of technologies to enable them to reduce their impact on the environment while increasing economic growth.

Another fundamental dimension of global environmental protection concerns intertemporal, or intergenerational, equity. That is, policies must consider not only the needs of the present generation but those of the future. Edith Brown Weiss, a leading scholar of international environmental law, defines three essential principles: (1) each generation should be required to conserve the diversity of the resource base so that it does not unduly restrict the options available to future generations; (2) each generation should maintain the planet's overall quality so that it is bequeathed in no worse condition than it was received; and (3) members of every generation should have comparable rights of access to the legacy of past generations and should conserve this access for future generations.[19] The latter principle implies a degree of intragenerational equity as a condition for intergenerational equity; that is, no group should either be denied a right to present environmental resources or be asked to bear a disproportionate share of environmental burdens (a principle often referred to as *environmental justice*).

The concept of sustainable development was born of these concerns. First set out in *World Conservation Strategy*, published by the International Union for the Conservation of Nature (IUCN) in cooperation with the World Wildlife Fund and UNEP in 1980, the concept was popularized in the Brundtland Report of 1987. The famous definition of sustainable development is from this report: "Sustainable development is development that meets the needs of the present without compromising the ability of future generations to meet their own needs." This was immediately followed by the statement that two key concepts were embedded within it: "the concept of 'needs,' in particular the essential needs of the world's poor, to which overriding priority should be given"; and "the idea of limitations imposed by the state of technology and social organization on the environment's ability to meet present and future needs." [20]

Several elements in this definition are critical for an understanding of sustainable development. First, the concept clearly represents an attempt to bridge the concerns and interests of developed and developing nations, but it applies to both (that is, industrial as well as less developed countries must change their production and consumption patterns). Second, it attempts to reconcile economic growth and environmental protection rather than viewing them as trade-offs; indeed, the Brundtland Report argues that neither is possible without the other. Third, the concept is strongly anthropocentric. It starts from the premise that human needs must be met in order to address environmental problems. Thus improvement in the living conditions in poor countries, and especially of women and marginal social and economic groups, is an essential precondition for ecological preservation.

Fourth, the limits to growth are not ultimately physical or biological but social and technological; it is assumed that environmental problems can be solved. Finally, the concept is extremely general, lacking specific content on how sustainable development is to be attained or who is responsible for achieving it. This vagueness was deliberate: it allows the idea to be adopted by virtually everyone as a way of bringing people together to seek common ground. In this formulation it is clearly a political and social construct, not a scientific concept or blueprint.[21]

There are numerous other definitions of sustainable development; by one count there are at least seventy in circulation.[22] These formulations reflect the different values and priorities of the holders. For example, in 1991 the IUCN published a sequel to *World Conservation Strategy* entitled *Caring for the Earth*, which put more emphasis back on ecological limits: sustainable development was defined as "improving the quality of human life while living within the carrying capacity of supporting ecosystems." The more general idea of "sustainability" has also been the subject of considerable controversy; *Caring for the Earth* defines it simply as "a characteristic of a process or state that can be maintained indefinitely."[23] This implies such basic principles as "rates of utilization of renewable resources must not be greater than rates of regeneration"; "waste emissions must not be greater than the assimilation capacities of the environment"; and "rates of use of non-renewables must not be greater than the rate of creation of renewable substitutes."[24]

Whatever the conceptual and ideological differences below the surface, there have been numerous attempts to translate sustainable development into policy initiatives. The most important political effort to do so occurred at the UN Conference on Environment and Development in 1992. UNCED produced both a general declaration of principles (Rio Declaration on Environment and Development) and Agenda 21, a massive effort to define strategies and policies for implementing sustainable development. Governments throughout the world pledged to formulate sustainable development plans and programs, and a new Commission on Sustainable Development was established by the UN General Assembly to monitor these commitments. Many other regional, national, and local organizations have adopted the principles and goals of sustainable development since 1992, including the European Union. Organizations such as UNEP, the IUCN-World Conservation Union, the World Bank, the Organization for Economic Cooperation and Development, and the U.S. National Academy of Sciences have also been actively working to identify specific empirical "indicators" for measuring progress toward sustainable development.[25]

Despite these efforts, there is a general sense of disappointment, if not despair, regarding implementation of Agenda 21 since the Rio summit. International aid flows for sustainable development projects have failed to come anywhere close to the levels considered necessary in 1992; indeed, official development assistance has *declined* in absolute terms.[26] A sense of pessimism thus pervaded the World Summit on Sustainable Development (WSSD) held in Johannesburg on the tenth anniversary of UNCED. The

WSSD understandably focused on implementing existing obligations rather than launching new programs, although some new policy goals, financial commitments, and public-private partnerships were agreed upon. The summit also produced a Johannesburg Declaration on Sustainable Development and a Plan of Implementation to guide future investments.[27]

Most of the chapters in this book discuss efforts to incorporate the idea of sustainable development into international environmental institutions, treaties, and policies. The case studies in Part III evaluate particular national and regional policies and projects from this perspective, further illustrating the obstacles to realizing sustainable development in both North and South.

Overview of the Book

This section outlines the main themes and concepts of the three parts of the book and briefly summarizes each of the individual contributions.

International Environmental Institutions and Regimes

International environmental organizations take many forms. Some of the oldest, like European river basin commissions or the International Joint Commission formed by the United States and Canada in 1909 to preserve the Great Lakes, are bilateral or multilateral bodies created to encourage cooperation in managing a shared resource. Some, like the International Whaling Commission and International Tropical Timber Organization, concern the worldwide harvesting and trade of specific categories of living resources, while others protect "common pool" resources such as Antarctica and the high seas that are beyond national jurisdictions. The International Maritime Organization regulates shipping to reduce pollution as a result of both normal operations and accidents. Still others, like the World Meteorological Organization, conduct scientific research and monitor environmental change on a global scale. Finally, many are essentially ad hoc organizations, such as the secretariats and Conferences of the Parties (COPs) that are created to monitor and develop detailed protocols to treaties and conventions.

Most of these international bodies are *intergovernmental* organizations (IGOs), meaning that they are created by member states and are accountable to them. In most cases member states are formally equal in governing (though not financing) these institutions, but in some (notably the World Bank and the International Monetary Fund), weighted voting procedures are used that reflect donor contributions. This has become a contentious issue in negotiations over multilateral funding mechanisms to channel special economic assistance to the South. The Global Environment Facility, which provides funding primarily for implementation of the climate change and biodiversity conventions in developing countries, was restructured after 1992 to give recipient countries more influence in financial decisions.

In Chapter 2, Marvin S. Soroos looks at the evolution of global institutions since the Stockholm era and focuses on the record and current state of five principal IGOs: the United Nations General Assembly, the United Nations Environment Programme, the UN Commission on Sustainable Development (CSD), the Global Environment Facility (GEF), and the World Bank. Overall, he finds substantial accomplishments in regard to focusing worldwide attention on environmental problems; framing new principles, policies, and laws; facilitating international treaties and agreements; coordinating environmental monitoring and promoting scientific research; and providing modest technical and financial support for sustainable development projects. But the picture is a very mixed one. The new institutions, GEF and CSD, have gotten off to a slow start in promoting sustainable development. And while the World Bank has made considerable efforts to develop environmentally sensitive loan policies, it continues to support many destructive projects, so that it is doubtful whether, on balance, it can be viewed as furthering sustainable development. Overall, despite great progress since the 1960s, it appears that the state of critical environmental IGOs has deteriorated rather than improved in the post-Rio period. Soroos suggests that a new central UN agency such as an Environmental Security Council may be needed to deal effectively with coming problems, but he doubts that agreement could be reached on creating such an institution. The alternative is to strengthen existing institutions and improve coordination among them.

There are now at least 200 Multilateral Environmental Agreements (MEAs) or treaties of global significance.[28] These international agreements have established a fairly comprehensive body of international environmental law covering the atmosphere, oceans and seas, international watercourses, hazardous wastes and materials, wildlife conservation, biodiversity and habitat protection, desertification, the polar regions, and outer space.[29] However, international law differs from domestic law in that it is normally binding only upon participating states and in that it applies to national governments, not individuals or corporations. (There are some exceptions, for example, in human rights law.) Moreover, there is no international court that can force states to comply with their obligations. The International Court of Justice, or World Court, hears cases and renders opinions that carry great weight, but sovereign states must ultimately agree to accept them. Nevertheless, even nonbinding declarations and principles (often called "soft law") can influence the behavior of governments.

Philippe Sands and Jacqueline Peel provide a history of the development of international environmental law and its most important principles in Chapter 3. They point out that prior to the establishment of the United Nations in 1945, there was no international forum in which to raise international environmental issues. Although the UN Charter does not explicitly mention the environment or conservation of resources, the UN convened its first environmental conference in 1949 and hosted many negotiations prior to the Stockholm conference in 1972. Most of the current environmental treaties were signed between 1972 and 1992, and recent decisions of the International Court of Justice confirm that the environment is now considered within the mainstream of international law. Sands and Peel explain the sources of international law, the role of different actors in formulating and implementing it, and the most important emerging principles of environmental law. They then outline the development of international legal standards in six broad fields: protection of flora and fauna, the marine environment, freshwater resources, air quality, waste management, and hazardous substances. Finally, they conclude that implementation and enforcement of this body of international law will be the most critical issue in the next phase of its development, suggesting that both international courts and nonjudicial bodies such as tribunals of the World Trade Organization will have to play a stronger role than heretofore.

Chapter 4 by David Downie analyzes the nature of international environmental policy regimes. Building on previous scholarship, Downie defines such regimes as "a set of integrated principles, norms, rules, procedures, and institutions that actors create or accept to regulate and coordinate action in a particular issue area of international relations." He explains in detail the meaning of each of these terms, using as an example the global regime to protect the ozone layer. He also outlines the structure of a dozen other environmental regimes before discussing a wide range of political, economic, procedural, scientific, and cultural factors that can undermine the effectiveness of regimes and make international cooperation difficult. While not denying the success of some existing regimes, his chapter casts a cold eye of realism on the strategic difficulties in achieving effective international policy.

In Chapter 5, John McCormick argues that the failure of the nation-state system since World War II—including its dependent environmental organizations—has led to the rapid rise of local, national, and international nongovernmental organizations (NGOs) to fill the vacuum. These groups, ranging from thousands of local grassroots organizations to large federations of national organizations such as the International Union for Conservation of Nature and the World Wide Fund for Nature, play an increasingly important role in setting the environmental agenda, participating in negotiations that create environmental regimes, and monitoring the implementation of treaties and agreements and environmental conditions generally. NGOs are now essential actors in international environmental regimes whether they have official status or not. Collectively, McCormick and others argue, they provide the backbone of an emerging global civil society in which the loyalties of individuals transcend national boundaries.

This does not mean that international NGOs are homogeneous in their beliefs, goals, or methods. McCormick distinguishes several different philosophies of environmentalism, as well as basic differences between groups in developing and developed countries and among different socioeconomic groups. Focusing on some of the larger international NGOs (INGOs), he provides numerous examples of how they carry out different functions and specialize in different issue areas. They also collaborate with one another and with IGOs in various campaigns, often forming broad international alliances (for example, to save tropical rain forests and endangered species). However, they are also handicapped by the lack of any central environmental authority on the international level, by the consequent need to influence a large number of national governments, by the power of countervailing interest groups, and by the weakness of international legal enforcement.[30]

Global Environmental Policy: Cases and Questions

The range of international environmental policies currently in force is vast, covering, among other things, protection of endangered plants and animals; protection against transboundary pollution of air, water, and soil; protection of the atmosphere against acidification, ozone depletion, and climate change; protection of the oceans against oil spills and the dumping of radioactive and other hazardous materials; conservation of fisheries; regulation of trade in dangerous chemicals, pesticides, and hazardous wastes; measures to combat desertification; and protection of Antarctica. In addition, new policies are emerging for consideration of environmental protection under the rules of international trade and for promoting sustainable development initiatives pursuant to Agenda 21.

Policies may take the form of binding treaties or secondary legislation, or they may take the form of policy declarations or voluntary programs to achieve certain results. They usually require implementation by actors at many levels, including businesses, local governments, and grassroots organizations as well as national governments. Evaluation of the *effectiveness* of policies is complex and can be measured in many ways: for example, by whether states are in legal compliance with treaties, whether monetary and other resources are being spent on programs, or by the actual results of the policy measured in terms of environmental improvements. Policies are also *learning processes* in that the actors involved continually gain new knowledge about problems and engage other parties in parallel efforts to achieve goals.

Global warming, or climate change resulting from a gradual buildup of greenhouse gases (GHGs) in the Earth's atmosphere, is perhaps the most serious, complex, and contentious of all international environmental policy issues. In Chapter 6, Michele Betsill traces the origins of concern over this problem and analyzes policy responses since the First World Climate Conference in 1979. She discusses the development of scientific research as a basis for negotiations leading to the Framework Convention on Climate Change (FCCC) in 1992. The chapter explains the principles underlying this historic agreement before analyzing the first binding agreement restricting GHG emissions made pursuant to the FCCC, the Kyoto Protocol of 1997. Although the United States announced in 2001 that it would neither ratify nor implement the Kyoto treaty, and the protocol cannot enter into legal force without ratification by either the United States or Russia, Betsill argues that the Kyoto agreement and subsequent negotiations have had many important indirect effects on policy actors at other levels of government and in the private sector. For example, many cities and private corporations have adopted GHG reduction strategies despite the lack of international agreement on these issues. Betsill thus concludes that "global governance of climate change is a complex, multilevel process no longer confined solely to multilateral treaty-making."

Another policy regime showing recent promise is that for control of hazardous chemical use throughout the world. In Chapter 7, David Downie, Jonathan Krueger, and Henrik Selin trace the development of three international treaties that form the core of this policy regime: the 1989 Basel Convention on the Control of Transboundary Movements of Hazardous Wastes and Their Disposal, the 1998 Rotterdam Convention on the Prior Informed Consent Procedure for Certain Hazardous Chemicals and Pesticides in International Trade, and the 2001 Stockholm Convention on Persistent Organic Pollutants (POPs). Their careful analysis of the many steps involved demonstrates how scientific and political consensus can build and strengthen through the international policy process. Essentially, what began as a fairly narrow effort to control irresponsible "dumping" of highly toxic industrial wastes in developing countries has broadened into a coordinated effort to manage the use of certain dangerous chemicals and pesticides. As such, the chemicals regime is a prime example of how environmental regimes can accelerate the accumulation of learning and knowledge, build capacity in developing countries for informed decision making and management, and improve equity in international trade and risk bearing. Unfortunately, as the authors point out, there are still many gaps and loopholes in the treaties; ratification and implementation remain weak; and more funding and support will be needed to make them fully effective.

International trade in dangerous substances is only one example of how economic globalization has led to a host of new concerns over environmental impacts. Many environmentalists fear that recent international trade agreements such as the North American Free Trade Agreement (NAFTA) in 1993 and establishment of the World Trade Organization (WTO) in 1994 will accelerate global environmental degradation in several ways: by the sheer increase in consumption of resources and production of wastes that will result from accelerated economic growth; by shifting capital and production to "pollution havens" with weak environmental laws; and by establishing rules of international trade that may conflict with and override existing multilateral environmental agreements and environmental legislation in individual countries. For example, laws restricting trade in endangered species or banning products harvested by environmentally damaging methods might be found to violate international free trade principles.[31]

In Chapter 8, Daniel C. Esty takes a somewhat more optimistic view of the potentials for balancing international trade and environmental protection. He carefully analyzes the concerns of environmentalists that liberalized trade and increasing competitive pressures will undermine existing environmental protections and summarizes the counterarguments of free trade advocates. NAFTA was the first such agreement to integrate environmental and trade policy. Esty evaluates the Environmental Side Agreement to NAFTA in some detail, generally finding it a more successful effort to balance economic and environmental goals than many critics have suggested.[32]

Moreover, in the new round of trade negotiations begun at Doha in 2001, in the new trade authority granted to President Bush in 2002, and at the World Summit on Sustainable Development in Johannesburg, the linkage between trade and environmental protection was explicitly recognized. Still, Esty concludes that the WTO needs reform—especially to increase transparency and access by NGOs—and that the underlying General Agreement on Tariffs and Trade may have to be revised to ensure the trade regime's compatibility with environmental treaties.[33]

The final chapter in Part II, by Michael Faure and Jürgen Lefevere, focuses on the broader problem of improving compliance with international environmental agreements.[34] The authors distinguish between treaty compliance, implementation, enforcement, and effectiveness. *Compliance* refers to the extent to which the behavior of states conforms to the rules set out in a treaty, whereas *implementation* involves specific actions taken by states within their own legal systems to make a treaty operative; *enforcement* denotes measures to force state compliance and implementation; and *effectiveness* focuses on whether the objectives of the treaty are actually achieved. Compliance does not guarantee effectiveness but is usually a necessary condition unless the treaty itself is so weak that compliance requires no changes in behavior.

Traditionally, international agreements have included some dispute settlement procedures or other provisions for invoking legal, economic, or political sanctions against noncompliant parties, but in practice such sanctions have rarely been enforced and are seldom effective in achieving treaty objectives. Faure and Lefevere discuss the many factors that can affect rates of compliance, including the number of parties involved, the capacities of national governments, the strength of NGOs, and the nature of the substantive provisions (primary rules) written into the treaties themselves. They show how there has been a shift from the traditional enforcement approach to a "managerial" or "facilitative" approach in some recent environmental agreements such as the Montreal Protocol on ozone-depleting substances and the Kyoto Protocol on climate change. These new "comprehensive noncompliance response" systems attempt to induce compliance through information and advice, technical assistance, and other incentives rather than by invoking negative sanctions (though the Kyoto treaty also contains a strong sanctions enforcement mechanism). However, it remains to be seen how effective these nonadversarial methods will be.

Implementing Global Policy: Cases and Controversies in Sustainable Development

Since the concept of sustainable development is broad and has quite different meanings when translated into different cultures and languages, it is difficult to evaluate national policies in terms of specific criteria or indicators of sustainability.[35] Some nations such as New Zealand and the Netherlands have adopted far-reaching sustainable development plans and programs, whereas others have dealt with sustainability issues in piecemeal and ad hoc fashion, if at all.[36] But apart from rhetorical justification of selected measures under the sustainable development label, many policies and projects at the national and local levels do, in fact, have major implications for sustainability. Decisions about energy supply or land use within a given country can impact other nations or the entire global system; this is especially true of very large nations such as China, Brazil, and the United States. Major projects within countries (even small states) also attract capital and technical support from international banks and corporations, thus involving the international community in what may appear to be local developments. It is important to study these linkages between national politics and international action as part of global environmental policy.[37]

Among developed nations, the United States has been among the most resistant to the idea of sustainable development and to ratification of multilateral environmental agreements in the past decade.[38] Although the leader in establishing many of the environmental treaties through the 1980s (including the Montreal Protocol), the United States has been an international laggard since the first Bush administration and has become openly hostile to multilateral institutions and policies in the second Bush administration. American policy also reflects a shift to conservative majorities in the U.S. Congress since 1994, making it virtually impossible to ratify any environmental treaties. Thus the United States has not ratified (and is not a party to) the Convention on Biological Diversity and its Biosafety Protocol, the Kyoto Protocol, or the Basel Convention on Hazardous Wastes. However, American avoidance of certain kinds of international environmental agreements predates recent conservative ascendancy and thus requires a deeper analysis of U.S. behavior.

Chapter 10 by Elizabeth DeSombre explores a wide range of hypotheses as to why the United States has initiated or supported some multilateral environmental agreements and opposed others over the past several decades. In particular, why has the United States taken a unilateral course on such major issues as climate change, biodiversity, and trade in hazardous wastes? In search of a consistent causal explanation, DeSombre examines these cases as well as others in which the United States has preferred a cooperative approach. After determining that most conventional explanations concerning American culture and ideology, scientific uncertainty, relative vulnerability to harm, and the projected costs of regulation fail to explain all cases, she suggests a more nuanced explanation that focuses on certain aspects of U.S. domestic politics. In general, the United States supports international agreements when it already has enacted domestic regulations in the same area and opposes international controls that go beyond domestic regulation or would be difficult to implement in our system. This pattern can in turn be explained by institutional peculiarities of the American system, especially the unique role that Congress plays in shaping foreign policy. DeSombre and others have noted that the Senate, especially, tends to be responsive to domestic business and industry pressures seeking to block international regulation. However, this pattern may be changing as some sectors of industry now favor action on climate change and other issues.

In contrast to the United States, the European Union (EU) has increasingly taken the lead on international as well as many aspects of domestic environmental policy. Chapter 11 by Regina Axelrod, Norman Vig, and Miranda Schreurs explains how the European integration process and its evolving institutional structure have contributed to this leadership role. Although the Treaty of Rome, which established the European Economic Community in 1957, made no mention of environmental policy, beginning in 1972 the Community adopted a series of environmental action programs and enacted numerous specific environmental laws as a way of harmonizing economic policies. Since 1986 several major treaty revisions have strengthened the legal capacity of the Community to legislate in the field of environmental protection. The Maastrict Treaty of 1992 transformed the European Community into a broader European Union, which has since grown from twelve to twenty-five states. The Union has also explicitly incorporated the goal of sustainable development into the treaty and has taken an increasingly active role in international environmental diplomacy on matters such as climate change. The policies of the EU and the United States have thus increasingly diverged on global environmental issues.[39]

Chapter 11 describes the structure and evolution of the EU in detail and analyzes policy developments since 1992. Although the Union is still an intergovernmental organization in the sense that decisions must ultimately be approved by the Council of Ministers representing the member states, in practice it functions as a supranational governance system in which most policies are adopted by majority voting in the council and the parliament. Moreover, the council's composition changes according to the subject at issue; thus it consists of environment ministers when it considers environmental legislation. As a result, EU environmental policies have been less subject to opposition group pressure than is the case in the United States. At the same time, the EU treaty requires integration of environmental policy into other policy sectors in order to promote sustainable development. Several new, innovative policies that go beyond measures in the United States are discussed in the chapter. Nevertheless, the authors argue that the EU still faces major hurdles in implementing sustainable development policies and in adapting governance structures and policy standards to the new member states.[40]

Chapter 12 shifts the focus to the "developing" world, or the "South," as opposed to the wealthy, industrialized "North." Adil Najam argues that the South has a well-developed collective identity and sense of purpose dating back to the Stockholm Conference on the Human Environment and the quest for a "New International Economic Order" (NIEO) in the 1970s. This unity is manifested primarily by the Group of 77 (G-77) block in the United Nations, now consisting of some 134 developing countries. Najam explains how preparations for the 1992 UN Conference on Environment and Development (UNCED) in Rio offered the South an opportunity to revive the North-South dialogue around the theme of sustainable development. From the South's perspective, the Rio conference provided a high point in its ability to shape the international agenda. Though most of its demands were not met, UNCED did link the economic development goals of the South to the environmental agenda of the North, and it established several important new principles of international environmental law such as the principle of "common but differentiated responsibility." Nevertheless, in looking back at the decade between Rio and the World Summit on Sustainable Development in 2002, Najam concludes that these principles and the "Rio Bargain" on sustainable development have largely been abandoned at the global level and have led to widespread disillusionment among developing countries.

Chapter 13 by Lawrence Sullivan addresses a specific case of sustainable development (or lack thereof) in a developing country—construction of the mammoth Three Gorges Dam in China. What is most interesting is that the Chinese government has increasingly sought to justify the dam—and refute its critics—by utilizing the language of sustainable development. While a case can be made for hydroelectric power to offset China's rapidly increasing consumption of fossil fuels, Sullivan raises questions about the project's sustainability on several grounds: that the giant reservoir behind the dam will become irreversibly polluted, that the financial costs may be unmanageable, that resettlement policies are inadequate and potentially a major source of social conflict, and that the failure of the dam structure itself would cause catastrophic human and environmental damage. In rapidly changing transitional societies such as China, state-sponsored definitions of sustainable development are likely to become major points of contention between governments and emerging social and political groups.

This may also be the case in the former socialist countries of central and eastern Europe that are in the process of transition to democracy and market economies.[41] In Chapter 14, Regina Axelrod discusses one fascinating example: the political controversy surrounding the Temelin nuclear power plant in the Czech Republic. Western governments, banks, and corporations, as well as various IGOs, are involved in upgrading Soviet-designed nuclear power reactors such as Temelin in the central and eastern European countries to ensure their safety and to provide alternative sources of energy to dirty coal-fired plants. However, as Axelrod explains, many serious technical and environmental problems raise questions about the wisdom of this strategy and have led to protests both inside and outside the Czech Republic. She looks at the project in the broader context of sustainable development and the evolution of Czech democracy and society since 1989. Essentially she finds a disturbing rejection of sustainable development policies by Czech governments since 1992, accompanied by an exclusion of environmental NGOs and the reassertion of state bureaucratic and technocratic methods of decision making. It does not appear that Czech citizens have either access to information or opportunities to participate in what are regarded as technical areas of regulation. This raises profound questions about both the democratization process and the priority being given to sustainability issues in the rush to marketization.

The Uncertain Future

The contributions to this book convey a very mixed and sobering message. Although great progress was made between the Stockholm and Rio conferences in establishing international environmental institutions, laws, and policies to address problems such as marine pollution and depletion of the ozone layer, it appears that advancement of the global environmental agenda has faltered badly since 1992. The concept of sustainable development turned out to be enormously complex and difficult to implement in the decade after the Rio summit. Its most basic requirements for raising the living standards of the world's poor have not been met, nor can it be said that environmental concerns are being effectively integrated into most sectors of economic and social development. Nor does the political will appear to exist to address the preeminent global environmental problem—climate change. Most international agencies, including the United Nations Environment Programme, Global Environment Facility, and Commission on Sustainable Development, are inadequately financed and torn by North-South divisions and other ideological conflicts. With the exception of the European Union and certain specific policy regimes, international environmental governance remains weak. National governments also vary greatly in their interpretation of, and commitment to, the idea of sustainable development, but few have given high priority to environmental sustainability in the post-Rio period. Most sadly, perhaps, the United States has abdicated what leadership it could previously claim in international environmental diplomacy. Conversely, local governments, private organizations, and a host of NGOs have become more important actors in defining the environmental norms of civil society.

Overall, the opening years of the twenty-first century have been a period of crisis and uncertainty for international environmental governance. Whether economic globalization, fueled by a growing world population and even more rapidly rising consumption levels, will prove compatible with the integrity of the Earth's ecological systems remains to be seen. What can be said is that global environmental governance will demand a great deal more attention in the future.

Notes

1. World Resources Institute et al., *World Resources 1998–99* (New York: Oxford University Press, 1998), 141, 188–189; World Resources Institute et al., *World Resources 1996–97: The Urban Environment* (New York: Oxford University Press, 1996); James Gorman, "Scientists Predict Widespread Extinction by Global Warming," *New York Times,* January 8, 2004; "Global Warming Called Growing Threat to Species," *Seattle Times,* January 8, 2004.
2. Lynton K. Caldwell, *International Environmental Policy,* 3d ed. (Durham, N.C.: Duke University Press, 1996).
3. See esp. Richard Elliot Benedick, *Ozone Diplomacy* (Cambridge: Harvard University Press, 1998).

4. World Commission on Environment and Development (WCED), *Our Common Future* (New York: Oxford University Press, 1987).
5. On UNCED and WSSD, see Philip Shabecoff, *A New Name for Peace: International Environmentalism, Sustainable Development, and Democracy* (Hanover, N.H.: University Press of New England, 1996); and James Gustave Speth, "Perspectives on the Johannesburg Summit," *Environment* 45, no. 1 (Jan.–Feb. 2003): 24–29.
6. World Resources Institute, *World Resources 2002–2004: Decisions for the Earth: Balance, Voice, and Power* (Washington, D.C.: World Resources Institute, 2003), 138.
7. Edith Brown Weiss, "The Emerging Structure of International Environmental Law," in *The Global Environment: Institutions, Law, and Policy*, ed. Norman J. Vig and Regina S. Axelrod (Washington, D.C.: CQ Press, 1999), 111.
8. World Resources Institute, *World Resources 2002–2004*, 140–141.
9. Ibid., 138–139; James Gustave Speth, *Red Sky at Morning: America and the Crisis of the Global Environment* (New Haven: Yale University Press, 2004), esp. chap. 5, "Anatomy of Failure"; Hilary French, *Vanishing Borders: Protecting the Planet in the Age of Globalization* (New York: Norton, 2000); Ronnie D. Lipschutz, *Global Environmental Politics: Power, Perspectives, and Practice* (Washington, D.C.: CQ Press, 2004).
10. See Lipschutz, *Global Environmental Politics*, and Speth, *Red Sky at Morning*.
11. See also Norman J. Vig and Michael G. Faure, eds., *Green Giants? Environmental Policies of the United States and the European Union* (Cambridge: MIT Press, 2004).
12. See, for example, Andreas Hasenclever, Peter Mayer, and Volker Rittberger, *Theories of International Regimes* (Cambridge: Cambridge University Press, 1997); and Ian H. Rowlands, *The Politics of Global Atmospheric Change* (Manchester: Manchester University Press, 1995).
13. For a recent statement of this position, see John J. Mearsheimer, "The False Promise of International Institutions," *International Security* 19 (1995): 5–49. Classic realist texts include Hans J. Morgenthau, *Politics among Nations: The Struggle for Power and Peace*, 5th ed. (New York: Knopf, 1978); and Kenneth N. Waltz, *Theory of International Politics* (New York: Random House, 1979).
14. For a standard text, see Robert O. Keohane and Joseph S. Nye, *Power and Interdependence: World Politics in Transition* (Boston: Little, Brown, 1977).
15. Oran R. Young, ed., *Global Governance: Drawing Insights from the Environmental Experience* (Cambridge: MIT Press, 1997); Oran R. Young, George J. Demko, and Kilaparti Ramakrishna, *Global Environmental Change and International Governance* (Hanover, N.H.: University Press of New England, 1996); and Paul F. Diehl, ed., *The Politics of Global Governance* (Boulder, Colo.: Rienner, 1997).
16. See, for example, Ronnie D. Lipschutz, with Judith Mayer, *Global Civil Society and Global Environmental Governance* (Albany: State University of New York Press, 1996); Margaret E. Keck and Kathryn Sikkink, *Activists beyond Borders: Advocacy Networks in International Politics* (Ithaca, N.Y.: Cornell University Press, 1998); and Lipschutz, *Global Environmental Politics*.
17. On the conflict preceding the Stockholm conference, see Caldwell, *International Environmental Policy*, 57–62.
18. See, for example, John Lemons and Donald A. Brown, eds., *Sustainable Development: Science, Ethics, and Public Policy* (Dordrecht, Netherlands: Kluwer Academic Publishers, 1995); Ian H. Rowlands, "International Fairness and Justice in Addressing Global Climate Change," *Environmental Politics* 6 (autumn 1997): 1–30; and Keekok Lee, Alan Holland, and Desmond McNeill, eds., *Global Sustainable Development in the 21st Century* (Edinburgh: Edinburgh University Press, 2000).
19. Weiss, "Emerging Structure of International Environmental Law," 106–107. For a full discussion, see Edith Brown Weiss, *In Fairness to Future Generations: International Law, Common Patrimony, and Intergenerational Equity* (Dobbs Ferry, N.Y.: Transnational Publishers, 1989).
20. WCED, *Our Common Future*, 43.

21. For an excellent collection of essays, see Susan Baker, Maria Kousis, Dick Richardson, and Stephen Young, eds., *The Politics of Sustainable Development* (London: Routledge, 1997). See also Thomas M. Parris, "Toward a Sustainability Transition: the International Consensus," *Environment* 45, no. 1 (Jan.–Feb. 2003): 12–22; and John C. Dernbach, ed., *Stumbling Toward Sustainability* (Washington, D.C.: Environmental Law Institute, 2002).
22. Thaddeus C. Trzyna, ed., *A Sustainable World: Defining and Measuring Sustainable Development* (Sacramento: California Institute of Public Affairs, 1995), 23 n. 1. See also David Pearce and Edward B. Barbier, *Blueprint for a Sustainable Economy* (London: Earthscan, 2000); Neil E. Harrison, *Constructing Sustainable Development* (Albany: State University of New York Press, 2000); and Simon Bell and Stephen Morse, *Measuring Sustainability: Learning from Doing* (London: Earthscan, 2003).
23. Tryzna, *Sustainable World*, 15.
24. Bell and Morse, *Measuring Sustainability*, 6.
25. Some of these are discussed in Trzyna, *Sustainable World*, and Bell and Morse, *Measuring Sustainability*. See also Joy E. Hecht, "Sustainability Indicators on the Web," *Environment* 45, no. 1 (Jan.–Feb. 2003): 3–4.
26. Paul G. Harris, *International Equity and Global Environmental Politics: Power and Principles of US Foreign Policy* (Aldershot, U.K.: Ashgate, 2001); Harris, "International Development Assistance and Burden Sharing," in *Green Giants?* ed. Vig and Faure, 252–275; and Adil Najam et al., "From Rio to Johannesburg: Progress and Prospects," *Environment* 44, no. 7 (September 2002): 26–38.
27. World Resources Institute, *World Resources 2002–2004*, 140–141; Speth, "Perspectives on the Johannesburg Summit"; Speth, "Environment and Globalization After Johannesburg," in *Worlds Apart: Globalization and the Environment*, ed. James Gustave Speth (Washington, D.C.: Island Press, 2003), 155–165.
28. For a recent United Nations review of current treaties, see United Nations Environment Programme (UNEP), "Multilateral Environmental Agreements: A Summary," UNEP/IGM/1/INF/1 30 March, (paper prepared for the Open-Ended Intergovernmental Group of Ministers or the Representatives on International Environmental Governance, First Meeting, New York, April 18, 2001) available online at http://www.unep.org/IEG/WorkingDocuments.asp (accessed March 11, 2004).
29. For an excellent legal text, see David Hunter, James Salzman, and Durwood Zaelke, eds., *International Environmental Law and Policy*, 2d ed. (New York: Foundation Press, 2002).
30. See Thomas Princen and Matthias Finger, *Environmental NGOs in World Politics* (London: Routledge, 1994); Paul Wapner, *Environmental Activism and World Politics* (Albany: State University of New York Press, 1996); and Keck and Sikkink, *Activists beyond Borders*.
31. See Speth, *Worlds Apart*, for a collection of essays on the environmental consequences of free trade.
32. See John J. Audley, *Green Politics and Global Trade: NAFTA and the Future of Environmental Politics* (Washington, D.C.: Georgetown University Press, 1997); and Jerry Mander and Edward Goldsmith, eds., *The Case against the Global Economy* (San Francisco: Sierra Club, 1996). For a recent assessment of NAFTA, see John J. Audley et al., *NAFTA'S Promise and Reality: Lessons from Mexico for the Hemisphere* (Washington, D.C.: Carnegie Endowment for International Peace, 2004).
33. See also Daniel Esty, "Toward a Global Environmental Mechanism," in *Worlds Apart*, ed. Speth, 67–82.
34. See David G. Victor, Kal Raustiala, and Eugene B. Skolnikoff, eds., *The Implementation and Effectiveness of International Environmental Commitments: Theory and Practice* (Cambridge: MIT Press, 1998); and Edith Brown Weiss and Harold K. Jacobson, *Engaging Countries: Strengthening Compliance with International Environmental Accords* (Cambridge: MIT Press, 2000).

35. For a comparison of European language translations, see Nigel Haigh, "'Sustainable Development' in the European Union Treaties," *International Environmental Affairs* 8 (winter 1996): 87–91.

36. Huey D. Johnson, *Green Plans: Greenprint for Sustainability* (Lincoln: University of Nebraska Press, 1995). See also Tim O'Riordan and Heather Voisey, eds., *Sustainable Development in Western Europe: Coming to Terms with Agenda 21,* special issue, *Environmental Politics* 6 (spring 1997); and William M. Lafferty and James Meadowcroft, eds., *Implementing Sustainable Development: Strategies and Initiatives in High Consumption Societies* (Oxford: Oxford University Press, 2000).

37. For some good examples, see Miranda A. Schreurs and Elizabeth A. Economy, eds., *The Internationalization of Environmental Protection* (Cambridge: Cambridge University Press, 1997).

38. See Gary C. Bryner, "The United States: 'Sorry—Not Our Problem,'" in Lafferty and Meadowcroft, *Implementing Sustainable Development.* However, there have been many sustainable development projects at the state and local level; see Daniel A. Mazmanian and Michael E. Kraft, eds., *Toward Sustainable Communities: Transitions and Transformations in Environmental Policy* (Cambridge: MIT Press, 1999); Kent E. Portney, *Taking Sustainable Cities Seriously: Economic Development, the Environment, and the Quality of Life in American Cities* (Cambridge: MIT Press, 2002); and Barry G. Rabe, *Statehouse and Greenhouse: The Emerging Politics of American Climate Change Policy* (Washington, D.C.: Brookings Institution, 2004).

39. See Vig and Faure, *Green Giants?*

40. See also Susan Baker and John McCormick, "Sustainable Development: Comparative Understandings and Responses," in *Green Giants?* ed. Vig and Faure, 277–302.

41. For a survey of recent developments in this region, see Liliana B. Andonova, *Transnational Politics of the Environment: The European Union and Environmental Policy in Central and Eastern Europe* (Cambridge: MIT Press, 2003); and Joann Carmin and Stacy D. Vandeveer, eds., *EU Enlargement and the Environment: Institutional Change and Environmental Policy in Central and Eastern Europe* (London: Frank Cass, 2004).

PART I. INTERNATIONAL ENVIRONMENTAL INSTITUTIONS AND REGIMES

2

Global Institutions and the Environment:
An Evolutionary Perspective

Marvin S. Soroos

The last half of the twentieth century saw a significant rise in the impacts of humanity on the natural environment. This trend is attributable in part to a burgeoning of the world's population from approximately 2.5 billion in 1950 to more than 6 billion by the century's end, with most of the increase taking place in Africa, Asia, and Latin America. Over the same period, the world's economy has grown sixfold (in constant dollars) and trade by a factor of fifteen.[1] The global push to industrialize and enhance living standards has devoured immense amounts of natural resources and released huge quantities of pollutants into the environment. With the growing magnitude of human activities, environmental degradation, once largely localized within the borders of states, has increasingly taken on transnational, regional, and even global proportions. Scientists warn that human beings have become the agents of fundamental alterations of the Earth, including depletion of the stratospheric ozone layer, global climate change, and loss of biological diversity.[2]

The world's political system has also undergone a major transformation over the past several decades. The dissolution of the far-flung colonial empires of Britain, France, the Netherlands, Belgium, and Portugal, as well as the splitting up of the Soviet Union and Yugoslavia, is reflected in the growth of the United Nations from 51 member states in 1945 to 191 in 2002. All of these independent states claim the sovereign right to decide on the use of natural resources located within their boundaries. This fragmentation of political authority among such a large number of sovereign states with diverse interests and a reluctance to relinquish authority over their natural resources have significantly complicated the task of achieving international cooperation on regional and global environmental problems.

The centrifugal tendencies of the nation-state system are partly counteracted by the emergence and maturation of international regimes, which provide a measure of "international governance" for addressing numerous environmental problems.[3] The term *international regimes* has been widely used to refer to the combination of international institutions, customary norms and principles, and formal treaty commitments that guide how states relate to a specific subject, problem, or region.[4] For example, there are international regimes for preserving biological diversity, reducing transboundary air pollution in Europe, the dumping of toxic substances in the oceans, and managing uses of outer space.

International institutions play a fundamental role in the creation, development, and operation of international environmental regimes. They include not only the global intergovernmental organizations (IGOs) of the United Nations system, but also regional ones, such as the European Union and the African Union (formerly the Organization of African Unity). Most of the IGOs that have played a role in the evolution of international environmental regimes were not established expressly to address environmental problems, but over time such problems were added to their agendas as ecological concerns arose. A relatively small number of IGOs have been created whose responsibilities are primarily or exclusively environmental, the most notable example being the United Nations Environment Programme (UNEP).

The work of these international institutions has been complemented by a rise in the number and influence of nongovernmental organizations (NGOs). Among these are scientific associations, such as the International Council for Science (formerly the International Council of Scientific Unions), and numerous environmental advocacy organizations, such as Greenpeace and the WWF (formerly the World Wildlife Fund). Collectively, NGOs have been described as an "international civil society" in view of their roles in drawing together people and groups from multiple countries around a common interest or cause.[5]

This chapter reviews the roles that global institutions play in addressing threats to the environment posed by human activities. It begins with a historical overview of the subject, with emphasis on how other issues—in particular the quest by a growing bloc of developing countries for economic development and equity—have shaped the response of global institutions to environmental problems. The chapter then presents case studies of five global institutions that are key players in addressing environmental concerns. The concluding section asks whether these and other international institutions are adequate to the challenge of responding to the increasingly ominous array of environmental threats and considers alternative forms of global environmental governance that may be more effective in addressing these threats.

Historical Perspective

The evolution of environmental issues on the agendas of international institutions can be better understood by dividing the postwar period into three eras defined by two major landmark meetings—the United Nations Conference on the Human Environment, which was convened in Stockholm in June 1972, and the United Nations Conference on Environment and Development, otherwise known as the Earth Summit, which was held in Rio de Janeiro in June 1992. The first, or *pre-Stockholm era*, extends to 1968, the year in which the UN General Assembly adopted a resolution to convene the Stockholm conference four years later. The second, or *Stockholm era*, from

1968 to 1987, encompasses the 1972 Stockholm conference, including the numerous preparatory meetings in the years preceding it, as well as the implementation of its recommendations over the following decade. The third, or *Rio de Janeiro era*, commences in 1987 with the release of the influential report of the Brundtland Commission (see Chapter 1), entitled *Our Common Future*,[6] which set the stage for the Earth Summit in 1992. The Rio de Janeiro period continues through the summit and follow-up efforts to implement the summit's lengthy and elaborate plan of action for achieving sustainable development, known as Agenda 21, including the World Summit on Sustainable Development in Johannesburg, South Africa, in 2002.[7]

The Pre-Stockholm Era (Prior to 1968)

International institutions have addressed environmental problems for more than a century; the earliest were the international commissions for the Rhine and Danube Rivers that were formed during the nineteenth century to foster cooperation among the riparian states on matters such as navigation, hydrology, flood control, and pollution.[8] Nevertheless, at the time the UN was established immediately after World War II, there was little awareness of environmental problems.[9] Even though the new organization was given a significantly broader mission than that of the League of Nations, especially on economic, social, and humanitarian matters, no mention was made of the natural environment in the UN charter.

In the following decades, IGOs, in particular the semiautonomous specialized agencies loosely coordinated by the United Nations, took up a growing number of specific environmental problems. These included the Food and Agriculture Organization, whose broad portfolio includes concerns for the relationships between food production and the environment; one of its projects is to facilitate the founding of a score of international fishery commissions to conserve marine fish stocks. The World Health Organization has investigated the impacts of air and water pollution on human health, while the International Labor Organization has sought to protect workers from environmental perils, such as dust and pesticides. The International Maritime Organization has sponsored a series of international agreements designed to regulate pollution of the oceans from vessels, especially oil tankers. The United Nations Educational, Scientific and Cultural Organization (UNESCO) has supported research on environmentally related matters, including the Man and the Biosphere Program. Outside the United Nations, the International Whaling Commission was established in 1946 to regulate the harvesting of whales whose stocks were becoming seriously depleted.[10]

In general, however, what international attention was given to environmental issues through the 1960s was directed toward rather narrowly defined ecological problems, such as the prevention of certain types of pollution or the conservation of specific species of wildlife. No major international organizations existed whose primary mission was broadly environmental, whereas in the economic realm, three powerful Bretton Woods institutions—the World Bank, the International Monetary Fund (IMF), and the General Agreement on Tariffs and Trade (GATT)—shaped the development of an increasingly integrated world economy. The existing forms of international environmental governance were rudimentary and fragmented across many largely independent IGOs, for whom environmental issues were secondary to their central missions in sectors such as transport, labor, weather, health, resources, energy, and science.

The Stockholm Era (1968–1987)

A wave of public concern about the environment, led by NGOs in Europe and North America, began building during the late 1960s and peaked during the early 1970s. Among the specific problems receiving attention were the dispersion of DDT and other toxic substances through ecosystems, radioactive contamination from the above-ground testing of nuclear weapons, and damage to forests and aquatic life from acid deposition. The immense oil spill from the grounding of the supertanker *Torrey Canyon* in the English Channel in 1967 was described by political scientist Richard Falk as the "Hiroshima of the environmental age." [11] The devastating effect of warfare on the environment in Vietnam became a contentious issue at the Stockholm conference, during which Sweden introduced the term *ecocide* in referring to American use of tactics such as defoliation and land clearing to deny guerrillas the cover of the jungle canopy.

More significant, this era saw a growing tendency to view the environment in a holistic way. This perspective had its origins in the International Geophysical Year of 1957–1958, an eighteen-month global scientific project sponsored by the International Council of Scientific Unions, which added considerable new scientific knowledge about the more remote realms of the planet, including Antarctica, the oceans, the atmosphere, and outer space. [12] This holistic perspective was also inspired by pictures from the moon and orbiting satellites showing the planet Earth as a fragile sphere drifting through the dark vastness of space, an image that prompted Barbara Ward to coin the phrase "spaceship Earth." [13] By the latter 1960s there was a growing uneasiness about the prospect that exponential population growth and booming industrial development would rapidly deplete the planet's natural resources and severely degrade its environment. [14]

Revelations that the increasingly serious problem of acidification in southern Scandinavia was being caused by pollutants from as far away as the British Isles and continental Europe prompted Sweden to propose the United Nations Conference on the Human Environment, which was held in Stockholm in 1972. Following up on the recommendations of the conference, the UN General Assembly established the United Nations Environment Programme to be a focal point for UN programs on the environment. The Stockholm conference became the prototype for a spate of major world conferences, sometimes referred to as "global town meetings," which focused worldwide attention on major international issues. Among those on environmentally related subjects were the World Population Conference in Bucharest in 1974, the World Food Conference in Rome in 1974, the United Nations Conference on Human Settlements in Vancouver in 1976, the United Nations Water Conference in Mar del Plata (Argentina) in 1977, and the United Nations Conference on Desertification in Nairobi in 1977. In each case, including the original Stockholm conference, a series of preparatory meetings was held to draft official documents, typically a declaration of principles and a plan of action, which were revised and adopted at the conference itself. The governments of most nations sent representatives to these conferences, as did UN agencies and other intergovernmental organizations with interest in a particular subject. Nongovernmental organizations, some of which were given limited opportunities to participate in the official governmental meetings, organized simultaneous public forums of their own that often had more interesting exchanges of ideas on the problems and solutions being considered.[15]

The surge in environmental concern during the Stockholm era came primarily from industrialized countries, which by the early 1970s had begun establishing environmental ministries, departments, or agencies (such as the U.S. Environmental Protection Agency) to address domestic problems such as air and water pollution. Developing countries were skeptical of the new environmental agenda because they viewed economic development and alleviation of poverty as much more pressing priorities. They were also concerned that a perception of the Earth's resources as finite and rapidly depleting and degrading, as suggested by the influential book *The Limits to Growth*, would become a rationale for denying them their right to develop high-consumption economies.[16] Moreover, by the time of the Stockholm conference, the developing countries were actively pressing their demands for a "new international economic order" that would entail significant reforms in the major global economic institutions. Developing countries refused to enter into a meaningful dialogue on the ecological issues of concern to the industrialized countries without strong assurances that international environmental initiatives would not occur at the expense of their legitimate aspirations for development.[17]

The wave of international environmental concern that peaked about the time of the Stockholm conference dissipated by the late 1970s, a change reflected in a declining number of relevant world conferences. Despite limited funding, however, UNEP made remarkable progress in implementing key parts of the action plan adopted at Stockholm. Several of the UN specialized agencies took on additional environmental projects. In many cases they worked in partnership with one another, UNEP, and even some NGOs, such as the World Conservation Union (formerly the International Union for the Conservation of Nature and Natural Resources). Nevertheless, the response of the UN system to environmental problems during this period continued to be fragmented and largely uncoordinated. Furthermore, international efforts in the realms of environment and economic development proceeded largely on separate institutional tracks despite the efforts of developing countries to link the two overarching priorities.

The Rio de Janeiro Era (1987 to the Present)

A second major wave of international environmental concern arose during the latter 1980s and reached a climax at the time of the Earth Summit in Rio de Janeiro in 1992. The problems receiving most attention during this period included ozone depletion, climate change, rapid shrinkage of tropical rain forests, the loss of biological diversity, the spread of deserts, and the decline of marine fisheries. The scientific community adopted the term *global change* to suggest that human activities could alter the functioning of the Earth system. This perspective has guided the International Geosphere-Biosphere Program, a continuing global scientific research effort headquartered in Stockholm, launched by the International Council for Science in 1986.[18]

The Rio era also saw significant shifts in the responses by international institutions to environmental problems. The first was a move to adapt international environmental initiatives to the aspirations of the South for economic development and equity, the overarching challenge being the pursuit of "sustainable development." This reorientation of UN environmental programs was proposed by the World Commission on Environment and Development, which was chaired by Norwegian prime minister Gro Harlem Brundtland and became widely known as the Brundtland Commission. The group addressed the misgivings of the developing countries about the UN's environmental agenda against the backdrop of their frustrations with the slow pace of economic development during the 1980s and the failure of the rich developed countries to respond to their demands for a reformed international economic order. The Brundtland Commission's report, *Our Common Future*, was notable for recognizing that poverty and underdevelopment in developing countries were important causes of environmental degradation. The report argued persuasively that environmental priorities could not be achieved without at the same time reducing poverty through sustainable economic growth in the developing countries and addressing inequities between rich and poor countries in the consumption of the planet's limited resources.[19]

The report of the Brundtland Commission provided the intellectual framework for the Rio de Janeiro conference, held in June 1992 on the twentieth anniversary of the landmark Stockholm conference. The conference drew 116 heads of state, the largest assemblage of world leaders to that date, which testified to the rise of the environment in the constellation of global issues before the United Nations. The gathering adopted a revised set of principles and the plan of action called Agenda 21, as well as major international treaties on climate change and biological diversity and a statement of forest principles. The UN General Assembly followed up by creating the Commission on Sustainable Development (CSD) to implement

Agenda 21, rather than assigning this responsibility to UNEP, which the developing countries regarded as being too narrowly focused on environmental problems to carry out the broad range of proposals adopted at the Rio de Janeiro conference. The commission's impact has been severely limited because governments have given it neither the authority to make binding decisions nor the financial resources to provide substantial funding for sustainable development.

In addition to the Earth Summit, several other global conferences convened during the 1990s included discussions of environmental issues within the context of a "people centered" emphasis of the United Nations. These included the World Conference on Human Rights in Vienna in 1993, the United Nations Conference on Population and Development in Cairo in September 1994, the World Summit on Social Development in Copenhagen in March 1995, and the Fourth World Conference on Women in Beijing in September 1995.[20] These conferences are also notable for the heightened involvement of NGOs at all stages, from the preparatory meetings through the implementation of the action programs that were adopted. The past decade also saw follow-up meetings held five years after the original world conferences to assess progress toward implementing their recommendations, which were generally disappointing. The goal of the World Summit on Sustainable Development (WSSD), which was convened in Johannesburg in 2002, was not to take ambitious new initiatives but to revitalize efforts to advance the recommendations contained in Agenda 21, adopted at the Earth Summit ten years earlier. At WSSD, which drew representatives from 191 countries, environmental issues took a back seat to the development problems of the poorer countries, who argued that they were not sharing in the growth stimulated by economic globalization and that inequalities between the world's rich and poor continued to widen. Most observers concluded that the meeting did little to advance the cause of sustainable development.[21]

Major Global Institutions

This section profiles five global institutions from among many whose activities have a significant bearing on the environment. The UN General Assembly is not only the arena in which numerous environmental issues are first raised, but also the body that instigates and reviews the response to them by the UN family of organizations, including the specialized agencies. The United Nations Environment Programme and the Commission on Sustainable Development are, respectively, the principal institutional products of the Stockholm and Rio de Janeiro conferences. The World Bank is a major global economic institution that has been seeking to "green" its image in response to strong criticism for its earlier failures to take environmental consequences into account in funding large-scale development projects. Finally, the Global Environment Facility has become a key instrument for dispersing funding for environmental projects in developing countries.

United Nations General Assembly

The General Assembly is the only one of the six principal organs of the United Nations in which all member states are represented. Since 1945 it has been the central meeting place of the international community and the only permanent forum in which a broad range of issues are raised, discussed, and debated. The institution has been known as the world's preeminent "debating society" because it provided the most visible international forum for the clashing views of East and West during the cold war and also because of the often contentious "North-South dialogue" between the industrial and developing countries. The General Assembly is, however, much more than an arena for airing conflicting perspectives. Although the organ lacks the authority to make decisions that bind its members, it has played a key role in framing and implementing international strategies for addressing a wide array of problems.

The General Assembly has convened numerous major world conferences to focus international attention on specific problems, including many in the environmental realm, beginning with the Stockholm conference in 1972. To the casual observer, these conferences may appear to be extravagant media events that have temporarily heightened interest in a given issue. The importance of these meetings cannot be fully appreciated, however, without viewing each of them as the most visible event in a much longer process that includes preparatory meetings that draft the documents to be taken up and approved at the conference, which normally lasts less than two weeks. Also to be considered are the steps that governments and international organizations take to implement the recommendations of the conferences, which are typically reviewed and evaluated at follow-up conferences held five years later. Thus the significance of any global conference should be judged by the sum of the new institutions created, programs launched or expanded, international treaties and policies adopted, and, ultimately, the results of these initiatives.[22]

The General Assembly facilitates the creation of international treaty law by sponsoring negotiating sessions. Notable examples are the three United Nations Law of the Sea conferences of 1958, 1960, and 1973–1982, the latter culminating in the signing of the comprehensive Convention on the Law of the Sea. The General Assembly sponsored negotiations that drafted the 1992 Framework Convention on Climate Change and a 1995 treaty on the conservation of straddling and highly migratory fish stocks. In addition, the General Assembly has adopted numerous resolutions setting forth non-binding regulations and standards, which are commonly referred to as "soft law" (see Chapter 3 on international environmental law). For example, a 1992 resolution calls for a moratorium on large-scale drift-net fishing on the high seas, a practice that had taken a heavy toll on marine life.[23]

The General Assembly plays a role in addressing environmental problems by delegating tasks and responsibilities to other institutions. It has been a primary creator of new IGOs, including those with key environmental responsibilities, such as the United Nations Environment Programme, the

Global Environment Facility, and the Commission on Sustainable Development. The General Assembly also convenes independent panels of prominent international political figures and experts to investigate and make recommendations on how to tackle major international problems; examples are the Brandt Commission on international development issues and the Brundtland Commission mentioned earlier.[24] The General Assembly frequently calls upon existing international organizations to assume additional environmental responsibilities. A 1961 General Assembly resolution, for example, called upon the World Meteorological Organization (WMO) to develop an improved global weather monitoring and reporting system that would take advantage of technological advancements in the fields of satellites, computers, and telecommunications. A 1962 resolution proposed that the WMO undertake the Global Atmospheric Research Program; it did so from 1967 to 1981, significantly increasing knowledge about atmospheric processes. Collectively, these programs have provided data and knowledge that have been critical to understanding the prospects for human-induced climate change.[25]

The General Assembly has been the arena of choice for developing countries not only because of the universality of its membership but also because each country has one vote regardless of economic or population size, level of development, or contributions to the United Nations budget. Thus it has been possible for the far more numerous developing countries to dictate the Assembly's agenda and, through their coalition, known as the Group of 77, to routinely pass by large majorities resolutions of interest to them. In the 1970s the General Assembly was the arena in which the developing countries pushed their proposals for a "new international economic order," widely known as the NIEO. These proposals were elaborated in several General Assembly resolutions, most notably the Charter on the Economic Rights and Duties of States, which was adopted by a 120–3 vote in 1974.[26] In the 1980s the General Assembly became the forum that oversaw the merging of the environmental and development agendas within the goal of sustainable development. Developing countries have been repeatedly frustrated, however, that their dominance in agenda setting and voting in the General Assembly has had limited results, especially in implementing the proposals contained in the NIEO, because the body's resolutions are not binding on the developed countries, whose cooperation is needed to implement them.

The United Nations Environment Programme

Following the Stockholm conference of 1972, the General Assembly created the United Nations Environment Programme (UNEP) to become the institutional focus for environmental activities within the UN system. To keep the new organization from competing directly with initiatives already under way in the well-established specialized agencies, UNEP's role was to be limited primarily to catalyzing, facilitating, and coordinating environmental programs both by countries and other international organizations. In keeping with this limited mission, UNEP was given a small staff and budget and was headquartered in Nairobi, far from the principal centers of UN activity, such as New York, Geneva, and Vienna.

With strong, effective leadership from its first two executive directors, Maurice Strong of Canada and Mostafa Tolba of Egypt, UNEP was remarkably successful in using its modest resources to carry out its mission. The organization has done much to gather, compile, and disseminate a variety of environmentally relevant information through the components of its Earthwatch program. Among these are the Global Environmental Monitoring System (GEMS), which coordinates numerous satellite-, Earth-, and ocean-monitoring networks that collect data on environmental variables such as climate, land cover, and air and water pollution. UNEP's International Registry of Toxic Chemicals (IRTC) is a repository of information on the environmental and health effects of numerous widely used chemical substances. INFOTERRA is a referral system available to those seeking information on how environmental problems are being dealt with around the world. Finally, UNEP's Global Resource Information Database (GRID) integrates environmental data for geographical units ranging from local to global levels in forms that are useful to planners and policymakers.[27]

UNEP has also been notably effective in stimulating the development of international environmental law and policy. In the mid-1970s UNEP launched its Regional Seas Programme, bringing together the diverse and conflict-prone states bordering the Mediterranean Sea to adopt a series of intergovernmental agreements. These agreements reduced the flow of both vessel- and land-based sources of pollution contaminating the largely self-contained sea.[28] What is known as the Mediterranean Blue Plan became the prototype for similar projects that address the environmental problems of other regional seas, including the Black Sea, the Red Sea, the Caribbean, the Persian Gulf, the West and Central African seas, the South Pacific, and the East Asian seas, which now collectively involve more than 140 coastal states.[29]

In 1981 the Governing Council of UNEP adopted an ambitious plan for the development of international environmental law, known as the Montevideo Programme. The plan established three priorities: prevention of marine pollution from land-based sources, protection of the stratospheric ozone layer, and the handling and disposal of toxic wastes. Efforts to stem the flow of chlorofluorocarbons (CFCs) and other ozone-depleting substances into the atmosphere led to the adoption of the 1985 Vienna Convention for the Protection of the Ozone Layer and two years later to the famous Montreal Protocol on Substances that Deplete the Ozone Layer. The latter document was amended several times in order to impose controls on additional substances that threaten the ozone layer, to make the phase-out of these chemicals complete, and to shorten the deadlines. The Montreal Protocol has been a timely and comprehensive response to the threat of ozone depletion and arguably the most significant accomplishment thus far in the development of international environmental law. The agreements exemplify the precautionary approach that addresses a serious environmental threat even before scientific evidence is fully conclusive.

UNEP also sponsored negotiations to regulate what had become a significant trade in hazardous waste, especially from industrialized countries to developing countries, which in many cases were unprepared to dispose of them safely. The negotiations led to the 1989 Basel Convention, which provides that such trade may take place only after the government of the recipient country has been informed of a proposed transfer of hazardous waste substances and has given its approval. These and other UNEP-brokered agreements, including the 2001 Stockholm Convention on Persistent Organic Pollutants, have contributed to making the environment one of the most dynamic growth areas of international law in recent decades.[30]

UNEP has been sensitive to development issues and continues to be the only global UN agency whose headquarters are in a developing country. It was UNEP's Governing Council in 1982 that proposed what became the Brundtland Commission to delve into the relationship between environment and development. Nevertheless, UNEP's role was challenged, as the environmental agenda of the United Nations was redirected toward the pursuit of sustainable development during preparations for the Rio de Janeiro Earth Summit. Developing countries looked upon UNEP as being overly attentive to the concerns of the industrialized countries with global environmental problems, such as stratospheric ozone depletion and human-induced climate change, and not sufficiently responsive to the environmental problems of developing countries, such as desertification and land erosion, or to their aspirations for economic development. Thus the General Assembly created a special negotiating committee for the climate-change negotiations beginning in 1991, rather than assigning them to UNEP, despite UNEP's decade-long involvement with the issue. Moreover, rather than placing UNEP in charge of implementing Agenda 21, the General Assembly created a new body, the Commission on Sustainable Development (CSD), to undertake this responsibility, even though the United States and other industrialized countries were exerting strong pressure for the UN to streamline its operations.[31]

The creation of the CSD, described further in the next section, has made it possible for UNEP to concentrate on its original mission to be the environmental conscience within the United Nations system. Agenda 21 called on UNEP to continue its role as both a coordinator and a catalyst of environmental activities within the UN system, to further develop the various components of the Earthwatch program, and to facilitate the drafting and negotiating of environmental treaties.[32] Nevertheless, UNEP has been a subject of considerable controversy between industrial and developing countries in recent years in ways that have threatened its future. The conflict came to a head in the spring of 1997, when the United States, the United Kingdom, and Spain threatened to withhold funds for the organization until reforms were made to strengthen the role of environmental ministers in determining UNEP's policies while weakening the power of Nairobi-based diplomats who reflected the interests of developing countries.[33] Amid continuing complaints that UNEP had lost its way, its executive director, Elizabeth Dowdeswell of Canada, declined to seek a second five-year term and was replaced in 1998 by Klaus Töpfer of Germany. Töpfer has generally kept UNEP on a steady course within its prescribed mission, helping to facilitate the development of new international policy, including the 2001 Stockholm Convention on Persistent Organic Pollutants. UNEP also continues to augment international knowledge on environmental issues, including, for example, helping to establish a task force to investigate the environmental problems in Iraq following the recent wars and the policies of Saddam Hussein.[34]

The Commission on Sustainable Development

The General Assembly established the Commission on Sustainable Development (CSD) in 1992 to monitor and facilitate efforts to implement the diverse goals and recommendations of the Earth Summit, in particular Agenda 21, the Declaration on the Environment and Development, and the Statement of Forest Principles. Headquartered in New York, CSD consists of representatives from fifty-three member states of the United Nations who serve staggered three-year terms. More than 1,000 nongovernmental organizations are accredited to participate in the work of the commission. Lacking both the power to make binding decisions and its own financial resources to fund programs, CSD was charged to further the recommendations of the Earth Summit by promoting dialogue and encouraging partnerships among governments, UN agencies, the NGO community, and the numerous groups identified in Agenda 21, such as women, youth, indigenous peoples, workers, and business and industry.[35] CSD reports directly to the UN Economic and Social Council but also makes some recommendations directly to the General Assembly.

Beginning with its first session in June 1993, the CSD has provided a forum for the discussion of a wide range of issues related to sustainable development. In view of the breadth of subjects covered by Agenda 21, the commission set up a multiyear schedule focusing attention on three or four environmental problems each year. Accordingly, health, human settlements, fresh water, and hazardous wastes were taken up at its 1994 session. Certain cross-sector issues also appear on the agenda each year, such as trade and the environment, poverty, population dynamics, financial resources, and the transfer of environmentally sound technologies. Member governments and the United Nations have convened additional conferences between the annual sessions of the CSD to focus attention on subjects such as chemical safety, drinking water and environmental sanitation, and the transfer of technologies to replace lead in gasoline. Among the subjects addressed in recent years are management of freshwater resources, sustainable development of small island developing countries, government subsidization of fishing fleets, the role of industry in sustainable development, and the promotion of an international agreement on the sustainable management of forests.

The CSD was also charged with monitoring the progress made by industrial and developing countries to implement Agenda 21. Toward this end, CSD invested heavily in developing a format that countries can use to report periodically on measures they have taken to implement recommendations contained in Agenda 21. At first, the industrialized countries were reluctant to institute a procedure that might generate embarrassing criticism of their performance, while developing countries were leery of a reporting system that could become the basis for imposing environmental conditions for economic assistance. Over time, however, a protocol for the reports was agreed upon, and by 2002, 137 countries had submitted such reports.[36]

The CSD has proven to be a lively and open forum for continuing discussions among governments, international organizations, and NGOs on how to carry out the plan of action on environment and development set forth in Agenda 21. It has stimulated the creation of sustainable development commissions in well over 100 countries, including a body in the United States led by the vice president. In addition, nearly 2,000 cities in 64 countries have adopted environmental plans. The CSD facilitated formation of the World Business Council for Sustainable Development, a coalition that has grown to 160 corporations based in 30 countries and representing 20 major industrial sectors.

Aside from these encouraging organizational developments, however, little progress has been made toward implementing key provisions of the documents agreed to at the Earth Summit.[37] Indeed, environment and development indices seem to have deteriorated further since 1992. The environment is increasingly stressed because of continued growth of the world's population, substantial increases in consumption of fossil fuels, and the alarming rate at which tropical rain forests and biological species are disappearing. Developing countries are discouraged by the failure of the industrialized countries to follow through on their commitments to increase economic assistance substantially and to facilitate the transfer of environmentally benign technologies.[38] Levels of foreign economic assistance actually declined during the 1990s.

Nonetheless, these disturbing trends do not necessarily reflect badly on the efforts of the CSD, which lacks the power and resources to effect substantial change on its own. The problem lies in the failure of governments to follow through on commitments made at Rio de Janeiro and the gulf that continues to exist between North and South on the relative priority that should be given to preserving the environment as opposed to economic development and reducing poverty.

The World Bank

The World Bank, whose official name is the International Bank for Reconstruction and Development (IBRD), was established in 1946 to provide funding for reconstruction of the war-devastated countries of western Europe. Its initial priority was to rebuild the infrastructure of these countries, such as roads, bridges, dams, water systems, and power plants, which private investors were reluctant to fund. Later the World Bank shifted its attention to providing loans that would speed up the development of African and Asian countries, many of which emerged from colonialism during the late 1950s and 1960s. Over the years, the World Bank has directed its loans mostly toward large infrastructure projects and the exploitation of natural resources rather than the development of human capital through programs in such sectors as health and education. Loans are normally made directly to governments at interest rates approaching commercial levels. The World Bank expects its loans to generate sufficient economic activity to enable the recipient countries to pay them off in a timely way. In 1960 the World Bank opened a separate "window" known as the International Development Agency (IDA) to provide loans to the least-developed countries at zero interest, with an extended repayment schedule.

The World Bank has provided nearly $400 billion in loans to developing countries and economic institutions, making it by far the world's largest single source of development assistance. The IDA has provided an additional $100 billion in development loans to the world's poorest countries. While the Bank has done much to facilitate economic development, it has also been one of the most criticized international institutions for funding numerous ill-conceived projects. Critics attribute the Bank's misjudgments in part to a compulsion to lend the large amounts of capital it has had available. Many of the projects have fallen far short of generating the revenues needed to pay them off. Such projects have added to the chronic debt burdens of developing countries, which for many became especially burdensome in the 1980s after dramatic decreases in the world price of oil and other commodities they depend upon for export revenue. Critics also point to the large numbers of people, currently more than 2 million, who have been displaced without adequate provision for their relocation as a result of World Bank projects, in particular the construction of large dams for power generation and irrigation. It is also alleged that World Bank projects tend to benefit those who are already well off in developing societies, while further impoverishing the poorest classes.[39]

The World Bank has drawn especially heavy criticism for its failure to anticipate the ecological impacts of projects, including several that are frequently cited for having had catastrophic environmental consequences. During the 1980s the Bank provided $500 million to Indonesia to assist in the relocation of 3.5 million peasants from heavily populated Java to the nation's outer islands of Sumatra, Kalimantan, Sulawesi, and West Papua. Unfortunately, the soils of these islands are not suitable for food crop rotations, leaving the settlers few options but to engage in slash-and-burn agriculture, which, along with commercial logging, has devastated the forests. At times, violence has broken out between the transplanted people and the original inhabitants of the regions. The World Bank also supported a large population relocation project in Brazil, known as Polonoroeste, providing $440 million for the construction of a 1,500-kilometer road deep within the northwestern Amazon state of Rodônia. As in Indonesia, the tropical soils were unsuitable for sustained cultivation, and many of the tens of thousands of settlers drawn to the region by government promises of land engaged in slash-and-burn methods of agriculture over an area the size of the United Kingdom. The result has been destroyed forests and displaced indigenous forest dwellers. Large tracts of Amazon forest have also been destroyed by Brazil's Greater Carajas project, which included a large iron-ore mine, a railway, and a deep-water port. To develop the infrastructure for the project, the World Bank provided more than $300 million.[40]

Growing concern over global climate change has drawn attention to World Bank projects that have added significantly to anthropogenic greenhouse gas emissions. The Bank has funded numerous projects for oil wells, refineries, coal mines, power stations, and road building, which have led countries to develop economies heavily dependent on fossil fuels. The Bank has been especially supportive of India's coal industry, from mining operations to power plants; one example is the $850 million in loans it provided for the notorious Singrauli complex of twelve open-pit coal mines and eleven coal-fired power plants. The complex, known as "the inferno," emits 10 million tons of carbon into the atmosphere each year and has denuded a large area that previously was lushly forested and home to indigenous peoples and numerous plant and animal species. China, Indonesia, Pakistan, the Philippines, and Poland are among numerous other countries that have constructed large coal- or oil-fired power plants with loans from the World Bank. The destruction of forest cover, as occurred in the projects in Indonesia and Brazil, also contributes significantly to atmospheric greenhouse gas levels both by releasing the carbon contained in the trees when they are burned and by diminishing an important carbon sink provided by ongoing living material and photosynthesis.[41]

In 1987 the incoming World Bank president, Barber Conable, acknowledged that not enough scrutiny had been given to the environmental consequences of the projects the Bank had funded. To address the problem, environmental divisions were established for each of the Bank's four regional operational offices—Sub-Saharan Africa, Asia, the Middle East, and Latin America and the Caribbean— and charged with assessing the environmental impacts of all loan applications. The Bank's annual report for 1992 stressed the importance of the relationship between environment and development in line with the report of the Brundtland Commission and the theme of the Earth Summit at Rio de Janeiro. The Bank played a central role in the creation of the Global Environment Facility (described in the next section) and assumed responsibility for administering its grant programs. During the 1990s the Bank expanded its portfolio of so-called green projects that it has funded in areas such as land management, forestry, biodiversity, water resources (both freshwater and marine), pollution management, and poverty reduction through sustainable development. In 2002 projects with environmental and natural resource management objectives and components (in addition to those funded by the GEF) amounted to $14 billion, which is approximately 14 percent of the Bank's total portfolio of $100 billion. Natural resources, the environment, and sustainable development were the emphases of the Bank's 2003 annual report, *Sustainable Development in a Dynamic World*.

Despite the efforts to improve its environmental record and embrace the goal of "sustainable development," questions persist as to whether the World Bank has actually enacted sufficient reforms. Some critics question whether the new environmental units and policies have had a meaningful impact on the culture of the Bank, which still appears to be oriented toward making new loans with little critical attention to environmental and human impacts. For example, the Bank provided loans for the controversial Sardar Sarovar dam project in India until an independent commission, chaired by former U.S. representative Bradford Morse, issued a report in 1992 that strongly criticized the lending agency for violating its own rules on environmental impact assessment and its standards for the resettlement of displaced peoples.[42] The fiftieth anniversary of the Bretton Woods Conference, in 1994, became the occasion for a campaign by a coalition of more than 200 NGOs that suggested that the World Bank had outlived its usefulness and questioned whether these institutions could be reformed to play more constructive roles in furthering sustainable development.[43] And even as efforts are made to negotiate treaties that would reduce emissions of greenhouse gases, funds provided by the Bank in support of energy efficiency and the development of sustainable energy sources continue to be a very small fraction of the amount loaned for large-scale fossil fuel projects.[44]

The Global Environment Facility

In 1990, at the suggestion of France and Germany, the World Bank took the lead in setting up an experimental program, the Global Environment Facility (GEF), to provide funds on favorable terms to low- and middle-income countries for environmental projects that would have global benefits. At the time, developing countries were insisting that their acceptance of several of the major environmental treaties being promoted by the industrialized countries was conditioned upon new and additional sources of international assistance that would enable them to comply with provisions of the treaties. GEF funds have been targeted at four major environmental priorities: protection of the stratospheric ozone layer, limiting emissions of greenhouse gases, preservation of biological diversity, and protection of international waters. The industrialized countries sponsoring the GEF saw it as a way to avoid the inefficiencies of establishing a separate fund for each major environmental treaty.[45] It was hoped that GEF assistance would induce developing countries to embark on projects that would benefit the larger community of nations. Without such assistance, developing countries would have little incentive to allocate their limited resources for environmental projects in view of other compelling national priorities.

The World Bank has shared responsibility for operating the GEF with the United Nations Development Programme (UNDP) and UNEP. The World Bank, which has been the dominant partner, administers the GEF's trust fund and manages the program's application process. The UNDP oversees technical assistance projects and coordinates them with the national environment programs of the recipient countries. UNEP's role has been to provide scientific and technical oversight, as well as guidance in identifying and selecting projects to be funded. To assist in carrying out its responsibility, UNEP established a fifteen-member Scientific and Technical Advisory Panel to provide advice on broad scientific and technical issues.

The GEF's first phase, which ran from July 1991 through July 1993, was designed as a trial to see if it could be an effective mechanism for dispersing assistance in support of major environmental treaties. During this period the GEF allocated $750 million for projects, with global warming and biological diversity projects each receiving approximately 40 percent of the funds, while international waters projects received most of the remaining 20 percent. Very few funds were allocated to protecting the stratospheric ozone layer in view of the existence of a separate multilateral fund linked to the Montreal Protocol. The GEF quickly encountered criticism, especially from NGOs, for rushing into making what were considered to be ill-conceived grants before criteria for awarding them had been established.[46]

The future of the GEF became a North-South issue at the Earth Summit in 1992 in the context of discussion over funding for Agenda 21. To developing countries, the GEF's emphasis on global environmental problems under the leadership of the World Bank reflected the priorities of the industrialized countries. It provided no support, however, for tackling the more localized environmental problems considered by developing countries to be more pressing, such as desertification, soil loss, and urban air pollution. Developing countries argued for the creation of a general purpose Green Fund not dominated by the World Bank model of weighted voting, which would support a broader range of proposals associated with sustainable development. Moreover, their governments were critical of the World Bank's secretive ways. As the providers of funding for the GEF, the industrialized countries insisted on retaining substantial authority over GEF decision making by continuing it under the auspices of the World Bank; they also insisted on keeping the program focused on preserving the global commons.[47]

The deadlock over the future of the GEF was finally broken at the Earth Summit, when governments agreed that the GEF should undergo a major restructuring. It took an additional eighteen months of intense negotiations for seventy-three participating countries to work out the specifics on how to restructure the GEF as a permanent institution that would balance the interests of the donor and recipient countries. The restructuring provided for two decision-making bodies. One is the Assembly, which includes all member countries and meets every third year to review the general policies of the GEF. The Assembly's first meeting was held in New Delhi in 1998, the second in Beijing in 2002. The second body is the smaller Governing Council, which meets much more frequently and is the GEF's primary governing organ. Of the thirty-two seats on the council, fourteen were allocated to industrialized countries, sixteen to developing countries, and two to the transitional countries of the former Soviet bloc. In the absence of a consensus, decisions of the council require simultaneous double majorities, one comprising a majority of the member states, the other the votes of countries that make at least 60 percent of all contributions to the GEF. Thus the interests of both the developing and the donor countries are protected.

The GEF has emerged from the turmoil and contentiousness of its initial experimental phase to become a useful complement to other sources of financial assistance for environmental projects in developing countries, including various multilateral funds, UN agencies, regional development banks, nongovernmental organizations, and bilateral assistance programs. As of 2002, the GEF had grown to 173 member states and had a portfolio of more than 1,000 projects in 140 countries, valued at more than $16 billion. Funds related to climate change have gone to projects that increase carbon-absorbing forest cover, known as carbon sinks, that encourage energy conservation, or that promote the harnessing of solar and other renewable sources of energy. Grants directed toward promoting biological diversity have gone largely to projects for the protection of habitats, such as the establishment of parks and nature preserves and facilities for ecotourism. Among the projects to protect international waters have been initiatives to cut back on ship wastes in major trading seaports and to reduce organic and toxic pollution in the Danube River system and the Black Sea.[48] The GEF has also added a new funding window dedicated to persistent organic pollutants (POPs) and implementation of the 2001 Stockholm POPs Convention.

Prospects for Change

International institutions have accomplished much over the past several decades toward facilitating cooperation among nations in addressing environmental problems that transcend their borders and affect the global commons. These include the international institutions whose missions are primarily environmental, most notably UNEP and the GEF, as well as numerous other organizations that have taken up environmental problems as part of their broader missions, such as the UN General Assembly and several of the specialized agencies of the United Nations family of organizations. Other major global organizations, such as the three Bretton Woods institutions—the World Bank, the International Monetary Fund, and the GATT/World Trade Organization—have been adopting reforms in the face of strong criticism for pursuing their economic missions in ways that have further aggravated environmental problems.

Nevertheless, the ecological predicament of humanity appears to be deepening, despite the monitoring networks, scientific research projects, environmental treaties and standards, reporting mechanisms, and funding programs that have been sponsored by these international institutions. While the efforts of international institutions have contributed to solving some environmental problems, most conspicuously the preservation of the stratospheric ozone layer, they have been largely ineffective in brokering effective international responses to others; among these are human-induced climate change, which is arguably the preeminent ecological problem confronting humanity as it enters the twenty-first century. The failure of the Johannesburg summit in 2002 to make much progress on either the environmental or sustainable development fronts does not bode well for reconciling the developed North's concerns about global environmental problems with the South's aspirations for development.

The question arises as to whether international institutions, as presently constituted, possess the capacity to deliver the global collective environmental benefits that they are being asked to provide. In the prevailing anarchical world order, states for the most part cannot be compelled against their will to enter into cooperative arrangements to address international problems. Thus international agreements are the product of complex and time-consuming negotiations among disparate countries with conflicting interests that typically produce weak documents reflecting the lowest common denominator of perceived interests. Countries tend to seek treaties that maximize the responsibilities of other nations while minimizing their own obligations, thus playing the role of free rider.

Concern over impending global ecological crises has prompted proposals for strengthening international institutions. One potential direction would be to establish a strong central organ within the United Nations system, possibly in the form of an Environmental Security Council. This would take the place of the Trusteeship Council, which has all but completed its mission of decolonization. Such a body would elevate the environment from being a peripheral, cross-sectoral issue to being one of the core priorities of the United Nations, along with peacekeeping and economic development. Another approach would create institutions with the power to make binding decisions that are needed to effectively address environmental problems such as depletion of the ozone layer and climate change. Such an institution was proposed at an international conference attended by leaders from seventeen states meeting in The Hague in 1988. The absence of the United States, the Soviet Union, and China—the world's three leading emitters of carbon dioxide—did not bode well for the implementation of such a proposal.[49]

It is difficult to conceive of circumstances in which states would be willing to relinquish or pool their sovereignty to substantially strengthen global institutions charged with mounting a more effective response to the deepening environmental crisis confronting humanity. If anything, there is some public disillusionment with global institutions and policies in both industrial and developing countries because of their perceived failure to be responsive to local needs and preferences. The best hope appears to lie in strengthening existing institutions and enhancing coordination between them. Nongovernmental organizations can be expected to play a significant role in mobilizing support for stronger international policies and programs and monitoring compliance with them. Whether such a decentralized, problem-specific approach to addressing global environmental policies will be adequate to the challenges that lie ahead remains to be seen. Unfortunately, at least for now, there appears to be no viable alternative.

Notes

1. Lester R. Brown, Michael Renner, and Christopher Flavin, *Vital Signs 1998* (Washington, D.C.: Worldwatch Institute, 1998), 75, 77.
2. See Constance Mungall and Digby J. McLaren, eds., *Planet under Stress: The Challenge of Global Change* (New York: Oxford University Press, 1990).
3. See Oran Young, *International Governance: Protecting the Environment in a Stateless Society* (Ithaca, N.Y.: Cornell University Press, 1994); and Lamont C. Hempel, *Environmental Governance: The Global Challenge* (Washington, D.C.: Island Press, 1996).
4. See Stephen D. Krasner, ed., *International Regimes* (Ithaca, N.Y.: Cornell University Press, 1983).
5. See Paul Wapner, *Environmental Activism and World Civic Politics* (Albany: State University of New York Press, 1996); and Ronnie D. Lipschutz, with Judith Mayer, *Global Civil Society and Global Environmental Governance: The Politics of Nature from Place to Planet* (Albany: State University of New York Press, 1996).
6. World Commission on Environment and Development, *Our Common Future* (New York: Oxford University Press, 1987).
7. United Nations, *Agenda 21: Programme of Action for Sustainable Development*, 1993, E.93.I.11.
8. Lynton Keith Caldwell, *International Environmental Policy*, 3d ed. (Durham, N.C.: Duke University Press, 1995), 160–161.
9. For an overview of perceptions of environmental issues during this era, see John McCormick, *Reclaiming Paradise: The Global Environmental Movement* (Bloomington: Indiana University Press, 1979), 25–46.
10. See Patricia Birnie, "The UN and the Environment," in *United Nations, Divided World: The UN's Roles in International Relations*, 2d ed., ed. Adam Roberts and Benedict Kingsbury (New York: Oxford University Press, 1993), 355–358.
11. Richard A. Falk, *This Endangered Planet: Prospects and Proposals for Human Survival* (New York: Vintage Books, 1971), 284. For an account of accidents involving supertankers, see Noël Mostert, *Supership* (New York: Warner Books, 1975).
12. See Wallace W. Atwood Jr., "The International Geophysical Year in Retrospective," *Department of State Bulletin* 40 (1959): 682–689.
13. Barbara Ward, *Spaceship Earth* (New York: Columbia University Press, 1966).
14. An influential book on world population growth was Paul R. Ehrlich's *The Population Bomb* (New York: Ballantine Books, 1968).
15. See A. LeRoy Bennett, *International Organizations: Principles and Issues*, 3d ed. (Englewood Cliffs, N.J.: Prentice Hall, 1984), 293–323.
16. Donella H. Meadows et al., *The Limits to Growth* (New York: Universe Books, 1972).
17. See Marian A. L. Miller, *The Third World in Global Environmental Politics* (Boulder, Colo.: Rienner, 1995).
18. Thomas F. Malone, "Mission to Planet Earth: Integrating Studies of Global Change," *Environment* 28 (October 1986): 6–11, 39–42.
19. See *Our Common Future*.
20. See John Tessitore and Susan Woolfson, eds., *A Global Agenda: Issues before the 49th General Assembly of the United Nations* (New York: University Press of America, 1994), 154.

21. See International Institute for Sustainable Development, "Summary of World Summit on Sustainable Development, 26 August–4 September 2002," *Earth Negotiations Bulletin* 22 (September 6, 2002), http://www.iisd.ca/linkages/vol22/enb2251e.html.

22. See Bennett, *International Organizations.*

23. See Blaine Sloan, *United Nations General Assembly Resolutions in Our Changing World* (Ardsley-on-Hudson, N.Y.: Transnational, 1991).

24. Independent Commission on International Development Issues, *North–South: A Programme for Survival* (Cambridge: MIT Press, 1980).

25. See Marvin S. Soroos, *The Endangered Atmosphere: Preserving a Global Commons* (Columbia: University of South Carolina Press, 1997), 58–61.

26. See Marvin S. Soroos, *Beyond Sovereignty: The Challenge of Global Policy* (Columbia: University of South Carolina Press, 1986), 195–226.

27. See Peter M. Haas, "Institutions: United Nations Environment Programme," *Environment* 36 (September 1994): 43–45.

28. See Peter M. Haas, *Saving the Mediterranean: The Politics of International Environmental Cooperation* (New York: Columbia University Press, 1990).

29. "United Nations Environment Programme: Two Decades of Achievement and Challenge," *Our Planet* 4, no. 5 (1992): 9.

30. See Carol Annette Petsonk, "The Role of the United Nations Environment Programme (UNEP) in the Development of International Environmental Law," *American University Journal of International Law and Policy* 5 (1990): 351–391.

31. See Konrad von Moltke, "Why UNEP Matters," in *Green Globe Yearbook 1996*, ed. Helge Ole Bergesen and Georg Parmann (New York: Oxford University Press, 1996), 58–59.

32. Dale Boyd, "UNEP after Rio," *Our Planet* 4, no. 4 (1992): 8–11.

33. Fred Pearce, "Environmental Body Goes to Pieces," *New Scientist,* February 15, 1997, 11.

34. Olga Kharif, "Healing Iraq's Wounded Earth," *Business Week,* April 20, 2003.

35. See Chris Mensah, "The United Nations Commission on Sustainable Development," in *Greening International Institutions, London: Earth*, ed. Jacob Werksman, (London: EarthScan, 1996), 21–37.

36. See UN Sustainable Development Web site: http://www.un.org/esa/agenda21/nationalinfo/.

37. See http://www.wbcsd.ch/aboutus/index.htm. Such was the conclusion of the General Assembly's Special Session on "Rio Plus Five," held in New York in 1997, and the World Summit on Sustainable Development in Johannesburg in 2002.

38. Alexandra Marks, "Rio+5: Wake-up Call for Earth Cleanup," *Christian Science Monitor,* June 24, 1997, 1, 10–11.

39. See Catherine Caufield, *Masters of Illusion: The World Bank and the Poverty of Nations* (New York: Holt, 1996); Doug Bandow and Ian Vàsquez, eds., *Perpetuating Poverty: The World Bank, the IMF, and the Developing World* (Washington, D.C.: CATO Institute, 1994).

40. Horta, "The World Bank and the International Monetary Fund," in Werksman, *Greening International Institutions,* 138–139. The most influential book on this subject is Bruce Rich, *Mortgaging the Earth: The World Bank, Environmental Impoverishment, and the Crisis of Development* (Boston: Beacon Press, 1994).

41. See Christopher Flavin, "Banking against Global Warming," *World Watch* 10 (November/December 1997): 25–35.

42. See Hilary F. French, "The World Bank: Now Fifty, but How Fit?" *World Watch* 7 (July–August 1994): 10–18.

43. David R. Francis, "IMF and World Bank 50th Birthday Bash: Critics Crash Parties," *Christian Science Monitor,* October 3, 1994, 4.

44. See Flavin, "Banking against Global Warming."

45. "The Global Environmental Facility," *Our Planet* 3, no. 3 (1991): 10–13.

46. See Andrew Jordan, "Paying the Incremental Costs of Global Environmental Protection: The Evolving Role of the GEF," *Environment* 36 (July/August 1994): 12–20, 31–36.

47. David Fairman, "The Global Environment Facility: Haunted by the Shadow of the Future," in *Institutions for Environmental Aid,* ed. Robert O. Keohane and Marc A. Levy (Cambridge: MIT Press, 1996), 57–58. See also Helen Sjöberg, "The Global Environmental Facility," in Werksman, *Greening International Institutions,* 148–162.
48. Mohamed T. El-Ashry, "Welcome Address," Global Environment Facility Assembly, Beijing, October 2002. See http://www.gefonline.org/assembly/assembly.htm.
49. See Hilary F. French, "An Environmental Security Council," *World Watch* 2 (September/October 1989): 6–7.

3

Environmental Protection in the Twenty-first Century: Sustainable Development and International Law

Philippe Sands and Jacqueline Peel

This chapter examines the historical development, central principles, and current implementation of international environmental law. Only a few decades ago a discussion of this topic would probably have begun with a question as to whether the subject of international environmental law even existed: there were no treatises or journals specifically on the subject, only a very small number of law school seminars were taught, and most public international law texts avoided addressing the environment, with little risk of being criticized for incompleteness.

Today the situation is entirely different. The International Court of Justice has confirmed the "obligations of States to respect and protect the natural environment." [1] Moreover, it has declared that states' "general obligation . . . to ensure that activities within their jurisdiction or control respect the environment of other States or of areas beyond national control is now part of the corpus of international law relating to the environment." [2] This latter obligation, it is now clear, is applicable at all times and to all activities, even the use of nuclear weapons.[3] These general obligations have been further developed in the context of the international community's commitment, at the United Nations Conference on Environment and Development (UNCED, also known as the Earth Summit) held at Rio de Janeiro in 1992, to integrate environment and development and to cooperate "in the further development of international law in the field of sustainable development." [4]

This chapter is divided into three sections. The first section briefly describes the historical development of international environmental law and the institutional context within which that development has taken place. The second section examines certain general principles of international law that have emerged, or are emerging, in relation to environmental matters. The last section sets out basic rules of international environmental law in fields such as protection of flora and fauna, protection of freshwater resources and the marine environment, air quality, waste and hazardous substances.

International Environmental Law: Context, History, and Sources

International legal efforts to protect the environment go back at least to the 1880s, when a dispute was submitted to international arbitration as a consequence of the United States' efforts to prevent British vessels from exploiting fur seals in international waters of the Bering Sea. Although the

Pacific Fur Seal Arbitration Tribunal did not find in favor of the unilateral U.S. approach to conservation, it did adopt regulations for the "proper protection and preservation" of fur seals.[5] These regulations have served as an important precedent for the subsequent development of international environmental law, reflecting a recognition that environmental problems transcend national boundaries.

Yet the basic challenge for the twenty-first century remains one of reconciling the inherent and fundamental interdependence of the global environment with the fact that many land, sea, and air spaces are part of the sovereign areas of independent states.[6] This challenge raises issues about the nature of international society and the structure of the international legal order, the content and reach of international environmental law, and the relationship between international environmental law and other areas of international law, particularly in the economic and social domains.

The International Legal Order

International law and international organizations provide the basis for cooperation between the various members of the international community in their efforts to protect the global environment. At each level the task becomes progressively more complex as new actors and interests are drawn into the process. Whereas just two states, representing the interest of local fishing communities, negotiated the early fisheries conventions in the middle of the nineteenth century, more than 150 states were involved in negotiations sponsored by the UN General Assembly that led to the 1992 UN Framework Convention on Climate Change and its 1997 Kyoto Protocol (see Chapter 6).

In both cases, however, the principles and rules of public international law are intended to serve similar functions. The overall objective of the international legal order is to provide a framework within which the various members of the international community may cooperate, establish norms of behavior, and resolve their differences. As with national law, the functions of international law are legislative, administrative, and adjudicative. The legal principles and rules that impose binding obligations requiring states and other members of the international community to conform to certain norms of behavior are accomplished through the legislative function. These obligations place limits upon the activities that may be conducted or permitted because of their actual or potential impact upon the environment. Such impact may be entirely within national borders, across territorial boundaries, or in areas beyond national jurisdictions.

The administrative function of international law allocates tasks to the various actors to ensure that standards imposed by the principles and rules of international environmental law are carried out. The adjudicative function of international law aims, in a limited way, to provide mechanisms or forums for the pacific settlement of differences or disputes that arise between members of the international community involving the use of natural resources or the conduct of activities affecting the environment.

Sovereignty and Territory

In the traditional international legal order, states are sovereign and equal, imbued with equal rights and duties as members of the international community, notwithstanding differences of an economic, social, or political nature. The sovereignty and equality of states means that each has *prima facie* exclusive jurisdiction over its territory and the natural resources found there. States also have a duty not to intervene in the area of exclusive jurisdiction of other states. In principle, this means that each state has the competence to develop policies and laws in regard to the natural resources and environment of its own territory. That territory comprises

- land within the boundaries of a state, including the subsoil
- internal waters, such as lakes, rivers, canals
- territorial sea, which is adjacent to the coast, including its seabed, subsoil, and the resources thereof
- airspace above a state's land, internal waters, and territorial sea, up to the point at which the legal regime of outer space begins

States may also have more limited sovereign rights and jurisdiction over other areas, including a contiguous zone adjacent to their territorial seas; the continental shelf, its seabed and subsoil; certain fishing zones; and "exclusive economic zones."

As a result of these arrangements, certain areas fall outside the territory and exclusive jurisdiction of any state. These areas, which are sometimes referred to as the global commons, include the high seas and its seabed and subsoil, the atmosphere, outer space, and, according to a majority of states, the Antarctic.

This apparently straightforward international legal order was a satisfactory organizing structure until technological developments, and their environmental effects, permeated national boundaries. The traditional structure does not coexist comfortably with an environmental order that consists of a biosphere of interdependent ecosystems that do not respect artificial territorial boundaries between states.[7] As an ecological matter, if not a legal one, many natural resources and their environmental components are shared, and the use by any one state of the natural resources within its territory will invariably have consequences for the use of natural resources and their environmental components in other states. Ecological interdependence therefore poses a fundamental problem for international law, as no one state, acting within its territorial boundaries, can adequately address global environmental problems. International cooperation and the development of shared norms of behavior are indispensable.

Historical Development

The deficiencies of the traditional international legal order in responding to environmental challenges led to the rapid development of new, "greener" rules of international law. The process of "greening" international law occurred over four periods, responding to particular factors that influenced legal developments.[8] In the early stages of the development of international environmental law, the field lacked a coordinated legal and institutional framework. The 1972 Stockholm conference and then UNCED attempted to create such a framework.

To 1945. The first distinct period in the greening process began with nineteenth-century bilateral fisheries treaties and the Pacific Fur Seal Arbitration.[9] It concluded with the creation of the new UN family of international institutions in 1945. This period might be characterized as one in which states first acted internationally upon their understanding that the process of industrialization and the rapid expansion of economic activities relying on natural resources required placing limits on the exploitation of flora and fauna and the adoption of appropriate legal instruments.

Until the establishment of the United Nations in 1945, no international forum existed in which to raise environmental concerns, and most of the agreements adopted in this initial period did not create arrangements to ensure that legal obligations were complied with or enforced. Many initiatives grew from activities by private citizens, an early harbinger of the more intensive activism of nongovernmental organizations that marks international negotiations today.

Creation of the United Nations: 1945–1972. The establishment of the UN introduced a second period in the development of international environmental law, which culminated in the 1972 UN Conference on the Human Environment. During this period many international organizations with competence in environmental matters were created, and legal instruments were adopted to address particular sources of pollution and the conservation of general and particular environmental resources. These included oil pollution, nuclear testing, wetlands, the marine environment and its living resources, freshwaters, and the dumping of waste at sea.[10]

The UN provided a forum for discussing the consequences of technological progress and introduced a period characterized by proliferation of international organizations, engagement with environmental issues, and action to address the causes of pollution and environmental degradation. The relationship between economic development and environmental protection began to be understood. However, the UN Charter did not, and still does not, explicitly address environmental protection or the conservation of natural resources.

In 1949 the UN convened its first environmental conference, the Conservation and Utilization of Resources, which presaged the 1972 Stockholm conference and the 1992 UNCED.[11] The 1949 conference was significant because it recognized the UN's competence in regard to environmental and natural resource issues. In 1954 the UN General Assembly convened its first major conference, the Conference on the Conservation of the Living Resources of the Sea, which led to the conservation rules adopted in the 1958 Geneva Conventions on the High Seas.[12]

Stockholm to Rio. The third period began with the 1972 Stockholm conference and concluded with UNCED in 1992. In this twenty-year span the UN attempted to put in place a system to address a growing range of environmental issues in a more coordinated and coherent way. A raft of regional and global conventions addressed new issues, and new techniques of regulation were employed.

The 1972 Stockholm conference, convened by the General Assembly, adopted three nonbinding instruments: a resolution on institutional and financial arrangements, the Declaration of Twenty-six Guiding Principles (including Principle 21), and an Action Plan setting forth 109 recommendations for more specific international action.[13] These represented the international community's first effort at constructing a coherent strategy for the development of international policy, law, and institutions to protect the environment.

For international environmental law, the most significant development proved to be the creation of the United Nations Environment Programme (UNEP). UNEP has subsequently been instrumental in the establishment and implementation of its Regional Seas Programme, including some thirty-two regional treaties, as well as important global treaties addressing ozone depletion, trade in hazardous waste, and biodiversity.

Stockholm catalyzed other global treaties adopted under the UN's auspices. One of the most important, if often overlooked, agreements is the 1982 United Nations Convention on the Law of the Sea (UNCLOS).[14] This established a unique comprehensive framework for the establishment of global rules to protect the marine environment and marine living resources, including detailed institutional arrangements and provisions on environmental impact assessment, technology transfer, and liability. These provisions have provided an influential basis for the language and approach of many other environmental agreements.

By 1990, when preparations for UNCED formally began, there existed a solid body of rules of international environmental law. States were increasingly subject to limits on the right to allow or carry out activities that harmed the environment. New standards were in place, and a range of techniques sought to implement those standards. Environmental issues, moreover, had begun to intersect with economic matters, especially trade and development lending. But in spite of these relatively impressive achievements, environmental matters remained on the periphery of the international community's agenda and the activities of most institutions.

UNCED and Beyond. UNCED, in 1992, launched a fourth period for international environmental law, requiring that environmental concerns be integrated into all international activities. International environmental law merged with international law in the new field of sustainable development.

In December 1987 the UN General Assembly endorsed the Brundtland Report, and the following year it called for a global conference on environment and development.[15] UNCED was formally proposed in December 1989 by General Assembly Resolution 44/228, and after four preparatory negotiating sessions, representatives from 176 states, several dozen international organizations, and several thousand NGOs converged on Rio de Janeiro for two weeks in June 1992. UNCED adopted three nonbinding instruments: the Rio Declaration on Environment and Development (the Rio Declaration); a Non-legally Binding Authoritative Statement of Principles for a Global Consensus on the Management, Conservation, and Sustainable Development of All Types of Forest (the Forest Principles); and Agenda 21.[16] Two treaties were also opened for signature at UNCED: the Convention on Biological Diversity and the United Nations Framework Convention on Climate Change.[17] These two treaties have formed the basis for further elaboration of international environmental law in their respective fields through the adoption of protocols and implementing arrangements. The recently adopted Marrakesh Accords, for example, elaborate emission reduction obligations under the 1997 Kyoto Protocol and include an unprecedented level of detail and complexity for an international instrument in the environmental field. [18]

Since UNCED, progress in developing and implementing the international concept of sustainable development has not been as promising. The 2002 World Summit on Sustainable Development (WSSD) held in Johannesburg produced a "Plan of Implementation," but in fact it contained few new commitments. This may have been a result of the breadth of the negotiating agenda, which included poverty eradication, agricultural practices, and public health issues. The Summit's failure to agree on concrete actions for implementing "sustainable development" calls into question the capacity of such a broad concept to provide a basis for the future development of international environmental law.

International Actors

Although states remain far and away the most important actors, the history of international environmental law reflects the central roles played by international organizations and nongovernmental actors. As with the human rights field, international environmental law provides clear evidence of an evolution from the view that international society comprises only a community of states to one that encompasses individuals, groups, and corporate and other entities within and among those states. This new reality is now reflected in many international legal instruments, especially the Rio Declaration and Agenda 21, which call for the further development of the role of international organizations and nongovernmental actors in virtually all aspects of the international legal process relating to environment and development. [19]

Different actors have different roles and functions, both as subjects and objects of international environmental law. These functions and roles include, principally, participating in the law-making process; monitoring implementation, including reporting; and ensuring enforcement of obligations. The extent to which each actor contributes to that process turns upon the extent of its international legal personality and the rights and obligations granted to it by general international law, as well as the rules established by particular treaties and other rules.

States. States continue to play the primary and dominant role in the international legal order. It is still states that create, adopt, and implement international legal principles and rules, create international organizations, and permit other actors to participate in the process. In 2003 there were 191 member states of the United Nations, and several others with observer status.[20] The members include both developed and developing countries. Developed countries include the twenty-four industrialized member states of the Organization for Economic Cooperation and Development (OECD)[21] and the thirteen states that previously formed part of the Soviet bloc. The latter are commonly referred to as "economies in transition." Some 133 member states are the developing countries that form an association referred to as the Group of 77, which often works as a single negotiating block within the United Nations.[22] Forty-nine of the most vulnerable developing countries are designated "least developed countries," or LDCs. Within the UN system states are also grouped regionally, usually for the purpose of elections to UN bodies. The five groupings are Latin America and the Caribbean, Africa, Asia, western Europe and others, and central and eastern Europe.

In environmental negotiations these rather simple distinctions tend to break down as states pursue what they perceive to be vital national interests, including their strategic alliances. However, the divide between industrialized nations of the OECD and the developing countries of the Group of 77 remains a prominent part of most environmental negotiations at the international level. The UNCED negotiations, for instance, illustrated the extent of the differences that often exist between developed and developing countries on contentious issues such as atmospheric emissions, conservation of marine mammals, protection of forests, institutional arrangements, and financial resources.

International Organizations. The international organizations involved in environmental matters make up a complex and unwieldy network at the global, regional, subregional, and bilateral levels. It is unlikely that any international organization today will not have some responsibility for environmental matters. The lack of coordination between international organizations in the environmental field makes it difficult to assess their role by reference to any functional, sectoral, or geographic criteria. To help understand their activities and interests, they can, however, be divided into three general categories: (1) global organizations under the auspices of, or related to, the United Nations and its specialized agencies, such as UNEP, the Food and Agriculture Organization, and the International Maritime Organization; (2) regional organizations outside the UN system, including the OECD, the Council of Europe, the Organization of African Unity, the Organization of American States, and the Association of Southeast Asian Nations; and (3) organizations established by environmental and other international agreements, such as the Intergovernmental Panel on Climate

Change and the numerous administrative and subsidiary bodies set up under environmental treaties.

International organizations perform a range of different functions and roles—judicial, legislative, and administrative—in the development and management of international legal responses to environmental issues and problems. The actual functions of each institution will depend to a great extent upon the powers granted to it as subsequently interpreted and applied by the parties and the practice of the organization. Nevertheless, five separate but interrelated legal functions and roles are performed by most international organizations:

- providing a forum for general cooperation, coordination, and consultation (formal and informal) between states on matters of international environmental management
- receiving and disseminating information between states and between states and the organization
- creating international legal obligations, including "soft law" or nonbinding commitments, by developing policy initiatives, standards, and treaty-specific rules
- ensuring the implementation of, and compliance with, standards and obligations developed by the organization
- providing an independent forum, or mechanism, for the settlement of disputes, usually between states

Nongovernmental Organizations. Nongovernmental organizations (NGOs) have historically played an important role in developing international environmental law and continue to do so in a variety of ways (see Chapter 5). In the past few decades at least six different types of NGO have emerged as actors in the development of international environmental law: the scientific community, nonprofit environmental groups and associations, private companies and business concerns, legal organizations, the academic community, and individuals. In addition, transnational corporations are more and more the object of international environmental regulation. Because they conduct activities across national boundaries in an increasingly interdependent world, the need for minimum international standards of behavior has been recognized. Transnational corporations have themselves begun to consider the need for further development of international environmental law governing their activities, although most of the efforts to date have produced only voluntary guidelines for corporate behavior.[23]

Sources of International Environmental Law

International law consists of rules, rights, and obligations that are legally binding on states and other members of the international community in their relations with each other. The sources of international law include:

- bilateral or multilateral treaties

- binding acts of international organizations
- rules of customary international law
- judgments of an international court or tribunal

The most important binding source of international law is treaties—formal international agreements also referred to by such names as conventions or protocols. These can be adopted bilaterally, regionally, or globally. With more than 191 states now in existence, the number of bilateral environmental agreements runs into the thousands, supplemented by dozens of regional agreements and a smaller but increasing number of global treaties. Countries of the European Union and other industrial nations have adopted a large body of regional environmental rules that frequently provide a basis for measures adopted in other parts of the world. Regional treaties are less well developed in Africa, the Caribbean, and Oceania and are even more limited in Asia and parts of the Americas. Industrial activity is prohibited by treaty in Antarctica.

The second principal source of international law in the environmental field is acts of international organizations. Almost all international environmental agreements establish institutional organs with the power to adopt certain rules, make decisions, or take other measures. Such acts, sometimes referred to as secondary legislation, can provide an important source of international law. Some of the more far-reaching international measures affecting the use of natural resources have been adopted in the form of acts of international organizations rather than by treaty.

Many environmental treaties allow the institutions they create to have a choice of adopting acts with or without binding legal effects. Binding acts of international organizations derive their legal authority from the treaty on which their adoption was based and can therefore be considered part of treaty law. Those acts that do not have binding legal consequences could, however, subsequently be relied upon as reflecting a rule of customary international law.

The primary role of treaties and acts of international organizations as sources of international law should not obscure the important, albeit secondary, role played by customary international law. Customary law fulfills a number of functions by creating binding obligations and contributing to the codification of obligations in the form of treaty rules and other binding acts. The significance of customary law lies in the fact that, as a general matter, it establishes obligations for all states (or all states within a particular region) except those that have persistently objected to a practice and its legal consequences. Article 38(1)(b) of the statute establishing the International Court of Justice identifies the two elements of customary international law: state practice and *opinio juris*—the belief that the practice is required as a matter of law. Establishing the existence of a rule of customary international law requires evidence of consistent state practice. Such practice will rarely provide clear guidance as to the precise content of any particular rule.

The case law of international courts and tribunals and arguments presented to such bodies identify some general principles and rules of international environmental law. The importance of arbitral awards, particularly in the development of international environmental law, should not be understated. Important principles were elaborated by arbitral tribunals in the previously mentioned Pacific Fur Seal case, in the Lac Lanoux arbitration between France and Spain (concerning the use of a shared river) and the much-cited Trail Smelter case between the United States and Canada (concerning transboundary air pollution). The latter articulated the principle that "no state has the right to use or permit the use of territory in such a manner as to cause injury by fumes in or to the territory of another of the properties or persons therein, when the case is of serious consequence and the injury is established by clear and convincing evidence." [24]

Judgments of the International Court of Justice have also contributed to the development of international environmental law, particularly in the Icelandic fisheries cases (on fisheries conservation), the nuclear test cases of 1974 and 1995 (on the legality of atmospheric nuclear tests), the 1997 Danube Dam case (concerning a large hydroelectric project with potential impacts on biodiversity), and the opinions on the legality of the use of nuclear weapons.

These sources of binding obligation are supplemented by nonbinding sources of soft law, reflected in guidelines, recommendations, and other nonbinding acts adopted by states and international institutions. Rules of soft law play an important role by pointing to the likely future direction of formally binding obligations, by informally establishing acceptable norms of behavior, and by "codifying" rules of customary law. The most important sources of soft law are found in the 1972 Stockholm Declaration; the World Charter for Nature, adopted by the UN General Assembly in 1982; and the 1992 Rio Declaration.

International Environmental Law: General Principles

Several general principles and rules of international law have emerged, or are emerging, specifically in relation to environmental matters. They are general in the sense that they are potentially applicable to all members of the international community across all ranges of activities and in that they address the protection of all aspects of the environment. [25]

Sovereignty and Responsibility for the Environment

The rules of international environmental law have developed in pursuit of two principles that pull in opposing directions: that states have sovereign rights over their natural resources and that states must not cause damage to the environment. These objectives are reflected in Principle 21 of the Stockholm Declaration and Principle 2 of the Rio Declaration and provide the foundation of international environmental law.

The first element (sovereignty) reflects the preeminent position of states as primary members of the international legal community. It is tempered by the second element (environmental protection), which places limits on the exercise of sovereign rights. In an environmentally interdependent world, activities in one state almost inevitably produce effects in other states or in areas beyond national jurisdiction (such as the high seas).

In the form presented by Principle 21 and Principle 2, the responsibility to prevent damage to the environment of other states or of areas beyond national jurisdiction has been accepted as an obligation by all states.[26] As indicated in the introduction, the International Court of Justice has now confirmed that the second element reflects customary international law.[27]

The emergence of this responsibility has historical roots that predate the Stockholm conference. These relate to the obligation of all states "to protect within the territory the rights of other states, in particular their right to integrity and inviolability in peace and war" and the principle endorsed by the arbitral tribunal in the Trail Smelter case.[28]

Good Neighborliness and International Cooperation

The principle of "good neighborliness," as enunciated in Article 74 of the UN Charter, concerning social, economic, and commercial matters, has been extended to environmental matters by rules promoting international cooperation. It applies particularly to activities carried out in one state that might have adverse effects on the environment of another state or in areas beyond national jurisdiction. The commitment to environmental cooperation is reflected in many international agreements and is supported by state practice. In general, the obligation includes commitments to implement treaty objectives or to improve relations outside a treaty or in relation to certain tasks. Specifically, the obligation can require information sharing, notification, consultation or participation rights in certain decisions, the conduct of environmental impact assessments, and cooperative emergency procedures, particularly where activities might be ultrahazardous. The construction of nuclear power plants on borders is an example of cooperative obligations that are reasonably well developed, at least in some regions.

The extent of compliance with this obligation was one of the central issues in the dispute between Hungary and Slovakia over construction of the Gabcikovo Dam, referred to the International Court of Justice in 1993.[29] Construction of the dam, as well as a second dam at Nagymaros, required the diversion of the Danube River, which Hungary claimed would produce dire environmental consequences. Hungary alleged that Czechoslovakia (now just Slovakia) violated its obligation to cooperate in good faith in the implementation of principles affecting transboundary resources. In its 1997 judgment, the Court found that Hungary had not been entitled to terminate construction work on the dams or to terminate the treaty, and that Slovakia was operating an alternative dam illegally. The parties subsequently undertook negotiations to implement the judgment, which implied that Hungary was not required to build a second dam. However, in the absence of agreement, in September 1998 Slovakia returned to the International Court with a further request that the Court lay down guidelines on the conduct of the negotiations.

More recently, the International Tribunal for the Law of the Sea (ITLOS) considered Ireland's allegation that the United Kingdom failed to cooperate in protecting the Irish Sea by refusing to share information and failing to carry out a proper environmental impact assessment of the proposed operation of a nuclear fuel recycling plant at Sellafield in England. ITLOS affirmed that "the duty to cooperate is a fundamental principle in the prevention of pollution of the marine environment" under UNCLOS and general international law. In the interests of "prudence and caution," the Tribunal ordered the parties to cooperate in exchanging information about the environmental risks and effects of the operation of the plant and in devising appropriate measures to prevent pollution of the marine environment. [30]

Sustainable Development

The International Court of Justice in the Gabcikovo-Nagymaros case described this principle as expressing the "need to reconcile economic development with protection of the environment." [31] The ideas underlying the concept of "sustainable development" have a long history in international law, dating back at least to the Pacific Fur Seal Arbitration in 1893. The concept came of age with UNCED and the international agreements that it spawned.

What "sustainable development" means in international law today is a more complicated matter. Where it has been used, it appears to refer to at least four separate but related objectives that, taken together, might constitute the legal elements of the concept of "sustainable development" as used in the Brundtland Report. [32] First, as invoked in some agreements, it refers to the commitment to preserve natural resources for the benefit of present and future generations. Second, in other agreements, sustainable development refers to appropriate standards for the exploitation of natural resources based upon harvest or use. Third, yet other agreements require an "equitable" use of natural resources, suggesting that a state must consider the needs of other states and people. A fourth category of agreements requires that environmental considerations be integrated with economic and other development plans, programs, and projects, and that development needs be taken into account in applying environmental objectives.

Common but Differentiated Responsibility

This principle has emerged from applying the broader principle of equity in general international law and recognizing that the special needs of developing countries must be considered if these countries are to be encouraged to participate in global environmental agreements. The principle is reflected in a handful of agreements, including treaties dealing with climate change that require parties to protect the climate system "on the basis of equity and in accordance with their common but differentiated responsibilities and respective capabilities" and place the burden of reducing greenhouse gas emissions primarily on developed countries.[33]

The principle of common but differentiated responsibility includes two important elements. First, states have a common responsibility to protect certain environmental resources. Second, it is necessary to take account of differing circumstances, particularly in relation to each state's contribution to causing a particular environmental problem and its ability to respond to the threat. Application of the principle of common but differentiated responsibility has important, practical consequences. It leads to the adoption and implementation of environmental standards that impose different commitments for states, and it provides a basis for providing financial and technical assistance to developing and least developed countries to assist them in implementing the commitments.

Precautionary Principle

This principle emerged in international legal instruments only in the mid-1980s, though it had previously been relied upon in some domestic legal systems. The core of this emerging legal principle, which some believe reflects customary international law,[34] is reflected in Principle 15 of the Rio Declaration, one part of which provides that "[w]here there are threats of serious or irreversible damage, lack of full scientific certainty shall not be used as a reason for postponing cost-effective measures to prevent environmental degradation." The precautionary principle aims to provide guidance to states and the international community in the development of international environmental law and policy in the face of scientific uncertainty and is, potentially, the most radical of environmental principles. Some invoke it to justify preemptive international legal measures to address potentially catastrophic environmental threats such as ozone depletion or climate change. Opponents, however, have decried the principle, arguing that it promotes overregulation of a range of human activities.

Notwithstanding the controversy, the principle has been endorsed in a large number of international agreements. Among these is the Biosafety Protocol to the Convention on Biological Diversity, which permits parties to ban imports of genetically modified organisms where there is a "lack of scientific certainty due to insufficient relevant scientific information and knowledge" concerning health or environmental impacts.[35] Similar language is found in the provisions of the 2001 Stockholm Convention on Persistent Organic Pollutants regarding placing controls on additional chemicals in the future,[36] although the words "precautionary principle" are not used due to objections raised by the United States, Australia, and other countries.[37]

International judicial acceptance of the precautionary principle has been more cautious. The principle was not mentioned in the majority decision in the Gabcikovo-Nagymaros case, despite considerable scientific uncertainty over the environmental impact of the project.[38] Likewise, the Appellate Body of the World Trade Organization, in the Beef Hormones case, declined to take a position on whether the principle amounts to customary international law, commenting that the international status of the principle is "less than clear." [39] The International Tribunal for the Law of the Sea was more forthcoming in the Southern Bluefin Tuna case, citing "prudence and caution" as a basis for its decision requiring Japan to cease an experimental fishing program that potentially endangered stocks of the migratory tuna species.[40]

Polluter Pays Principle

This principle states that the costs of pollution should be borne by those responsible for causing the pollution and the consequential costs. The precise meaning, international legal status, and effect of the principle remain open to question, since international practice based upon the principle is limited. It is doubtful whether it has achieved the status of a generally applicable rule of international law, except perhaps in relation to states in the European Union, the UN Economic Commission for Europe (UNECE), and the OECD. It has nevertheless attracted broad support and underlies rules on civil and state liability for environmental damage, on the permissibility of state subsidies, and the growing acknowledgment by developed countries of the "responsibility that they bear in the international pursuit of sustainable development in view of the pressures their societies place on the global environment," as well as the financial and other consequences that flow from this acknowledgment.[41] Supporting instruments include Principle 14 of the Rio Declaration, OECD Council Recommendations, the EC Treaty of Rome (as amended) and related instruments, and the 1992 agreement establishing the European Economic Area.

Basic Rules and Emerging Legal Standards

As international environmental law has developed, standards have been adopted to address a widening range of environmental resources. These standards tend to address particular resources, the most important being flora and fauna, water quality, air quality, hazardous substances, and waste.

Protection of Flora and Fauna

The protection of flora and fauna was the subject of the earliest international environmental regulation, and there are now widely accepted standards that prohibit interference with endangered species in particular. Important global instruments regulate wetlands, trade in endangered species, the conservation of biodiversity generally, and, most recently, transboundary movement of genetically modified organisms.[42] However, efforts to adopt a convention on forests at UNCED proved to be fruitless in the face of sustained opposition from many developing countries.

Protection of the Marine Environment

International law to prevent pollution of oceans and seas is now relatively well developed at the global and regional levels. At the global level the 1982 UN Convention on the Law of the Sea, which entered into force in November 1994, establishes a comprehensive framework to address marine pollution from various sources, including dumping at sea, land-based sources, vessels, and offshore installations, such as oil rigs.[43] Detailed obligations for these sources of pollution were adopted both prior to and after UNCLOS. At the global level there are agreements on the dumping of waste at sea, protection of the environment during salvage operations, and oil pollution preparedness and response.[44] However, no global agreement regulates pollution from land-based sources, which is particularly consequential because this accounts for more than 70 percent of the total.

Acts adopted by international organizations have also contributed significantly to the development of this area of international law. Notable examples include the 1982 decision by the International Whaling Commission to adopt a moratorium on commercial whaling and the 1985 decision of the parties to the 1972 London Dumping Convention to adopt a moratorium on the dumping of radioactive waste at sea.

At the regional level early agreements addressed dumping from ships and pollution from land-based sources.[45] These have since been supplemented by an extensive network of conventions adopted under the UNEP Regional Seas Programme, which was initiated in 1975 and now includes programs covering thirteen regional seas: the Caribbean, East Asian, East African, Kuwait, Mediterranean, Red Sea and Gulf of Aden, South Asian, South Pacific, Southeast Pacific, West and Central African, Northwest Pacific, Black Sea, and Northeast Pacific. More than 140 coastal states now participate in this UNEP program, and framework conventions and supplementary protocols are in force for the Caribbean, Kuwait, the Mediterranean, the Red Sea and Gulf of Aden, the Southeast Pacific, the South Pacific, West and Central Africa, the Indian Ocean and East Africa, and the Black Sea.[46] Additional commitments have been adopted for the EU and Antarctic regions.

Protection of Freshwater Resources

Freshwater resources include rivers, lakes, and groundwaters. Many individual rivers and river systems are now subject to special rules governing their use and the maintenance of water quality. Noteworthy examples include the Rhine in Europe, the Zambezi in Africa, and the Plate in South America, each of which has been subject to treaty protection for many years. More recently, efforts have been made to develop rules that apply to all rivers

in a particular region or to all rivers globally.[47] Lakes have also been subject
to protective regimes, especially in North America and other areas where
acid rain and other deposits have threatened to cause long-term damage.[48]
Protection of groundwaters remains less well developed in international law.

Air Quality

International law for the protection of the atmosphere addresses transboundary air pollution, ozone depletion, and climate change. Measures now
place limits for many states on permissible atmospheric emissions of certain
substances. This has important implications for production patterns and,
particularly, energy use.

In this area of international regulation, the first instrument was the
regional 1979 UNECE Convention on Long-Range Transboundary Air
Pollution, which has since been supplemented with protocols on sulfur
dioxide, nitrogen oxides, volatile organic compounds, heavy metals, persistent organic pollutants, and ground-level ozone.[49] The transboundary air
pollution model was relied upon in global efforts to protect the ozone layer
with the 1985 Framework Convention for the Protection of the Ozone
Layer, as supplemented by the 1987 Montreal Protocol, subsequently
amended in 1990, 1992, 1997, and 1999.[50] The 1992 Framework Convention on Climate Change and its 1997 Kyoto Protocol also have global
application. The 1992 convention entered into force in March 1994,
aiming to limit industrial countries' emissions of carbon dioxide and other
greenhouse gases; it also created a framework for cooperation and commitments to ensure that greenhouse gas concentrations in the atmosphere
do not lead to dangerous anthropogenic interference with the climate
system.[51] These soft commitments are to be implemented by the Kyoto
Protocol, which establishes emission reduction targets for certain developed countries for the commitment period 2008 to 2012.[52] Parties are permitted to use a range of innovative "flexibility mechanisms" (including
emissions trading) to reach their targets, although significant domestic
abatement action will still be necessary.

Waste

Binding international regulation of waste management is currently limited to regulating or prohibiting trade in certain wastes, as well as provisions
prohibiting the disposal at sea of certain hazardous wastes. These measures
encourage waste prevention and minimization by increasing costs and are
likely precursors to measures that might limit industrial wastes produced,
including packaging.

The principal international agreement establishing regulations and
prohibitions on trade in hazardous waste is the 1989 Basel Convention,
which requires that importing countries be notified of, and grant consent
for, shipments before they occur (prior informed consent).[53] A proposed

amendment to the Convention, known as the "Basel Ban," seeks to go further, prohibiting hazardous waste exports from OECD countries to non-OECD countries (see Chapter 7 for a full discussion).[54] At a regional level the 1991 African Bamako Convention prohibits imports of hazardous waste, which is redefined to include all substances whose use is banned in the exporting country.[55] Global regulation of radioactive waste movements is governed by a nonbinding 1990 International Atomic Energy Agency Code of Practice, which establishes regulatory guidelines and is far less stringent than any of the treaty agreements.[56] More stringent regulation of transboundary movements of spent nuclear fuel was established by the Joint Convention on the Safety of Spent Fuel Management and on the Safety of Radioactive Waste Management.[57]

Hazardous Substances

Until recently, the management of hazardous substances other than waste, including chemicals and pesticides, was not subject to any binding global legal instruments. In 2001 a Convention on Persistent Organic Pollutants (POPs) was adopted to regulate the production, use, and transboundary movement of POPs (chemicals that remain intact in the environment for long periods and bioaccumulate in living organisms).[58] The Convention establishes controls on the production, import, export, and disposal of these substances. Another new convention establishes a Prior Informed Consent (PIC) procedure for international trade in toxic pesticides and other hazardous chemicals.[59] The PIC Convention will allow countries to refuse imports of hazardous chemicals that they cannot manage safely and imposes labeling requirements on exports of these substances to promote their safe use. The two conventions supplement a large body of detailed, nonbinding regulations and other instruments dealing with the management of hazardous substances, including, in particular, international trade and chemical safety at work.[60] (See Chapter 7 for a detailed discussion of both Conventions.)

Conclusion

In a relatively short space of time, a significant body of principles and rules of international law has been put in place for the protection of the environment and conservation of natural resources. These rules have been primarily developed by and are addressed to states, although increasingly international environmental law encompasses a much broader range of actors, including nongovernmental organizations, treaty bodies, and corporate entities. Over the past decade, in particular, the rules of international environmental law have become increasingly complex and technical, as environmental considerations are addressed in economic and other social fields.

Although UNCED and its follow-up (WSSD) have not provided a clear sense of direction as to likely future developments, an emerging feature of international environmental law in the twenty-first century is its increased focus on issues of implementation and enforcement. Already we are seeing a shift from the legislative domain to the judicial and quasi-judicial domain, with international courts and other such bodies filling the gaps left by legislators. Further signs of this trend are the increasingly detailed noncompliance mechanisms adopted under treaties dealing with atmospheric pollution.[61] Nevertheless, judging by decisions of international tribunals, there is still some way to go before the more established judicial bodies will feel comfortable dealing with environmental issues and providing leadership in this next phase.[62] Indeed, it may well be that the greatest contribution to applying the principle of sustainable development will come from bodies traditionally outside the field of international environmental law, such as the World Trade Organization dispute settlement bodies.[63] As environmental issues are increasingly integrated into aspects of economic and development institutions and law, the field in which international environmental law has developed will continue to broaden, creating new challenges for those involved in its development and application.

Notes

1. "Request for an Examination of the Situation in Accordance with Paragraph 63 of the Court's Judgment of 20 December 1974 in the Nuclear Tests (*New Zealand v. France*) Case," Order of September 22, 1995, *International Court of Justice Reports* (hereafter *ICJ Reports*) (1995): 306, para. 64 (hereafter *Nuclear Tests II*).
2. *Legality of the Threat or Use of Nuclear Weapons*, Advisory Opinion, July 8, 1996, *ICJ Reports* (1996): 226, para. 29.
3. *Legality of the Threat or Use of Nuclear Weapons*, para. 33.
4. See Principle 27 of the Rio "Declaration on Environment and Development," *Report of the UN Conference on Environment and Development*, A/CONF.151/26/Rev.1, 2:3 (1993), reprinted in *International Legal Materials* (hereafter *ILM*) 31 (1992): 874.
5. See "Pacific Fur Seal Arbitration (Great Britain v. United States)," *Moore's Report of International Arbitration Awards* 1 (1893): 755.
6. Philip Allott, *Eunomia: New Order for a New World* (New York: Oxford University Press, 1990), para. 17.52.
7. See generally Philippe Sands, "The Environment, Community, and International Law," *Harvard International Law Journal* 30 (1989): 393.
8. For a general history of international environmental law, see Philippe Sands, *Principles of International Environmental Law* (Cambridge: Cambridge University Press, 2003).
9. See further below ("Sources of International Environmental Law").
10. Important treaties during this period included the Geneva Conventions on the High Seas (see "Convention on the High Seas," Geneva, April 29, 1958, United Nations Treaty Series, *Treaties and International Agreements Registered or Filed or Reported with the Secretariat of the United Nations* [hereafter cited as UNTS], 450: 82; "Convention on Fishing and Conservation of the Living Resources of the High Seas," Geneva, April 29, 1958, UNTS, 559: 285; "Convention on the Continental Shelf," Geneva, April 29, 1958, UNTS, 499: 311). In 1963 the Nuclear Test Ban Treaty was adopted, paving the way politically for Australia and New Zealand to bring a case before the ICJ calling on France to stop all nuclear testing; see Australia v. France, *ICJ Reports* (1974): 253; New Zealand v. France, *ICJ Reports* (1974): 457.
11. *United Nations Yearbook, 1948–1949* (New York: United Nations, 1950), 481–482.

12. UN General Assembly Resolution 800 (IX), December 14, 1954; the conference report is in *International Protection of the Environment* 8: 3969. See also the Geneva Conventions on the High Seas, cited above in n. 10.

13. *Report of the UN Conference on the Human Environment,* UN Doc. A/CONF/48/14 at 2-65, and Corr. 1 (1972), reprinted in *ILM* 11 (1972): 1416. For an excellent account of the conference and the Declaration, see Louis B. Sohn, "The Stockholm Declaration on the Human Environment," *Harvard International Law Journal* (1973).

14. "United Nations Convention on the Law of the Sea," Montego Bay, December 10, 1982, reprinted in *ILM* 21 (1982): 1261.

15. UN General Assembly Resolution 42/187, December 11, 1987, endorsement of World Commission on Environment and Development, *Our Common Future*; UN General Assembly Resolution 43/196, December 20, 1988.

16. *ILM* 31 (1992): 881; *Report of the United Nations Conference on Environment and Development,* vol. 1.

17. *ILM* 31 (1992): 822, 849.

18. See *Report of the Conference of the Parties on its Seventh Session,* Marrakesh, October 29–November 10, 2001, FCCC/CP/2001/13. The decisions that make up the Accords are in four volumes: FCCC/CP/2001/13/Add.1–Add.4.

19. United Nations Conference on Environment and Development, "Agenda 21," chap. 38, paras. 38.42–38.44.

20. Up-to-date membership figures for the UN can be found at http://www.un.org/Overview/unmember.html.

21. Up-to-date membership figures for the OECD can be found at http://www.oecd.org/oecd/pages/home/displaygeneral/0,3380,EN-countrylist-0-nodirectorate-no-no-159-0,00.html.

22. Up-to-date membership figures for the G-77 can be found at http://www.g77.org/main/main.htm.

23. For example, the OECD Guidelines for Multinational Enterprises (2000).

24. Permanent Court of Arbitration, Palmas Case (1928), *HCR* 2: 93. "United States v. Canada," *Reports of International Arbitral Awards* 3 (1941): 1907; citing Clyde Eagleton, *Responsibility of States* (New York: New York University Press, 1928), 80.

25. For the general distinction between rules and principles, see Ronald Dworkin, *Taking Rights Seriously* (Cambridge: Harvard University Press, 1977), 24, 26.

26. *Nuclear Tests II, ICJ Reports* (1995): 306.

27. *Legality of the Threat or Use of Nuclear Weapons,* para. 29. See also "Case Concerning the Gabcikovo-Nagymaros Project" (Hungary/Slovakia), *ICJ Reports* (1997), paras. 53 and 112.

28. See n. 24 above and accompanying text

29. See original Hungarian Application, October 22, 1992, paras. 27, 29, and 30, in *Documents in International Environmental Law,* ed. Philippe Sands, Richard Tarasofsky, and Mary Weiss, vol. 2A (Manchester: Manchester University Press, 1995), 691, doc. 28.

30. "MOX Plant Case (Ireland v. United Kingdom) (Provisional Measures)," *ILM* 41 (2002): 405, paras. 82, 84, and 89.

31. "Case Concerning the Gabcikovo-Nagymaros Project," para. 140.

32. World Commission on Environment and Development, *Our Common Future.*

33. "Climate Change Convention," Art. 3(1), *ILM* 31 (1992): 881, and the "Kyoto Protocol," *ILM* 37 (1997): 22.

34. See Owen McIntyre and Thomas Mosedale, "The Precautionary Principle as a Norm of Customary International Law," *Journal of Environmental Law* 9 (1997): 221.

35. "Cartagena Protocol on Biosafety," Art. 10(6), *ILM* 39 (2001): 1027.

36. "Stockholm Convention on Persistent Organic Pollutants," Art. 8.7(a) and 8.9, *ILM* 40 (2001): 532.

37. A rift has emerged in this respect between the EU, which supports the idea of the "precautionary principle" as a principle of international law, and the United States

and other countries (particularly Australia, and to a lesser extent Canada and New Zealand), which see precaution merely as an approach to decision making.

38. See Afshin A-Khavari and Donald R. Rothwell, "The ICJ and the Danube Dam Case: A Missed Opportunity for International Environmental Law?" *Melbourne University Law Review* 22 (1998): 507, 530.
39. "EC Measures Concerning Meat and Meat Products (Hormones)", *Report of the Appellate Body*, WT/DS26/AB/R & WT/DS48/AB/R, January 16, 1998, para. 123.
40. "Southern Bluefin Tuna Cases (New Zealand v. Japan; Australia v. Japan) (Provisional Measures)", *ILM* 38 (1999): 1624, para, 77. Also see suggestions of Judge Weeramantry in his dissenting opinion in *Nuclear Test II, ICJ Reports* (1995): 342.
41. "Declaration on Environment and Development," Principle 7.
42. "Convention on Wetlands of International Importance," Ramsar, Iran, February 2, 1971, UNTS, 996: 245; "Convention on International Trade in Endangered Species of Wild Fauna and Flora," Washington, March 3, 1973, UNTS, 993: 243; "Convention on Biological Diversity," Rio de Janeiro, June 5, 1992, *ILM* 31 (1992): 822 (which also regulates the sustainable use of the components of biodiversity and the sharing of benefits arising from the use of genetic resources); "Biosafety Protocol," Montreal, January 29, 2000, *ILM* 39 (2001): 1027.
43. "United Nations Convention on the Law of the Sea," December 10, 1982, *ILM* 21 (1982): 1261.
44. "Convention on the Prevention of Marine Pollution by Dumping of Wastes and Other Matter," December 29, 1972, UNTS, 1046: 120 (in London on November 7, 1996, the parties to the Dumping Convention agreed to a protocol that will replace the Convention: *ILM* 36 [1997]: 1); "International Convention Relating to Intervention on the High Seas in Cases of Oil Pollution Damage," Brussels, November 29, 1969, reprinted in *ILM* 9 (1970): 25; "International Convention on Salvage," London, April 28, 1989, *International Journal of Estuarine and Coastal Law* (1989): 300; "International Convention on Oil Pollution Preparedness, Response, and Cooperation," London, November 30, 1990, *ILM* 30 (1991): 733.
45. The early Oslo and Paris Conventions have now been replaced by the "OSPAR Convention for the Protection of the Marine Environment of the North East Atlantic," Paris, September 22, 1992, *ILM* 32 (1993): 1228.
46. See generally Jorge Illueca, "A Regional Seas Renaissance," *Synergies*, UNEP, November 1999.
47. See "Convention on the Law of Non-navigational Uses of International Watercourses," reprinted in *ILM* 36 (1997): 700.
48. "Agreement between the United States and Canada Concerning the Water Quality of the Great Lakes," Ottawa, April 15, 1972, reprinted in *ILM* 11 (1972): 694.
49. "Convention on Long-Range Transboundary Air Pollution," Geneva, November 13, 1973, reprinted in *ILM* 18 (1979): 1442.
50. "Framework Convention for the Protection of the Ozone Layer," Vienna, March 22, 1985, reprinted in *ILM* 26 (1987): 1529; "Protocol on Substances That Deplete the Ozone Layer," Montreal, September 16, 1987, reprinted in *ILM* 26 (1987): 1550.
51. *ILM* 31 (1992): 881.
52. The Kyoto Protocol is currently not in force.
53. "Convention on the Control of Transboundary Movements of Hazardous Wastes and Their Disposal," Basel, March 22, 1989, reprinted in *ILM* 28 (1989): 649.
54. Decision II/12, Report of COP-2, UNEP/CHW.2/30, March 25, 1994. The Basel Ban is not yet in force.
55. "Convention on the Ban of the Import into Africa and the Control of Transboundary Movement and Management of Hazardous Wastes within Africa," Bamako, January 30, 1991, reprinted in *ILM* 30 (1991): 775.
56. International Atomic Energy Agency, Doc. GC(XXXIV)/920, June 27, 1990, *Yearbook of International Environmental Law* 1 (1990): 537.

57. Joint Convention on the Safety of Spent Fuel Management and on the Safety of Radioactive Waste Management, September 5, 1997, *ILM* 36 (1997): 1436.

58. Convention on Persistent Organic Pollutants, Stockholm, May 22, 2001, reprinted in *ILM* 40 (2001): 532.

59. Rotterdam Convention on the Prior Informed Consent Procedure for Certain Hazardous Chemicals and Pesticides in International Trade, Rotterdam, September 10, 1998, reprinted in *ILM* 38 (1999): 1.

60. 1985 UN Food and Agriculture Organization Code of Conduct on the Distribution and Use of Pesticides; 1987 UNEP London Guidelines for the Exchange of Information on Chemicals in International Trade, as amended in 1989; "Convention Concerning Safety in the Use of Chemicals at Work," Geneva, June 24, 1990, *Yearbook of International Environmental Law* 1 (1990): 295.

61. Notably the detailed compliance mechanism adopted under the Marrakesh Accords for implementation of the Kyoto Protocol: Decision 24/CP.7, Procedures and mechanisms relating to compliance under the Kyoto Protocol.

62. By contrast, the European Court of Justice and the European Court of Human Rights are beginning to address environmental issues across the range of their competencies.

63. Of particular significance are the two decisions of the Appellate Body in the Shrimp/Turtle dispute. See "United States–Import Prohibition of Certain Shrimp and Shrimp Products," *Report of the Appellate Body,* WT/DS58/AB/R, reprinted in *ILM* 38 (1999): 118, and "United States–Import Prohibition on Certain Shrimp and Shrimp Products," Recourse to Article 21.5 of the DSU by Malaysia, *Report of the Appellate Body,* October 22, 2001, WT/DS58/AB/RW.

4

Global Environmental Policy: Governance through Regimes

David Leonard Downie

Nearly exhausted after a remarkable twenty-four-hour final negotiation session, delegates from 137 countries grew quiet as John Buccini, chair of the International Negotiating Committee (INC), took the microphone on Sunday morning, December 10, 2000. After three years of negotiations, including this exhausting final week in Johannesburg, more than a few leaned forward in anticipation. "Ladies and gentlemen, you have just made a Convention." The room erupted in applause. The final draft of a new global environmental treaty, the Stockholm Convention on Persistent Organic Pollutants, had just been completed.[1]

These moments—the creation of new environmental treaties—are rightly seen as significant achievements. Indeed, countries must agree to specific goals and policies if real progress is going to be made. However, students and scholars would fail to understand global environmental policy in a given issue area if they focused only on a single treaty rather than the entire evolving set of principles, norms, rules, procedures, and institutions—the "international regime"—that countries and other actors create and implement for a specific issue.

This chapter provides an introduction to "regimes" in the context of global environmental policy. It provides a detailed definition of the term, delineates prominent examples in global environmental politics, and outlines obstacles to creating and implementing effective global environmental regimes.

International Regimes

An international regime is a set of integrated principles, norms, rules, procedures, and institutions that actors create or accept to regulate and coordinate action in a particular issue area of international relations. Principles are beliefs of fact, causation, and rectitude. Norms are standards of behavior. Rules are specific prescriptions or proscriptions for action. Procedures are prevailing practices, including those for making and implementing collective choice. Institutions are mechanisms and organizations for implementing, operating, evaluating, and expanding the regime and regime policy.[2]

These five regime elements are created, structured, and implemented through formal agreements, international organizations, private international law, soft law, and/or accepted norms of international behavior among actors involved in the issue area (governments, international organizations, nongovernmental organizations, multinational corporations, and others). States, as the dominant actors in the international system, are the primary and most important creators of international regimes, but they are not the only source, and the involvement of other actors often proves critical. Similarly, while formal, legally binding treaties often form the core of a regime, it can also be based on private international law, soft law, or other arrangements, provided that these are accepted by the actors in the issue areas as creating principles, rules, and procedures that guide their behavior. Examples include the rapidly growing body of international management and manufacturing standards, particularly those based on the ISO frameworks developed under the rubric of the International Organization of Standards.[3]

Regimes can thus be seen as dynamic, sector-specific regulatory and administrative systems. A regime is not patterned interaction, a single international agreement, or a single organization, although each of these is usually part of one. Rather, an international regime consists of the principles, norms, rules, and procedures contained in one or more interrelated agreements, organizations, standard practices, and shared understandings that together regulate international action in a particular issue area. The nuclear nonproliferation regime, for example, consists of the principles, norms, rules, and procedures contained or included in the Partial Test Ban Treaty, the Non-Proliferation Treaty, and the relevant activities of the International Atomic Energy Agency. When effective, regimes, through their principles, help to sharpen international goals in an issue area; shape international behavior toward a common goal through their rules and norms; manage state interactions; augment policy coordination and collaboration; reduce conflict; and facilitate the making of further agreements.

The ozone regime is one of the best-developed and most effective regimes in global environmental policy and can be used to illustrate the definition of a regime and its components. Many students and scholars correctly understand the Montreal Protocol as a ground-breaking global treaty that seeks to protect stratospheric ozone—the ozone layer that in turn protects the Earth from ultraviolet radiation. However, global ozone policy consists of much more.[4]

The ozone regime is the set of integrated principles, norms, rules, and procedures that nation-states have created to regulate and coordinate action in an attempt to protect stratospheric ozone from human-made chemicals such as chlorofluorocarbons (CFCs) and methyl bromide. The international agreements that delineate the main elements of the regime include the 1985 Vienna Convention for the Protection of the Ozone Layer, the 1987 Montreal Protocol on Substances that Deplete the Ozone Layer, and the binding amendments and adjustments to the protocol agreed to during fifteen meetings of the parties to the agreement. Of these, the most important agreements are the 1987 Montreal Protocol, the 1990 London Amendment and Adjustment, the 1992 Copenhagen Amendment and Adjustment, the 1995 Vienna Adjustment, and the 1999 Beijing Amendment and Adjustment.[5]

Also central to the ozone regime are operations of its constituent institutions. The Meeting of the Parties (an annual gathering of government representatives from countries that have ratified the protocol) is the supreme decision-making authority and can negotiate amendments and adjustments to the protocol as well as make binding decisions on issues related to its implementation. The Open-Ended Working Group (OEWG) holds discussions in preparation for the Meeting of the Parties (MOP). Three independent assessment panels—the Scientific, Environmental Effects, and Technology and Economic assessment panels—provide the Parties with periodic, comprehensive, and authoritative reviews of key issues, under instructions from the Parties and OEWG.[6] The Multilateral Fund provides financial assistance to developing countries to aid their transition from using ozone-depleting chemicals—under rules established by the protocol and decisions by the parties.[7] The implementing agencies—the World Bank, United Nations Development Programme (UNDP), United Nations Environment Programme (UNEP), and United Nations Industrial Development Organization (UNIDO)—execute work plans approved and funded by the Multilateral Fund's decision-making body, the Executive Committee, which is composed of representatives from fourteen governments. The Implementation Committee provides a forum for discussing issues of noncompliance and offers recommendations to the MOP. The Ozone Secretariat provides day-to-day administration of the regime and supports the MOP, OEWG, assessment panels, and Implementation Committee. The Multilateral Fund Secretariat performs similar functions for the operation of the Multilateral Fund and its Executive Committee.

The major principles (beliefs of fact, causation, and rectitude) of the ozone regime are enunciated in the Vienna Convention and the Montreal Protocol, particularly in the preamble. These include statements that the ozone layer is a critical component of the Earth's natural systems and should be protected; that certain human-made chemicals have the capacity to deplete the ozone layer and, in fact, have already done so; that political action should be based on the best scientific and technical information available; that regulations should be guided, in general, by precaution; and that all states have a common responsibility to help protect the ozone layer but have different responsibilities in doing so.

The norms of the ozone regime include all standards of behavior enunciated in the Vienna Convention, the Montreal Protocol, amendments to the protocol, and decisions by the Parties or Executive Committee that do not carry the binding nature of rules. The telling difference is the verb used to proscribe the action. For example, "Parties shall" indicates a rule. "Parties should" or "are requested to" indicates attempts to create norms.

The rules (specific prescriptions or proscriptions for action) of the ozone regime constitute the binding international law of global ozone policy. The rules are enunciated most prominently in the binding provisions of the Vienna Convention, the Montreal Protocol, and related amendments and adjustments to the protocol. The most important regime rules establish specific targets and timetables for countries to reduce and eventually eliminate the production and use of particular ozone-depleting substances (ODS).[8] They also include a variety of requirements regarding reporting, scientific assessments, assistance to developing countries, treaty implementation, and operation of the MOP. Rules are also created by binding decisions of the MOP and the Executive Committee of the Multilateral Fund on a variety of policy and procedural issues within their jurisdiction (which are established by the protocol).

Finally, the procedures of the ozone regime are the prevailing practices, including those for making and implementing collective choice. These include provisions for amending the treaty and reaching decisions, as well as the standard operating procedures of the regime's institutions: the MOP, OEWG, Ozone Secretariat, Executive Committee of the Multilateral Fund, Fund Secretariat, assessment panels, Implementation Committee, and implementing agencies. Moreover, because the ozone regime is nearly twenty years old, many operating procedures are fully entrenched and provide clear and well-regarded precedents for considering, developing, deciding upon, mandating, and implementing global ozone policy.

International Regimes in Global Environmental Policy

Regimes are found in most areas of international relations, including trade, finance, environment, human rights, managing the global commons such as the oceans and Antarctica, communications, travel, even security.[9] As a result, regimes have received a good deal of theoretical and empirical attention within the international organization subfield of international relations.[10] Of course, comparative levels of regime development and impact vary significantly across issue areas. Although some wildlife treaties date from early in the twentieth century, the prominence of transnational environmental politics has risen significantly since the 1972 Stockholm conference. Indeed, to date global environmental policy (of varying specificity and importance) exists for stratospheric ozone (including significant global agreements in 1985, 1987, 1990, 1992, 1995, 1997, 1999); climate change (1992, 1997); biodiversity, including species protection, habitat protection, and biosafety (1973, 1979, 1992); Antarctica (1991); desertification (1992); hazardous waste (1989, 1991); toxic chemicals (1998, 2001); financial transfers, especially the agreements creating and reorganizing the Global Environment Facility (GEF), as well as other issues. Negotiations on these and other global issues continue, as do talks on numerous regional and bilateral issues.

International environmental policy in each of these areas increasingly takes place through an international regime. In addition to the ozone regime, prominent examples of international environmental regimes and their constituent agreements and organizations include the following (by no means an exhaustive list):

- The climate change regime, which seeks to mitigate human-induced climate change by limiting anthropogenic emissions of

greenhouse gases such as carbon dioxide and methane and protecting associated sinks. Components of the climate regime include
the principles, norms, rules, and procedures contained in the 1992
Framework Convention on Climate Change and the 1997 Kyoto
Protocol, as well as the international organizations tasked with supporting these agreements, including the Climate Secretariat, Intergovernmental Panel on Climate Change (IPCC), GEF's climate
program, as well as the Conference of Parties and its numerous subsidiary bodies.

- The hazardous waste regime, which seeks to protect human health
  and the environment from wastes that are toxic, poisonous, explosive,
  corrosive, eco-toxic, or infectious. The hazardous waste regime centers on the global 1989 Basel Convention on the Control of Transboundary Movements of Hazardous Wastes and Their Disposal,
  which requires or urges parties to minimize the generation of hazardous wastes, work to ensure their environmentally sound management and disposal, and control, reduce, or ban their transnational
  movement, including taking measures to prevent and punish illegal
  traffic. The regime includes the Basel Ban Amendment and the Basel
  Protocol on Liability and Compensation (neither of which has
  entered into force). It also includes the Basel Convention Secretariat,
  Basel Convention Regional Centers, the Conference of Parties, and,
  to a lesser extent, several regional treaties. (See Chapter 7 for an outline of the Basel Convention.)
- A toxic chemical regime, which centers on the 1998 Rotterdam
  Convention on the Prior Informed Consent Procedure for Certain
  Hazardous Chemicals and Pesticides in International Trade
  (PIC); the 2001 Stockholm Convention on Persistent Organic
  Pollutants (POPs); the 1989 Basel Convention; the PIC, POPs,
  and Basel Secretariats; UNEP Chemicals; the POPs-related port-
  folio of the GEF; the International Programme on Chemical
  Safety (IPCS); the Inter-Organization Programme on the Sound
  Management of Chemicals (IOMC); the Intergovernmental
  Forum on Chemical Safety (IFCS); and the nascent Strategic
  Approach to International Chemicals Management initiative
  (SAICM). (See Chapter 7 for an outline of the Rotterdam and
  Stockholm Conventions.)
- A global biodiversity regime that centers on the 1992 Convention
  on Biodiversity, the 2000 Cartagena Protocol on Biosafety, the
  Biodiversity Secretariat, and associated funding activities by the
  GEF. The regime could also be considered to include a number of
  species-specific and habitat protection treaties, including the 1973
  Convention on International Trade in Endangered Species of Wild
  Fauna and Flora (CITES), the 1979 Bonn Convention on the

Conservation of Migratory Species of Wild Animals, and the 1991 Ramsar Wetlands Convention.

- Several endangered species regimes, including those centered on the aforementioned CITES, the Whaling Convention, the Migratory Species Convention, and several seal conventions, including some from early in the twentieth century.

- The ocean pollution regime, which includes the London Ocean Dumping Convention (regulating waste disposal in the oceans); the 1973, 1978, and 1990 International Conventions for the Prevention of Marine Pollution from Ships (MARPOL, regulating ship discharges); and relevant activities of the International Maritime Organization (IMO).

- The Mediterranean Sea regime, which consists of more than a dozen individual agreements, including the 1976 Barcelona Convention for the Protection of the Mediterranean Sea Against Pollution; the 1976 Protocol Concerning Cooperation in Combating Pollution of the Mediterranean Sea by Oil and Other Harmful Substances in Cases of Emergency; the 1976 Protocol for the Prevention of Pollution of the Mediterranean Sea by Dumping from Ships and Aircraft; and the 1980 Protocol for the Protection of the Mediterranean Sea from Land-based Sources. Several other regional sea regimes have also been created.[11]

- An emerging forestry regime or "governance system," which includes the forest principles adopted at UNCED;[12] several increasingly prominent voluntary certification bodies and systems, perhaps most prominently the Forest Stewardship Council; and an increasing number of major private actors.

- The desertification regime, which includes the 1994 Convention to Combat Desertification, its constituent institutions, and the associated funding activities of the GEF.

- The Antarctic Treaty regime, which arose from broader political and economic issues but includes important environmental components, including the 1972 Convention for the Conservation of Antarctic Seals; the 1980 Convention on the Conservation of Antarctic Marine Living Resources; the 1988 Wellington Convention on the Regulation of Antarctic Mineral Resource Activities; and the 1991 Protocol on Environmental Protection.

- The pan-European air pollution regime, which also includes Canada, Russia, and the United States, built around the 1979 Geneva Convention on Long-Range Transboundary Air Pollution (CLRTAP).[13] CLRTAP has provided the forum for creation of eight issue-specific protocols, including the 1984 Protocol for Long-Term Financing of Monitoring; the 1985 Sulfur Protocol; the 1988 Nitrogen Oxides Protocol; the 1991 Volatile Organic Compounds Protocol; the 1998 Heavy Metals Protocol; and the 1998 POPs Protocol.

Obstacles to Effective Global Environmental Policy

The existence of international regimes in many environmental issue areas should not obscure the fact that creating and implementing effective global environmental policy are not easy. It took many years to create each of the environmental regimes listed in the first section of this chapter, and several of them remain weak and rather ineffective (for example, the climate change, desertification, and global biodiversity regimes). It is important, therefore, to understand the obstacles to effective global environmental policy.

This section outlines factors that make it difficult for governments to create and implement effective international environmental policy and regimes. Four types of factors stand out: (1) systemic obstacles, (2) procedural obstacles, (3) lack of necessary and sufficient conditions, and (4) obstacles characteristic of international environmental issues. Please note that the individual and relative impact of each characteristic varies across countries and issue areas.

Systemic Obstacles

Several significant impediments to creating and implementing effective global environmental policy can be traced to core elements of the global political, ecological, and legal systems.[14]

The International Political System: Effective Cooperation Is Difficult

Anarchy is one defining characteristic of the structure of the international system. The absence of a world government with recognized authority to maintain order demands that states ultimately must rely only on self-help to ensure their safety. Many theorists argue that the exigencies of this situation and the resulting security dilemma have broad consequences for international relations.[15] Among the most familiar are that states tend to balance the power of others through alliances and armaments; states prefer and strive for independence over interdependence; and effective cooperation among states is difficult to achieve.[16]

It is the last of these consequences that concerns us here. Even without relying upon the assumptions of human imperfections or negative motivations found in the realism of Thomas Hobbes, Reinhold Niebuhr, and Hans Morgenthau, many theorists argue that the consequences of the structure of the international system alone can constrain states from following cooperative paths.[17] Oran Young notes that "one of the most robust findings of the social sciences is reflected in the proposition that rational actors engaging in interactive decision-making in the absence of effective rules or social conventions can and often do fail to realize feasible joint gains, thus ending up with outcomes that are suboptimal (and sometimes highly destructive)."[18]

Thus states often do not cooperate successfully for many different reasons: fear of being double-crossed;[19] desire to gain benefits without paying a fair share of the costs (free riding);[20] concern that other countries might gain relative positional advantages;[21] incentives to pursue gains that may be rational individually but result in destruction of a collective good or common-pool resource;[22] misperception of the motives, intentions, or actions of other governments;[23] market failure;[24] and lack of a global government with recognized authority to punish violators and maintain order.

Environmental politics takes place within the international arena. Its green veneer does not divorce it from the pressures that system structure places on state actors. Cooperative solutions do not arise without concerns for comparative costs. States do engage in distributive bargaining. They do compromise possible solutions by linking them to extraneous political, security, and economic issues. They do fail to locate mutually advantageous policies. In short, international environmental politics is still international politics, and, therefore, creating and implementing effective global policy and regimes remain difficult.

Global Political and Ecological Systems

Ecological systems have their own logic and laws and exist independently of the international political and legal systems. Simply put, the causes, consequences, and geographic scope of environmental problems do not respect national boundaries. This somewhat simplistic observation nevertheless captures an important truth: the structure of the global political system, composed of independent sovereign states, is not well suited to address complex, interdependent, international environmental problems whose causes, impacts, and solutions transcend unrelated political boundaries.

Global Legal Systems and the Requirements for Effective International Environmental Policy

Principle 21 from the 1972 Stockholm conference is often cited as one of the most important foundations of modern international law. It reads: "States have, in accordance with the Charter of the United Nations and the principles of international law, the sovereign right to exploit their own resources pursuant to their own environmental policies, and the responsibility to ensure that activities within their jurisdiction or control do not cause damage to the environment of other states or of areas beyond the limits of national jurisdiction"[25] (such as the atmosphere or oceans). Note the profound contradiction between the two halves of this sentence. The fundamental principle of international law is sovereignty. States have, to a significant extent, unique and unfettered legal control over activities within their borders. This has been, and continues to be, particularly true when it comes to economic development and the use of natural resources (as both raw materials and as sinks for pollution).

At the same time, actions taken within a country—from emitting greenhouse gases to clearing rain forests to discharging pollutants into the air or water—can have international environmental implications. Legitimate actions within one country can create environmental problems for another. Effective international policy, therefore, often requires limiting what a state does within its own borders. This is how the structure of international law, in the form of sovereign legal control, can conflict with the requirements for effective international environmental policy. Overcoming this obstacle is among the more difficult challenges in global environmental policy.

Procedural Obstacles

The structural obstacles outlined above give rise to specific procedural problems once nation-states actually attempt to address an international environmental issue. Two stand out: the lowest common denominator and the time-lag problems.

Lowest Common Denominator

All states are sovereign entities. They can choose to join or not join international environmental agreements. At the same time, the active participation of many countries is usually necessary to address a regional or global problem. This often means that the countries most interested in addressing a problem must gain the cooperation of countries with less, little, or even no interest. Thus international and global environmental policy often represents, at least at the start, the lowest common denominator measures that the relevant countries are willing to accept.

For example, during the early stages of negotiations on protecting the ozone layer, from 1983 to 1985, there were two major coalitions. The United States, the Nordic states, Canada, and Switzerland supported creating international controls on CFCs and other ozone-depleting substances (ODS), while the European Community and its member states, supported quietly by Japan and the USSR, largely opposed them. (Most other countries were either undecided or, as in the case of China and India, uninterested in regulation and largely uninvolved in the negotiations.) In March 1985, representatives of forty-three states and dozens of international governmental and nongovernmental organizations met in Vienna to review and adopt a framework treaty that affirmed the importance of protecting the ozone layer but did not include specific measures on potential threats. Until the last moments, the United States, Canada, and the Nordic countries considered forcing delegates to vote on adding a protocol mandating binding controls on certain uses of CFCs. They abandoned this strategy, however, understanding that such controls without participation by the European Community, and probably without Japan and the Soviet bloc, would not significantly impact the global problem and probably threaten the ability of the Framework Convention to produce a binding protocol in the future. The most reluctant, necessary actor, Europe, set the lowest common denominator for global policy.

Slow Development and Implementation: Time Lags

The sovereignty of states and the fact that each can choose to join or not join an international environmental agreement also contribute to a significant time lag between the identification of an international environmental problem and the impact of international policy. In short, it is neither an easy nor a quick process to create and implement global policy. Negotiations must be convened, policies agreed to, and treaties formally ratified by governments—and by enough governments so that the treaty can enter into force and be effective, treaty implementation initiated, and policy implemented effectively over a long enough period of time to impact the environmental problem.

Yet during this process the issue at hand does not wait. While the policy process drags on, greenhouse gases continue to build up, biodiversity continues to decline, toxic pollutants continue to accumulate. The years, even decades, required by the global policymaking process, even when it is successful, present a significant procedural obstacle to effective global environmental policy and regimes.

The Absence of Necessary Conditions: Concern, Contractual Environment, and Capacity

As Peter Haas, Robert Keohane, and Marc Levy argue, effective international environmental policy, when reduced to its most basic and obvious elements, "requires three fundamental conditions. . . . First, government concern must be sufficiently high to prompt states to devote scarce resources to solving the problem. . . . Second, there must be a hospitable contractual environment. . . . States must be able to make credible commitments, to enact joint rules with reasonable ease, and to monitor each other's behavior at moderate costs . . . without debilitating fear of free riding or cheating by others. . . . Third, states must possess the political and administrative capacity . . . necessary for the implementation of international norms, principles and rules." [26]

These conditions can be considered necessary (but not sufficient) for effective international environmental policy. Although it is easy to oversimplify the terms, concern, contractual environment, and capacity encapsulate important, even critical, requirements for successful environmental policy. While these are not obstacles themselves, the absence of any one of them presents significant obstacles to the creation and implementation of effective environmental regimes.

General Characteristics of International Environmental Issues

International environmental issues also possess inherent characteristics that make effective cooperation difficult. These characteristics are not unique to environmental issues, but they are prominent in, and common to, environmental issues. Individually or in combination, these characteristics can exacerbate systemic constraints on international cooperation as well as inhibit the creation of sufficient concern, a hospitable contractual environment, and sufficient capacity. Of course, the individual and relative impact of each characteristic in obstructing effective environmental policies varies across countries and issue areas.

This section delineates these obstacles and illustrates their impact, using examples from the development of the ozone regime. Please note that the categories represent somewhat artificial but useful heuristic divisions. Thus their components and impacts are interrelated rather than mutually exclusive.

Scientific Complexity and Uncertainty

Environmental issues often involve both complex scientific issues and significant uncertainty about their ultimate impact. New environmental issues often exist, almost by definition, at the edge of current knowledge of chemistry, biology, physics, and natural systems.

Scientific complexity can create uncertainty concerning the content, scope, severity, and time frame of individual problems. In such situations, reaching agreement on international policy can be difficult. It can be difficult to infer causation, to attribute responsibility, and to design solutions. Lack of firm knowledge can undermine concern. Large degrees of uncertainty allow other, more certain economic or political interests to maintain priority in the policy hierarchy. Complexity can challenge the capacity of government bureaucracies to understand the problem or to implement common solutions properly. Uncertainty and complexity can lead different states to perceive the payoff matrix differently, perhaps reducing incentives to risk cooperation and increasing incentives to free ride, thereby harming the contractual environment. Climate change, biodiversity loss, and ocean fish stocks are three examples of issues in which continuing uncertainty hampers international negotiations despite general agreement that complete inaction could lead to significant if not disastrous outcomes.

Scientific complexity and uncertainty certainly affected the development of the global ozone regime. The CFC-ozone theory emerged suddenly in 1974.[27] The claim that a relatively small number of inert molecules released near ground level would threaten stratospheric ozone in the next century through a complex set of chemical reactions appeared to many an unlikely proposition. Atmospheric chemistry was poorly understood at the time, and the theory left a significant number of potentially critical chemical interactions and feedback mechanisms to be investigated. No depletion had been observed in nature, and obtaining proof that any future depletion was the result of CFCs rather than natural fluctuations could be difficult.

For many years, scientists investigated and debated many issues surrounding the CFC-ozone theory, including reaction rates, secondary reactions, feedback mechanisms, CFC sinks, and related points of atmospheric chemistry and physics. Not surprisingly, predictions for ozone depletion varied significantly for many years, even among scientists convinced of the accuracy of the general theory. These uncertainties provided opponents of ODS controls with significant leverage to argue that national and international regulations were unnecessary and that further discussion should wait for atmospheric chemistry to become better understood and for scientists to provide proof that CFCs had caused measurable ozone depletion.[28]

Linked Economic and Political Interests

A second and equally critical obstacle is that environmental problems are inextricably linked to important economic and political interests. Environmental issues, and therefore environmental negotiations, do not exist independent of other economic and political activities and interests. Rather, environmental issues exist *because* of these activities and interests. Environmental problems are produced as externalities of individuals, corporations, and nations pursue other interests.

Few, if any, individuals or organizations harm the environment as an end in itself. People do not get up in the morning, leave their homes, and announce, "I intend to pollute today." What people do say, however, is "I intend to manufacture today. I intend to produce energy. I intend to farm. I intend to drive my car to work." Environmental degradation is one consequence of these pursuits. It is the consequence of such important local, corporate, national, and international economic and political activities as energy production, mining, manufacturing, farming, fishing, transportation, resource consumption, livestock husbandry, urbanization, weapons production, territorial expansion, and military conflict. The fact that many of these activities could be pursued successfully while producing less environmental degradation does not erase the links between the issues.

Thus international cooperation on environmental issues often must entail de facto cooperation on important economic and even security concerns. Addressing the possibility of climate change requires controlling fossil fuel consumption. Preventing more serious declines in ocean fish stocks requires limiting fishing economies. Safeguarding biodiversity requires addressing the economic pressures that lead to habitat destruction. Protecting or restoring regional seas and waterways, such as the Mediterranean, Baltic, and Red Seas, the Nile, and the Danube requires cooperative agreements and coordinated regulatory policy among large numbers of states with very different economic interests concerning the use of these waters.

Such issue linkage also affects concern, contractual environment, and capacity. For example, governments and their constituencies often express greater concern for economic and political interests than for environmental threats. In addition, as high economic costs become associated with collaborative action, actors face increasing incentives to "defect" or free ride, thus harming the contractual environment. Many governments lack the capacity to negotiate, enact, and enforce environmental regulations in the face of significant economic or political costs.

Cooperation to protect stratospheric ozone first appeared to be an extremely difficult case for exactly these reasons. Many of the world's largest and most influential corporations produced or used CFCs.[29] Many believed CFCs were technically or economically essential to products and processes intimately associated with modern life, including refrigeration, air conditioning, flexible and rigid foam, aerosol sprays, and the manufacture of transistors and computer chips. Either directly, through their production, or indirectly, through their use in manufacturing and consumer products, CFCs were involved in transactions worth billions of dollars and the maintenance of thousands of jobs.[30]

In addition, production of CFCs and many of the products that use them had become standardized, creating new actors who valued their continued availability. Production and use in the developing world were expected to soar in the 1990s, particularly in China, India, Argentina, Brazil, and the newly industrialized countries (NICs) of the Pacific Rim.[31] Indeed, some national development goals, such as widespread household refrigeration in China, appeared to depend on creating large, indigenous CFC production capacities in the third world. By the late 1980s many observers were convinced that very large production increases in developing countries were inevitable without further international agreements—and thus that the success of global ozone policy depended on addressing the associated economic and political interests of developing countries.[32]

Unequal Adjustment Costs

Solutions to international environmental problems frequently involve unequal adjustment costs. Solving a common problem does not mean there will be common costs for each country. This accentuates the difficulties inherent in international cooperation and significantly impacts the contractual environment. Because states can be concerned with relative or positional advantages, they may reject solutions that ask them to bear a relatively larger burden than other states.[33] Alternatively they may demand special compensation for joining the regime. Such difficulties are common in the creation of trading regimes. Their importance in environmental issues must also be recognized.

Comparative costs vary depending on the environmental issue area, level of industrialization, method of energy production, resource base, transportation policy, and other factors. Saudi Arabia would likely bear a much greater burden than Japan in global attempts to combat climate change. Indeed, one could argue that Saudi Arabia would be put out of business, while Japan could sell energy-efficient technology. Brazil would likely pay a higher price than the United States in protecting global biodiversity. Western societies, particularly the United States, would bear a higher burden in any systematic global attempt to reduce or equalize energy and resource consumption.

Such inequalities existed in the ozone issue. Countries with warmer climates required more CFCs for air conditioning and realized their comparative costs would be higher. This produced incentives to free ride, delay, or avoid the economic dislocations that could be associated with the transition to substitutes. Developing countries that had plans to produce CFCs in large quantities but lacked the ability to develop substitutes were at a disadvantage compared with the developed nations from whom they would have to buy the substitutes (thereby returning to the bottom of the product cycle).

Extended Time Horizons and Time Horizon Conflicts

For many environmental problems, the most serious impacts will not occur for many years. This extended time horizon can make it difficult for societies and policymakers to bear short-term costs to fix such a problem, despite the fact that it would often be most effective and least costly to take significant action to address the problem before the most serious consequences occur.

In addition, the elected officials and government bureaucrats who are responsible for making decisions on when and how to address environmental problems often operate in a much shorter time frame—a two-, four-, or six-year election cycle and a one- or two-year budget cycle—than do global environmental problems. This is not to cast aspersions on these individuals, their ability, or their priorities, but rather to acknowledge that even the most enlightened officials usually face time pressures and perspectives far different from those required to address a problem with a fifty- or a hundred-year horizon.

These conflicts present political difficulties, especially if the threat is not well defined or the costs of abatement measures are very high. Policymakers can find it difficult to enact policies that entail significant short-term costs in order to achieve long-term benefits. They and the electorate will definitely bear the short-term costs (perhaps threatening the policymaker's reelection), but they may not be around to enjoy the long-term benefits. This can reduce concern and harm the contractual environment. Such a timing conflict certainly produced obstacles to cooperation on ozone depletion. In the 1970s and early 1980s many corporations and governments, facing the prospect of incurring high short- and medium-term costs in order to prevent a (potential) problem from emerging sometime in the next century, came out against CFC controls and instead proposed further study.

Nonlinear Patterns of Change

Many environmental problems do not develop in a linear, predictable pattern. Stratospheric ozone depletion, particularly the appearance of the ozone hole, sudden declines in fish stocks, and rapid climate change are but a few of the past or potential examples. Nonlinear change makes it difficult to predict the timing and impact of environmental problems. This, in turn, can make it difficult to develop and implement effective policy. This is particularly true if the proposed policy is controversial or expensive, as opponents can cite the uncertainty of the impact and its timing as reasons to forgo action.

Large Number Problems

Solutions to international environmental problems often require the participation of a large number of state and private actors. The problems associated with creating cooperation in such situations are well known. Large numbers present significant incentives for free riding—not participating in the policy, and thereby avoiding the costs, while hoping to enjoy the benefits. This can be particularly dangerous when the environmental policy aims to manage and protect a common pool resource—such as oceans or the atmosphere, which all can use but no one controls—if fears that others will cheat can lead actors to believe they face a "use it or lose it" situation.[34] Large numbers can also harm the contractual environment and decrease the possibility of effective environmental cooperation due to increased transaction costs, difficulties in identifying and reaching consensus, increased likelihood of free riding, and problems in detecting and sanctioning violators. Large numbers also increase the likelihood of significant differences in culture, environmental values, and economic and institutional development among the states. Again, the logic tempting states to cheat (and continue to pollute) is exacerbated if the benefits of cooperation are suspect or the adjustment costs high or uneven.

Global issues (such as biodiversity, climate change, ozone depletion, ocean issues, and population) present special problems. Solutions must not only involve a large number of state and private actors but also (by definition) overcome North-South divisions. Although neither group is uniformly cohesive, many global negotiations exhibit strong differences along North-South lines concerning financial assistance, technology transfer, institutional structure, and the relative importance of environmental protection. (See Chapter 12 for a detailed discussion.)

Ozone depletion, by definition a global environmental problem, possessed all these obstacles. Although a manageable group of companies dominated CFC production, broader ODS production (halons, carbon tetrachloride, methyl chloroform, and methyl bromide) involved many actors. Moreover, nearly all countries and a very large number of different types of corporations consumed ODS. Finally, because most large developing nations intended to significantly increase their ODS production and consumption, North-South politics became an unavoidable concern.

Different Core Beliefs

States and groups within states (including cultural, religious, regional, economic, and political groups) sometimes possess different core beliefs and values relevant to environmental cooperation. Religions differ. Cultural beliefs differ. Values differ. Opinions differ regarding the environment and the relative importance of precaution in setting public policy. These differences matter and can create obstacles to effective global environmental policy. For example, some individuals in certain Asian societies believe products from now endangered animal species have significant medicinal, psychological, or sexual properties. This creates a market for these animals and undercuts international controls designed to protect them. Many Catholics and members of other religious groups oppose certain policies designed to control human population growth. Some groups have strong cultural links to whaling, fishing, or timbering. Some political ideologies treat "economic development" and freedom from government regulations as higher priorities than "environmental protection." Others contend the reverse.

Core beliefs, values, and cultures are clearly important in international environmental negotiations, perhaps to a degree greater than most discussions acknowledge. They can not only inhibit the identification and implementation of cooperative solutions but also obstruct attempts to begin discussions by limiting concern for particular environmental issues.

Capacity Problems

Finally, even when states can agree on what measures should be taken, they do not have equal abilities to enact them. As noted, the success of international environmental rules depends, in part, on the effectiveness of domestic implementation. Some developing and eastern European countries lack effective domestic institutions to enact and enforce environmental rules. They do not have the internal capacity to gather and disseminate environmental information, to create the laws called for in international environmental treaties, and to detect, punish, and deter violators. Capacity can also affect the contractual environment if some states believe that others will be unable to enact or enforce their commitments and thus are likely candidates to free ride.

Intersecting Obstacles

In addition to their individual impact, the characteristics of global environmental issues outlined above can also create intersecting or crosscutting obstacles to effective cooperation. For example, complexity, uncertainty, issue linkages, and the possibility of unequal adjustment costs offer opportunities for aggressive or less risk-averse states to seek positional advantages while enhancing fears of positional disadvantages (sucker's payoff) among risk-averse or less well-informed states. Long-time horizons and scientific complexity offer policymakers opportunities to postpone economically and politically expensive solutions. Complex, lengthy, and expensive remedies, involvement by many actors, and disparate state interests and capacities reduce the likelihood of agreement and increase the opportunity for, and attractiveness of, free riding (should an agreement be created).

Conclusion

Effective global environmental policy is not easy to design or implement, but it does exist. Protection of the ozone layer, trade in endangered species, and addressing pollution in regional seas are but three significant examples. These and other global regimes prove that the international community has the ability to address complex global environmental problems with innovative and successful policies.

Nevertheless, it is important to understand the obstacles to effective global environmental policy—systemic obstacles, procedural obstacles, a lack of necessary and sufficient conditions, and characteristic obstacles—so that we can better understand these successes as well as the significant challenges that remain. It is also important to look at global environmental policy, particularly the type of policy created and implemented by states and international organizations, not as a single, static international treaty but as a complex regime. By examining and understanding the comparative creation, content, evolution, and impact of these regimes, students and policymakers can gain insight into the sources of effective global environmental policy.

Notes

1. David Downie, personal notes and observation during POPs INC-5.
2. Compare definition and use of the term regime in John Gerard Ruggie, "International Responses to Technology: Concepts and Trends," *International Organization* 29 (1975): 557–583; Ernst Haas, "On Systems and International Regimes," *World Politics* 27 (1975): 147–174; Robert Keohane and Joseph Ny Jr., *Power and Interdependence: World Politics in Transition* (Boston: Little, Brown, 1977); Oran Young, "International Regimes: Problems of Concept Formation," *International Organization* 32 (1980): 331–356; Stephen Krasner, *International Regimes* (Ithaca, N.Y.: Cornell University Press, 1983); Robert Keohane, *After Hegemony* (Princeton: Princeton University Press, 1984); Jack Donnelly, "International Human Rights: A Regime Analysis," *International Organization* 40 (1986): 599–642; Stephan Haggard and Beth Simmons, "Theories of International Regimes," *International Organization* 41 (1987): 491–517; Thomas Gehring, "International Environmental Regimes: Dynamic Sectoral Legal Systems," in *Yearbook of International Environmental Law*, vol. 1, ed. G. Handl (London: Graham & Trotman, 1990); and David Downie, "Road Map or False Trail: Evaluating the Precedence of the Ozone Regime as Model and Strategy for Global Climate Change," *International Environmental Affairs* 7 (fall 1995): 321–345. Regarding the definition, John Ruggie introduced international regimes as "set[s] of mutual expectations, rules and regulations, plans, organizational energies and financial commitments, which have been accepted by a group of states" (Ruggie, "International Responses to Technology," 570). Ernst Haas initially defined regimes as "collective arrangements among nations designed to create or more effectively use scientific and technical capabilities" (Haas, "On Systems and International Regimes," 147). Robert Keohane and Joseph Nye first defined regimes instrumentally, "[b]y creating or accepting procedures, rules or institutions for certain kinds of activity, governments regulate and control transnational and interstate relations. We refer to these governing arrangements as international regimes." In the same book they also define a regime as a "network of rules, norms, and procedures that regulate behavior" (Keohane and Nye, *Power and Interdependence*, 5 and 19). Oran Young first defined regimes as "social insti-

tutions governing the actions of those interested in specifiable activities . . . [that] may or may not be accompanied by explicit organizational arrangements" (Young, "International Regimes," 332–333). In 1983 a group of leading scholars working with Robert Krasner attempted to standardize and extend regime study. Most definitions, including the one presented here, are variants of the so-called Krasner definition presented in that volume (Krasner, *International Regimes*, 2).

3. See the ISO home page at http://www.iso.ch/iso/en/ISOOnline.openerpage.

4. For discussions of the Montreal Protocol and the ozone regime, see Richard Benedick, *Ozone Diplomacy*, 2d ed. (Cambridge: Harvard University Press, 1998); Karen Litfin, *Ozone Discourses* (New York: Columbia University Press, 1994); David Downie, "UNEP and the Montreal Protocol: New Roles for International Organizations in Regime Creation and Change," in *International Organizations and Environmental Policy*, ed. Robert V. Bartlett, Priya A. Kurian, and Madhu Malik (Westport, Conn.: Greenwood Press, 1995); David Downie, "The Power to Destroy: Understanding Stratospheric Ozone Politics as a Common Pool Resource Problem," in *Anarchy and the Environment: The International Relations of Common Pool Resources*, ed. J. Samuel Barkin and George Shambaugh (Albany: State University of New York Press, 1999); and David Downie, "Road Map or False Trail."

5. Text of the ozone treaties, amendments, and adjustments, as well as reports from each Meeting of the Parties, OEWG meeting, and Implementation Committee meeting are available online from the Ozone Secretariat, at http://www.unep.org/ozone/index.shtml.

6. See, for example, http://www.teap.org/.

7. See the Multilateral Fund home page at http://www.unmfs.org/.

8. ODS controlled under the protocol include chlorofluorocarbons (CFCs), once very widely used as refrigerants, industrial solvents, aerosol propellants, and in the manufacture of rigid and flexible foam; HCFCs, less ozone-depleting CFC substitutes; halons, used for fire control; methyl bromide, an inexpensive, widely used, and very toxic fumigant; carbon tetrachloride; and methyl chloroform. The Montreal Protocol and/or its amendments mandate severe restrictions and in most cases the eventual elimination of the production and use of these chemicals.

9. See Krasner, *International Regimes*.

10. Influential discussions of the use of regime in international relations include Ernst Haas, "Why Collaborate? Issue-linkage and International Relations," *World Politics* 32 (1980): 357–405; Robert Keohane, "The Theory of Hegemonic Stability and Changes in International Economic Regimes," in *Changes in the International System*, ed. Ole Holsti (Boulder, Colo.: Westview Press, 1980); Krasner, *International Regimes;* Keohane, *After Hegemony;* Friedrich Kratochwil and John Gerard Ruggie, "International Organization: A State of the Art on an Art of the State," *International Organization* 40 (1986): 753–776; and Haggard and Simmons, "Theories of International Regimes."

11. Examples include the Baltic Sea regime, which emerged from the 1974 Helsinki Convention on the Protection of the Marine Environment of the Baltic Sea Area.

12. This is officially known as the "Non-Legally Binding Authoritative Statement of Principles for a Global Consensus on the Management, Conservation and Sustainable Development of all Types of Forests." Report of the United Nations Conference on Environment and Development, Annex II, UN Document A/CONF.151/26 (vol. III) of August 14, 1992; available at http://www.un.org/documents/ga/conf151/aconf15126-3annex3.htm.

13. For updated and detailed information, see http://www.unece.org/env/lrtap/.

14. Some would also argue that the current structure of the international economic system—particularly a global capitalism that emphasizes consumerism, lowest-cost production, globalization, and resource extraction while largely failing to cost in environmental degradation—also presents a structural impediment to effective global environmental policy. Although these characteristics can present obstacles to effec-

tive policy, I believe that they are not as structurally inherent as the other factors. Indeed, at times, such as in the expansion of the ozone regime, they have supported global environmental policy by helping to speed the introduction of environmentally friendly technology.

15. Classic examples include Thucydides, Machiavelli, and Hobbes. Influential modern examples include Hans Morgenthau, *Politics Among Nations*, 5th ed. (New York: Knopf, 1973); Robert Jervis, "Cooperation under the Security Dilemma," *World Politics* 30 (1978): 167–186; Kenneth Waltz, *Theory of International Politics* (Reading, Mass: Addison-Wesley, 1979); and Glenn Snyder, "The Security Dilemma in Alliance Politics," *World Politics* 36 (1984):461–495.
16. Waltz, *Theory of International Politics*.
17. For example, Reinhold Niebuhr, *Moral Man and Immoral Society* (New York: Scribner's, 1960 [1932]); and Morgenthau, *Politics Among Nations*.
18. Oran Young, "Global Environmental Change and International Governance," *Millennium* 19 (1990): 337–346, 338.
19. Glenn Snyder and Paul Diesing, *Conflict Among Nations: Bargaining, Decision Making, and System Structure in International Crises* (Princeton: Princeton University Press, 1977); Jervis, "Cooperation under the Security Dilemma"; and Kenneth Oye, ed., *Cooperation Under Anarchy* (Princeton: Princeton University Press, 1986), 1–22.
20. Mancur Olson, *The Logic of Collective Action* (Cambridge: Harvard University Press, 1965).
21. Joseph M. Grieco, "Anarchy and the Limits of Cooperation," *International Organization 42* (summer 1988): 485–507
22. J. Samuel Barkin and George Shambaugh, eds., *Anarchy and the Environment: The International Relations of Common Pool Resources* (Albany: State University of New York Press, 1999).
23. Robert Jervis, *Perception and Misperception in International Politics* (Princeton: Princeton University Press, 1976).
24. Keohane, *After Hegemony*.
25. United Nations Document A/CONF.48/14, p. 118. This principle later became Principle 2 of the Rio Declaration, but with the words "and developmental" inserted before "policies," thus making it even more self-contradictory.
26. Peter Haas, Robert Keohane, and Marc Levy, eds., *Institutions for the Earth: Sources of Effective International Environmental Protection* (Cambridge: MIT Press, 1993), 19–20.
27. Mario Molina and F. Sherwood Rowland, "Stratospheric Sink for Chlorofluoromethanes: Chlorine Atomic Catalyzed Destruction of Ozone," *Nature* 249 (June 28, 1974): 810–812.
28. The best secondary literature on the interplay of scientific and technical debates in the development of the ozone regime includes Lydia Dotto and Harold Schiff, *The Ozone War* (New York: Doubleday, 1978); Paul Brodeur, "Annals of Chemistry: In the Face of Doubt," *New Yorker,* June 9, 1986, 70–87; and Karen Litfin, *Ozone Discourses: Science and Politics in Global Environmental Cooperation* (New York: Columbia University Press, 1994).
29. For example, DuPont, ICI, Atochem, General Motors, Toyota, General Electric, and Proctor and Gamble.
30. Estimates of specific figures vary widely.
31. As far back as 1976, ODS were produced in Argentina, Brazil, Czechoslovakia, East Germany, Mexico, and India, although the United States, the United Kingdom, West Germany, France, Japan, the USSR, and the Netherlands accounted for over 90 percent of total production. For discussion, see David Downie, "Comparative Public Policy of Ozone Layer Protection," *Political Science* 45 (1993): 186–197.
32. Based on personal communications, global ozone negotiations, London, June 1990. See also Benedick, *Ozone Diplomacy.*
33. Grieco, "Anarchy and the Limits of Cooperation."
34. Downie, "The Power to Destroy: Understanding Stratospheric Ozone Politics as a Common Pool Resource Problem."

5

The Role of Environmental NGOs in International Regimes

John McCormick

The environment has been an issue of critical public concern since the 1970s. As the physical and social sciences have revealed more about the damaging effects of human activity on the environment, opinion polls have found growing levels of public support for government action in response to these effects. However, the record of local and national governments in addressing the causes and consequences of environmental damage has been mixed at best. Lip service has been paid to the importance of environmental management, but practical action has often fallen short of government pronouncements. As the former executive director of the United Nations Environment Programme (UNEP) noted in 1992, political commitment "to set up ministries and to enter into international agreements has not always led to an equal commitment to action. Environment ministries exist, but their role in national decision-making is frequently marginal. Agreements have been entered into freely, but the will to enforce them has often been lacking."[1]

At the national level, the development of effective environmental policies has been undermined by a lack of political will, by questions about the science of environmental problems, and by a failure (or an unwillingness) to understand and quantify the costs and benefits of preventive or remedial action. At the international level, the handicaps to effective action have been even greater, for several reasons. First, there is no global legal system (other than international treaties or the terms of membership of international organizations), and there is no global authority responsible for proposing and enforcing environmental regulations affecting multiple states. Second, national governments and corporations are less motivated to act on transboundary or global issues than on national issues because they face few legal obligations, confront no direct political pressures from voters and other constituencies outside their own borders, and find it easier to ignore or transfer the costs of inaction to another party. It is simpler and cheaper, for example, to build tall smokestacks that will carry pollution across borders than to control the sources of that pollution. Finally, because many environmental problems are shared by multiple states, or are common to multiple states, individual states lack the motivation to act unless they can be assured that their neighbors will take similar action.

Against this background, private citizens have stepped into the breach by attempting to generate pressure for political change through the work of nongovernmental organizations (NGOs). These NGOs have undertaken

research into environmental problems, lobbied local and national governments, exerted pressure on international organizations and multinational
corporations, raised and spent the funds needed to implement practical
management measures, monitored the actions of governments and corporations, built political coalitions in support of public policy, and promoted
public awareness of environmental problems. The need to address international problems has led in turn to the creation of international NGOs,
formed to bring together the collective interests of national lobbies with a
view to influencing multiple governments and publics and to drawing
attention to the many environmental problems that are international,
regional, or global in nature. The work of these NGOs, it has been argued,
has influenced values and social behavior among large groups of people,
generating a global civil society in which the behavior of states has become
less important.[2]

This chapter examines the roots, the structure, the work, and the effects
of environmental NGOs. It argues that they have collectively played an
important role in influencing the nature of various international regimes—
such as those dealing with trade and development—and have become important sources of pressure for international action on environmental
management. As such, they have contributed to the development of a global
civil society within which humans have increasingly come to appreciate that
most economic and social problems—and environmental problems in particular—are not limited by national boundaries but are part of the common
experience of humanity and must be addressed accordingly.

The Rise of International Regimes

The period since 1945 has seen an unprecedented growth in the
number and the activity of international organizations, whose presence has
obliged us to rethink the way we try to understand global politics. We still
see the world in terms of states, we still see ourselves as citizens of one
country or another, and the study of international relations has been heavily
influenced by realist analyses, which argue that the state is the fundamental
unit of analysis. Realists believe that global politics is best understood by a
study of the nature of relations among states: forming alliances, going to war,
imposing sanctions, protecting and promoting individual interests, and pursuing self-interested goals of security, open markets, and autonomy.

A different approach is offered by idealist theory, which focuses on
individuals, groups, and communities rather than the state. Idealism argues
that values predominate over military strength and strategic resources and
that humans can place higher causes above self-interest, can pursue ideals in
the interest of improving the quality of life, and can thus work to avoid conflict. Idealists support the development of international organizations as a
means to bridging differences among states and avoiding destructive competition. Idealism is also based on a belief in the notion of globalism, where
institutions and ideals other than the state attract the loyalty of humans.[3]

The idealist view has been promoted in part by increased doubts about the wisdom and efficiency of the modern state system, whose critics charge it with four key failings:

- During the cold war (1945–1990), the superpowers were unable to guarantee global peace through anything less than mutually assured nuclear destruction.
- The state system has failed to respond effectively to demands for self-determination from national groups divided by state lines (such as the Kurds, the Basques, and the Hutus) and has promoted the kind of nationalism that has encouraged conflict and war rather than cooperation and compromise.
- The state system has failed to resolve pressing economic and social issues, so that the rich industrial states have become richer, while one in every three people—according to World Bank calculations—remains poor.
- The state system has failed to develop an effective response to issues that transcend state lines. The modern industrial state may have improved the quality of life of many of its citizens, but it has done so at the expense of encouraging people to think of themselves as competing citizens of individual states rather than as cooperating members of the human race.

Among the consequences of these failures has been a worsening of transboundary environmental problems, driven by a combination of three main factors. First, there has been a lack of scientific agreement about the causes and effects of environmental problems, which has encouraged states—out of concerned self-interest—to err on the side of caution in making their policy calculations. Scientific debate, for example, has encouraged the United States to be slow in reaching agreement on global warming, concerned as many American political and corporate leaders have been about the loss of comparative economic advantage arising from the costs of controlling emissions of greenhouse gases such as carbon dioxide.

Second, states have worried about economic costs, both internally and relative to other states. The United States, for example, was slow to take action on acid pollution in the 1980s in part because of the potential costs to auto-manufacturing and coal-producing states (Michigan and West Virginia) and the lack of political concern for Canada, which received many of the emissions generated by power stations in upwind U.S. states. Similarly, Britain was largely unmoved during the same period by the appeals of downwind Scandinavian states to reduce its pollution emissions; it took action only when it discovered forest damage within its own borders and was compelled to do so by European Union law.[4]

Third, while states are members of international organizations and signatories of international treaties, there is no authority or executive that has significant powers of coercion over states, obliging them to meet the terms of either membership or signature. Furthermore, the signature of treaties often commits governments to adhere to principles rather than to meet specific objectives. This problem is exemplified by the 1979 Convention on Long-Range Transboundary Air Pollution, which committed signatories to "endeavour to limit, and as far as possible, gradually reduce and prevent air pollution . . . [using] the best available technology which is economically feasible." Governments may have obligations as signatories of international treaties and conventions, but they are not obliged to sign, will do so only when acceptable compromises have been reached, and during negotiations may work to ensure that the obligations are as weak as possible.

One of the consequences of weaknesses in the state system since World War II has been the growth in the number, reach, and activities of non-governmental organizations. Known also as interest groups or pressure groups, NGOs consist of groups of people (or coalitions of organizations) who come together outside the formal structures of government in an institutionalized and regularized manner in an effort to achieve social, economic, or political change. They may try to effect change just among their own members, mobilizing citizens or member organizations to act in their collective interests, but they will often try to influence public opinion, the media, elected officials, and bureaucrats with a view to influencing the actions of government.

Weaknesses in the state system since World War II have also contributed to a growth in the number, reach, and activities of international organizations (IOs). In their attempts to address and remove the causes of interstate conflict and to address matters of shared interest collectively, national governments have created and joined IOs dealing with everything from defense, trade, and economic development to humanitarian issues, education, environmental management, and consumer safety. According to the Union of International Associations, there were just over 200 international organizations in the early twentieth century; by 1964 the number had grown to nearly 2,000, by 1987 it had risen to 27,000, and by 1999 it stood at more than 50,000.[5]

IOs broadly take the form of intergovernmental organizations (IGOs), international nongovernmental organizations (INGOs), or multinational corporations (profit-making organizations that function in more than one country). IGOs are made up of states or national government bodies, generally lack autonomy in decision making, have few assets, lack the power to impose taxes or enforce their rulings, and are normally used as forums within which states can negotiate or cooperate with one another. The most influential IGOs are those in the network of United Nations specialized agencies, such as the World Bank, the Food and Agriculture Organization (FAO), and the United Nations Development Programme. Equally important IGOs have been created to deal with defense issues (the North Atlantic Treaty Organization, or NATO), global trade (the World Trade Organization, or WTO), and regional economic development (the Organization for Economic Cooperation and Development, or OECD).

Jacobson has identified five major categories of IGOs:

- *Informational:* agencies that gather, analyze, exchange, and disseminate data, such as the UN specialized agencies and the OECD.
- *Normative*: agencies that define standards and declare international principles and goals.
- *Operational:* agencies that have the power to oversee the implementation of certain functions, such as administering financial or technical assistance (for example, the World Bank and the International Monetary Fund).
- *Rule creating:* bodies involved in the enactment of formal treaties that are binding on the states that ratify them, such as agreements made under the auspices of GATT (now WTO) and NATO.
- *Rule supervisory:* organizations that have the authority to monitor compliance with treaties and other rules, again such as GATT/WTO and NATO.[6]

INGOs normally have memberships consisting of individuals or private associations rather than states and have only the first three of the functions identified by Jacobson. They are rarely in the position to create or supervise the implementation of rules other than those relating to their own operations or those of their members. The most important rules are made by governments and by agreement among governments, so INGOs function outside the rule-making process, offering expert advice, undertaking research, and monitoring the application of these rules. Some are made up of delegations from participating national and local NGOs (examples include the International Chamber of Commerce and the World Federation of Trade Unions), while others work to rise above national identity and to become truly global in their memberships and interests.

IOs have been critical actors in the emergence of international regimes. If national regimes are defined as the common expectations, principles, norms, laws, objectives, and organizations that bind a national government and its citizens, then international regimes can be defined as the same factors applied to a group of states. Hughes defines an international regime as "the principles, norms, rules, and decision-making procedures that facilitate extensive reciprocity in a given issue area."[7] It might be argued that we live in a single global regime driven by the balance of power and expectations among the more than 190 independent states of the world, but regime theory has also been applied to specific issue areas, such as trade (as influenced by decisions taken within the auspices of the WTO), monetary relations (the International Monetary Fund), and transportation (the International Civil Aviation Organization).

International regimes emerge when states need to reach agreement on common problems in a fashion that goes beyond ad hoc action but does not extend to obliging them to relinquish sovereignty to a more permanent decision-making system. At one end of the scale, the ad hoc multilateral Western responses to problems such as the crises in Bosnia, Iraq, and Liberia could not be defined as regimes, while—at the other end—the surrender of national sovereignty involved in the development of the European Union has taken its member states far beyond the creation of a regime.

Environmental issues have become the subject of several different international regimes. This reflects the difficulty in compartmentalizing environmental issues and divorcing them from other issues (such as international trade), as well as the fact that the international response to environmental problems has often demanded managing what are known as "common-pool resources." These are resources that do not belong to any one state but are instead part of the global domain. Prime examples include the atmosphere and oceans outside territorial waters, but it has also been suggested that the tropical rain forests of the Amazon basin, central Africa, and Southeast Asia—because of their role in global weather patterns—are also part of the global commons.

The Growth of the Environmental Movement

The earliest attempts to build cooperation among national governments date back to the nineteenth and early twentieth centuries, but it has been only since 1945 that internationalism has come into its own. Motivated initially by the desire to avoid conflict, then pushed into the competing ideological camps of the cold war, then driven by the rising demands of newly independent African and Asian states for recognition and aid, and finally driven into cooperation through growing international trade and a revolution in international communication, states have found themselves drawn into greater cooperation on issues of mutual interest.

One of those issues has been the environment, which was approached for much of the nineteenth and early twentieth centuries largely as a local matter. Driven by the findings of the scientific revolution of the nineteenth century, by concerns about the effects on urban life of the spread of industry, and the effects on nature of agricultural intensification, local and national nongovernmental organizations were created in the United States, Canada, and several European countries. Among the first NGOs with a focus on the environment were the Society for the Protection of Birds (created in Britain in 1889) and the Sierra Club (founded in the United States in 1892).[8]

A variety of pressures subsequently indicated that a broader perspective was needed if environmental problems were to be addressed effectively. First, private citizens and scientists began to realize that many problems were common to two or more countries and began communicating with each other and sharing ideas about how best to respond. Second, these communications led to the realization that many problems could not be addressed by individual countries acting alone. Finally, following World War II, the growth of international trade meant that consumer demand in one country often created, or worsened, problems in another.

The Europeans were the first to begin looking outside their borders, both to their colonies and to their immediate neighbors. For example, the protection of colonial wildlife was the motivation for the creation in Britain in 1903 of the world's first international conservation NGO, the Society for the Preservation of the Wild Fauna of the Empire. Meetings among European nature protectionists led in 1913 to the creation of the Commission for the International Protection of Nature. INGOs such as these took a broader view than their national precursors; they encouraged environmentalists to look beyond their immediate circumstances and concerns and promoted cooperation among environmentalists with shared interests in multiple countries.

The growth in the number and reach of environmental IGOs and INGOs accelerated following World War II. There were IGOs that predated the war—for example, the International Joint Commission was created in 1909 to encourage cooperation between the United States and Canada on the management of the Great Lakes—but the postwar IGOs were more ambitious in their scope and objectives. The UN Food and Agriculture Organization, for example, was created in 1945 not only to deal with an immediate food supply crisis but also to look at long-term supply, and its founders quickly realized that a more globalized approach was needed for the management of natural resources.[9]

In 1947 the Commission for the International Protection of Nature was reorganized as the International Union for the Protection of Nature, becoming the first INGO with a global outlook on environmental problems. Renamed the International Union for the Conservation of Nature (IUCN) in 1956, it became the precursor to many more environmental INGOs, notably the World Wildlife Fund (WWF, later renamed the Worldwide Fund for Nature outside the United States), created in 1961 to raise funds for IUCN projects.

The 1960s saw a rapid rise in public interest in environmental problems in industrial countries, driven by the publication of books such as Rachel Carson's *Silent Spring* (which drew attention to the use of chemicals in agriculture), concerns about the threat of fallout from nuclear testing, a series of well-publicized environmental disasters (including several major marine oil spills), and advances in scientific knowledge.[10] New NGOs were created in response, and public interest reached a new peak in 1972 with the convening in Stockholm, Sweden, of the United Nations Conference on the Human Environment, attended by representatives from 113 countries and more than 400 intergovernmental and nongovernmental organizations.[11] The Stockholm conference was the first meeting at which a combination of governments and NGOs from around the world sat down to address the global aspects of the emerging environmental crisis.

Among the many consequences of the Stockholm conference, three in particular stand out. First, the presence of so many national and international NGOs drew new public and political attention to their work and encouraged them to be more persistent in their efforts to work with one another and to influence public policy. Second, the presence of many newly independent African and Asian governments encouraged the industrial countries—for the first time—to acknowledge that poorer emerging countries had a different set of priorities and that underdevelopment was as much a cause of environmental problems as overdevelopment. For the United States and Europe, the major problems were a consequence of industrialization and the accelerated exploitation of resources—air and water pollution in particular. For Africa and Asia, by contrast, the major problems were a consequence of poverty and population growth, contributing, for example, to deforestation and soil erosion. Third, the conference resulted in the creation in 1973 of the United Nations Environment Programme, which went on to redefine the United Nation's interest in environmental issues and to offer NGOs and INGOs a new forum in which they could attempt to influence public policy.

Environmental NGOs were also active before, during, and after the convening of the United Nations Conference on Environment and Development (UNCED, or the Earth Summit), held in Rio de Janeiro in 1992. The formal input of NGOs began as early as 1982 with the ten-year review of the Stockholm conference, which led to the creation in 1983 of the World Commission on Environment and Development (or the Brundtland Commission). Charged with reporting on progress in achieving the objectives of sustainable development, the commission finished its work in October 1987 and was replaced by a new body called the Center for Our Common Future (COCF).

NGOs influenced the Brundtland Commission through the testimony they provided, but they played a more active role in the work of COCF. The Center's mission was to publicize the goals of the Brundtland Commission, which it did in part through establishing contacts with partners, including NGOs and INGOs. With the announcement in 1989 that the Earth Summit was to be held in 1992, NGOs played an active role in preparatory hearings, working through COCF and the Environment Liaison Centre International, which was a conduit for contacts between NGOs and UNEP. NGOs also directly lobbied negotiators at the preparatory meetings for UNCED and had further influence as members of national delegations involved in those meetings.[12]

Since the Rio conference, NGOs have played a central role in publicizing the extent to which the goals and objectives of the conference have found (or failed to find) their way into public policy. Another opportunity to make their case came with the September 2002 World Summit on Sustainable Development, held in Johannesburg, South Africa. The meeting took a critical look at UNCED, its deliberations given greater focus by the presence once again of many NGOs.

The Global NGO Community

There is no authoritative source on the size of the global environmental NGO community, but the number of groups has grown at least in concert with the growth of NGOs more generally, and probably even faster. The *World Directory of Environmental Organizations* described 2,500 environmental organizations in its 2001 edition.[13] However, these are the bigger

NGOs, and many are themselves umbrella bodies for smaller local and grass-roots organizations, whose numbers are constantly changing. The European Environmental Bureau, for example, which acts as a conduit for contacts between NGOs and the major bodies of the European Union, has 134 NGO members from 25 countries.[14] If one extrapolates from cases such as these, also taking into account national and regional umbrella bodies around the world, the total number of environmental NGOs in the world probably runs well into six figures.

It would be wrong to suggest that there is a homogeneous global community of environmental NGOs that is driven by complementary goals and uses similar methods. While it is true that they share a common vision of encouraging a workable relationship between humans and their environment, NGOs use many different methods, often have different priorities and objectives, and vary substantially in size, goals, durability, stability, credibility, and ideological orientations (see Table 5-1).[15] In many cases they have disagreed on both methods and goals.

The most fundamental division within the NGO community is the philosophical one that exists between groups based in the industrial countries of the North and those based in the emerging states of the South. The former tend to focus on the environmental consequences of industrial development and to argue that adjustments are needed in the goals of the free market, including greater regulation of industry, changes in the nature of consumerism, and investment in pollution control. Meanwhile, the latter argue that many environmental problems result from poverty, the shift of polluting industries from the North to the South, and the demands of northern consumers. While the former argue the need for placing curbs on economic growth, the latter argue that the worst problems are created by industry and excessive consumption in the North and by inequalities in the global economic system. The philosophical difference was clear to one of the participants at UNCED in 1992: "While the North set the agenda with high profile statements on the need to tackle population growth and deforestation, without committing substantial new funds to do so, the South's insistence on the need for justice, relief of crippling international debt, new financial resources for sustainable development including environmental protection, and technology transfer went unheeded." [16]

In addition to these global philosophical groupings, it is important to distinguish among groups driven by differences in philosophy regarding the methods by which change is best achieved. In his study of the NGO community in the United States, for example, Rosenbaum identifies three "enclaves": the ideological mainstream of "pragmatic reformist" organizations, the deep ecologists, and the radicals.[17] The pragmatists consist of the largest, most conservative, most politically active and publicly visible groups, which prefer to work within established political processes to influence public policy. In the United States, these include members of what is informally known as the Group of Ten, the biggest and most visible mainline NGOs, such as the National Wildlife Federation, the Sierra Club, and the

Table 5-1 Philosophies, Structures, and Methods of Environmental NGOs

Philosophy	Structure	Method
Northern NGOs focusing on the environmental consequences of industrial development and consumerism	Federations of national/international groups. Created to facilitate communication and cooperation among member bodies	Working with elected officials, bureaucrats, and employees of corporations
Southern NGOs focusing on the environmental consequences of poverty and inequalities in the global economic system	Universal membership	Raising and spending money on groups, with widespread, global membership and interests
Conservative, pragmatic groups working to achieve change within established political processes	Intercontinental membership groups. Interests go beyond a particular region, but are not necessarily global	Campaigning and organizing public protests
Green organizations seeking fundamental changes in relationship among humans and between humans and the environment	Regionally defined membership groups. Interests restricted to one continent or region	Promoting media coverage of environmental issues
Radical organizations that use confrontation to draw attention to the problems of the environment and argue that conventional political processes are part of the problem	Internationally oriented national groups. National NGOs partly or wholly focused on international issues	Litigation and monitoring the implementation of environmental law
NGOs representing the views of socioeconomic groups with an interest in the environmental debate, such as women, minorities, and business		Information exchange
		Undertaking research
		Acquiring/managing property
		Generating grassroots involvement

National Audubon Society. (They have their counterparts in Europe in the form of the Royal Society for the Protection of Birds in Britain, Bund für Vogelschutz in Germany, and the Worldwide Fund for Nature.)

The deep ecologists include groups that emphasize the place of humans as a part of nature, believe that all forms of life have an equal right to exist, challenge the underlying institutional structures and social values upon which governments are based and economies function, and argue the need for fundamental social change as a prerequisite for effective environmental management. While other groups generally accept the existing sociopolitical order and do not question the dominant values of society, ecologists reject those values; they criticize existing political structures, consumerism, and materialism and propose the development of a new environmental paradigm more compatible with the realities of environmental limits.[18] In several countries, these views have combined with grassroots movements to produce "green" political parties that see themselves as the vanguard of a new society in which humans take a holistic approach to their relationship with one another and their environment. Their members see green politics as a clarion call for good sense in a world driven by consumption and acquisition, where greed threatens to undermine the foundations of life on Earth. Their critics see them as a threat to economic development, jobs, and livelihoods and as a brake on human progress.

The third of Rosenbaum's enclaves—the radicals—consists of groups that have become disenchanted with the methods and goals of mainstream environmentalism and believe in the use of direct action as a means to bring about urgently needed political and social change. Radicalism is apparently difficult to sustain. Notable among such groups in the 1970s were Friends of the Earth (FoE) and Greenpeace, which had a reputation for headline-grabbing tactics such as interfering with whaling activities and having their members tie themselves to bridges to protest shipments of nuclear waste; since then, they have become less confrontational and more willing to work within established political procedures. Greenpeace still believes that "determined individuals can alter the actions and purposes of even the most powerful by 'bearing witness,' that is, by drawing attention to an abuse of the environment through their unwavering presence at the scene, whatever the risk."[19] However, the best known of the radicals now is Earth First!, founded in 1980, which argues that extreme methods are needed to deal with extreme problems and has opted for militant action, variously termed *ecotage* or *monkey wrenching*, such as hammering metal spikes into trees to discourage lumber companies from cutting them down.

Finally, the NGO community is also divided among groups that represent the viewpoints of specific socioeconomic groups, such as women, racial minorities, the poor, consumers, or business. For example, the Women's Environment and Development Organization was set up in 1990 to lobby for the inclusion of gender equity concerns in the documents for the Earth Summit, and the organization has gone on to become a network of 20,000 individuals and groups in more than 100 countries that believe in the need to encourage environmental activism among women's groups. Similarly, the World Business Council for Sustainable Development acts as a federation representing the interests of business councils and corporations in the debate over environmental issues and sustainable development. Within these philosophical and stylistic groupings, NGOs also vary in their internal structures and the methods and strategies they use.

Internal Structures

A structural typology developed by the Belgian-based Union of International Associations divides INGOs as follows:

Federations of International and National Organizations. These are bodies set up to facilitate communication and cooperation among their member bodies. They can be global networks of national offices of the same NGO, such as Greenpeace, the Worldwide Fund for Nature, or Friends of the Earth. These three have national offices, respectively, in thirty-two, fifty-three, and fifty-five countries, but the national offices are autonomous and have their own funding and strategic priorities. Cooperation is promoted by international secretariats in Amsterdam and, for WWF, Switzerland.

Federations also take the form of umbrella bodies, bringing together different organizations that act either as conduits for contacts between those NGOs and an IGO (for example, the Environment Liaison Centre International, with NGO members in 104 countries, provides a point of contact between NGOs and the UN Environment Programme),[20] or as a channel for contacts among NGOs, as is the case with the more than 530 NGO members of the African NGOs Environment Network.[21]

Universal Membership Organizations. These are bodies that have a widespread, geographically balanced membership. The prime example is the World Conservation Union (which has undergone several name changes and now confusingly calls itself the World Conservation Union while retaining the IUCN acronym of its previous identity, the International Union for Conservation of Nature and Natural Resources).

IUCN is one of the oldest environmental INGOs, tracing its roots back to the creation in 1947 of the International Union for the Protection of Nature. Headquartered in Switzerland, it is an unusual hybrid of governmental and nongovernmental members. Its membership in 2003 consisted of seventy-five governments (the United States, for example, is a state member), 108 government agencies (including the U.S. Environmental Protection Agency, the Indian Ministry of Environment and Forests, the Kenyan Ministry of Tourism and Wildlife, the Russian Ministry of Natural Resources, and so on), and 773 national and international NGOs.[22] This arrangement not only brings together equivalent organizations from different states but also allows national NGOs to take part in the work of an organization that includes their own governments and government agencies. IUCN also has six commissions (covering issues such as protected areas, education, communication, and law) within which networks of more than 8,000 technical, scientific, and policy experts are brought together to provide IUCN with the information it needs for its work.

IUCN provides governments and NGOs with information, acts as a clearinghouse for the exchange of ideas, and carries out its own environmental management projects, notably the creation of national parks and other protected areas and gathering of information on the status of threatened species and ecosystems. It has also been active in the drafting of international treaties, such as the Convention on Biological Diversity and the Convention on International Trade in Endangered Species.

It is one of the more conservative INGOs, shying away from controversy and—unlike the FoE or Greenpeace—doing little to draw media attention to itself. This is because it is not a campaigning organization so much as it is a meeting place for government bodies and NGOs, less engaged in changing policy and public opinion than in facilitating the exchange of ideas and information.

Intercontinental Membership Organizations. These are bodies whose interests go beyond a particular region but not to the point where they become universal membership groups. Among these are environmental INGOs with more focused interests, such as BirdLife International and Wetlands International. BirdLife International is a network of "partner" organizations in ninety-nine countries that work collectively to gather and share information and to build strong national bodies working to protect birds and their natural habitats. It has a global secretariat in Britain and regional offices in Ecuador, Indonesia, and Belgium.[23] Wetlands International, a federation bringing together national delegations in forty-eight countries, promotes research and information exchange and has played an active role in the development and application of the 1971 Ramsar Convention on Wetlands of International Importance. It is headquartered in the Netherlands and has eighteen subregional offices around the world.[24]

Regionally Defined Membership Organizations. These are bodies whose interests are restricted to a particular continent or region, such as the African Wildlife Foundation (Kenya), the Caribbean Conservation Association (Barbados), and the European Environmental Bureau (Belgium). The latter facilitates contacts between groups in the member states of the European Union (EU) and the main policymaking bodies of the EU.

Internationally Oriented National Organizations and National NGOs that Are Partly or Wholly Focused on International Issues. The former include the Sierra Club and the Natural Resources Defense Council, and the latter include the World Resources Institute and the Worldwatch Institute (all based in the United States). The Sierra Club is mainly active on the domestic political front in the United States but also campaigns on issues such as human rights and the environment, environmentally compatible trade policies, global warming, and population growth control. The World Resources Institute, meanwhile, focuses on policy research, publishing, among other things, the well-respected annual World Resources series.

In addition, it is important to appreciate that NGOs also have different interests and priorities as well as different constituencies. At one end of the scale are the single-issue groups, which pursue a specific, focused objective, such as clean water, opposition to toxic waste storage sites, or even the welfare of a single species of wildlife (as is the case with the U.S.-based Mountain Lion Preservation Foundation and Bat Conservation International). At the other end of the scale are environmental organizations that take a broader view of the place of humans in their environment, quality of life issues, and the damaging consequences of human activities. Many of these groups grew out of the expansion of environmental consciousness during the 1960s and address issues as broad as nuclear power, acid pollution, toxic waste disposal, chemicals in the environment, oil spills, and global warming.

A phenomenon that emerged in large part since the mid-1970s has been the creation of groups with an interest in promoting sustainable development. This is a term that replaced *conservation* in the dictionary of environmentalism and means development that takes place within the carrying capacity of the natural environment. The sustainable development lobby focuses on managing resources for continued use. For example, it supports the management of forests and fisheries with a view to preventing clear-cutting and overfishing, arguing that sustainable use will allow them to be a constant source of resources. Although the term is usually applied to African, Asian, and Latin American states, it has been a central factor in environmentalism in industrial states for decades.

Methods and Strategies

As well as having different structures, environmental NGOs also differ in the means they use to achieve their objectives. A distinction is commonly made among groups that attempt to persuade, to bargain, and to coerce,[25] but groups have multiple methods available to them.

Working with Elected Officials, Bureaucrats, and Employees of Corporations. Lobbying is the method most commonly used by groups at the national level, with care being taken not to compromise their nonprofit or charitable status. In the United States, several major NGOs have created political action committees to channel funds to political parties and candidates running for office; they also work to provide support and information for favored candidates. Elsewhere, umbrella NGOs such as the European Environmental Bureau and Environment Liaison Centre International act as a conduit between their member bodies and IGOs.

Groups can also exert influence by providing advice and expert testimony during legislative hearings and the development of international treaties, or by submitting proposals to government departments and working with government commissions.[26] Several groups are active, for example, on Antarctic issues: the Scientific Committee on Antarctic Research is an independent advisory body that approves all scientific activity in the Antarctic, and the Antarctic and Southern Ocean Coalition represents more than 240 NGOs at meetings of the signatories of the 1959 Antarctic Treaty.[27] Similarly, many groups have maintained a close relationship with the International Whaling Commission, which monitors the application of the International Convention for the Regulation of Whaling and allows NGOs to participate in its meetings.

A notable example of how NGOs have developed a constructive relationship with an IGO is found in the World Bank. In 1983, six U.S. NGOs—including the National Wildlife Federation and the Natural

Resources Defense Fund—exerted pressure on the World Bank to pay more attention to the environmental effects of its projects, using hearings before the U.S. Congress on World Bank appropriations to draw attention to some of those projects.[28] The World Bank subsequently encouraged NGO involvement in an increasing number of its projects and now meets regularly, mainly with NGOs based in Washington, D.C. Since the creation of the United Nations, and most notably since the 1972 Stockholm conference, NGOs have been increasingly active in attending and observing international conferences and in holding parallel NGO conferences. For example, more than 1,000 NGOs attended negotiations held in Geneva and New York in preparation for the 1992 Earth Summit, and more than 22,000 representatives from more than 9,000 NGOs attended the summit itself.[29]

Raising and Spending Money. The Worldwide Fund for Nature was founded to raise money that could then be channeled to conservation activities. It was originally charged with raising funds for IUCN projects but quickly went off on an independent course of its own. While it still has a close relationship with IUCN, it is very much a separate organization with its own set of methods and priorities.[30]

As its title implies, WWF initially raised money to spend on projects aimed at protecting animal and plant species. It discovered very early, however, that threatened wildlife could not be protected in isolation and that natural habitats had to be protected first. This meant eliciting the support of local communities and using economic arguments in favor of environmental management. It was no good trying to protect birds and animals in a Brazilian rain forest, for example, unless local farmers could be convinced that the rain forest had more economic value to the local community if it was maintained intact rather than being cut down for timber or to clear land for farming. The result was that WWF became increasingly involved in lobbying local and national governments and in promoting international treaties to achieve its interests.

WWF has its international headquarters in Switzerland and a network of offices in more than fifty countries. It raises funds through a combination of grassroots activities and national and international campaigns, which have gone beyond a focus on individual species and have moved into habitat protection (for example, endangered seas and forests campaigns), attempts to encourage tourists not to buy the products of endangered species, and recently even global environmental issues such as climate change.

Campaigning and Organizing Public Protests. These methods are most commonly associated with groups such as Friends of the Earth and Greenpeace, which are among the best-known environmental NGOs in industrial countries because of their focus on generating publicity for their causes. Both were founded at about the same time (FoE in 1969 and Greenpeace in 1971), and both have since gone on to open national offices all over the world (FoE in sixty-eight countries and Greenpeace in forty). Between them they now have nearly 4 million individual members, and they use similar methods to draw attention to similar problems.

FoE was founded in the United States after a fallout between the Sierra Club and its executive director, David Brower. The Sierra Club is one of the oldest U.S. environmental NGOs (dating back to 1892) but had become too conservative for Brower's tastes. He argued that the solution to environmental problems lay not in temporary remedies but in fundamental social change and that vigorous campaigning was needed to achieve maximum publicity.[31] Similar motivations led to the creation of Greenpeace, which was born as the Don't Make a Wave Committee, a group that sailed a ship into northern Pacific waters to protest nuclear weapons tests. It has since used a combination of public protests and political lobbying to draw attention to issues such as deforestation in Russia, Canada, and Brazil; the dangers of nuclear energy and toxic wastes; and the problem of overfishing.

Promoting Media Coverage of Environmental Issues. Almost every NGO uses this channel, mainly through providing information and being available for interviews. Studies have repeatedly found that environmental groups believe the media is generally sympathetic to their cause, and most groups actively use the media to get their message across to the public, mobilize potential allies, give legitimacy and support to their work, and influence policymakers.[32]

Litigation and Monitoring the Implementation of Environmental Law. The former is a method used particularly by groups in the United States, such as the Environmental Defense Fund and the Natural Resources Defense Council, which have exploited citizen suit provisions included in several major pieces of federal environmental law since the early 1970s. These allow private citizens to sue private parties for noncompliance with the law and to recover legal fees and even fines, which then help fund their activities.[33]

Among groups that monitor the implementation of laws at the international level are the Wildlife Trade Monitoring Unit, Trade Records Analysis of Flora and Fauna in Commerce (TRAFFIC), and the Environmental Investigation Agency. These groups were at the forefront of efforts to stop international trade in ivory in the 1980s and to monitor compliance with the ivory trade ban imposed under the Convention on International Trade in Endangered Species (CITES) in 1989.[34]

Information Exchange. NGOs can play an important role in information exchange and dissemination, helping to strengthen the operations of other groups. A prime example is the Indonesian Forum for the Environment (WALHI), an umbrella body for several hundred other groups, which organizes education and training programs, provides technical assistance to its members on issues such as fund raising, and coordinates the activities of its members in lobbying government officials and bringing lawsuits.[35]

Undertaking Research. The British-based International Institute for Environment and Development carries out research on behalf of governments, international agencies, and NGOs on issues such as forestry, sustainable agriculture, and human settlements. Similarly, the Austrian-based International Institute for Advanced System Analysis undertakes scientific research on a variety of environmental problems, such as air pollution.

Acquiring and Managing Property. One of the biggest NGOs in Britain is the National Trust, which buys or is given buildings of historical significance and land of natural significance and manages such property in perpetuity. In the United States, the Nature Conservancy and Ducks Unlimited purchase land that is then set aside as wildlife habitat.

Generating Local Community Involvement in Environmental Protection. Several organizations focus on mobilizing grassroots support for their objectives. Such groups are most common in rural and urban communities in poorer countries and have been active, for example, in mobilizing forest dwellers in Brazil, India, and Malaysia to block the activities of lumber companies. The most famous of these was Chipko Andalan, the movement to "hug trees" in India in 1973–1974, which encouraged local villagers (mainly women) to band together to physically block the felling of trees by timber companies. In Kenya, the Green Belt Movement encourages people (again, mainly women) to find public areas and plant seedlings to form tree belts. Local community mobilization has also been effective in stopping the building of nuclear power stations, new highways, and toxic waste dumps in industrial countries.[36]

Environmental Groups and International Regimes

The last thirty years have seen the evolution of a large and varied community of environmental NGOs that has exerted a powerful influence on national governments, intergovernmental organizations, and negotiations on international environmental agreements. As suggested in this chapter, these NGOs have goals, philosophies, styles, structures, and methods that are often very different from one another. In some respects, this has been their strength, enabling them to develop a variety of methods to deal with a variety of problems at a variety of levels. It has also been a weakness, however, because the fragmentation of the environmental NGO community has prevented it from presenting a united front to policymakers and has thus impeded its policy impact.[37]

At the national level, NGOs have government institutions and bodies of law that they can monitor, influence, lobby, and attempt to change. They can appeal to elected officials, use their members and funds to exert influence on the electoral process, and work through the media, elected officials, the courts, and the bureaucracy to influence the policy process. They exist within a civil society, an organized society over which a state rules and in which citizens participate. In most cases, NGOs were created because citizens felt that the state was not dealing effectively with a particular problem—such as environmental management—and they organized in order to use their numbers to put pressure on the state or to respond themselves to the shortcomings of the state.

The same cannot be said for NGOs working at the international level, where they face at least three major handicaps. First, there is no central authority to which NGOs can appeal, other than the United Nations and its specialized agencies, which have only limited powers and certainly lack the kind of elected officials needed to provide a connection between an institution and those who live under its authority. For environmental NGOs, the United Nations Environment Programme comes closest to being an international authority, but it suffers a number of critical handicaps: it is a junior member of the UN system, it has no executive powers, it has little scope for carrying out its own projects, and it was intended from the outset to be an agent of cross-cutting policy coordination, working through the other UN specialized agencies.[38] UNEP has achieved the most when it has been a facilitator, bringing together governments and institutions with shared interests and encouraging them to negotiate and reach agreement on those interests. It cannot compel governments to act against their will.

Second, international treaties and organizations are the result of agreements among states, and citizens of those states can influence such compacts only indirectly through their own national governments. It is true that NGOs have worked around this handicap and have played an active role in, for example, the development of international treaties, as reflected in their presence at the Stockholm, Rio de Janeiro, and Johannesburg conferences. However, there is no formal provision for public review and comment on such treaties, nor is there a formal mechanism by which citizens or NGOs can bring suit before the World Court against IGOs or states failing to meet their obligations.[39]

Finally, while there is a body of international law and a series of international courts with various jurisdictions, there are no international bureaucrats with the power to ensure the implementation of that law. Nor is there an identifiable constituency of citizens that NGOs can mobilize to bring pressure to ensure implementation.

NGOs have nevertheless been able to exploit their strengths in several ways to overcome the handicaps inherent in exerting influence over an international regime:

- They have acted as information brokers, becoming the source of much of the research upon which policy decisions are taken. Reports to the Stockholm conference and the Earth Summit, and the intergovernmental discussion leading up to many of the most important international environmental treaties, have been heavily influenced by research generated by NGOs and by NGO influence over media coverage of these events.
- They have been whistle-blowers, helping IGOs keep track of progress (or the lack thereof) in the implementation of international treaties in signatory states. Indeed, it is arguable that without NGO pressure, there would be little obligation upon states to agree to substantial goals, and there would be little transparency in the process of agreeing and implementing international treaties.
- They have promoted democracy (albeit in limited form) in the work of IGOs and the deliberations preceding agreement of international

treaties by ensuring that the views of their members have been taken into consideration.

- They have played a valuable role as opponents of national government policy, drawing attention to the failures of domestic policies and exerting international pressure to change those policies.
- They have provided models for new government programs, using their resources and links with other NGOs to develop and offer solutions to environmental problems. In many instances, NGOs have themselves carried out the work of government by undertaking necessary research, raising funds, and carrying out practical environmental management projects.
- They have built international coalitions that have occasionally bypassed states and helped make up for some of the weaknesses of IGOs.

In the absence of an international body of environmental law backed up by a global governmental authority with responsibility for—and powers of—enforcing that law, much of the responsibility for promoting environmental concern at the international level since World War II has fallen to—or been adopted by—an increasingly complex network of nongovernmental organizations. These organizations operate at several different levels, use many different methods, and have multiple objectives and underlying principles. As well as identifying problems, proposing solutions, and monitoring the responses of states and the international community, environmental NGOs have contributed to the promotion of international regimes and a global civil society within which states and their citizens have redefined their relationships to one another and have helped us better understand the nature of global society.

Notes

1. Mostafa K. Tolba et al., *The World Environment 1972–1992: Two Decades of Challenge* (London: Chapman and Hall, 1992).
2. Paul Wapner, "Politics Beyond the State: Environmental Activism and World Civic Politics," *World Politics* 47 (1995): 311–340.
3. Gordon C. Schloming, *Power and Principle in International Affairs* (San Diego: Harcourt Brace, 1991); see chap. 2 for a discussion of the characteristics of realism and idealism.
4. John McCormick, *Acid Earth: The Politics of Acid Pollution,* 3d ed. (London: Earthscan, 1997).
5. See Union of International Associations Web site: http://www.uia.org (2003).
6. Harold K. Jacobson, *Networks of Interdependence: International Organizations and the Global Political System,* 2d ed. (New York: Knopf, 1984), 88–90.
7. Barry B. Hughes, *Continuity and Change in World Politics: Competing Perspectives,* 4th ed. (Englewood Cliffs, N.J.: Prentice Hall, 1999), 268.
8. For details, see John McCormick, *The Global Environmental Movement,* 2d ed. (New York: John Wiley, 1995), chap.1.
9. Ibid., 29–36.
10. Ibid., chap. 3.

11. Ibid., 119.
12. For more details on the role of NGOs in UNCED, see Matthias Finger, "Environmental NGOs in the UNCED Process," in *Environmental NGOs in World Politics*, ed. Thomas Princen and Matthias Finger (London: Routledge, 1994).
13. Ted Trzyna, ed., *World Directory of Environmental Organizations*, 6th ed. (London: Earthscan, 2001).
14. See European Environmental Bureau Web site: http://www.eeb.org (2003).
15. For further discussion, see Princen and Finger, *Environmental NGOs in World Politics*, 6–9.
16. Andrew Simms, "If Not, Then When? Non-Governmental Organizations and the Earth Summit Process," *Environmental Politics* 21 (spring 1993): 94–100.
17. Walter A. Rosenbaum, *Environmental Politics and Policy*, 5th ed. (Washington, D.C.: CQ Press, 2003), 29–32.
18. Russell J. Dalton, *The Green Rainbow: Environmental Groups in Western Europe* (New Haven: Yale University Press, 1994); Stephen Cotgrove, *Catastrophe or Cornucopia: The Environment, Politics, and the Future* (New York: Wiley, 1982); Lester Millbrath, *Environmentalists: Vanguard for a New Society* (Albany: State University of New York Press, 1984); Ronald Inglehart, *The Silent Revolution: Changing Values and Political Styles among Western Publics* (Princeton: Princeton University Press, 1977).
19. See Greenpeace Web site: http://www.greenpeace.org:80/gpi.html (2003).
20. See Environment Liaison Centre International Web site: http://www.elci.org (2003)
21. Donald T. Wells, *Environmental Policy: A Global Perspective for the Twenty-First Century* (Upper Saddle River, N.J.: Prentice Hall, 1996).
22. See IUCN Web site: http://www.iucn.org (2003).
23. See BirdLife Web site: http://www.birdlife.net (2003).
24. See Wetlands International Web site: http://www.wetlands.org (2003).
25. Ralph Turner, "Determinants of Social Movement Strategies," in *Collective Behavior*, ed. T. Shibutani (Englewood Cliffs, N.J.: Prentice Hall, 1970).
26. Dalton, *Green Rainbow*, 189–195.
27. See Antarctic and Southern Ocean Coalition Web site: http://www.asoc.org (2003).
28. Bruce Stokes, "Storming the Bank," *National Journal*, December 31, 1985, 3521–3522; and Ken Conca, "Greening the UN: Environmental Organizations and the UN System," in *NGOs, the UN, and Global Governance*, ed. Thomas G. Weiss and Leon Gordenker (Boulder, Colo.: Lynne Rienner, 1996).
29. Princen and Finger, *Environmental NGOs in World Politics*, 4.
30. McCormick, *Global Environmental Movement*, 46–48.
31. Ibid., 170–172.
32. Dalton, *Green Rainbow*, 185–186.
33. Michael S. Greve, "Private Enforcement, Private Rewards: How Environmental Suits Become an Entitlement Program," in *Environmental Politics: Public Costs, Private Rewards*, ed. Michael S. Greve and Fred L. Smith (New York: Praeger, 1992), 105–109.
34. Thomas Princen, "The Ivory Trade Ban: NGOs and International Conservation," in Princen and Finger, *Environmental NGOs in World Politics*.
35. See Indonesian Forum for the Environment Web site: http://www.walhi.or.id (2003).
36. For more details on citizen action movements, see Michael Edwards and John Gaventa, eds., *Global Citizen Action* (London: Earthscan, 2001).
37. Lynton K. Caldwell, *Between Two Worlds: Science, the Environmental Movement, and Policy Choice* (Cambridge: Cambridge University Press, 1990), 89–97.
38. McCormick, *Global Environmental Movement*, chap. 6, n. 7.
39. Hilary French, "The Role of Non-State Actors," in *Greening International Institutions*, ed. Jacob Werksman (London: Earthscan, 1996).

PART II. GLOBAL ENVIRONMENTAL POLICY: CASES AND QUESTIONS

6

Global Climate Change Policy: Making Progress or Spinning Wheels?

Michele M. Betsill

Global climate change presents a significant challenge to the international community. Anthropogenic emissions of greenhouse gases (GHGs) are causing a warming of the Earth's surface at an unprecedented rate.[1] Most scientists predict that if left unchecked, climate changes produced by this warming could include disruptions in rainfall and temperature patterns, a global rise in sea level, and an increased frequency of severe weather events, such as droughts, hurricanes, and floods.[2] In turn, these and other impacts of climate change could have serious implications for food security, freshwater supplies, human health, and species survival.

Climate change is a *global* environmental problem. Its causes, effects, and potential solutions transcend state boundaries, creating a need for international cooperation. Achieving such cooperation has proven difficult, however. Indeed, several factors create incentives for states and other actors to avoid taking meaningful steps to control their GHG emissions. For example, political and ethical questions remain regarding who bears responsibility for mitigating the threat. While industrialized countries emitted the vast majority of GHGs in the past, these will be surpassed by emissions from developing countries in the not too distant future. Second, since most GHGs remain in the atmosphere for a long time, the benefits of reducing emissions today will go to future generations rather than to those who must bear the cost of achieving such reductions. Third, the issue of climate change remains intimately linked with the global energy system. Any requirement to reduce emissions will likely impact the cost and availability of energy, a central component of the global economy. Finally, scientists remain uncertain about the rate and magnitude of climate change and the regional distribution of potential impacts.

This chapter examines the development of the global climate change regime, focusing on the agenda-setting and negotiation phases (Table 6-1).[3] According to Oran Young, "Agenda formation covers the steps by which an issue initially makes its way onto the international political agenda."[4] Thus the chapter begins with a discussion of how the problem of climate change emerged on the international agenda through a gradual buildup of scientific concern and then the transfer of that concern to the political arena. The subsequent section examines the negotiation phase and the two global environmental agreements it has produced to date: the 1992 United Nations Framework Convention on Climate Change (UNFCCC) and its 1997 Kyoto Protocol. The third section evaluates the effectiveness of the climate change regime, arguing that its significance goes beyond the direct effects of the UNFCCC and the Kyoto Protocol. While these agreements are clearly central to the international regime, the global governance of climate change includes activities carried out by both state and nonstate actors at a variety of levels, all aimed at mitigating and/or adapting to the risk of global climate change. The chapter concludes with a brief look at future challenges facing the international community as it seeks to address climate change.

Table 6-1 Key Events in the Formation of the Global Climate Change Regime

Agenda-setting phase	1896	• Arrhenius identifies enhanced greenhouse effect
	1957–1958	• Revelle and Seuss study
		• International Geophysical Year
		• Regular monitoring of atmospheric CO_2 levels begins at Mauna Loa
	1979	• First World Climate Conference
	1980–1985	• Villach scientific conferences
	1987	• Villach and Bellagio policy conferences
	1988	• Toronto Conference
		• IPCC created
	1988–1992	• All industrialized states (except United States) adopt domestic targets and timetables for controlling GHG emissions
	1990	• IPCC First Assessment Report
Negotiation phase	1991–1992	• UNFCCC negotiations
	1994	• UNFCCC enters into force
	1995-1997	• Kyoto Protocol negotiations on commitments
	1996	• IPCC Second Assessment Report
	1998–2001	• Kyoto Protocol negotiations on operationalization
	2001	• IPCC Third Assessment Report
		• United States withdraws from Kyoto Protocol
	2004	• Kyoto Protocol's entry into force contingent upon Russian ratification
Operationalization phase	2008–2012	• First commitment period under the Kyoto Protocol

Agenda Setting: From the Scientific to the Political Arena

The agenda-setting phase of the global climate change regime saw the expansion of concern about the problem from the scientific to the political arena (see Table 6-1). The threat of global warming is rooted in what is commonly referred to as the "greenhouse effect." Molecules of particular gases that exist naturally in the atmosphere (GHGs) trap heat like the panes of a greenhouse. This "natural" greenhouse effect keeps the Earth's surface temperature 30 degrees Celsius warmer than would otherwise be the case and is thus essential to preserving life on Earth. Global climate policy—the climate change regime—is concerned with the "enhanced" greenhouse effect, first identified in 1896 by Swedish chemist Svante Arrhenius. Arrhenius claimed that humans were altering the makeup of the atmosphere through the burning of coal, which would increase CO_2 concentrations.[5] He speculated that a doubling of CO_2 could lead to a 4-degree to 6-degree Celsius warming of the Earth's surface temperature.

International Scientific Cooperation

The scientific community generally ignored Arrhenius's claim of an enhanced greenhouse effect until the 1950s. In 1957 Roger Revelle and H. E. Seuss raised concern that the oceans would not be capable of absorbing the high levels of CO_2 being emitted through industrialization processes and that these emissions would thus alter the composition of the global atmosphere. They concluded, "Human beings are now carrying out a large scale geophysical experiment of a kind that could not have happened in the past nor be reproduced in the future."[6] Later that same year, the International Council of Scientific Unions launched the 1957–1958 International Geophysical Year (IGY). One of the research activities initiated as part of the IGY was the establishment of an observatory at Mauna Loa, Hawaii, to monitor atmospheric CO_2 concentrations. These observations, along with other types of data, soon revealed that CO_2 levels had risen significantly since the industrial revolution.[7] Observations of higher atmospheric CO_2 concentrations were accompanied by findings of increased mean global surface temperature, as had been predicted by Arrhenius.

Based on these emergent findings, delegates and scientists attending the 1979 First World Climate Conference, which had been organized by the World Meteorological Organization, established the World Climate Program and called on the world's governments "to foresee and prevent potential man-made changes in climate that might be adverse to the well-being of humanity."[8] In collaboration with the United Nations Environment Programme and the International Council of Scientific Unions, the World Climate Program organized a series of scientific conferences in Villach, Austria, in the early 1980s. By 1985, these meetings had produced an emerging scientific consensus that climate change posed a legitimate threat to the international community.[9] Two follow-up conferences were held in 1987: one in

Villach (September 28 to October 2) and one in Bellagio, Italy (November 9–13), to consider what policy steps might be appropriate given the state of scientific knowledge on climate change. As a result, scientists participating in the Bellagio conference recommended that governments "immediately begin to reexamine their long-term energy strategies with the goals of achieving high end-use efficiency, reducing multiple forms of air pollution and reducing CO_2 emissions." [10]

The process of placing climate change on the international political agenda culminated in the World Conference on the Changing Atmosphere, held in Toronto, Canada, in June 1988. Although the Toronto Conference, as it came to be known, was sponsored by the Canadian government, it was organized by individuals who had participated in the Villach/Bellagio conferences and thus built directly on the outcomes of those meetings. Participants, including scientists, policymakers, industry representatives, and environmentalists, suggested the first concrete target and timetable for controlling GHG emissions. The "Toronto target," which continues to figure prominently in international debates, called upon states to reduce their CO_2 emissions 20 percent below 1988 levels by 2005.[11]

In the aftermath of the Toronto Conference, the United Nations convened formal international negotiations. The first session, held in 1991, marked the beginning of the "negotiation phase" of the climate regime. During this period, a number of industrialized countries adopted domestic targets and policies for limiting GHG emissions. By 1992, all but the United States had adopted such targets, with members of the European Union (EU) committing to stabilizing their emissions at 1990 levels by 2000.[12] The United States had initiated a domestic debate and a significant research program but had not yet developed an action plan for controlling emissions.[13]

The Intergovernmental Panel on Climate Change

Scientific research continues to play an important role in the climate change regime. In November 1988 the World Meteorological Organization and the United Nations Environment Programme created the Intergovernmental Panel on Climate Change (IPCC) to synthesize and assess the state of scientific knowledge on climate change and evaluate response strategies. (The IPCC does not conduct original scientific research.) The IPCC has completed three major assessments (1990, 1996, and 2001), as well as numerous technical reports, and is generally viewed as the authoritative scientific body on the issue of climate change, giving the IPCC a privileged position in the policy process. To date, more than 2,000 scientists from around the world have participated in IPCC assessments. The IPCC is currently working on its fourth assessment report, scheduled for publication in 2007.

The work of the IPCC is primarily carried out by three working groups and is overseen by a bureau consisting of the chairman of the IPCC (currently Dr. Rajendra K. Pachauri of India), three vice chairs, as well as the chairs and co-chairs of each of the three working groups, and the Special

Task Force on National Inventories.[14] The IPCC Secretariat, located in Geneva, has the responsibility for planning, overseeing, and managing all IPCC activities. The IPCC meets in plenary session annually and establishes the mandate for the working groups. Working Group I focuses on the science of climate change. Working Group II assesses issues related to impacts, vulnerability, and adaptation to climate change. Working Group III reviews options for mitigating climate change.

According to the IPCC Third Assessment Report (2001), atmospheric CO_2 concentrations have increased 31 percent since 1750, due primarily to human activities such as fossil fuel combustion and deforestation.[15] In the twentieth century, global mean surface temperatures have risen 0.6 degree Celsius, with the 1990s being the warmest decade on record.[16] Overall, atmospheric concentrations of GHGs are increasing at a rate that is unprecedented in the last 20,000 years. The IPCC has linked these increases to a number of observed changes in the global climate, including a rise in sea level; a decrease in snow cover; more frequent, persistent, and intense El Niño episodes; and more frequent and severe droughts in parts of Africa and Asia. These trends are projected to increase into the next century.[17]

The effects of global warming are likely to be harmful to humans and the ecosystems on which they depend. Sea-level rise threatens the physical existence of several small-island states located in the Pacific and Indian Oceans, as well as the availability of fresh water in low-lying coastal areas, which are home to between 50 and 70 percent of the world's population. Changes in precipitation patterns will negatively affect agricultural productivity in many regions, leaving a large number of people at greater risk of food insecurity and famine, and will expand the habitat of insects carrying infectious diseases such as dengue fever and malaria. Developing countries are most vulnerable to the impacts of climate change because of their limited options for adapting to anticipated changes.[18]

Negotiating a Global Climate Policy

The process of developing a coordinated global response to climate change has focused on negotiation of the UNFCCC and the Kyoto Protocol. As a "framework" convention, the UNFCCC establishes the basic architecture within which international efforts to address global climate change take place. The Kyoto Protocol outlines specific obligations consistent with the guiding principles set forth in the UNFCCC. Together, these documents form the core of the global climate change regime, setting forth the principles, norms, rules, and decision-making procedures that govern interactions between members of the international community on this issue. More than 190 countries have participated in international climate negotiations, along with hundreds of nongovernmental organizations (NGOs). Many states have organized themselves into negotiating blocks (Table 6-2), while NGOs have created "observer constituencies" (Table 6-3) in order to facilitate coordination among participants with relatively common interests.

Table 6-2 State Negotiating Blocks

Group Name	Members	Position
EU	15 member states of the European Union*	Support targets and timetables for emissions reductions
JUSCANZ/JUSSCANNZ	Japan, United States, Canada, Australia, and New Zealand; Switzerland and Norway joined during the Kyoto Protocol negotiations	Concerned that targets and timetables for emissions reductions will have negative economic impacts
Umbrella Group	Russia, Iceland, Ukraine, and JUSSCANNZ	Support the use of market mechanisms to achieve emissions reductions
OPEC	Members of the Organization of Petroleum Exporting Countries	Oppose targets and timetables for emissions reductions because of fear they will severely reduce export markets for oil and natural gas upon which their economies are heavily dependent
AOSIS	Alliance of Small Island States: 42 low-lying and/or island developing states that are particularly vulnerable to the impacts of climate change, especially sea-level rise	Support strict targets and timetables for emissions reductions as a matter of survival
G-77 and China	Developing countries	Support targets and timetables for emissions reductions in industrialized countries only; priority on social and economic development

Sources: Michele M. Betsill, "Greens in the Greenhouse: Environmental NGOs, Norms and the Politics of Global Warming" (Ph.D. diss., University of Colorado-Boulder, 2000); Joyeeta Gupta, *Our Simmering Planet: What to Do About Global Warming?* (London: Zed Books, 2001); Sebastian Oberthür and Hermann E. Ott, *The Kyoto Protocol: International Climate Policy for the 21st Century* (New York: Springer, 1999).

*The European Union expanded to 25 member states in 2004.

Negotiating the United Nations Framework Convention on Climate Change

Under a United Nations General Assembly mandate, the Intergovernmental Negotiating Committee for a Framework Convention on Climate Change (INC) met six times between February 1991 and May 1992. The negotiations took place as part of the preparations for the 1992 United

Nations Conference on Environment and Development (the Earth Summit), held in Rio de Janeiro. The UNFCCC was one of two international treaties opened for signature at the conference (the Convention on Biological Diversity was the other).[19] The UNFCCC entered into force in March 1994 and has been ratified by more than 185 countries. Key elements of the Convention, and thus of global climate policy, include its objective, principles, and commitments and the creation of an organizational structure for the regime.

Objective. Article 2 of the UNFCCC establishes the objective of the climate change regime as

> stabilization of greenhouse gas concentrations in the atmosphere at a level that would prevent dangerous anthropogenic interference with the climate system. Such a level should be achieved within a time-frame sufficient to allow ecosystems to adapt naturally to climate change, to ensure that food production is not threatened and to enable economic development to proceed in a sustainable manner.[20]

Note that the goal is to stabilize GHG *concentrations* rather than *emissions.* Emissions and concentrations are clearly related—increased emissions will lead to increased atmospheric concentrations. However, stabilizing GHG emissions will not stabilize atmospheric concentrations because of the long life of many GHGs in the atmosphere. Indeed, in its First Assessment Report, released in 1990, the IPCC estimated that stabilizing atmospheric CO_2 concentrations at then current levels would have required an immediate reduction of global emissions by 60 percent.

Note also that the UNFCCC does not state what constitutes "dangerous" interference with the climate system or at what level atmospheric GHG concentrations must be stabilized to avoid such interference. Countries could not agree on more specific language due to significant differences on the need for action. Nevertheless, many in the scientific community argue that some damage to the Earth's ecosystems and human societies is inevitable at this point and that the international community needs to act to prevent even more substantial impacts.[21]

Principles. Article 3 of the UNFCCC sets forth principles that should guide the international community in its efforts to mitigate climate change. The principle of *common but differentiated responsibilities* acknowledges that while all members of the international community have an obligation to protect the climate for present and future generations, countries listed in Annex I (industrialized countries and formerly communist countries with economies in transition) have a responsibility to take the lead in addressing climate change. This stems from their historical responsibility for emitting greenhouse gases, as well as the assumption that they possess the financial and technological capabilities to control those emissions.

The UNFCCC also states that *equity* should be a guiding principle in the development of a global response to climate change. However, equity has

Table 6-3 NGO Observer Constituencies

Constituency		Position	Alignment with state negotiating blocks
Environmental NGOs: Organized under the umbrella of the Climate Action Network		Support strict targets and timetables for emissions reductions; seek to hold states accountable for their commitments	EU, G-77 and China, and/or AOSIS (depending on the issue)
Business and Industry NGOs:	e.g., the Global Climate Coalition	Oppose targets and timetables for emissions reductions; question scientific basis of climate change	JUSSCANNZ and OPEC groups
	e.g., the Business Environmental Leadership Council	Support the use of market mechanisms to ensure that emissions reductions can be achieved at the lowest cost	Umbrella group
	e.g., groups representing renewable energy industry	Support targets and timetables for emissions reductions; see economic opportunities in developing technologies to achieve reductions	EU, AOSIS, some partnerships with environmental NGOs
Local Governments and Municipal Authorities: Represented by the International Council on Local Environmental Initiatives		Support targets and timetables for emissions reductions; seek to gain wider recognition for the contributions of local authorities in controlling emissions	EU and environmental NGOs
Indigenous Peoples' Organizations		Seek to ensure that rules on the use of forests in achieving emissions reductions do not infringe upon the rights of indigenous peoples	Some alignment with G-77 and China and environmental NGOs

Sources: Michele M. Betsill, "Greens in the Greenhouse: Environmental NGOs, Norms and the Politics of Global Warming" (Ph.D. diss., University of Colorado-Boulder, 2000); Peter Newell, *Climate for Change: Non-state Actors and the Global Politics of the Greenhouse* (Cambridge, England: Cambridge University Press, 2000); Kal Raustiala, "Nonstate Actors in the Global Climate Regime," in *International Relations and Global Climate Change,* ed. Urs Luterbacher and Detlef F. Sprinz (Cambridge: MIT Press, 2001), 95–118; UNFCCC, "Non-governmental Organization Observer Constituencies" (Bonn, Germany: UNFCCC Secretariat, 2003). Available from http://unfccc.int/resource/ngo/const.pdf (accessed May 8, 2003).

been interpreted in a variety of ways and remains an unsettled matter. For example, many developing countries argue that equity would be best achieved through a per capita allocation of GHG emissions rights, noting their low historical contribution to the climate problem, current low levels of per capita GHG emissions compared with industrialized countries, and lack of resources. Per capita emissions allocations would enable developing countries to raise their living standards, thereby reducing their vulnerability to the impacts of climate change.[22] However, achieving a convergence of per capita emissions would require even more significant reductions on the part of industrialized countries than have been adopted thus far.

The UNFCCC also recognizes the specific needs and special circumstances of developing countries that may be particularly vulnerable to climate change, either to adverse impacts, such as drought, or because their economies are dependent on the production and export of fossil fuels (states belonging to the Organization of Petroleum Exporting Countries [OPEC]). In addition, the Convention embraces the *precautionary principle,* stating that the absence of full scientific certainty should not be used as an excuse to avoid taking action to mitigate the threat and/or impact of climate change.

The principles of the UNFCCC also reflect the relationship between climate change and economic conditions. Measures taken to deal with climate change should be *cost effective,* ensuring the greatest benefit at the lowest cost. This has been a particularly important point for members of the JUSS-CANNZ group, as well as some of the EU member states. In addition, all countries are seen to have a right to *sustainable development,* and measures to address climate change should promote that objective. This was a particularly important issue for the G-77 and China during the UNFCCC negotiations.[23] Finally, the Convention emphasizes the importance of *maintaining an open international economic system.*

Commitments. The UNFCCC imposes three key obligations on parties. First, all Annex I parties (industrialized countries and formerly communist countries with economies in transition) must adopt policies and measures "with the aim of returning individually or jointly to their 1990 levels of these anthropogenic emissions of carbon dioxide and other greenhouse gases not controlled by the Montreal Protocol" (Article 4.2(b)). No binding timetable is set for achieving stabilization, but Article 4.2(a) does call upon parties to recognize "that the return by the end of the present decade [2000] to earlier levels of anthropogenic emissions of carbon dioxide and other greenhouse gases" would contribute to mitigating the threat of climate change.

Second, Annex I parties must provide "new and additional financial resources" as well as technology to help developing countries meet their commitments under the Convention (Article 4(3)). Note that consistent with the principles outlined above, the UNFCCC differentiates between industrialized and developing countries, placing the primary burden for addressing global climate change on the industrialized countries.

Third, under Articles 4 and 12, all parties must regularly report on their national emissions inventories and programs to mitigate climate change.

Thus, under these and other articles, developing countries do have a general obligation to address global climate change.

During negotiation of Annex I country commitments, some participants—particularly the EU, AOSIS, and environmental NGOs—argued for binding targets and timetables for reducing emissions. The United States, however, with support from other JUSCANZ countries, called for voluntary commitments to stabilize emissions without any clear timetable. The United States and others objected to binding targets and timetables on the grounds that binding reductions were premature, given what they viewed as uncertainties about whether humans were causing climate change, and would have devastating economic effects.[24] The U.S. position was heavily influenced by the Global Climate Coalition (GCC), a business and industry group representing members of the fossil fuel industry. Eventually, countries accepted the JUSCANZ position. Given that the United States was responsible for more than one-quarter of 1990 global GHG emissions and that countries feared being placed at a competitive disadvantage if they accepted binding reductions while the United States did not, participants reasoned that it was essential to keep the United States engaged in the process of developing an international response to climate change, even if that meant formalizing a weaker target in the Convention.[25]

Organizational Structure. The UNFCCC creates the central institutional architecture for global climate policy. Article 7 establishes the Conference of the Parties (COP) as the supreme body, with responsibility for reviewing the implementation of the UNFCCC (and any related legal instruments) and making decisions to promote its effective implementation. The COP usually meets annually, although, as was the case following the collapse of negotiations at COP-6, parties can agree to convene extraordinary sessions. The Secretariat (Article 8), located in Bonn, Germany, administers the Convention, making meeting arrangements and compiling and transmitting information. The UNFCCC also established two other important subsidiary bodies—the Subsidiary Body for Scientific and Technological Advice (SBSTA, Article 9) and the Subsidiary Body for Implementation (SBI, Article 10), which meet at least twice a year and assist the COP with assessing the state of scientific and technological knowledge related to climate change, as well as the effects of measures taken under the Convention and subsequent legal decisions. The Global Environment Facility (GEF) acts as the financial mechanism for the UNFCCC on an interim basis (Articles 11 and 21). Developing countries were disappointed that the Convention did not create an independent financial mechanism. They feared that industrialized states, as the principal donors to the GEF, would use their leverage to control the allocation of resources.[26]

Negotiating the Kyoto Protocol: From Rio to Marrakesh

Broad acceptance of nonbinding reductions did not last long. At the first Conference of the Parties to the UNFCCC (COP-1), held in Berlin in 1995, delegates adopted the Berlin Mandate, which stated that commitments contained in the Convention were insufficient to meet its long-term objective and initiated a process of negotiating a protocol to the UNFCCC that would contain binding targets and timetables for reducing GHG emissions beyond 2000.

Following two years of extremely complex and intense negotiations, parties adopted the Kyoto Protocol to the UNFCCC at COP-3, held in Kyoto, Japan, in December 1997.[27] The Kyoto Protocol requires industrialized countries and countries with economies in transition to reduce their aggregate GHG emissions 5.2 percent below 1990 levels over the period 2008–2012. The protocol provides "flexible mechanisms" to assist countries in meeting their commitments cost-effectively. These include emissions trading, joint implementation, and the Clean Development Mechanism (CDM) (see below). The protocol also allows parties to receive credit for emissions absorbed by "sinks."[28] However, the rules and operational details for the mechanisms and sink credits were left to subsequent negotiations, and it quickly became apparent that many states would not ratify the protocol without resolution of these issues.

The Buenos Aires Plan of Action, agreed upon at COP-4 in Argentina in 1998, set COP-6 as the deadline for resolving these and other issues related to making the Kyoto Protocol operational. In addition to finalizing the rules on the use of flexible mechanisms and assigning credits for emissions absorbed by sinks, parties agreed to develop a compliance system and common standards for accounting and crediting emissions reductions.

Although parties met in several formal and informal negotiating sessions in 1999 and early 2000, by the time they arrived at COP-6 in The Hague, Netherlands, in November 2000, many key issues remained unresolved. After two weeks of nearly continuous debate over more than 300 pages of highly technical draft text, the talks broke down. Most observers identified questions related to the use of sinks as the ultimate reason for failure.[29] The future of the Kyoto Protocol became even more uncertain in the spring of 2001, when newly elected U.S. president George W. Bush announced that the United States would not continue to support the Kyoto process (a 1997 Senate resolution had already made ratification unlikely); he called the protocol "fatally flawed" on the grounds that it failed to include emissions reduction commitments for developing countries and would damage the U.S. economy.

In what was billed as a "rescue effort,"[30] countries met at COP-6, part II, in Bonn in July 2001 and reached a political agreement about how to move forward. The Bonn Agreement was a package of decisions aimed at clarifying the rules for emissions trading, the use of sinks, financing, and compliance. Politically, the agreement was seen as a tremendous victory, demonstrating to the United States that the rest of the international community was committed to a multilateral approach to global climate change. The political agreement reached in Bonn was formalized at COP-7, held in Marrakesh, Morocco, in November 2001. With the adoption of the Marrakesh Accords, parties finalized the rules for the Kyoto Protocol and cleared the way for industrialized countries to move forward with the ratification process.

The Kyoto Protocol

While the UNFCCC laid out the general architecture of the climate change regime, the Kyoto Protocol identified mechanisms to be used to achieve its overall objective. The central elements include commitments, rules on flexible mechanisms and compliance, and the creation of new organizations.[31]

Commitments. Article 3 of the Kyoto Protocol requires industrialized countries to reduce their aggregate GHG emissions at least 5.2 percent below 1990 levels by 2008–2012. These commitments are differentiated in that each country has an individual target (see Table 6-4). In addition, some countries with economies in transition were permitted to select a year other than 1990 as a baseline. These differentiated targets are widely recognized as "purely political," the result of tough bargaining in closed-door sessions involving the EU leadership, the United States, and Japan during the final days (and ultimately hours) of the Kyoto negotiations. They are not based on scientific or economic analysis and are far below what the IPCC says is necessary to stabilize atmospheric concentrations of GHGs.

The Marrakesh Accords also address uncertainties and controversy regarding whether and how parties can get credit for emissions absorbed by biotic sinks in the land use (provided that activities in this sector do not undermine the environmental integrity of the protocol, especially in terms of protecting biodiversity). Under the Marrakesh Accords, emissions and offsets in the following activities may be taken into account: afforestation, reforestation, deforestation, crop management, forest management, grazing land management, and revegetation.

Flexible Mechanisms. Consistent with the principle of cost-effectiveness, the Kyoto Protocol gives parties considerable flexibility in choosing how to achieve their emissions reduction commitments. The "Kyoto mechanisms" or "flexible mechanisms" include emissions trading (Article 17), joint implementation (Article 6), and the Clean Development Mechanism (CDM; Article 12). Emissions trading permits countries that exceed their allowed emissions to purchase emissions credits from countries whose emissions are below their allotted amount.[32] Industrialized countries may also invest in emissions reduction activities in other industrialized countries under the rules of joint implementation. The investing country receives emissions reduction units (ERUs) that can be applied toward its target (the ERUs are subtracted from the host country's assigned amount). The CDM allows industrialized countries to invest in emissions-reducing activities in developing countries in return for certified emissions reductions (CERs) that may then be used toward meeting its target.[33]

During the initial negotiation of the Kyoto Protocol, the United States, supported by other members of the Umbrella Group and industry representatives, pushed strongly for a broad set of flexibility measures. The EU, most developing countries, and environmental groups objected, arguing that extensive reliance on such mechanisms would allow rich countries to buy their way out of making any meaningful commitments domestically, thereby violating

Table 6-4 Emissions Reduction Targets in the Kyoto Protocol

Country	Emissions reduction (% below 1990 levels)	Country	Emissions reduction (% below 1990 levels)
Australia	+8	Liechtenstein	8
Austria	8	Lithuania	8
Belgium	8	Luxembourg	8
Bulgaria	8	Monaco	8
Canada	6	Netherlands	8
Croatia	5	New Zealand	0
Czech Republic	8	Norway	+1
Denmark	8	Poland	6
Estonia	8	Portugal	8
European Community	8	Romania	8
Finland	8	Russia	0
Germany	8	Slovakia	8
Greece	8	Slovenia	8
Hungary	6	Spain	8
Iceland	+10	Sweden	8
Ireland	8	Switzerland	8
Italy	8	Ukraine	0
Japan	6	United Kingdom	8
Latvia	8	United States	7

Source: UNFCCC, *The Kyoto Protocol to the Convention on Climate Change* (Bonn, Germany: UNFCCC Secretariat, 1997), Annex B.

the "polluter pays" principle. In the final hours of the COP-3 in Kyoto, flexibility mechanisms were included in the protocol in exchange for U.S. support of reduction, rather than stabilization, targets. As noted, negotiations to finalize the rules about how these mechanisms could be used were extremely contentious. Of particular concern was the issue of "additionality." While the Marrakesh Accords do not place a specific limit on the use of flexible mechanisms, they clearly state that countries should achieve a significant portion of their emissions reductions through domestic measures. The use of the mechanisms should be in addition to, not instead of, such measures.

Another controversy concerned the possibility for "hot air" emissions trading, which refers to the ability of a country whose emissions are below its legally binding limits to trade the difference.[34] At the time the Kyoto targets were negotiated, emissions in Russia and the Ukraine were more than 30 percent below 1990 levels due to economic decline. Yet each country secured a stabilization commitment under the protocol. As a result, both

Russia and the Ukraine have a supply of surplus hot-air emissions—emissions that exist only on paper—that could be sold to countries like Japan and the United States who might have difficulty meeting their targets through actual domestic reductions.

Countries also differed on how to treat sinks within the CDM. In a compromise between the Umbrella Group and the EU/G-77 and China, the Marrakesh Accords limit the types of activities that may be applied for afforestation and reforestation during the first commitment period and state that the credits earned for these activities "may not exceed 1 percent of a party's base-year emissions." [35]

Compliance. While the issue of compliance was largely ignored in the Kyoto Protocol, the subsequent Marrakesh Accords set forth a compliance system consisting of a Compliance Committee with two branches—the facilitative and enforcement branches—each having ten members. The facilitative branch helps parties fulfill their commitments under the protocol. The enforcement branch determines whether parties are in compliance with their commitments. Parties that are found to be in noncompliance with their reporting obligations become ineligible to use the flexible mechanisms. Parties that fail to meet their emissions reduction targets in the first commitment period are required to make up the difference during the second commitment period, with a 30 percent penalty.[36] This is one of the strongest compliance systems in any multilateral environmental agreement.

Organizational Structure. The negotiations to finalize the Kyoto Protocol added several new institutions to the organizational structure of the global climate change regime. The CDM Executive Board will accredit operational entities to participate in CDM projects and develop procedures to encourage small-scale projects, particularly in the areas of energy efficiency and renewable energy.[37] It will consist of ten representatives from the various state blocks that participate in the climate change negotiations (see Table 6-2).

For developing countries, one of the major objectives has been to secure financial resources to assist in meeting current and future commitments under the climate change regime. To that end, the Marrakesh Accords call for an increase in funds to the GEF as well as the creation of three new funds.[38] The Special Climate Change Fund is designed to finance activities related to adaptation, technology transfer, development of policies and measures in a number of different sectors, and diversification of economies. The Least-Developed Country Fund assists these countries in the preparation and implementation of national action plans as required under the UNFCCC, while the Adaptation Fund provides resources for activities related to adaptation.

Ratification and Entry into Force. Article 25 states that the Kyoto Protocol will enter into force when it has been ratified by at least fifty-five countries, including parties accounting for 55 percent of 1990 emissions from industrialized countries. To date, 119 parties have ratified the protocol, including more than twenty industrialized countries accounting for over 44 percent of 1990 emissions.[39] The United States and Australia have formally announced that they do not intend to ratify the protocol. Thus entry into force depends on ratification by Russia, which accounted for 17 percent of 1990 emissions.

Effectiveness of the Global Climate Change Regime

Evaluating the effectiveness of international environmental regimes is difficult and raises a host of methodological challenges.[40] Of particular import is whether one chooses to focus solely on the direct impacts of a particular cooperative arrangement, in this case the UNFCCC and the Kyoto Protocol, on targeted actors and ultimately the environment, or if one also includes consideration of more indirect effects that may be generated as a result of the negotiation process and reflected in society more broadly. This section contends that while the direct effects of the UNFCCC and the Kyoto Protocol may be limited, the indirect effects have prompted a shift in the governance of climate change beyond nation-states, opening up greater possibilities for meaningful action in the future to address the problem.

Effects on Targeted Actors and GHG Emissions

A legalistic definition of effectiveness focuses on whether states are complying with the rules of the regime.[41] The vast majority of countries in the world have ratified the UNFCCC and submitted national communications containing emissions inventories and an overview of policies and measures taken to address climate change. Thus compliance with this basic requirement is quite high. However, critics argue that much of the information in these communications is not useful, is incomplete, and often cannot be compared across states.[42]

In terms of commitments to control greenhouse gases, the performance to date is less encouraging. Only the United Kingdom, Germany, and Russia achieved the goal of stabilizing their greenhouse gas emissions at 1990 levels by 2000. In each case, however, such progress had little to do with adopting innovative climate policies and more to do with economic circumstances.[43] Moreover, a recent report by the Convention Secretariat questions the ability of industrialized countries to meet the Kyoto Protocol target, noting that "the combined emissions of Europe, Japan, the US and other highly industrialized countries could grow by 17 percent from 2000–2010."[44] Emissions from EU countries, which had decreased 3.5 percent since 1990, rose in 2000 and 2001.[45] U.S. emissions decreased 1.6 percent between 2000 and 2001 but remained 13 percent higher than 1990 levels.[46]

In some cases compliance may be a misleading measure of regime effectiveness. Where standards set in an international treaty are low, high levels of compliance may be meaningless.[47] Alternatively, analysts can consider whether agreements prompt changes in behavior among targeted actors by comparing their behavior with business-as-usual scenarios.[48] For example, although U.S. greenhouse gas emissions in 1999 were 11 percent above 1990 levels, the Clinton administration argued that they would have been even higher were it not for its 1993 Climate Change Action Plan, developed in compliance with the UNFCCC, which consisted of more than fifty voluntary measures designed to stabilize emissions.[49]

Assessments of regime effectiveness might also consider "the degree to which the degrading or polluting processes and consequences are arrested or reversed."[50] In other words, does the regime actually help ameliorate the problem that gave rise to its creation? On this basis, the short-term effectiveness of the global climate change regime must be called into question. Global GHG emissions continue to increase, and although the precise meaning of "dangerous anthropogenic interferences with the climate system" has yet to be defined, preventing such interference is generally expected to involve emissions reductions well beyond the level called for in the Kyoto Protocol. Critics also note that an overreliance on flexibility mechanisms could further compromise the environmental integrity of the climate change regime.[51] Moreover, even if the Kyoto targets were achieved, atmospheric concentrations will continue to rise as emissions from developing countries increase. Some analysts question the regime's focus on developing targets and timetables for controlling GHG emissions, noting that targets can become ceilings and are hard to measure. Negotiating targets and timetables may divert attention from other activities with potentially greater impact in terms of addressing the climate change.[52]

Broader Effects

Despite the regime's shortcoming in the near term, it is possible that the processes and institutions created under the UNFCCC and the Kyoto Protocol will facilitate international action to address climate change in the long term. This optimistic perspective stems from viewing international regimes as catalysts for learning and generating shared understandings rather than simply a set of specific rules and obligations.[53] As Underdal argues,

> International negotiation processes are often large-scale exercises in *learning*, through which at least some parties modify their perceptions of the problem and of alternative policy options and perhaps see their incentives change as well. As a consequence, the process itself may lead governments as well as nongovernmental actors to make unilateral adjustments in behavior—even in the absence of any legal obligation to do so. The aggregate impact of such side effects may well be more important than the impact of any formal convention or declaration signed in the end.[54]

Through the negotiation of the UNFCCC and the Kyoto Protocol, the international community has come to view the problem of climate change as a legitimate threat. Together, these agreements send a clear message to states as well as industry that business as usual (for example, unregulated emission of GHGs) is no longer acceptable.[55] Moreover, the climate change regime has given rise to new actors, institutions, and interests that are likely to play a significant role in addressing the threat of climate change over the long term.

Nation-states increasingly behave in ways that suggest they have accepted a responsibility to address climate change by limiting their GHG emissions. Over the past decade, all industrialized countries have institutionalized responsibility for addressing climate change within their respective governments and adopted policies for controlling emissions. This is true even in some oil-producing countries, which are attempting to secure resources to protect their economies, as well as in laggard countries, such as the United States. Despite the Bush administration's objection to the Kyoto Protocol, the United States remains engaged on the issue of climate change, continuing to participate in ongoing negotiations related to the UNFCCC and enacting domestic programs aimed at curbing the greenhouse gas intensity of the American economy.[56] Many developing countries have also institutionalized the need to address climate change and are taking steps to limit their emissions, even though they are not formally required to do so under the UNFCCC and the Kyoto Protocol.[57]

The climate change regime has given rise to a new discourse linking economic growth with the achievement of emissions reductions, illustrated in the striking shift in the position of many business and industry groups over the past decade.[58] During the UNFCCC negotiations, the business groups that participated in the process primarily consisted of members of the fossil-fuel industry who organized themselves under the umbrella of the GCC. Members of the GCC were united in their opposition to international regulations on GHG emissions. Over the course of the Kyoto Protocol negotiations, the business and industry community diversified, with groups representing members of the renewable energy industry as well as the insurance industry coming out in support of international GHG regulations. In addition, a number of companies whose profits derive from the production and consumption of fossil fuels left the Global Climate Coalition (which eventually disbanded in December 2001) and have begun working to find economically viable ways to control GHG emissions. A particularly visible result of this shift is the Business Environmental Leadership Council, an initiative of the Pew Center on Global Climate Change in Washington, D.C. Established in 1998, the Pew Center works with thirty-eight major corporations, including British Petroleum, DuPont, Boeing Company, Toyota, and Weyerhauser. British Petroleum and DuPont have made voluntary pledges to reduce GHG emissions within their operations by 10 percent and 65 percent, respectively. In 2002 each company announced that it had met its target, eight years ahead of schedule.[59]

Recognition of the need to address climate change has also filtered down to the local level. More than 560 municipal governments throughout the world (accounting for 8 percent of global GHG emissions) participate in the Cities for Climate Protection campaign sponsored by the International Council for Local Environmental Initiatives (ICLEI).[60] These communities have committed to developing policies and programs to reduce GHG emissions and in the process have recognized linkages between environmental protection and economic growth. Toronto was one of the first cities to take on the issue of global climate change. Reflecting on the decision to address what is typically seen as a global issue, then Mayor Barbara Hall noted,

> Initially, we felt a sense of pride in being among the first to respond to the call for action issued by eminent climate scientists gathered at a major international conference held in Toronto in June 1988. After a while, though, we realized that investing in energy efficiency has many benefits for our city. These include reducing municipal expenses, creating jobs, nourishing a new industry, not to mention cutting air pollution; warmer summers are causing more smog locally.[61]

The governance of climate change has expanded beyond the realm of treaty-making between nation-states. As additional actors engage in efforts to address climate change, new opportunities emerge to enhance the effectiveness of the global climate change regime through public-private partnerships, bottom-up pressure, and transnational networks. In other words, the global governance of climate change has evolved into a complex, multi-level process.[62]

The Road Ahead

Agreement on the operational details of the Kyoto Protocol marked the beginning of a new phase in international climate change policy. Many members of the international community are now looking beyond 2012 and thinking more broadly about the future global response to climate change. One of the most important agenda items concerns participation by developing countries.[63] At COP-8, held in New Delhi, India, in November 2002, the EU and members of the Umbrella Group sought to initiate discussions about options for developing countries to control their GHG emissions. Most developing countries refused to discuss the issue, emphasizing instead their immediate needs to eradicate poverty and promote economic and social development. Ironically, the United States reinforced the developing countries' position, arguing that economic development is a prerequisite to addressing environmental problems such as climate change. Many observers believe that addressing such equity concerns will be a precondition for getting developing country commitments.[64]

The international community must also consider more fully how the climate change regime overlaps regimes in other issue areas, including biodiversity, forests, and desertification.[65] To the extent that norms and rules developed in the context of the climate change regime are consistent with those developed to deal with other global environmental problems, there is a potential for synergy that could enhance international efforts to address these issues. However, such synergies cannot be assumed. Since most environmental regimes have been developed as problem-specific, there is also the possibility that the rules and norms developed in a particular issue area are contradictory to those developed in other issue areas. The existence of a regime to deal with climate change may make it more difficult to address other, equally pressing problems, such as biodiversity loss.

Finally, it is important to recognize that the global governance of climate change is a complex, multilevel process no longer confined solely to multilateral treaty-making. Decisions affecting GHG emissions and strategies for adapting to the impacts of climate change are made by a myriad of state and nonstate actors working at all levels, from the global to the local, and often connected through transnational networks.[66] Thus our understanding of the global climate change regime must shift away from a hierarchical, state-centric perspective. Many local governments and members of the private sector are working on creative solutions for addressing the threat of global warming. However, these actors are not working in isolation, and their efforts are facilitated or constrained by policies and programs at other levels of government and actions in other spheres. In other words, the effective governance of global climate change over the long term will require that political attention focus on the mobilization of resources and creativity far beyond the relatively narrow confines of the UNFCCC and the Kyoto Protocol. While these agreements have been essential in defining the core of the climate change regime, it is unlikely that they alone will solve the problem of global warming.

Notes

1. The major greenhouse gases are carbon dioxide (CO_2), methane (CH_4), nitrous oxide (N_2O), chlorofluorocarbons (CFCs), and water vapor. Regulations within the climate change regime focus on a "basket" of six gases: CO_2, CH_4, N_2O, hydrofluorocarbons (HFCs), perfluorocarbons (PFCs), and sulfur hexafluoride (SF_6).
2. Intergovernmental Panel on Climate Change (hereafter IPCC), *Summary for Policy Makers: A Report of Working Group I of the Intergovernmental Panel on Climate Change* (Cambridge: Cambridge University Press, 2001). Available from http://www.ipcc.ch (accessed May 15, 2001).
3. A third phase of regime formation involves operationalization, or moving from a negotiated agreement to changes in practice. There will be some discussion of the operationalization of the two major international treaties on climate change, but it will not be treated as a distinct phase here. It should be noted that these phases are for analytical purposes only and that in practice there are considerable overlap and feedbacks.
4. Oran R. Young, "Rights, Rules and Resources in World Affairs," in *Global Governance: Drawing Insights from the Environmental Experience,* ed. Oran R. Young (Cambridge: MIT Press, 1997), 11.
5. Svante Arrhenius, "On the Influence of Carbonic Acid in the Air on the Temperature on the Ground," *Philosophical Magazine* 251 (1896): 236–276.
6. Quoted in Michael Oppenheimer and Robert H. Boyle, *Dead Heat: The Race against the Greenhouse Effect* (New York: Basic Books, 1990), 36.
7. Robert T. Watson and Core Writing Team, eds., *Climate Change 2001: Synthesis Report* (Cambridge: Cambridge University Press, 2001), 4–8.
8. World Meteorological Organization, *Proceedings of the First World Climate Conference—A Conference of Experts on Climate and Mankind, 12–23 February 1979* (Geneva: World Meteorological Organization, 1979), 709.
9. World Climate Program, *Report of the International Conference on the Assessment of the Role of Carbon Dioxide and of Other Greenhouse Gases on Climate Variations and Associated Impacts* (Geneva: World Meteorological Organization, 1986).

10. Jill Jaeger, *Developing Policies for Responding to Climatic Change: A Summary of the Discussions and Recommendations of the Workshops Held in Villach (28 September–2 October 1987) and Bellagio (9–13 November 1987), under the Auspices of the Beijer Institute, Stockholm* (Geneva: World Meteorological Organization, 1988), 37.

11. World Meteorological Organization, *Proceedings of the World Conference on the Changing Atmosphere: Implications for Global Security* (Geneva: World Meteorological Organization, 1988), 296.

12. International Energy Agency, *Climate Change Policy Initiatives,* vol.1: *OECD Countries* (Paris: International Energy Agency, 1994).

13. Michele M. Betsill, "Greens in the Greenhouse: Environmental NGOs, Norms and the Politics of Global Climate Change" (Ph.D. diss., University of Colorado-Boulder, 2000), chap. 4.

14. On the IPCC and the assessment process, see Shardul Agrawala, "Context and Early Origins of the Intergovernmental Panel on Climate Change," *Climatic Change* 39 (1988): 605–620; Shardul Agrawala, "Structural and Process History of the Intergovernmental Panel on Climate Change," *Climatic Change* 39 (1988): 621–642; and Tora Skodvin, "The Intergovernmental Panel on Climate Change," in *Science and Politics in International Environmental Regimes: Between Integrity and Involvement,* ed. Steinar Andresen, Tora Skodvin, Arild Underdal, and Jørgen Wettestad (Manchester: Manchester University Press, 2000), 146–180.

15. IPCC, *Summary for Policy Makers,* 7–8.

16. Instrumental records began in 1861.

17. IPCC, *Summary for Policy Makers,* 12–14.

18. IPCC, *Summary for Policy Makers. Climate Change 2001: Impacts, Adaptation and Vulnerability* (Cambridge: Cambridge University Press, 2001), 8.

19. An anticipated third agreement on forests failed to materialize.

20. United Nations, *United Nations Framework Convention on Climate Change* (Bonn: UNFCCC Secretariat, 1992), Art 2. Available from http://www.unfccc.int (accessed September 9, 2003).

21. See Donald A. Brown, *American Heat: Ethical Problems with the United States' Response to Global Warming* (Lanham, Md.: Rowman & Littlefield, 2002).

22. Ambuj Sagar, "Wealth, Responsibility, and Equity: Exploring an Allocation Framework for Global GHG Emissions," *Climatic Change* 45 (2000): 511–527; P. R. Shukla, "Justice, Equity and Efficiency in Climate Change: A Developing Country Perspective," in *Fair Weather? Equity Concerns in Climate Change,* ed. F. L. Toth (London: Earthscan, 1999), 150–155; Gary W. Yohe, David Montgomery, and Ed Balistreri, "Equity and the Kyoto Protocol: Measuring the Distributional Effects of Alternative Emissions Trading Regimes," *Global Environmental Change* 10 (2000): 121–132.

23. Tariq Osman Hyder, "Looking Back to See Forward," in *Negotiating Climate Change: The Inside Story of the Rio Convention,* ed. I. M. Mintzer and J. A. Leonard (Cambridge: Cambridge University Press, 1994).

24. It was not until the second IPCC assessment report, released in 1995, that the scientific community made its now infamous statement that the "the balance of evidence suggests a discernible human influence on global climate." See IPCC, *Climate Change 1995: The Science of Climate Change, Summary for Policy Makers* (Cambridge: Cambridge University Press, 1996), 10.

25. William A. Nitze, "A Failure of Presidential Leadership," in Mintzer and Leonard, *Negotiating Climate Change,* 187–200; Matthew Paterson, *Global Warming and Global Politics* (London: Routledge, 1996), 100.

26. Joyeeta Gupta, *Our Simmering Planet: What to Do about Global Warming?* (London: Zed Books, 2001), 75–76.

27. For a detailed discussion of the negotiating process, see Sebastian Oberthür and Hermann E. Ott, *The Kyoto Protocol: International Climate Policy for the 21st Century* (New York: Springer, 1999).

28. "Sinks" refer to biotic masses, such as forests, that absorb carbon dioxide from the atmosphere.
29. Michael Grubb and Farhana Yamin, "Climatic Collapse at The Hague: What Happened, Why and Where Do We Go from Here?" *International Affairs* 77, no. 2 (2001): 261–276.
30. Davis A. Wirth, "The Sixth Session (Part Two) and the Seventh Session of the Conference of the Parties to the Framework Convention on Climate Change," *American Journal of International Law* 96, no. 3 (2002): 648–660.
31. For a more detailed analysis of these elements, see Michael Grubb, Christiaan Vrulijk, and Duncan Brack, *The Kyoto Protocol: A Guide and Assessment* (London: Royal Institute of International Affairs, 1999); and Oberthür and Ott, *Kyoto Protocol*. For a more critical review, see David G. Victor, *The Collapse of the Kyoto Protocol and the Struggle to Slow Global Warming* (Princeton: Princeton University Press, 2001).
32. For a more detailed analysis of emissions trading in the climate change regime, see Victor, *Collapse of the Kyoto Protocol*, 25–54.
33. Oberthür and Ott, *Kyoto Protocol*, 165–186.
34. Ibid., 187–206.
35. Wirth, "The Sixth Session (Part Two) and the Seventh Session of the Conference of the Parties to the Framework Convention on Climate Change," 64.
36. Climate Change Secretariat, *A Guide to the Climate Change Convention and Its Kyoto Protocol: Preliminary Version* (Bonn: UNFCCC Secretariat, 2002). Available from <http://unfccc.int/resource/guideconvkp-p.pdf> (accessed September 8, 2003).
37. UNFCCC, *Kyoto Protocol Mechanisms* (Bonn: UNFCCC Secretariat, 2003). Available from http://unfccc.int/issues/mechanisms.html (accessed May 8, 2003).
38. Wirth, "The Sixth Session (Part Two) and the Seventh Session of the Conference of the Parties to the Framework Convention on Climate Change," 650–651.
39. For updated information from the UNFCCC Secretariat, see http://unfccc.int/resource/kpstats.pdf.
40. See Edward Miles, Arild Underdal, Steinar Andresen, Jørgen Wettestad, Jon B. Skjærseth, and Elaine Carlin, *Environmental Regime Effectiveness: Confronting Theory with Evidence* (Cambridge: MIT Press, 2001); David G. Victor, Kal Raustiala, and Eugene B. Skolnikoff, eds., *The Implementation and Effectiveness of International Environmental Commitments* (Cambridge: MIT Press, 1998); Oran R. Young, ed., *The Effectiveness of International Environmental Regimes: Causal Connections and Behavioral Mechanisms* (Cambridge: MIT Press, 1999).
41. Edith Brown Weiss and Harold K. Jacobson, eds., *Engaging Countries: Strengthening Compliance with International Environmental Accords* (Cambridge: MIT Press, 1998), 4–5.
42. Victor, *Collapse of the Kyoto Protocol*, 112–113.
43. Grubb et al., *Kyoto Protocol*, 81; Paterson, *Global Warming and Global Politics*, 69.
44. UNFCCC Secretariat, "Rich Countries See Higher Greenhouse Gas Emissions: Upward Trend Set to Continue," press release, Bonn, June 3, 2003.
45. European Environment Agency, *Annual European Community Greenhouse Gas Inventory 1990–2001 and Inventory Report 2003: Submission to the UNFCCC Secretariat* (Brussels: European Environment Agency, 2003).
46. Environmental Protection Agency (hereafter EPA), *U.S. Emissions Inventory 2003*, EPA report no. EPA 430-R-03-004 (Washington, D.C.: Environmental Protection Agency, April 2003), E-2.
47. Marvin S. Soroos, "Global Climate Change and the Futility of the Kyoto Process," *Global Environmental Politics* 1, no. 2 (2001): 1–9.
48. Victor et al., *Implementation and Effectiveness of International Environmental Commitments*, 7.
49. EPA, *Inventory of U.S. Greenhouse Gas Emissions and Sinks: 1990–1999* (Washington, D.C.: Environmental Protection Agency, 2001).

50. Gabriela Kütting, *Environment, Society and International Relations: Towards More Effective International Environmental Agreements* (London: Routledge, 2000), 36.

51. Soroos, "Global Climate Change and the Futility of the Kyoto Process," 1–9.

52. Frank N. Laird, "Just Say No to Greenhouse Gas Emissions Targets," *Issues in Science and Technology* 17, no. 2 (2000). Online edition available from http://www.nap.edu/ issues/17.2/laird.htm (accessed 7 March 2002); Daniel Sarewitz and Roger A. Pielke Jr., "Breaking the Global-warming Gridlock," *Atlantic* (July 2000): 55–64.

53. Oran R. Young, *The Institutional Dimensions of Environmental Change: Fit, Interplay and Scale* (Cambridge: MIT Press, 2002), 31.

54. Arild Underdal, "One Question, Two Answers," in *Environmental Regime Effectiveness: Confronting Theory with Evidence*, ed. Edward L. Miles, Arild Underdal, Steinar Andresen, Jørgen Wettestad, Jon. B. Skjærseth, and Elaine M. Carlin (Cambridge: MIT Press, 2002), 5 (emphasis in original).

55. Michele M. Betsill, "The United States and the Evolution of International Climate Change Norms," in *Climate Change and American Foreign Policy*, ed. P. G. Harris (New York: St. Martin's, 2000), 205–224; Oberthür and Ott, *Kyoto Protocol*, 287–300; Hermann E. Ott, *The Kyoto Protocol to the UN Framework Convention on Climate Change: Finished and Unfinished Business* (Wuppertal, Germany: Wuppertal Institute for Climate, Environment and Energy, 1999).

56. George W. Bush, quoted in "Clear Skies Initiative: Executive Summary," White House press release, February 14, 2002. Available from http://www.whitehouse.gov/ news/releases/2002/02/climatechange.html (accessed March 14, 2002).

57. Bonizella Biagini, *Confronting Climate Change: Economic Priorities and Climate Protection in Developing Countries* (Washington, D.C.: National Environmental Trust, 2000).

58. Matthew Paterson, "Climate Policy as Accumulation Strategy: The Failure of COP 6 and Emerging Trends in Climate Politics," *Global Environmental Politics* 2 (2001): 10–17.

59. Eileen Claussen, "Solving the Climate Equation: Mandatory and Practical Steps for Real Reductions," Remarks to the Alliant Energy Conference, Madison, Wisconsin, April 15, 2003. Available from http://www.pewclimate.org/media/ transcript_04142003.cfm (accessed May 15, 2003).

60. Harriet Bulkeley and Michele M. Betsill, *Cities and Climate Change: Urban Sustainability and Global Environmental Governance* (London: Routledge, 2003).

61. International Council for Local Environmental Initiatives, Statement by Barbara Hall, former mayor, Toronto, Ontario, Canada. Available from http://www.iclei.org/ mayors/mtoronto.htm (accessed September 8, 2003).

62. Bulkeley and Betsill, *Cities and Climate Change*, 189–193.

63. Tom Jacob, "Reflections on Delhi," *Climate Policy* 3 (2003): 103–106; Hermann E. Ott, "Warning Signs from Delhi: Troubled Waters Ahead for Global Climate Policy" (Wuppertal, Germany: Wuppertal Institute for Climate, Environment and Energy, 2003), 2. Available from http://www.wupperinst.org/download/Warning-Signs-Ott.pdf (accessed September 8, 2003).

64. Shukla, "Justice, Equity and Efficiency in Climate Change," 146.

65. G. Kristin Rosendal, "Overlapping International Regimes: The Case of the Intergovernmental Forum on Forests (IFF) between Climate Change and Biodiversity," *International Environmental Agreements: Politics, Law and Economics* 1, no. 4 (2001): 447–468.

66. Michele M. Betsill and Harriet Bulkeley, "Transnational Networks and Global Environmental Governance: The Cities for Climate Protection Program," *International Studies Quarterly*, forthcoming.

7

Global Policy for Hazardous Chemicals

David Leonard Downie, Jonathan Krueger, and Henrik Selin

Hazardous chemicals pose significant, if often overlooked, threats to human health and the environment. Toxic, explosive, and/or flammable chemicals are produced or used in virtually every country in the world. Such chemicals are released into the environment through the normal use of certain products (for example, pesticides), common industrial and manufacturing practices that involve or produce hazardous substances, combustion processes, leakage from waste streams (including medical, shipping, and household wastes), mismanagement, accidents, and intentional dumping.

Once hazardous chemicals have been dispersed into the environment, complete cleanup of them is extremely difficult, if not impossible, and their harmful effects can continue for years or even decades. Some chemicals can travel long distances from their emission source via air currents, waterways, and migratory animals. Many are also persistent, remaining in the environment for long periods before breaking down into less dangerous substances. Some chemicals have the ability to build up in fatty tissues of individual animals, with increasing concentrations upward through food webs.[1]

Creating and implementing effective international policy for hazardous chemicals can be surprisingly difficult. Some hazardous chemicals, such as pesticides used to control disease-carrying pests, exist for important and legitimate reasons, and controlling them involves balancing competing priorities. Sensitivity to chemicals often varies across species, gender, and age, and many chemicals exist in commercial mixtures with different physical, chemical, and biological properties and effects, making risk assessments difficult. More broadly, since a comprehensive policy requires the introduction of interrelated controls for each stage of a chemical's life cycle—production, use, trade, and disposal—effective policy faces a variety of technical, policy-design, and implementation obstacles.

This chapter focuses on global policy for management of hazardous chemicals. It examines the creation and implementation of three multilateral environmental agreements (MEAs) that constitute the key institutional and legal elements of current global chemicals policy: the 1989 Basel Convention on the Control of Transboundary Movements of Hazardous Wastes and Their Disposal, the 1998 Rotterdam Convention on the Prior Informed Consent Procedure for Certain Hazardous Chemicals and Pesticides in International Trade, and the 2001 Stockholm Convention on Persistent

Organic Pollutants.[2] The chapter ends by analyzing key areas in which concerted action under the three agreements could significantly strengthen the effectiveness of global chemicals policy.

Hazardous Chemicals on the International Agenda

The large-scale, systematic development and use of chemicals for commercial purposes began after World War II and has accelerated ever since.[3] Today human-made chemicals appear integral to everyday life, particularly in industrialized countries, with up to 100,000 chemicals in regular commercial production and use worldwide.[4] The Organization for Economic Cooperation and Development (OECD) estimates that global sales of the chemicals industry, valued in the billions in 1998, employed 10 million people and accounted for 9 percent of all international trade.[5] Almost 80 percent of the global total output of the chemicals industry is produced by sixteen countries: the United States, Japan, Germany, China, France, the United Kingdom, Italy, Korea, Brazil, Belgium, Luxembourg, Spain, the Netherlands, Taiwan, Switzerland, and Russia. Chemicals are widely used in industrial processes to facilitate and increase production; in products derived from life sciences, such as pharmaceuticals, pesticides, and biotechnology products; and in consumer products such as soap, detergents, and skin care products.[6]

Early in the twentieth century, scientists and industry considered the new pesticides and industrial chemicals to be generally harmless to humans and nontarget pests. Indeed, Paul Müller won the Nobel Prize for Medicine and Physiology in 1948 for his work related to development of dichlorodiphenyl trichloroethane (DDT) as a pesticide. Warnings of the potential dangers posed by the increasing use of pesticides and other chemicals began to appear in the early 1960s, most famously by Rachel Carson in her ground-breaking book, *Silent Spring*.[7] International concern about industrial chemicals increased significantly in 1968, when many people in Yosho, Japan, were poisoned after eating rice contaminated with high levels of polychlorinated biphenyls (PCBs) that had leaked from a heat exchanger.[8]

In the late 1960s and early 1970s, risk assessments led many industrialized countries to adopt domestic regulations on a relatively small set of hazardous chemicals, including DDT and PCBs. During this period, the OECD became the first international organization to pay serious attention to the environmental and human health impacts of hazardous chemicals. Most of the initial OECD efforts focused on stimulating information exchange and improving and harmonizing domestic technical, scientific, and policy measures among its member states (i.e., industrialized countries).[9] In the United States, DDT was banned in 1972, and PCBs were prioritized in the 1976 Toxic Substances Control Act.[10]

Global attention to hazardous chemicals was further stimulated by the 1972 United Nations Conference on the Human Environment, held in Stockholm, Sweden. The Action Plan produced at the conference called for improved international efforts to develop and harmonize procedures for assessing and managing hazardous substances and to make more resources available to developing countries for building domestic capacity. In response, the United Nations Environment Programme (UNEP) created the International Register of Potentially Toxic Chemicals (IRPTC) in 1976 to collect and process information on hazardous chemicals and disseminate it to countries seeking such information.

In the 1970s and early 1980s, several multilateral agreements that sought to protect oceans, regional seas, and rivers from dumping and pollution included references to hazardous chemicals.[11] More focused efforts began later in the 1980s in response to rising concern for, and evidence of, the potential dangers of hazardous chemicals. Discussions within the United Nations Food and Agriculture Organization (FAO) and UNEP led to the development of the 1985 International Code of Conduct for the Distribution and Use of Pesticides and the 1987 London Guidelines for the Exchange of Information on Chemicals in International Trade. Both the Code of Conduct and the London Guidelines included procedures aimed at making information about hazardous chemicals more freely available. Unfortunately, many developing countries lacked the regulatory infrastructure to make such assessments or to create and implement effective domestic policy. [12] In contrast, many European and North American countries continued to strengthen domestic and regional controls on hazardous chemicals.

Problems relating to the transnational transport and trade in hazardous wastes, including chemical wastes, gained increasing attention in the 1980s, particularly in response to several prominent cases of mismanaged and illegal shipments to developing countries. In 1987 UNEP's governing council concluded several years of work by adopting the voluntary Cairo Guidelines and Principles for the Environmentally Sound Management of Hazardous Wastes, which centered on the principle of prior notification and consent by states before the import or transit of hazardous wastes.[13] To strengthen the Cairo Guidelines, UNEP's governing council authorized global negotiations on a legally binding agreement. This process produced the 1989 Basel Convention on the Control of Transboundary Movements of Hazardous Wastes and Their Disposal.

The UN Conference on Environment and Development (UNCED), held in Rio de Janeiro in 1992, continued to advance global activities on hazardous chemicals. Agenda 21, adopted at UNCED, included a chapter on chemicals; six priorities were outlined, including the creation of new intergovernmental forums to facilitate discussion and coordination among the many national and international agencies working on some aspect of chemicals management.[14] To this end, the Intergovernmental Forum on Chemical Safety (IFCS) was established in 1994.[15] In 1995 the Inter-Organization Programme for the Sound Management of Chemicals (IOMC) was set up to help coordinate efforts of the many international organizations working on chemical-related issues.[16]

Following UNCED, concern about hazardous chemicals continued to grow in response to ongoing expansion in their production, use, and trade, as well as new evidence regarding the long-range transnational transport of emissions and their negative impact on the environment and human health. Particular attention was paid to the risks faced by sensitive groups such as small children and pregnant women.[17] Efforts to address these issues included the expansion of several existing multilateral treaties, such as the Basel Convention and northern regional seas agreements, as well as the development of two new global agreements, the 1998 Rotterdam Convention on the Prior Informed Consent Procedure for Certain Hazardous Chemicals and Pesticides in International Trade and the 2001 Stockholm Convention on Persistent Organic Pollutants.

The 2002 World Summit on Sustainable Development (WSSD) called for further action. Among other goals, WSSD agreed that countries should aim "to achieve by 2020 that chemicals are used and produced in ways that lead to the minimization of significant adverse effects on human health and the environment." [18] As part of this process, countries are expected to work toward full implementation of the Basel, Rotterdam, and Stockholm Conventions.

The Basel Convention

The 1989 Basel Convention on the Control of Transboundary Movements of Hazardous Wastes and Their Disposal seeks to protect human health and the environment by minimizing the generation of hazardous wastes, including chemical wastes, and controlling and reducing their transboundary movement.[19] Export of hazardous wastes is prohibited to Antarctica and to parties that have banned such imports.[20] Hazardous waste transfers to other parties are subject to prior notification and consent controls: a party must not export hazardous wastes to another party without the consent of the importing state. Waste exports to non-parties are prohibited unless they are subject to an agreement that is at least as stringent as the Basel Convention. Parties are expected to work toward reducing the generation of hazardous wastes and ensuring the environmentally sound management of wastes that remain.

Chemicals are subject to the Basel Convention if they can be categorized as hazardous wastes under the terms of the treaty.[21] Table 7-1 provides examples of materials thus classified under the Basel Convention. The Basel Convention entered into force in May 1992. Currently, there are 160 parties to the Convention, including all the major producers and exporters of hazardous wastes except the United States.[22]

A particular concern that led to the Basel Convention was an upswing in shipments of hazardous wastes from industrialized countries to developing countries, including several highly publicized incidents of illegal dumping.[23] In one of the most notorious examples, the cargo ship *Khian Sea* left port in 1986 in search of a disposal site for 14,000 tons of inciner-

Table 7-1 Indicative Wastes under the Basel Convention (Adapted from Annex I and Annex III)

Waste streams that can produce hazardous waste	Waste constituents that may be hazardous	Some characteristics of hazardous waste
Residues arising from industrial waste disposal operations	Copper compounds	Explosive
	Zinc compounds	Flammable
Tarry residues arising from refining	Arsenic and arsenic compounds	Poisonous
		Infectious
Chemical substances arising from research and development	Metal carbonyls	Corrosive
	Mercury and mercury compounds	Toxic (delayed or chronic)
Substances and articles containing PCBs	Lead and lead compounds	Eco-toxic
Pharmaceutical products	Inorganic cyanides	
Wood-preserving chemicals	Asbestos	
	Ethers	
Organic solvents	Halogenated organic solvents	
Inks, dyes, pigments, paints, lacquers, varnish	Acidic solutions or acids in solid form	
Mineral waste oils, emulsions	Cadmium and cadmium compounds	

Source: Originally published in *Global Governance: A Review of Multilateralism and International Organizations,* Volume 8, Number 3, July–September 2002, page 334. Copyright © 2002 by Lynne Rienner Publishers. Used with permission.

ator ash, originally from Philadelphia, that contained lead and cadmium. The ship spent almost two years at sea, during which it changed its name twice, dumping 4,000 tons of ash on a beach in Haiti and the remaining 10,000 tons somewhere between the Suez Canal and Singapore.[24]

The rise in legal and illegal North-South shipments of hazardous wastes resulted from several factors.[25] As the generation of hazardous wastes reached record levels in many industrialized countries, domestic regulations became more stringent, forcing older waste disposal facilities to close even as local opposition often prevented new ones. As a result, the economic and political costs associated with proper disposal grew rapidly in industrialized countries. This produced strong incentives for exporting hazardous wastes to developing countries with lower labor costs, less stringent environmental regulations and enforcement, and less local opposition. Similar incentives also appeared for recycling particular wastes that, even if contaminated, still had commercial value as a secondary raw material. Waste metals and decommissioned ships are two prominent examples of hazardous wastes sold to developing countries for recycling.

In the early 1980s, UNEP became one of the first international organizations to address these issues. It did so initially by facilitating development of the voluntary Cairo Guidelines for international transport of hazardous waste based on prior notification and consent. Seeking to strengthen the voluntary measures, UNEP helped to convene formal negotiations on a global, legally binding convention in 1987. Two years of contentious negotiations followed before governments adopted the Basel Convention in 1989.

During the early phases of negotiations, many African countries and Greenpeace advocated a complete ban on transferring hazardous wastes across national boundaries, arguing that only a ban would stop "toxic imperialism" in developing countries. Most industrialized countries preferred a system that imposed controls but not an outright ban, claiming that this would allow for the economically sensible continuation of international transport and trade in wastes, mainly among industrialized countries. In the end, the larger coalition of developing countries could not convince the industrialized bloc on the need for a broad ban. Thus the Basel Convention initially focused on categorizing wastes, eliminating their export to parties that overtly banned such shipments, and creating a prior notification and consent system for all other shipments.[26]

Parties to the Basel Convention have gradually strengthened its legal requirements and developed improved institutional structures for its implementation. At the first Conference of the Parties (COP-1), in December 1992, developing countries and the Nordic states successfully pushed for the adoption of Decision I/22, which requested that industrialized countries refrain from exporting hazardous wastes to developing countries for disposal.[27] At COP-2, efforts continued toward a mandatory ban on exports. Led by the G-77 and Nordic states, delegates agreed to Decision II/12, which immediately banned the export of all hazardous wastes from OECD countries to non-OECD countries for final disposal and banned the export of hazardous wastes intended for recycling by the end of 1997. However, because this policy was enunciated by a decision of the COP rather than by a formal amendment to the Convention, some countries questioned whether the decision was sufficiently binding and continued pressing for stronger actions under the Convention. COP-2 also adopted detailed technical guidelines on several priority waste streams—including organic solvents, household trash, and waste oil—designed to help industry and government officials manage hazardous wastes in an environmentally sound manner.

Responding to criticism that Decision II/12 was not stringent enough, COP-3, in September 1995, adopted the so-called Ban Amendment, which formally prohibits the export of hazardous wastes for final disposal and recycling from parties that are industrialized countries (as listed in Annex VII) to all other parties. Nonetheless, because of an apparent desire by both industrialized countries and some developing countries to maintain the economically valuable trade in hazardous wastes for recycling, ratification of the Ban Amendment has been slow, and it has not yet entered into force.

COP-4, in February 1998, identified priority waste streams via two new annexes, further clarifying the scope and priories of the Convention. Annex VIII lists specific wastes characterized as hazardous under the Basel Convention. Annex IX lists wastes not covered by the Convention. A third list, which is not kept in an annex but by the Secretariat as a working list, contains wastes awaiting classification. At COP-5, in December 1999, delegates adopted the Basel Protocol on Liability and Compensation in response to concerns by developing countries that they lacked sufficient funds and technologies for coping with illegal dumping or accidental spills. The protocol establishes provisions for liability and compensation for damage resulting from the transnational movement of hazardous wastes, including incidents occurring because of illegal traffic.

COP-6, held in December 2002, agreed upon a strategic plan that set a prioritized agenda for implementing the Basel Convention over the next decade. The plan stresses the need to tackle priority waste streams, such as obsolete pesticides, lead-acid batteries, used oil, PCBs, and electronics. COP-6 also adopted new technical guidelines for the environmentally sound management of hazardous wastes. There are now guidelines for sixteen different types of hazardous wastes, including biomedical and health-care wastes and obsolete ships. Governments also endorsed a special initiative through which leading mobile phone manufacturers will increase their responsibility for mobile phone recovery.

In addition, COP-6 streamlined the institutional architecture of the Convention, created a compliance mechanism to review and assist implementation, and confirmed the role of the Basel Convention Regional Centers (BCRCs) to facilitate implementation in developing countries and countries with economies in transition. BCRCs engage in a wide range of activities, including capacity-building, public education, data collection, reporting, promoting environmentally sound waste management, facilitating the transfer of cleaner production technologies, and helping to provide training for customs officials, local municipalities, and other stakeholders. There are now thirteen BCRCs located in different parts of Latin America, Africa, Asia, and Europe.[28] Additional centers may be created in the future.

Yet despite the strides taken since its inception in 1989, implementation of the Basel Convention suffers from important shortcomings. First, actions remain more focused on regulating the trade of hazardous wastes than on reducing their generation or safely managing their disposal. Second, the Ban Amendment and the Protocol on Liability and Compensation remain significantly short of the levels needed to enter into force. Third, too little has been done to improve the capacity of developing countries to limit and manage properly either imported or domestically generated hazardous waste. Finally, because a substance can be regulated under the Convention only if it satisfies Basel's particular definitions of both "waste" and "hazardous," the Convention allows some hazardous substances to escape regulation.

The Rotterdam PIC Convention

The 1998 Rotterdam Convention on the Prior Informed Consent Procedure for Certain Hazardous Chemicals and Pesticides in International Trade aims to reduce harm from such trade by allowing countries to make informed decisions about exporting or importing particular chemicals.[29] Negotiated between 1995 and 1998 under UNEP and FAO auspices, the Rotterdam Convention makes legally binding a similar procedure that earlier had been operating on a voluntary basis.

In 1989 both the FAO Code of Conduct and the UNEP London Guidelines were amended to include a voluntary Prior Informed Consent (PIC) procedure to help countries decide on the importing of chemicals that have been banned or severely restricted. This voluntary PIC system was a victory for environmental and consumer NGOs who had been advocating it for nearly a decade. Moreover, developing countries felt that a new, potentially effective mechanism had been established that would allow them to better regulate these imports.[30] At the same time, however, many believed that in the long run a voluntary system would be insufficient. Thus, in response to these concerns, Chapter 19 of Agenda 21 called on states to create a mandatory PIC procedure to supplement and eventually replace the voluntary guidelines.

Questions about the potential scope of a binding PIC convention were present from the outset of the negotiations. At first, developing countries sought a ban on the export of domestically prohibited chemicals from countries that are members of the OECD to other countries, but no such ban had been envisaged by UNEP or the FAO. Subsequently, the EU proposed that a PIC convention should contain a framework provision that would allow for the negotiation and addition of protocols on chemicals at later stages. This idea was also supported by environmental NGOs. However, strong opposition came from the United States, Canada, Australia, and other non-European OECD countries, who argued that it would create an expanding and increasingly costly bureaucratic process. With no consensus on potential changes, delegates eventually agreed that the negotiations would simply transform the existing voluntary procedure into a legally binding agreement without changing the scope. The resulting Rotterdam Convention was signed by fifty-four countries and the European Commission in September 1998.

Under the Rotterdam Convention, export of a listed chemical can take place only with the prior informed consent of the importing party. This "shared responsibility" of the exporter and importer allows the international community to obtain and formally disseminate decisions by countries about receiving future shipments of certain chemicals and ensures compliance with such decisions by exporting countries. One observer has noted that "if it operates properly, PIC could be one of the largest organized transfers of useful regulatory information to developing countries, which in turn could contribute to the ultimate goal of the PIC system—improving management of hazardous chemicals and pesticides."[31] The Rotterdam Convention also requires that parties with more advanced programs for regulating chemicals provide technical assistance to other countries for developing the infrastructure and capacity to manage chemicals in a more environmentally sound manner.

The Convention's core regulatory procedure can be divided into two phases: information exchange and prior informed consent. First, parties notify the PIC Secretariat about any national regulatory action that bans or severely restricts a particular toxic chemical or substance. After a required number of notifications of regulatory actions have been received, a decision is made to include the chemical in the PIC list and is sent to all parties. During the second stage, potential importing parties formally declare if they (a) consent to receive future imports of the chemical; (b) do not consent; or (c) will consent under certain conditions. The Secretariat then distributes the responses, and potential exporters must abide by the decisions.

Given its emphasis on regulating trade in hazardous chemicals, negotiators needed to formulate the Rotterdam Convention carefully so that it would not clash with the binding rules of the international trading system in the form of GATT regulations and the World Trade Organization (WTO). To avoid conflict with WTO rules, decisions taken by an importing country under the Rotterdam Convention must be trade-neutral. This means that if a party does not consent to accept imports of a specific chemical, it must also stop domestic production of that chemical and cease to accept imports from any non-party.[32]

The Rotterdam Convention did not enter into force until February 2004.[33] Nevertheless, countries have already taken steps to expand the number of chemicals (originally twenty-seven) controlled under the Convention; at least thirty-one chemicals are currently subject to the PIC procedure (including at least twenty-one pesticides, five industrial chemicals, and five severely hazardous pesticide formulations).[34]

In an improvement on the voluntary procedure, the Convention sets out clear criteria for the information required in notifications of national regulatory actions (bans or severe restrictions) *and* the criteria that a chemical must meet in order to be on the PIC list. A Chemical Review Committee is responsible for reviewing national regulatory actions and proposals for listing chemicals or severely hazardous pesticide formulations notified by parties. The criteria for judging whether or nor the actions meet the Convention's requirements are laid out in various annexes of the Convention.

Another important change from the voluntary procedure is that notification of regulatory action from one country will no longer be sufficient to trigger consideration of that chemical for inclusion on the PIC list. At least two notifications from two different PIC regions are now required. Nevertheless, it is likely that more substances will be added as the provisions of the Rotterdam Convention are implemented in this decade and beyond.

The Stockholm POPs Convention

The 2001 Stockholm Convention seeks to protect human health and the environment from persistent organic pollutants (POPs) by regulating their production, use, trade, and disposal. POPs comprise a set of extremely toxic, long-lasting chemicals that can travel long distances from their emission source and accumulate in animals, ecosystems, and people.[35] Although some POPs have been known to be hazardous since at least the 1960s, concern has increased significantly in the past two decades. While extensive variations occur in substances, species, and exposures, the observed or potential impacts of POPs on wildlife and humans include reproductive disorders, birth defects, cancers, developmental impairment, damage to central and peripheral nervous systems, impairment of the immune system, and endocrine disruption.[36]

POPs were discussed during some preparatory sessions for UNCED, but movement toward consideration of global regulations did not began in earnest until May 1995, when UNEP's governing council reacted to growing scientific data and called for an international assessment of twelve POPs—the dirty dozen.[37] In response, the IOMC established a UNEP/IFCS ad hoc working group on POPs. In November 1995 the Intergovernmental Conference to Adopt a Global Programme of Action for Protection of the Marine Environment from Land-Based Activities also considered POPs as part of its far broader agenda. The Washington Declaration issued from the conference included a call for talks on a legally binding treaty targeting the dirty dozen.

In June 1996 the IFCS working group concluded that international action—including a global, legally binding instrument—was needed to reduce the risks posed by POPs to human health and the environment. In February 1997 the governing council of UNEP endorsed the IFCS report and specifically requested that UNEP, together with WHO and other relevant international organizations, set up an intergovernmental committee to negotiate an international, legally binding instrument on POPs. These preparations, as well as subsequent negotiations, benefited significantly from work done under the regional Convention on Long-Range Transboundary Air Pollution (CLRTAP), which covers Europe, North America, and the Russian Federation. Negotiations on a regional CLRTAP POPs Protocol began in the early 1990s, and delegates signed the final agreement in June 1998.[38]

Formal negotiations on a global POPs treaty began in Montreal in June 1998. Difficult issues included how to design control measures to reduce or eliminate particular POPs; creating and designing possible exemptions to allow for some continued use of certain POPs in specific applications; developing science-based criteria and an acceptable regulatory process for examining and possibly adding other POPs in the future; and deciding upon the institutional mechanisms for providing technical and financial assistance to developing countries. Governments adopted the POPs Convention in Stockholm in May 2001. Seeking speedy implementation, UNEP, the Global Environment Facility (GEF), other intergovernmental organizations, and many governments began to implement the Stockholm Convention even before it entered into force in May 2004.

The Stockholm Convention targets the production, use, release, and trade of twelve POPs and establishes scientifically based criteria and a specific procedure for placing controls on additional chemicals in the future.[39] Specifically, all parties must:

- ban the production and use of nine POPs: the pesticides aldrin, chlordane, dieldrin, endrin, heptachlor, mirex, and toxaphene; and the industrial chemicals, PCBs and hexachlorobenzene (HBC), which is also a pesticide.
- restrict the production and use of DDT, so that it is used only for selected vector control, especially against malaria mosquitoes.
- minimize, and where feasible eliminate, releases of dioxins and furans— two unintentionally produced by-products of many industrial processes and combustion.
- promote the adoption and use of the best available technologies and practices for replacing existing POPs, reducing emissions of POPs, and managing and disposing of POP wastes in an environmentally sound manner.
- ban the import or export of POPs controlled under the Convention, except for narrowly defined purposes or environmentally sound disposal. In addition, exports to non-parties can take place only if the countries provide certification regarding the intended use of the chemical and their commitment to minimize emissions and comply with the Convention's waste disposal provisions.
- take efforts specifically aimed at preventing the development and commercial introduction of new POPs.
- draw up national legislation and develop implementation plans for fulfilling obligations under the Convention.

Despite the broad consensus regarding the need to control POPs, many countries argued for provisions that allow continued, limited use of selected POPs. In addition to the broad health-related exemption granted for DDT, a specific exemption for PCBs allows countries to maintain existing equipment containing PCBs until 2025.[40] Parties are also allowed to exercise "country-specific exemptions" that permit the continued use of specific POPs for narrowly defined applications for five years, after which an extension can be granted by the COP.[41]

The Convention also establishes scientifically based criteria and a specific step-by-step procedure for identifying and evaluating additional POPs for possible controls.[42] A POPs Review Committee made up of technical experts will meet on a regular basis to consider nominated chemicals in detail, develop risk profiles and risk management evaluations of candidate POPs, and outline proposals for possible action to be decided upon by the COP. Some delegations, such as the European Commission and EU member states, preferred a process that emphasized the precautionary principle and would allow the addition of chemicals to the Convention relatively quickly. Others, such as the United States and Australia, wanted a more regulated mechanism that required explicit risk analyses, high thresholds of toxicity and persistence, and evidence of clear, existing harm before a chemical could be added. In the end, the process created was a compromise between the two positions.

Another critical feature of the Convention is the financial mechanism to assist developing countries and countries with economies in transition in meeting their treaty obligations. Industrialized countries must provide new financial resources, albeit at unspecified levels, and promote the transfer of technical assistance. Although nearly all negotiators acknowledged the importance of providing financial and technical assistance, there were diverse views regarding the proper level and delivery mechanisms. Developing countries expressed concern about the GEF's willingness to respond to their needs and those specific to the Convention and strongly supported creating a new stand-alone financial institution patterned after the one developed under the Montreal Protocol. The industrialized donor countries, however, argued that the GEF would provide important efficiencies, expertise, and other benefits. In the final compromise, the GEF was designated as the main financing mechanism, although only on an interim basis.[43] In all likelihood, however, the GEF will remain the main financial mechanism for the Convention.

Challenges and Opportunities: Implementing Effective Global Chemical Policy

Effective management of intentionally produced hazardous chemicals requires the introduction of comprehensive controls throughout their entire life cycle—production, use, trade, and disposal—since all these activities directly or indirectly can endanger the environment and human health. Regulations must also be set for unintentionally produced by-products through emissions standards.[44] Despite the existence of the Basel, Rotterdam, and Stockholm Conventions and related regional treaties, significant problems associated with hazardous chemicals remain, including the following:

- Only a very small minority of chemicals that are known, or seriously suspected, to be hazardous are targeted by the major international agreements.
- The global production and use of hazardous chemicals continue to expand, and for most chemicals only scant data are available on emission sources and quantities, dispersion in the environment, and related exposures and effects on ecosystems and humans.[45]
- Respect for and use of the PIC process is far from uniform or effective. At the same time, global sales in chemicals have grown almost ninefold since 1970s, and OECD predicts that trade will continue to increase considerably over the next two decades.[46]
- The global generation of hazardous wastes, including wastes of hazardous chemicals or wastes containing hazardous chemicals, continues to climb.[47]
- Although the export of hazardous wastes from industrialized countries to developing countries has declined somewhat, other types of transnational movements continue relatively unabated.[48]
- Illegal dumping and disposal of hazardous wastes still exist on a large scale, and the application of proven methods for the environmentally sound management of wastes remains inadequate in large parts of the world.

- Ratification and implementation of the Basel Ban Amendment and the Rotterdam and Stockholm Conventions remain far below the level needed for true treaty effectiveness (beyond simple entry into force).
- The provision of capacity building activities and effective technical and financial assistance to developing countries for hazardous chemicals and wastes management remains insufficient and inadequately targeted. At the same time, while OECD expects that the OECD countries will continue to be the largest producers and consumers of chemicals, the rate of production and consumption is expected to grow much faster in developing countries over the next two decades.[49]

However, opportunities exist to make more rapid and effective progress in reducing the production, use, and release of hazardous chemicals, limiting their international transport, and improving environmentally sound management and disposal of them. This section outlines related areas in which more concerted efforts could help build the necessary foundation to make such progress during the next decade.

Increase Participation in Global Chemical Policy

To date, far too few countries have ratified the Rotterdam PIC and Stockholm POPs Conventions for them to be effective on a global scale.[50] In addition, while 160 countries have ratified the Basel Convention, the United States and more than thirty developing countries are not parties. More significantly, the Basel Convention Ban Amendment has not even received sufficient ratification to enter into force, while even fewer countries have signed the Protocol on Liability and Compensation.[51] For global policy on hazardous chemicals to be more effective, governments, international organizations, and other stakeholders need to take measures to improve ratification and implementation of the Rotterdam, Stockholm, and Basel Conventions, including the Basel Convention Ban Amendment and Protocol on Liability and Compensation.

Improve the Harmonization, Coordination, and Scope of Global Chemical Agreements

Efforts to accelerate global policy development and implementation on hazardous chemicals would benefit from improved harmonization and coordination of the Basel, Rotterdam, and Stockholm Conventions and related regional treaties. This would allow for more effective use of limited resources, help avoid unnecessary duplication of tasks, and help prevent unintended, counterproductive conflicts between the chemicals multilateral environmental agreements.[52]

A global political initiative to address issues relating to coordination and harmonization is under way. In February 2001 the UNEP governing council discussed ways to enhance synergies and coordination across the chemicals agreements and other related activities. At the third meeting of the Open-ended Intergovernmental Group of Ministers or their Representatives on International Environmental Governance, held in September 2001, chemicals were chosen as a pilot area to investigate possibilities and benefits of "clus-tering" agreements. A report examining the need for a strategic approach to international chemicals management (SAICM) was presented to the Global Ministerial Environment Forum in 2002. As a result, the UNEP governing council decided in February 2003 to initiate a series of preparatory meetings, which began in November 2003, to consider draft elements of such a strategic approach. An international conference is scheduled to convene in 2006 to consider the recommendations that emerge from these meetings.[53]

Actions to harmonize and coordinate the chemicals agreements need to address both membership and regulatory gaps. Different ratification patterns in the relevant agreements cause membership gaps across the spectrum of international chemicals treaties. As a result, countries have pledged to fulfill obligations under certain agreements but have not ratified others. This can impede the effective implementation of the agreements (and thus protection of the environment and human health), as the different agreements cover separate and important parts of the full life cycle of chemicals. In addition, regulatory gaps exist in the current system because the Basel, Rotterdam, and Stockholm Conventions cover partially different sets of chemicals. This means that some industrial chemicals and pesticides are not controlled throughout their entire life cycle of production, use, trade, and disposal.

There is also a need to expand the scope of the agreements beyond the substances currently subject to global controls. The Basel, Rotterdam, and Stockholm Conventions represent only a first step toward global chemicals safety. Many chemicals known to be hazardous are subject to incomplete international and domestic regulations and warrant more sustained attention and controls, for example, several brominated flame retardants.[54]

Increase Data Availability and Reporting

Large data gaps exist concerning the overall production, use, manage-ment, and trade of hazardous chemicals, as well as their environmental and human health consequences. The lack of data about a majority of commer-cial chemicals is a major challenge for policymaking, as it makes it very dif-ficult, and sometimes even impossible, to conduct adequate risk assessments and design effective risk reduction measures.[55] Finding ways to increase data availability and conduct more effective risk assessments to inform policy-making should be high on the agenda for the next decade. Efforts are under way in some regional forums such as the European Union, but this remains a global problem.[56]

Studies of institutional effectiveness demonstrate that regimes that uti-lize systems of regular reporting and monitoring of the actions of member states have better levels of domestic implementation.[57] Even though the

Basel Convention is more than a decade old, reporting is scattered, incomplete, and often based on different definitions of hazardous wastes and different standards of measuring (or estimating) their generation, management, and disposal.[58] Implementing regular and harmonized reporting should be a priority under the Basel, Rotterdam, and Stockholm Conventions. This would facilitate making more accurate assessments of global levels and trends in the production, use, transport, management, and disposal of hazardous chemicals. It would also make it easier to monitor progress in implementing the Conventions and improve the ability to direct international policies toward areas where they will have the most impact. Achieving this would require well-targeted funding and technical assistance for developing countries as part of the overall provision of assistance for implementation of the Basel, Rotterdam, and Stockholm Conventions.

Improve the Provision, Coordination, and Effectiveness of Technical Assistance and Capacity Building in Developing Countries

Many developing countries possess inadequate resources for designing effective domestic chemicals policy and ensuring the successful implementation of such policy. These problems will become even more pressing in the future if the OECD is correct in its prediction that chemicals production and use will increase sharply in developing countries over the next two decades.

As the goals and implementation requirements of the different global agreements are largely related and mutually reinforcing, significant progress could be made through more targeted coordination of technical assistance and capacity building in developing countries. Working with international organizations such as the United Nations Institute for Training and Research (UNITAR), UNEP Chemicals, GEF, and donor countries, the Basel Convention Regional Centers (BCRCs), through their mandates and design, have the potential to act as crucial nodes in coordinating developing country implementation of all chemicals agreements—a role that several BCRCs are pursuing.

Using BCRCs for this purpose could augment effective implementation while achieving economies of scale, facilitating valuable synergies, and avoiding costly duplication of efforts and materials. Equally important, an increased role for the BCRCs could increase regional relevance and support for the goals of the different agreements. Such efforts will require explicit guidance from the parties to the GEF and other intergovernmental organizations to ensure that financial and technical assistance is targeted toward coordinated implementation of the Conventions rather than to the priorities of the particular intergovernmental organizations.

The regional centers also offer unique institutional possibilities to link environmental protection with action on sustainable social and economic development in the area of hazardous chemicals and wastes. For example, building on the guidelines for dismantling ships that were agreed upon at Basel COP-6, BCRCs could help reduce environmental threats relating to hazardous wastes and human health issues by working to improve the often dreadful working conditions in the ship-breaking industry. Another example would be addressing the increasing use of China as a dumping ground for "e-waste" shipped from the United States, Europe, and Japan, sometimes with severe environmental and human health consequences.[59]

Increase Corporate Responsibility for Environmentally Sound Recycling and Disposal

Manufacturers, particularly in industrialized countries, are often in the best position to ensure that their products are disposed of or recycled in an environmentally sound manner. This may be particularly true in the technology and medical sectors, where the use of hazardous chemicals and the disposal of hazardous wastes pose particularly challenging and increasing international problems.

Introducing more market-based incentives and other regulations so that companies producing and using selected hazardous chemicals would be held responsible for them and for products containing such chemicals throughout their entire life cycle could play a significant role in improving management of these substances. The mobile-phone initiative undertaken at Basel COP-6 represents a welcome precedent in this regard. In developing countries, major intergovernmental organizations such as GEF, UNITAR, and UNEP, together with the BCRCs, could play key roles in disseminating regionally relevant information, technology, and financial assistance to support cleaner production, waste reduction, and full life-cycle management in domestic and multinational industries.

Promote Reductions in the Creation of Hazardous Chemicals and Wastes

In the long term, the most effective way to protect human health and the environment from hazardous chemicals and wastes is to avoid producing them in the first place. Because OCED countries and multinational corporations produce the majority of chemicals and generate by far the largest amounts of hazardous wastes, they have a special responsibility for minimizing the use of hazardous chemicals and the generation of hazardous wastes. Yet despite strong language in the Stockholm Convention, the Basel Convention, Agenda 21, the Johannesburg Plan of Implementation, and other agreements regarding the need to reduce these substances, global production continues to increase, particularly in industrialized countries.

Making the reversal of these trends an acknowledged global priority would represent a significant step in protecting the environment and human health in all parts of the world. Such a reduction could be reached, in part, through the application of cleaner production methods and, more broadly, a shift from the predominantly reactive approach of controlling hazardous chemicals and wastes to a more proactive approach focused on preventing their introduction to the market. Such a shift would logically emphasize the importance of more effectively screening old and new chemicals in order to identify harmful substances and better target practices that generate hazardous wastes. Measures of this kind are also explicitly called for under the Basel and Stockholm Conventions.[60]

Conclusion: Toward Sustainable Global Chemical Policy

Current global policy for hazardous chemicals can best be described as fragmented coordination between Conventions, regional treaties, and relevant international and regional institutions.[61] The Basel, Rotterdam, and Stockholm Conventions form the core of this framework. Taken together, these agreements provide three sets of largely compatible principles, norms, rules, and procedures that regulate different substances and stages of the life cycle of hazardous chemicals—their production, use, trade, and disposal. Other new initiatives, such as SAICM and the recently adopted UN Globally Harmonized System of Classification and Labelling of Chemicals, also have the potential to help improve chemical safety worldwide.

With the core Conventions, the international community is now in a position to move some of its focus from creating policy for hazardous chemicals (although additional policy is needed) to successfully implementing that policy. Lasting implementation of the Basel, Rotterdam, and Stockholm Conventions could prove impossible, however, if greater attention is not paid to increasing global participation, establishing markedly improved coordination between relevant treaties and institutions, providing more effective and targeted financial and technical assistance to developing countries, achieving real reductions in the production of toxic chemicals and hazardous wastes, and adopting true cradle-to-grave management of those that remain.

Notes

1. Today biologists tend to use the term food webs rather than food chains.
2. Chemicals covered under these agreements are directly toxic to human health and the environment. This differentiates them from chlorofluorocarbons (CFCs), the chemicals subject to extensive international regulation under the Montreal Protocol and its amendments. CFCs are not toxic by themselves. Rather, they rise to the stratosphere and cause ozone depletion, in turn affecting human health and the environment.
3. This section presents only the most basic historical outline. For detailed discussion, see Rune Lönngren, *International Approaches to Chemicals Control: A Historical Overview* (Stockholm: National Chemicals Inspectorate/KemI, 1992).
4. Naturvårdsverket, POP: stabila Organiska Miljögifter: Stort eller litet problem (Stockholm: Rapport 4563, 1996): 10; European Commission (2001b), "White Paper: Strategy for a Future Chemicals Policy," Brussels, February 27, 2001 (Brussels: European Commission, 2001), 88.
5. Organization for Economic Cooperation and Development, *Environmental Outlook for the Chemical Industry* (Paris: OECD, 2001), 10.
6. Masa Nagai, "Environmental Law and International Trade in Hazardous Chemicals," in *UNEP's New Way Forward: Environmental Law and Sustainable Development*, ed. Lal Kurukulasuriya (Nairobi: UNEP, 1995), 248.

7. Rachel Carson, *Silent Spring* (Cambridge, Mass.: Riverside Press, 1962). This book, parts of which appeared first as a series of articles in the *New Yorker*, focused on the dangers to wildlife from the increasing use of pesticides. Other reports followed. See, for examples, Anonymous, "Report for a New Chemical Hazard," *New Scientist* 32, no. 525 (1966): 512; Sören Jensen, "The PCB Story," *Ambio* 1, no. 4 (1972): 123–131.

8. J. K. Nichols and P. J. Crawford, *Managing Chemicals in the 1980s* (Paris: OECD, 1983).

9. Organization for Economic Cooperation and Development, *OECD and Chemicals Control: The High Level Meeting of the Chemicals Group of the Environment Committee, 1980* (Paris: OECD, 1981).

10. Thomas R. Dunlap, *DDT: Scientists, Citizens, and Public Policy* (Princeton: Princeton University Press, 1981); J. G. Koppe and J. Keys, "PCBs and the Precautionary Principle," in *The Precautionary Principle in the 20th Century*, ed. P. Harremoës, D. Gee, M. MacGarvin et al. (London: Earthscan, 2002), 64–78.

11. These include the 1972 International Convention on the Prevention of Marine Pollution by Dumping of Wastes and Other Matter (London Convention) and the MARPOL Convention, which includes the 1973 International Convention for the Prevention of Pollution from Ships and its 1978 protocol. Early regional and river agreements that touched on hazardous chemicals include the 1972 Convention for the Prevention of Marine Pollution by Dumping from Ships and Aircraft (Oslo Convention), 1974 Convention for the Prevention of Marine Pollution from Land-based Sources (Paris Convention), 1974 Convention on the Protection of the Marine Environment of the Baltic Sea Area (Helsinki Convention), 1976 Convention on the Protection of the Rhine Against Chemical Pollution, 1976 Protocol for the Prevention of Pollution of the Mediterranean Sea by Dumping from Ships and Aircraft, and the 1978 Great Lakes Water Quality Agreement.

12. Jonathan Krueger and Henrik Selin, "Governance for Sound Chemicals Management: The Need for a More Comprehensive Global Strategy," *Global Governance* 8 (2002): 323–342.

13. Jonathan Krueger, *International Trade and the Basel Convention* (London: Royal Institute of International Affairs/Earthscan, 1999); and Katharina Kummer, *International Management of Hazardous Wastes: The Basel Convention and Related Legal Rules* (Oxford, England: Clarendon Press, 1995).

14. These six priority areas were: (1) expanding and accelerating international assessment of risks; (2) harmonizing chemical classification and labeling; (3) exchanging information on toxic chemicals and risks; (4) establishing risk reduction programs; (5) strengthening national capacity and capability for chemicals management; and (6) preventing illegal international traffic in toxic and dangerous products. See United Nations, *Agenda 21: Programme of Action for Sustainable Development* (New York: United Nations Publications, 1992), chap. 19.

15. For information, see the Intergovernmental Forum on Chemical Safety Web site: http://www.who.int/ifcs.

16. The IOMC includes UNEP, FAO, the International Labour Organization (ILO), WHO, United Nations Industrial Development Organization (UNIDO), UNITAR, and OECD. Other global institutions active on chemicals include the GEF, United Nations Development Programme (UNDP), and the World Bank. Of these, UNEP is the most active assisting the development of new global treaties. Regional institutions include the Arctic Council, European Union, Great Lakes Program, Helsinki Commission (HELCOM), North American Agreement on Environmental Cooperation (NAAEC)/Sound Management of Chemicals Initiative, OECD, and the Oslo-Paris Commission for the Protection of the Marine Environment of the North-East Atlantic (OSPAR).

17. T. Colborn, D. Dumanoski, and J. P. Myers, *Our Stolen Future* (New York: Dutton, 1996); Arctic Monitoring and Assessment Programme, *AMAP Assessment Report: Arctic Pollution Issues* (Oslo: AMAP, 1998).

18. Report of the WSSD (A/CONF.199/20), paragraph 23.

19. For detailed discussions of the creation, content, expansion, and impact of the Basel Convention and related hazardous waste issues, see Krueger, *International Trade and the Basel Convention;* Kummer, *International Management of Hazardous Wastes;* and Kate O'Neill, *Waste Trading among Rich Nations: Building a New Theory of Environmental Regulation* (Cambridge: MIT Press, 2000).

20. In the context of international treaties, "party" is a legal term that denotes a country that has ratified a particular treaty. It distinguishes countries that have ratified the treaty (parties) from those that have not (non-parties).

21. Wastes are designated as hazardous under the Basel Convention if they belong to certain categories (Annex I) and contain certain characteristics (Annex III). The Convention defines "wastes" as substances or objects that are, are intended to be, or are required to be disposed of by national law. The Convention defines "disposal" both as final destruction and as actions that result in "resource recovery, recycling, reclamation, direct re-use or alternative uses." Thus, to recycle and reuse something, in Basel terms, is also to dispose of it.

22. For an updated list of signatories and ratifications, see the Web site of the Secretariat of the Basel Convention: http://www.basel.int. For discussions of U.S. policy regarding Basel, see William N. Doyle, "United States Implementation of the Basel Convention: Time Keeps Ticking," *Temple International and Comparative Law Journal* 9, no. 1 (spring 1995): 141–161; and Kate Sinding, "The Transboundary Movement of Waste: A Critical Comparison of U.S. Interstate Policy and the Emerging International Regime," *New York University Environmental Law Journal* 5, no. 3 (November 1996): 796–832.

23. Despite the fact that at that time, as today, most of the waste trade took place between industrialized countries.

24. Mark Jaffe, "Tracking the Khian Sea: Port to Port, Deal to Deal," *Philadelphia Inquirer,* July 15, 1988, B1; and Joel Millman, "After Two Years, Ship Dumps Toxic Ash," *New York Times,* November 27, 1988, A22. For a discussion of its place in the development of international law, see Hao-Nhien Q. Vu, "The Law of Treaties and the Export of Hazardous Waste," *UCLA Journal of Environmental Law and Policy* 12 (1994): 389–458.

25. For a full discussion, see Krueger, *International Trade and the Basel Convention,* and Kummer, *International Management of Hazardous Wastes.*

26. Thereby not straying significantly from the draft *international* agreement that was also being developed by the OECD, abandoned in 1989.

27. The texts of Basel Convention COP decisions and meeting reports are available at the Secretariat Web site: http://www.basel.int.

28. CRCs are located in Nigeria, Egypt, Senegal, South Africa, China, Indonesia, the South Pacific, Slovakia, the Russian Federation, Uruguay, Argentina, El Salvador, and Trinidad and Tobago.

29. For more information on the development and content of the Rotterdam Convention, see Jonathan Krueger, "Information in International Environmental Governance: The Prior Informed Consent Procedure for Trade in Hazardous Chemicals and Pesticides," *Belfer Center for Science and International Affairs (BCSIA) Discussion Paper 2000-16* (Cambridge: Environment and Natural Resources Program, Kennedy School of Government, Harvard University, 2000); David Victor, "Learning by Doing in the Nonbinding International Regime to Manage Trade in Hazardous Chemicals and Pesticides," in *The Implementation and Effectiveness of International Environmental Commitments,* ed. David Victor, Kal Raustiala, and Eugene Skolnikoff (Cambridge: MIT Press, 1998); and Richard Emory Jr., "Probing the Protections in the Rotterdam Convention on Prior Informed Consent," *Colorado Journal of International Environmental Law and Policy* 23 (2001): 47–91.

30. Victor, "Learning by Doing in the Nonbinding International Regime to Manage Trade in Hazardous Chemicals and Pesticides," 223.

31. Ibid., 247.
32. Significant concerns were expressed during the negotiations regarding the potential relationship between the Rotterdam Convention and WTO provisions. See, for example, reporting in the *Earth Negotiations Bulletin* 15, nos. 2–5.
33. For an updated list of ratifications, see the Web site of the Rotterdam Convention Secretariat http://www.pic.int.
34. Chemicals covered by the PIC Convention include the pesticides aldrin, binapacryl, captafol, chlorobenzilate, chlordane, chlordimeform, DDT, dieldrin, dinoseb and dinoseb salts, 1,2-dibromoethane (EDB), ethylene dichloride, ethylene oxide, fluoroacetamide, hch, heptachlor, hexachlorobenzene, lindane, mercury compounds, toxaphene, pentachlorophenol, methyl-parathion, methamidophos, monocrotophos, parathion, phosphamidon, and 2,4,5-T; and the industrial chemicals crocidolite, polybrominated biphenyls (PBB), polychlorinated biphenyls (PCB), polychlorinated terphenyls (PCT), tris(2,3dibromopropyl) phosphate (as of June 2004). Of these, aldrin, chlordane, DDT, dieldrin, heptachlor, hexachlorobenzene, lindane, toxaphene, and PCBs are also covered by the Stockholm Convention.
35. POPs are usually defined (including in the Stockholm Convention) as possessing four key characteristics: toxicity, persistence, bioaccumulation, and long-range environmental transport.
36. For broader discussions, which include evidence of increasing concern, see David Downie and Terry Fenge, eds., *Northern Lights Against POPs: Combatting Toxic Threats in the Arctic* (Montreal: McGill-Queen's University Press, 2003); and Colborn et al., *Our Stolen Future*.
37. The dirty dozen are aldrin, chlordane, dieldrin, dioxins, DDT, endrin, furans, heptachlor, mirex, and toxaphene; and the industrial chemicals, PCBs and hexachlorobenzene.
38. The core of the CLRTAP POPs Protocol consists of controls on sixteen compounds. The protocol regulates the production and use of thirteen pesticides and industrial chemicals. No trade restrictions on these substances were introduced, but the issue was referred to the global process. In addition, the protocol covers four unintentional by-products (one substance, hexachlorobenzene, is regulated both as a pesticide and a by-product). See Henrik Selin and Noelle Eckley, "Science, Politics, and Persistent Organic Pollutants: Scientific Assessments and Their Role in International Environmental Negotiations," *International Environmental Agreements: Politics, Law and Economics* 3, no. 1 (2003): 17–42; and Henrik Selin, "Regional POPs Policy: The UNECE/CLRTAP POPs Agreement," in Downie and Fenge, *Northern Lights Against POPs: Combatting Toxic Threats in the Arctic*.
39. For detailed analysis of the Convention, see David Downie, "Global POPs Policy: The 2001 Stockholm Convention on Persistent Organic Pollutants,"in Downie and Fenge, *Northern Lights Against POPs: Combatting Toxic Threats in the Arctic*.
40. See Part II of Annex A. PCBs have been widely used in electrical transformers and other equipment, and while equipment using new PCBs is no longer produced, hundreds of thousands of tons of PCBs are still in use in existing equipment.
41. The Convention establishes a Register of Specific Exemptions that will be used to identify parties that have specific exemptions listed in Annex A or Annex B. Any state, on becoming a party, may register for one or more types of specific exemptions listed in Annex A or Annex B by notifying the Secretariat in writing. There is no limit on the type or number of these exemptions. All registrations of specific exemptions expire after five years unless a party indicates an earlier date in the Register or the COP grants an extension. When there are no longer any parties registered for a particular type of specific exemption, no new registrations may be made with respect to it. See Article 4.2–4.9.
42. See Article 8 and Annexes D, E, and F.
43. The parties will review the GEF's performance and do have the option of making a final decision to use or exclude the GEF.

44. Jonathan Krueger and Henrik Selin, "Governance for Sound Chemicals Management: The Need for a More Comprehensive Global Strategy," *Global Governance* 8 (2002): 323–342.
45. European Commission, "White Paper: Strategy for a Future Chemical Policy" Brussels, February 27, 2001 (Brussels: European Commission, 2001).
46. Organization for Economic Cooperation and Development, *Environmental Outlook for the Chemical Industry,* 11 and 16
47. Basel Convention Secretariat. *Global Trends in Generation and Transboundary Movements of Hazardous Wastes and Other Wastes* (Geneva: Basel Convention, 2002).
48. Ibid.
49. Organization for Economic Cooperation and Development, *Environmental Outlook for the Chemical Industry,* 36–37.
50. For an updated list of countries that have ratified the Rotterdam PIC Convention, see http://www.pic.int/en/ViewPage.asp?id=265. For an updated list of countries that have ratified the Stockholm Convention, see http://www.pops.int/documents/signature/signstatus.htm.
51. As of October 17, 2003, only forty-two countries had ratified the Ban Amendment (sixty-two are needed for entry into force), and only thirteen had signed the Protocol on Liability and Compensation. For updated lists of signatories and ratifications to the Basel Convention and its associated agreements, see the Web site of the Secretariat of the Basel Convention at http://www.basel.int.
52. Jonathan Krueger and Henrik Selin, "Governance for Sound Chemicals Management: The Need for a More Comprehensive Global Strategy," *Global Governance* 8 (2002): 323–342; Henrik Selin and Stacy D. VanDeveer, "Baltic Sea Hazardous Substances Management: Results and Challenges," *Ambio* (forthcoming 2004).
53. Documentation related to the "SAICM" process can be found at the UNEP Web site: http://www.chem.unep.ch/
54. Noelle Eckley and Henrik Selin, "All Talk, Little Action: Precaution and its Effects on European Chemicals Regulation" *Journal of European Public Policy* (forthcoming 2004).
55. Organization for Economic Cooperation and Development, *Environmental Outlook for the Chemical Industry* (Paris: OECD, 2001); European Environment Agency and the United Nations Environment Programme "Chemicals in the European Environment: Low Doses, High Stakes?" in *The EEA and UNEP Annual Message 2 on the State of Europe's Environment* (Copenhagen: EEA, 1999); European Commission, *White Paper on a Strategy for a Future Chemicals Policy* (Brussels, 2001).
56. European Commission, "White Paper: Strategy for a Future Chemicals Policy."
57. Victor, Raustiala, and Skolnikoff, eds., *Implementation and Effectiveness of International Environmental Commitments.*
58. For a full discussion, see Basel Convention, *Global Trends in Generation and Transboundary Movements of Hazardous Wastes and Other Wastes.*
59. Peter S. Goodman, "China Serves as Dump Site for Computers: Unsafe Recycling Practice Grows Despite Import Ban," *Washington Post,* February 24, 2003, A1.
60. Stockholm Convention, article 3.3. Such action should include the destruction of existing stockpiles of obsolete hazardous chemicals that can pose significant problems, particularly in developing countries.
61. Krueger and Selin, "Governance for Sound Chemicals Management: The Need for a More Comprehensive Global Strategy."

8

Economic Integration and Environmental Protection
Daniel C. Esty

No mention was made of the word *environment* in the original General Agreement on Tariffs and Trade (GATT)—the central pillar of the international trading system—put into place just after World War II. At that time, no one saw much connection between trade liberalization and environmental protection. For the next forty years, trade and environmental policymakers pursued their respective agendas on parallel tracks that rarely, if ever, intersected. In recent years, however, trade and environmental policymaking have increasingly appeared to be linked, and the two realms have often seemed to collide. Environmental advocates have come to fear that freer trade means increased pollution and resource depletion. Free traders worry that protectionism in the guise of environmental policy will obstruct efforts to open markets and integrate economies around the world.

This chapter explores the trade-environment relationship. It traces the origins of the tension between trade liberalization and environmental protection and identifies the events that triggered the conflict. It examines why environmentalists worry about free trade and why free traders worry about unrestrained environmentalism. Ways to reconcile trade and environmental goals are highlighted, and the North American Free Trade Agreement (NAFTA) is explored as a model in this regard.

Freer trade and economic integration more broadly offer the promise of improved social welfare, as do programs aimed at pollution abatement and improved natural resource management. While not theoretically inconsistent, in practice, these goals are often not in perfect alignment. Only through concerted policy attention and efforts to overcome conflicts and tensions can both aims be addressed simultaneously and progress be made toward sustainable development.

Origins of the Trade and Environment "Conflict"

The trade and environmental policy agendas have been driven together by a number of factors. First, the end of the cold war has augmented interest in environmental issues. Reduced East-West tensions allowed public officials (and citizens more generally) to shift their foreign policy gaze from traditional politico-military concerns to a more extensive array of international issues.[1] As a result of this wider international affairs perspective, a broader definition of "national security" has begun to emerge that encompasses environmental matters.[2]

Second, environmental issues have taken on increased salience in the last several decades. Climate change, drinking-water safety, chemical exposures, and other pollution problems have become a major focus of public concern. Trying to accommodate new issues on the public agenda often creates strain.[3] The precise focus of the public's environmental interest varies from nation to nation, and particularly from industrialized to developing countries. But almost every corner of the world has experienced a marked increase in the attention paid to environmental problems over the last several decades.

Third, recognition of a set of inherently global pollution and resource problems has further propelled environmental issues up the international policy agenda. Scientific advances have transformed the environmental policy landscape. From the threat of global climate change arising from a buildup of greenhouse gases in the atmosphere to ozone layer destruction, from emissions of chlorofluorocarbons (CFCs) and other related chemicals to the depletion of fisheries in most of the world's oceans, overexploitation of the "global commons" has added to the sense of priority given to the environment on the international scene.[4]

Fourth, a policy focus on "sustainable development" has led to an appreciation that environmental progress is easier to achieve under conditions of prosperity—and long-term economic growth depends on careful stewardship of the natural environment. The 1992 Earth Summit in Rio de Janeiro (formally known as the United Nations Conference on Environment and Development) highlighted the link between economic development and environmental protection generally, and trade and the environment more specifically.[5] When a new round of global trade negotiations was launched in 2001 in Doha, the trade-environment relationship was made an explicit element of the negotiating agenda.[6] The 2002 World Summit on Sustainable Development in Johannesburg consolidated the focus on the trade-environment linkage.

Finally, economic integration has also helped to transform environmental protection from a clearly domestic, highly localized issue into one of inherently international scope. In a world of liberalized trade, where the competition for market share is global, the stringency of environmental regulations in each nation, state, or province becomes an important determinant of the competitiveness of the enterprises located within that territory. Thus, for example, while hazardous waste management requirements have long been viewed as simply a function of local pollution control priorities and risk tolerances, today these policy choices are understood to have important consequences for the production costs of the enterprises that must meet the standards.[7] Concerns about competitiveness transform even the most local environmental issue into a matter of international significance. These worries take on added significance in the context of efforts to open markets and promote economic integration.

Triggering Events

Recent free trade initiatives and commitments to liberalized investment regimes have sharpened the trade-environment debate. President

George H. W. Bush's 1989 announcement that he intended to negotiate a free trade agreement with Mexico first brought "trade and environment" issues to the fore. The prospect of a free flow of goods across the U.S.-Mexico border struck fear in the hearts of environmentalists. They worried that a trade agreement with Mexico might mean an expansion of the highly polluted "maquiladora" (duty-free) zone along the border, lowering U.S. environmental standards ("harmonized" to match lax Mexican regulatory requirements) or, worse, a downward spiral in environmental standards on both sides of the border as industry claims of competitive disadvantage induced governments to relax their environmental rules. Pressed by Congress, the Bush administration committed to a program of environmental efforts parallel with the trade negotiations with Mexico and Canada that led to NAFTA.[8]

While NAFTA set the environmental pot on the trade fire, the decision of a GATT dispute resolution panel in the 1991 "tuna/dolphin" case caused a simmering issue to boil over. The GATT declared the U.S. law requiring an embargo on Mexican tuna that were caught in nets that killed dolphins to be illegal under the rules of international trade.[9] U.S. environmentalists saw the decision as an affront to American environmental "sovereignty." [10] How could an obscure set of trade experts sitting in Geneva judge a U.S. law (the Marine Mammal Protection Act) to be unacceptable? The environmental community saw this decision as proof that, in a conflict between trade and environmental goals, the trade liberalization principles would trump environmental values. Outraged environmentalists decried "GATTzilla" and began a campaign to "green" trade law and policymaking.[11]

Interest in the trade and environment relationship now has widened and evolved. Protesters concerned about the effects of globalization, including the environmental impacts of economic integration, helped cause the collapse of the World Trade Organization (WTO) ministerial meeting in Seattle in 1999. Similar protests are now a fixture at almost every meeting of international economic officials. In fact, the push for further free trade agreements, including a Free Trade Area of the Americas (FTAA) and new commitments to multilateral trade liberalization through the WTO, has continued to make "trade and environment" a hot issue on the international agenda.[12]

Some success has been achieved in making trade and environmental policymaking more mutually supportive.[13] Policymakers have learned that they ignore the trade-environment link at some peril. For example, negotiations within the Organization for Economic Cooperation and Development (OECD) to establish a Multilateral Agreement on Investment (MAI) faltered in the face of environmentalists' outcries over the lack of attention to pollution control and resource management issues in the draft treaty.

Efforts to make trade and environmental policies more compatible have, however, faced significant obstacles. The trade and environmental communities have distinct goals, traditions, operating procedures, and even languages. The ultimate good for environmentalists—"protection"—sounds a lot like the consummate bad—"protectionism"—which free traders seek to avoid. Both in terminology and substance, bringing these two worlds together continues to be a significant challenge.[14]

Core Environmental Concerns about Free Trade

Environmentalists worry that economic integration and more global-ized markets will make environmental protection harder to achieve. Their concerns can be boiled down to a few key propositions:[15]

Expanded trade will cause environmental harm by promoting economic growth that, without environmental safeguards, will result in increased pollution and the unsustainable consumption of natural resources. Environmentalists who adhere to a traditional "limits to growth" perspective would reject the possi-bility that environmental safeguards might make trade liberalization envi-ronmentally acceptable. They see free trade inescapably resulting in environmentally damaging economic growth. Of course, many environmen-talists today adhere to the "sustainable development" paradigm, which would accept the possibility that environmental improvements might arise from economic growth so long as pollution control and resource consumption issues are expressly addressed.[16] They also would recognize that poverty leads to short-term decision making that is often environmentally harmful. Thus, to the extent that trade promotes growth and alleviates poverty, it can yield environmental benefits.

Many environmentalists fear that the "disciplines" to which countries bind themselves as part of a trade agreement will result in a loss of regulatory sover-eignty. Specifically, they worry that the market access obligations and other trade principles designed to permit the free flow of imports and exports will override environmental policies and goals, resulting in the harmonization of environmental standards at or below baseline levels.[17] This outcome might arise, they believe, through negotiated commitments to common regulatory rules. Alternatively, they fear that a free trade zone might make it hard for high-standard countries to keep their strict environmental requirements in the face of industry claims of competitive disadvantage from producers in low-standard jurisdictions whose environmental compliance costs are lower.

Even where pollution does not spill across national borders, countries with lax environmental standards will have a competitive advantage in a global mar-ketplace, putting pressures on countries with high environmental standards to reduce the rigor of their environmental requirements. The fear of competitive disadvantage in an integrated North American marketplace was the central trade and environment issue in the course of the NAFTA debate. Ross Perot's memorable suggestion that low labor costs and lax environmental standards in Mexico would result in a "giant sucking sound" of U.S. factories and jobs going down the drain to Mexico resonated broadly.[18] Although there is little empirical evidence of companies moving to "pollution havens," academics continue to debate the seriousness of fears about a "race toward the bottom" in setting environmental standards.[19]

Variations in the stringency of regulations are not necessarily a problem. Differences in environmental standards can be seen as an important component of comparative advantage. Indeed, the fact that countries have different levels of commitment to environmental protection—and thus different pollution control costs—makes gains from economic exchange and trade possible. Competitiveness pressures may also induce "regulatory competition" among jurisdictions as governments work to make their location attractive to industry. In some circumstances, these pressures will induce governments to provide services and regulate efficiently. Competition of this sort enhances social welfare.[20] But in other circumstances, competition among horizontally arrayed jurisdictions (national governments versus national governments) may precipitate a welfare-reducing cycle of weakening environmental commitments, as political leaders seek to relax their environmental standards to attract investment and jobs.[21] In practice, governments rarely lower their environmental standards to improve their competitive position. They may, however, relax the enforcement of their standards or fail to raise standards to optimal levels for fear of exposing their industries to higher costs than foreign competitors face.[22]

The critical issue, therefore, is why environmental standards diverge. If the stringency of the rules varies because of differences in climate, weather, population density, risk preferences, level of development, or other "natural" factors, the variations in regulatory vigor should be considered legitimate and appropriate. Any competitive pressure created is simply the playing out of socially beneficial market forces. In contrast, divergent standards may also arise from regulatory authorities failing to monitor fully the harms that spill across their borders into other jurisdictions. These spillovers may result in "externalizing" part of the costs of pollution control. In addition, regulatory "incapacity" may lead to suboptimal environmental standards or lax enforcement of environmental requirements. And special interest manipulation of the regulatory process or other distortions in environmental policymaking may result in regulations that deviate from what would be the optimal environmental policies (what academics call "public choice" problems).

Underregulation that permits pollution to spill over into neighboring jurisdictions or into a global commons represents an unfair (and economically inefficient) basis on which to establish a competitive advantage. Likewise, suboptimal standards that arise from regulatory failures—including results driven by weak government performance and inadequate environmental decision making or outcomes manipulated by special interests through lobbying, campaign contributions, or outright corruption of public officials—break the promise of improved social welfare through interjurisdictional competition. And where competitors have selected, for whatever reason, suboptimal environmental policies, governments often respond strategically and set their standards with an eye on those adopted by their competition. In each of these circumstances, international cooperation in response to environmental challenges promises to improve policy outcomes. Insofar as trade negotiations generate the competitive pressures that trigger a "race toward the bottom", they also provide an occasion to advance the collective action required to avoid a welfare-reducing regulatory chill.

The likelihood of a "race" dynamic increases as economic integration deepens. If Jurisdiction A is a comparatively unimportant destination of Jurisdiction B's exports, or if Jurisdiction A is an insignificant international competitor, then differential environmental standards matter very little. B will be relatively unaffected by environmental policy choices in A. But if the level of interaction grows, so does B's exposure to "economic externalities" arising from suboptimal environmental policies in A. For example, in 1985 U.S. exports to China totaled $7 billion, and imports from China stood at $3 billion. In 2002 Chinese exports to the United States topped $125 billion, and U.S. exports to China amounted to $22 billion.[23] This extraordinary growth in U.S.-China trade makes U.S. industries much more sensitive to cost disadvantages that they suffer in relation to Chinese competitors—and will focus increasing attention on whether any such disadvantages that arise from environmental conditions are appropriate and legitimate.

If countries fail to carry out their international environmental obligations, trade restrictions may need to be used as a way to limit "free riding." Yet the market opening commitments made in the course of trade agreements may reduce the availability of trade measures as an environmental enforcement tool. Environmentalists fear that commitments to trade liberalization will limit the international community's leverage over countries that are refusing to sign on to or are not living up to international environmental agreements.

While recognizing the need to discipline "free riders" (those who are benefiting from but not paying for pollution control or shared resource management), trade officials argue that it is not appropriate to use trade policy tools as a way of achieving environmental goals. They reason that it is hard enough to keep markets open without trying to carry environmental burdens at the same time. Environmentalists respond that there are very few ways of exerting pressure in the international domain and that trade measures must be available as an enforcement tool.

The Free Trade Response

Free traders worry that the environmentalists' critiques of trade are misplaced and could result in the disruption of efforts to promote trade liberalization and to obtain the benefits promised by more open markets around the world. Trade advocates note, in particular, that trade and environmental policy goals can be made compatible. As the members of the World Trade Organization declared at the launch of the WTO in 1994:

> There should not be, nor need be, any policy contradiction between upholding and safeguarding an open, nondiscriminatory and equitable multilateral trading system on the one hand, and acting for the protection of the environment and promotion of sustainable development on the other.[24]

Free traders note that both trade liberalization and environmental protection efforts are aimed at promoting efficiency and reducing waste. They posit that, to the extent that environmental policies seem to be in tension with freer trade, the conflict generally arises from poorly constructed environmental policies rather than any inherently anti-environmental bias embedded in the trading system. Trade experts further observe that environmental policies that seek to internalize externalities through the application of the Polluter Pays principle represent virtually no conflict with freer trade.[25]

Trade supporters also maintain that, as an empirical matter, as the wealth of the society increases, its spending on environmental protection almost always goes up. Thus they contend that environmentalists should support freer trade as a way of achieving economic growth and greater wealth, some part of which can be devoted to expanded pollution control and resource conservation programs. More dramatically, trade advocates observe that poverty is the source of a great many environmental harms. And indeed, poor people often make bad environmental choices because of the short-term time frame forced upon them. For example, those who lack modern conveniences must cut down nearby trees to cook their evening meal. They are unable to focus on the longer-term consequences of deforestation, such as soil erosion and pollution of nearby bodies of water.

Professors Gene M. Grossman and Alan B. Krueger have demonstrated that some environmental problems seem to worsen during the early stages of development, peak at a per capita gross domestic product of about $8,000, and improve as countries become wealthier beyond that point.[26] Some problems are so localized and pressing that even the poorest countries will be under pressure to address them as economic growth begins and incomes start to rise. Governments, for example, seek to provide drinking water to their people at even the lowest levels of development. Other problems appear to follow the inverted-U "Kuznets" curve that Grossman and Krueger hypothesize, rising in the initial stages of industrialization but falling as wealth increases. Local air pollution problems seem to fall into this category. But other environmental problems continue to worsen even as incomes rise.[27] For instance, greenhouse gas emissions may go up at a less rapid rate, but they do not fall even when high income levels are achieved. Other scholars have argued that the relationship between environmental harms and income is somewhat more complicated.[28]

A more nuanced understanding of the relationship between economic growth and environmental protection leads to the conclusion that trade can be a mechanism for advancing economic growth and social welfare, but this result is not guaranteed. Economic gains *can* permit resources to be made available for investments in environmental protection. But welfare losses from trade-exacerbated environmental harms could outweigh the benefits of freer trade. To maximize the chances of net welfare gains, environmental policy must evolve in tandem with commitments to trade liberalization.[29]

NAFTA—First Steps

The need to address environmental issues in the NAFTA context led to a commitment to a set of environmental negotiations alongside the trade negotiations—a "parallel track." These talks generated a joint U.S.-Mexican commitment to address pollution issues along their shared border. The "integrated border environmental plan" cataloged comprehensively for the first time the spectrum of environmental concerns arising along the 2,000-mile border between the two countries. The initiative also produced a game plan for addressing the issues identified and a set of priorities to be undertaken jointly by Mexican and U.S. environmental officials.

In addition to the border plan, the parallel track negotiations led to an Environmental Side Agreement to NAFTA. The Side Agreement, concluded during the Clinton administration, set up a "development bank" to promote environmental infrastructure investments along the U.S.-Mexico border and established a Commission for Environmental Cooperation (CEC) to oversee the environmental issues associated with closer trade links across North America.[30] The CEC provides a mechanism for facilitating cooperation among the NAFTA countries on the full range of environmental issues and resource challenges facing them. It serves as a forum for regular high-level meetings, provides an independent secretariat to report on significant environmental issues confronting the NAFTA parties, ensures that environmental enforcement remains a priority in all three countries, and offers opportunities for public participation in the development and implementation of environmental laws and programs in Mexico, the United States, and Canada.

In addition to the parallel track environmental negotiations, environmental officials were included, for the first time, in the trade negotiations themselves. EPA negotiators participated in several of the issue-specific working groups. A senior EPA official served on the high-level negotiating team of the U.S. Trade Representative (USTR). Likewise, nongovernmental organizations, including environmental groups, were considered an important constituency in the course of the NAFTA debate—a role they had never played before. In addition, trade representative Carla Hills placed four environmental group leaders on her public advisory committees on various aspects of trade policymaking.[31]

Perhaps the most important procedural advance associated with NAFTA was the decision to undertake an environmental review of issues associated with freer trade across North America. This analysis helped to focus the negotiators on both large and small issues, ranging from the benefits of broadening Mexico's economic development beyond the maquiladora zone to finding ways to reduce the traffic jams (and resulting air pollution) caused by backups at customs in Texas, New Mexico, Arizona, and California. The value of this type of analysis is now widely recognized. In fact, the Clinton administration issued an executive order in 1999 requiring the USTR to carry out environmental reviews in advance of all future trade agreements.[32]

Substantive advances in the integration of environmental sensitivity into the trade system were also made in the course of the NAFTA process. The preamble to the agreement makes environmental considerations a central focus of the effort to promote freer trade. It calls on the parties to pursue their program of trade liberalization so as to promote "sustainable development" and to "strengthen the development and enforcement of environmental laws and regulations." [33]

The NAFTA parties further agreed that major environmental agreements with trade provisions should be given precedence if a conflict were to develop between the party's obligations under the environmental agreement and under NAFTA. Similarly, NAFTA makes clear in its chapter on "sanitary and phytosanitary" provisions that each party to the agreement retains an unrestricted right to set and maintain environmental health and safety standards at its own chosen level of protection. By clarifying that the NAFTA parties are free to make their own risk assessments and apply their own risk policies, NAFTA acknowledges that some legitimate national environmental policies will have impacts on trade but should still be permitted.

NAFTA's investment chapter also breaks new ground in addressing environmental issues.[34] Specifically, the investment provisions assure each country the right to adopt and enforce any pollution control or resource management measure it deems necessary to protect its environment. This language prevents trade commitments from trumping environmental policies and programs as long as the policies are based on scientific foundations and are not disguised barriers to trade. The treaty also contains a "pollution haven" proviso that declares that a NAFTA party cannot seek to attract investments by relaxing environmental standards or cutting back on enforcement. A structure of binding arbitration and the possibility of trade penalties being imposed for noncompliance back this provision.

NAFTA also establishes more environmentally sensitive dispute resolution procedures. Specifically, where environmental issues are in question in a trade dispute, the agreement provides procedures for convening a board of scientific or technical experts to advise the dispute settlement panel. It also forbids countries to take disputes out of NAFTA and into the WTO to obtain less environmentally protective ground rules.

The NAFTA efforts to make trade liberalization and environmental protection mutually compatible have generally worked quite well.[35] Fears of industrial migration to Mexico based on a promise of lax environmental standards have not been realized. Rather, NAFTA's broadly based program of environmental cooperation has greatly increased the focus on pollution control in Mexico. While many problems remain, and the attempt to finance new environmental projects on the U.S.-Mexico border has gotten off to a slow start, environmental conditions across large parts of Mexico are beginning to improve.

Some environmentalists remain concerned that environmental issues are still not being taken seriously in the trade context. In the 1997–1998 debate over "fast track" legislation to authorize negotiations to extend NAFTA to all of the Western Hemisphere, these complaints rang true. The Clinton administration proposals for a Free Trade Area of the Americas (FTAA), devoid of any environmental provisions, represented a significant step back from NAFTA. And the president failed to win the trade negotiating authority he sought.

In 2002 the new Bush administration won approval for "trade promotion authority," the new name for "fast track authority." As part of the package approved by Congress, the Bush administration agreed to binding negotiating objectives related to the environment, including assurances that any new trade agreement will:

- insist that U.S. trading partners effectively enforce their own environmental laws
- promote the sale of U.S. environmental goods and services
- support environmental capacity building
- address governmental practices that threaten sustainable development
- strengthen consultative mechanisms aimed at enhancing implementation of environmental and human health protection standards
- include an environmental review consistent with the procedures established under the Clinton administration
- protect multilateral environmental agreements [36]

In addition, the recent U.S.-Jordanian, U.S.-Singaporean, and U.S.-Chilean free trade agreements have included expressed environmental commitments.[37]

In all of these recent agreements, the NAFTA environmental provisions have provided a template. But none of the agreements include a strong institutional structure such as that found in the U.S.-Mexico-Canada context. Of course, the NAFTA Side Agreement's Commission for Environmental Cooperation has not been an unmitigated success. The CEC has undertaken several studies designed to ensure that environmental considerations are factored into trade policy across North America. But the CEC has also faced pressure not to pursue its environmental goals too aggressively. The lack of clear political support has driven the CEC to back away from several controversial trade and environment issues, including questions about a Mexican cruise ship pier in Cozumel and efforts to address clear-cutting in the U.S. Northwest and British Columbia. Whether the CEC will mature into an effective mechanism for environmental coordination between the United States, Mexico, and Canada remains to be seen.[38]

The Broader Policy Response

The World Trade Organization, the international body set up in 1994 to implement the General Agreement on Tariffs and Trade and to manage international trade relations, has come under considerable criticism for its lack of environmental sensitivity. Although the WTO has a Committee on Trade and the Environment (CTE), little substantive progress has been made toward the goal of more mutually supportive trade and environmental policies.

New disputes have increased the trade and environment tension. Notably, the European Union (EU) challenged U.S. efforts to block wine imports containing procymidone, an unregistered fungicide used on grapes.[39] The EU also challenged the U.S. Corporate Average Fuel Economy (CAFE) car mileage standards, arguing that this policy tool unfairly penalized European automobile manufacturers (for example, BMW, Mercedes, and Volvo) that sell only at the upper (low-gas-mileage) end of the car market. The United States brought a successful WTO claim against the EU for obstructing exports to Europe of U.S. beef found to contain growth hormones.[40] Canada forced the EU to back off on plans to forbid fur imports if the animal had been caught through the use of a leghold trap. Brazil and Venezuela won a case against the United States based on a claim of discrimination against foreign refiners in the EPA's implementation of the reformulated gasoline regulations under the 1990 Clean Air Act. And Thailand and several other countries in Southeast Asia got a WTO panel to agree that U.S. trade limitations imposed on shrimp fishermen who refused to use turtle excluder devices (TEDs) to protect endangered sea turtles were illegal under the GATT, although the WTO Appellate Body decision in this case endorsed the use of trade measures as a last resort to reinforce internationally agreed upon environmental standards.[41]

As the pace of economic integration increases, so does the number of trade-environment conflicts. The pressure for a more systematic commitment to building environmental considerations into the international trading system shows little sign of abating. In fact, the WTO has been criticized generally for failing to advance trade-environment harmony and specifically for focusing almost exclusively on the trade effects of environmental policy while paying little attention to the environmental consequences of trade policy.

At the 2001 launch of a new round of multilateral trade talks—the Doha Development Round—the European Union insisted that environmental issues be added to the agenda.[42] While the identified issues are carefully circumscribed, the fact that the environment is on the global trade agenda represents a break with the past. How far the Doha Round will go in "greening" the WTO remains to be seen.

Strengthening the Global Environmental Regime

Many observers of the trade and environment debate have concluded that part of the explanation for the ongoing conflict lies in the weakness of the international environmental regime. The centerpiece of international environmental protection efforts, the United Nations Environment Programme (UNEP), is in serious disarray.[43] Moreover, global environmental responsibilities are spread across a half-dozen other UN agencies (including the United Nations Development Programme, the United Nations Commission on Sustainable Development, and the World Meteorological Organization), the secretariats to various international environmental treaties (including the Climate Change Convention, the Montreal Protocol, the Desertification Treaty, and the Basel Convention), as well as the Bretton Woods institutions (the World Bank, the regional development banks, and the WTO). This fragmented institutional structure results in disjointed responses to global pollution and resource challenges, difficulty in clarifying policy and budget priorities, little coordination across related problems, and lost opportunities for synergistic responses.

The presence of a global environmental organization, able to operate in tandem with the WTO and to provide some counterbalance to the WTO's trade emphasis, would be advantageous.[44] But fears of lost national sovereignty and concerns about creating a new UN bureaucracy make the prospect of establishing a comprehensive and coherent international umbrella environmental institution any time soon seem remote. In the absence of a functioning global environmental management system capable of addressing trade and environment issues, much of the responsibility for integrating these two policy realms will continue to fall to the WTO. A serious effort to make the international trading system more environmentally sensitive would require action on many fronts.

First, the activities of the WTO must become more transparent—that is, more open and easily followed by average people. Currently, most of the activities of the international trading system occur behind closed doors. This secrecy generates hostility from those who feel excluded from WTO processes or who are simply put off by the prospect that important decisions are being made without public input or understanding. What's more, the WTO's legitimacy and authoritativeness would be broadly enhanced by allowing representatives of nongovernmental organizations (NGOs) to participate in or at least observe its proceedings.[45] This logic has been advanced by the United States with a series of proposals to open up the WTO. But to date, the efforts to promote transparency have been blocked by representatives from various developing countries.

This opposition reflects many concerns. Most notably, many free traders fear that the presence of environmentalists and others within the walls of the WTO would result in special interest manipulation of trade policymaking. It seems unlikely, however, that the presence of outside observers would really distort the decision processes of the international trading system. The system is not free of special interest manipulation now, and inviting environmental groups might produce some influence counteracting that of the existing producer and business lobbying and other activities. Allowing NGOs to make submissions when they have a position on issues being addressed by dispute settlement panels, or more broadly by the WTO governing council, would improve the knowledge base of the WTO and might assist the organization's decision making, especially in relation to environmental policy outcomes, which are so fraught with uncertainty.[46]

Over the longer term, the WTO must find a more refined way of balancing trade and environmental goals. The current mechanism (found in Article XX of the GATT) requires a country whose environmental policies have been challenged as an obstacle to free trade to demonstrate that it has selected the "least GATT-inconsistent" policy tool available. This standard sets an almost impossibly high hurdle for environmental policies because, in almost every case, there is some environmental strategy or approach that would intrude less on trade. A variety of proposals have been advanced that would amend Article XX and make it easier for legitimate environmental policies to be maintained in the face of trade challenges.[47]

In addition, while the trade system permits restrictions on imports when the product itself fails to meet national environmental standards, current GATT rules forbid discrimination against imports based on the environmental conditions associated with their production process or method (PPM). This means that imports of cars without the requisite pollution control devices can be banned. Similarly, imports of strawberries containing chemical residues can be barred. But GATT rules do not permit a country to block imports of cars because the steel that goes into them was made in polluting mills. Nor do the rules allow imported strawberries to be turned back just because the farmers polluted nearby rivers with pesticides and fertilizers. The prohibition against PPM-based environmental requirements is, however, untenable in a world of ecological interdependence.

Today the issue of *how* things are made is just as important as *what* is traded. If a semiconductor is produced using chlorofluorocarbons in violation of the ozone-layer-protection provisions of the Montreal Protocol, GATT rules would not permit an importing nation to bar the offending chip.[48] Even if the current blanket prohibition on PPM-based regulation were swept aside, the WTO would face lingering questions at the trade-environment interface.[49] Whose regulatory standards should be adopted? Who will determine compliance with agreed-upon standards? And who assesses penalties or takes other enforcement actions when a violation is uncovered?

These questions persist even if the standards in question arise from an international agreement. The WTO remains vulnerable to challenges arising from the imposition of trade measures under multilateral environmental agreements. This is especially true in those cases where a WTO member is not a party to the environmental accord. A strong possibility exists that under current interpretations of the GATT a country facing trade penalties for failing to sign or adhere to a multilateral environmental agreement would be able to argue that those imposing the trade sanctions for environmental reasons are in violation of their GATT obligations. Thus a nation that failed to join the Montreal Protocol banning the use of ozone-layer-depleting chemicals might be able to "free ride" on the environmental protection efforts of others and dodge trade sanctions imposed by parties to the protocol. In response to this issue, the WTO could adopt a provision, such as that found in NAFTA, which declares that trade measures taken in accordance with multilateral environmental agreements are not NAFTA violations. Beyond finding ways to balance conflicting trade and environmental goals more effectively, those seeking to make trade and environmental policies more mutually reinforcing could identify many places where trade and environmental policy aims dovetail. Notably, the elimination of subsidies for timber, water, agriculture, and energy and the more careful regulation of fisheries would yield both substantial trade benefits and environmental improvements. Agricultural price supports, for instance, encourage farmers to plant on marginal lands, which often require heavy doses of chemicals to be productive. Reduced agricultural subsidies would diminish the incentives to farm marginal lands and reduce trade distortions, providing new agricultural export opportunities for many developing countries.

Managing Interdependence

Despite the breadth of activities linking trade and environment policies in recent years and the reasonably favorable results arising on this score from NAFTA, some policymakers continue to dismiss the significance of the trade-environment relationship. The call for separation of economic and environmental interests is, however, not just normatively wrong but practically impossible. The relationship between environmental and trade issues in the context of deepening economic integration is inescapable and multilayered. Ignoring these linkages threatens to reduce social welfare, limit the gains from trade, and cause unnecessary environmental degradation. Ignoring the environmental implications of trade policymaking poses an acute threat to current and future economic integration efforts, not to mention environmental programs.

The fundamental challenge is to manage interdependence on multiple levels, representing both shared natural resources and a common economic destiny. Governance in this context requires working across divergent priorities—North versus South, economic growth versus environmental protection, and present interests versus future ones. Sustainable development has emerged as the shorthand way of refining a systems-oriented policy approach that considers these conflicting needs simultaneously. Making trade and environmental policies work together, therefore, stands as a classic example of the on-the-ground challenge of sustainable development.

Notes

1. Geoffrey D. Dabelko and David D. Dabelko, "Environment Security: Issues of Conflict and Redefinition," in *Environmental Change and Security Project Report*, ed. P. J. Simmons (Washington, D.C.: Woodrow Wilson Center, 1995), 3. But note that the events of 9/11 and the ensuing "war on terror" may have reduced the policy space open to the environment.
2. See Norman Myers, "Environment and Security," *Foreign Policy* 68 (spring 1989): 23; Jessica T. Mathews, "Redefining Security," *Foreign Affairs* 68 (spring 1989): 162.
3. Kym Anderson and Richard Blackhurst, "Trade, the Environment, and Public Policy," in *The Greening of World Trade Issues*, ed. Kym Anderson and Richard Blackhurst (Ann Arbor: University of Michigan Press, 1992), 3.

4. Daniel C. Esty, *Greening the GATT: Trade, Environment, and the Future* (Washington, D.C.: Institute for International Economics, 1994), 17–20; Andrew Hurrell and Benedict Kingsbury, *The International Politics of the Environment* (Oxford, England: Clarendon Press, 1992).
5. Richard N. Gardner, *Negotiating Survival: Four Priorities after Rio* (New York: Council on Foreign Relations, 1992); "Rio Declaration on Environment and Development," UNCED, UN Doc. A/Conf. 151/5/Rev. 1, reprinted in *International Legal Materials* 31 (1992): 874, 878; "Agenda 21," UNCED, UN Doc. A/Conf. 151/26/Rev. 1 (1992).
6. Doha WTO Ministerial Declaration, WT/MIN(01)/DEC/1, November 14, 2001, paragraphs 31–33.
7. For a discussion of the far-reaching repercussions of the improper management of hazardous waste, see André Dua and Daniel C. Esty, *Sustaining the Asia Pacific Miracle* (Washington, D.C.: Institute for International Economics, 1997), 41–42.
8. John J. Audley, *Green Politics and Global Trade: NAFTA and the Future of Environmental Politics* (Washington, D.C.: Georgetown University Press, 1997); "Binational Statement on Environmental Safeguards that Should Be Included in the North American Free Trade Agreement," issued by Canadian Nature Federation, Canadian Environmental Law Association, Sierra Club-Canada, Rawson Survival-Canada, Pollution Probe-Canada, National Audubon Society, National Wildlife Federation, Community Nutrition Institute, and Environmental Defense Fund, May 28, 1992.
9. Robert Housman and Durwood Zaelke, "The Collision of the Environment and Trade: The GATT Tuna/Dolphin Decision," *Environmental Law Reporter* 22 (April 1992): 10268.
10. Steve Charnovitz, "Environmentalism Confronts GATT Rules," *Journal of World Trade* 28 (January 1993): 37.
11. For an entertaining depiction of how GATTzilla might devour cities and leave destruction in its wake, see Esty, eds., *Greening the GATT,* 34.
12. Dua and Esty, *Sustaining the Asia Pacific Miracle;* Yoichi Funabashi, *Asia-Pacific Fusion: Japan's Role in APEC* (Washington, D.C.: Institute for International Economics, 1995).
13. For a discussion of NAFTA's environmental dimensions and effects, see Carolyn Deere and Daniel C. Esty, eds., *Greening the Americas: NAFTA's Lessons for Hemispheric Trade* (Cambridge: MIT Press, 2002).
14. Daniel C. Esty, "Bridging the Trade-Environment Divide," *Journal of Economic Perspectives* 15 (summer 2001): 113–130.
15. Esty, *Greening the GATT,* 42–55.
16. It is interesting to see how "trade and environment" issues have split the environmental community, separating those who accept the promise of sustainable development from those who believe that economic growth is inherently environmentally harmful. See Audley, *Green Politics and Global Trade: NAFTA and the Future of Environmental Politics.*
17. For instance, in the debate over NAFTA, some environmentalists expressed concerns regarding the likelihood of a deterioration in meat inspection standards along the U.S.-Mexico border. See Lori Wallach, *The Consumer and Environmental Case against Fast Track* (Washington, D.C.: Public Citizen, 1991), 16. But some scholars instead contend that trade can uplift product standards. See Alan O. Sykes, *Product Standards for Internationally Integrated Goods Markets* (Washington, D.C.: Brookings Institution, 1995); David Vogel, *Trading Up: Consumer and Environmental Regulation in a Global Economy* (Cambridge: Harvard University Press, 1995). Further excellent considerations of harmonization issues are provided in Jagdish Bhagwati and Robert E. Hudec, eds., *Fair Trade and Harmonization: Prerequisites for Free Trade?* (Cambridge: MIT Press, 1996).
18. Ross Perot, *Save Your Job, Save Our Country: Why NAFTA Must Be Stopped—Now!* (New York: Hyperion, 1993).

19. Various aspects of this debate are reviewed in Daniel C. Esty and Damien Geradin, *Regulatory Competition and Economic Integration: Comparative Perspectives* (Oxford: Oxford University Press, 2001).

20. Charles M. Tiebout, "A Pure Theory of Local Expenditures," *Journal of Political Economy* (October 1956): 416; Wallace E. Oates and Robert M. Schwab, "Economic Competition among Jurisdictions: Efficiency Enhancing or Distortion Inducing," *Journal of Public Economy* 27 (April 1988): 333; Richard L. Revesz, "Rehabilitating Interstate Competition: Rethinking the 'Race to the Bottom' Rationale for Federal Environmental Regulation," *New York University Law Review* 67 (December 1992): 1210.

21. Daniel C. Esty, "Revitalizing Environmental Federalism," *Michigan Law Review* 95 (December 1996): 629–634.

22. Lyuba Zarsky and Jason Hunter, "Environmental Cooperation at APEC: The First Five Years," *Journal of Environment and Development* (September 1997): 222–252.

23. International Monetary Fund, *Direction of Trade Statistics* (Washington, D.C.: International Monetary Fund, 1996).

24. Marrakesh Decisions Concurrent to Establishing the WTO, "Decision on Trade and Environment," April 14, 1994, reprinted in *International Legal Materials* 33 (1994): 1255.

25. Steve Charnovitz, "Free Trade, Fair Trade, Green Trade: Defogging the Debate," *Cornell International Law Journal* 27 (1994): 459–525; Sanford Gaines, "The Polluter-Pays Principle: From Economic Equity to Environmental Ethos," *Texas International Law Journal* 26 (summer 1991): 463.

26. Gene M. Grossman and Alan B. Krueger, "Economic Growth and the Environment," *Quarterly Journal of Economics* 110 (May 1995): 353, 369.

27. Dua and Esty, *Sustaining the Asia Pacific Miracle*, 73–77.

28. Theo Panayotou, "Demystifying the Environmental Kuznets Curve: Turning a Black Box into a Policy Tool," *Environment and Development Economics* 2 (1997): 4, 465–484; M. A. Cole et al., "The Environmental Kuznets Curve: An Empirical Analysis," *Environment and Development Economics* 2 (1997): 4, 401–416; S. M. DeBruyn et al., "Economic Growth and Emissions: Reconsidering the Empirical Basis of Environmental Kuznets Curves," *Ecological Economics* 25 (1998): 2, 161–175.

29. Esty, "Bridging the Trade-Environment Divide," 119.

30. NAFTA Supplemental Agreements, "North American Agreement on Environmental Cooperation," September 13, 1993, reprinted in *International Legal Materials* 32 (1993): 1480.

31. *Inside U.S. Trade*, August 23, 1991, 7; Trade and Environment Committee of the National Advisory Council for Environmental Policy and Technology, *The Greening of World Trade*, Report to the EPA (Washington, D.C.: EPA, 1993).

32. Executive Order 13141—Environmental Reviews of Trade Agreements, November 16, 1999.

33. NAFTA Preamble, December 17, 1992, reprinted in *International Legal Materials* 32 (1993): 296 and 605.

34. NAFTA Chapter 11, however, became a source of controversy because its loose drafting seemed to create a risk that legitimate environmental regulation might trigger compensation requirements. For further discussion on this point, see Howard Mann and Monica Araya, "An Investment Regime for the Americas: Challenges and Opportunities for Environmental Sustainability," in *Greening the Americas: NAFTA's Lessons for Hemispheric Trade*, ed. Carolyn L. Deere and Daniel C. Esty (Cambridge: MIT Press, 2002).

35. Gary C. Hufbauer et al., *NAFTA and the Environment* (Washington: Institute for International Economics, 2001); Deere and Esty, "Trade and the Environment: Reflections on the NAFTA and Recommendations for the Americas," in Deere and Esty, *Greening the Americas: NAFTA's Lessons for Hemispheric Trade*, 329.

36. John Audley, "Environment's New Role in U.S. Trade Policy," Trade, Equity, and Development Policy Brief no. 3, Carnegie Endowment for International Peace, September 2002.

37. John Audley, "Evaluating Environmental Issues in the US-Singapore Free Trade Agreement," Trade, Equity, and Development Issue Brief, Carnegie Endowment for International Peace, April 2003; John Audley, "Opportunities and Challenges to Advance Environmental Protection in the US-Central America Free Trade Negotiations," Trade, Equity, and Development Issue Brief, Carnegie Endowment for International Peace, February 2003.

38. Gary C. Hufbauer et al., *NAFTA and the Environment: Seven Years Later* (Washington, D.C.: Institute for International Economics, 2000); Laura Carlsen and Hilda Salazar, "Limits to Cooperation: A Mexican Perspective on the NAFTA's Environmental Side Agreement and Institutions," in Deere and Esty, *Greening the Americas: NAFTA's Lessons for Hemispheric Trade*.

39. An "unregistered" fungicide is one that has not gone through EPA safety testing to establish a safe residue level under the Federal Insecticide, Fungicide, and Rodenticide Act, 7 U.S.C. §§136 et seq. (1996).

40. Michael B. Froman, "International Trade: The United States–European Community Hormone Treated Beef Conflict," *Harvard International Law Journal* 30 (spring 1989): 549–556.

41. For a compilation of many important and interesting trade disputes see Esty, *Greening the GATT*, app. C, 257–274. See also Carrie Wofford, "A Greener Future at the WTO: The Refinement of WTO Jurisprudence on Environmental Exceptions to the GATT," *Harvard Environmental Law Review* 24, no. 2 (2000): 563–592.

42. Doha WTO Ministerial Declaration, WT/MIN(01)/DEC/1, November 14, 2001, paragraphs 31–33.

43. Even UNEP acknowledges that "global governance structures and global environmental solidarity remain too weak to make progress a world-wide reality. . . . The gap between what has been done thus far and what is realistically needed is widening." See UNEP, *Global Environment Outlook* (New York: Oxford University Press, 1997).

44. For a review of global environmental governance issues, see Daniel C. Esty and Maria Ivanova, eds., *Global Environmental Governance: Options & Opportunities* (New Haven: Yale School of Forestry and Environmental Studies, 2002).

45. Steve Charnovitz, "Two Centuries of Participation: NGOs and International Governance," *Michigan Journal of International Trade* 18 (winter 1997): 183–286; Daniel C. Esty, "Non-governmental Organizations at the World Trade Organization: Cooperation, Competition, or Exclusion," *Journal of International Economic Law* 1 (1998): 123–147; James Cameron and Ross Ramsey, "Participation by NGOs in the WTO," Working Paper, Global Environment and Trade Study (GETS), New Haven, 1995.

46. Christophe Bellmann and Richard Gerster, "Accountability in the WTO," *Journal of World Trade* 30 (December 1996): 31–74. On the advantages of NGO "co-opetition," see Daniel C. Esty and Damien Geradin, "Regulatory Co-opetition," in *Regulatory Competition and Economic Integration: Comparative Perspectives*, ed. Daniel C. Esty and Damien Geradin (Oxford: Oxford University Press, 2001).

47. Daniel C. Esty, "Making Trade and Environmental Policies Work Together: Lessons from NAFTA," in *Trade and Environment: The Search for Balance*, ed. Damien Geradin et al. (London: Cameron, 1994), 382.

48. Duncan Brack, *International Trade and the Montreal Protocol* (London: Royal Institute of International Affairs, 1996).

49. Some softening of the WTO rules has begun to emerge, especially in the Appellate Body decision in the Shrimp/Turtle case. See Wofford, "A Greener Future at the WTO."

9

Compliance with Global Environmental Policy

Michael Faure and Jürgen Lefevere

The United Nations Conference on the Human Environment, held in Stockholm in 1972, set off an unprecedented development of new international environmental treaties. Before 1972, only a dozen international treaties with relevance to the environment were in force; twenty-five years later more than a thousand such instruments could be counted.

With the intensified use of international treaties as a means to combat environmental degradation, concerns have arisen regarding the compliance of states with the commitments to which they agreed. Even within relatively strong regional organizations such as the European Union (EU), compliance problems regularly overshadow successes in the adoption of new instruments. In a hearing on the subject conducted in 1992 by the British House of Lords, a member of the European Parliament even warned that "we have now reached the point in the EC where, if we do not tackle implementation and enforcement properly, there seems very little point in producing new environmental law." [1]

In recent decades international actors have tried new approaches to drafting, implementation, and enforcement in an attempt to improve compliance with international environmental treaties. This activity has been mirrored by advances in the scholarly study of factors that affect state compliance and increased discussion of such factors in both academic and policymaking circles.

This chapter examines the theory and practice of national compliance with international environmental treaties. In doing so, the chapter uses as its primary examples the United Nations Framework Convention on Climate Change (FCCC) and its Kyoto Protocol, the EU environmental regime, and the Montreal Protocol on Substances that Deplete the Ozone Layer. We begin by discussing the theory of compliance as it has been developed in both the academic literature and in practice.[2] We then provide an overview of sources for compliance and noncompliance. Finally, we examine methods developed to date that seek to improve compliance with international environmental treaties.

Theory of Compliance

The term *compliance* is often not used in a consistent way but is confused with related terminology such as *implementation, effectiveness,* or even *enforcement.* To avoid unnecessary confusion, one should be careful in using these terms. They refer to different aspects of the process of achieving international political and legal cooperation.

Implementation refers to the specific actions (including legislative, organizational, and practical actions) that international actors and states take to make international treaties operative in their national legal system. Implementation by relevant international actors includes, for instance, the provision of financial resources by the Global Environment Facility (GEF) in accordance with the rules adopted under the FCCC. Implementation by states establishes the link between the national legal system and the international obligations. The aim of establishing this link should be compliance.

Compliance is generally defined as the extent to which the behavior of a state—party to an international treaty—actually conforms to the conditions set out in this treaty. Some authors make a distinction between compliance with the treaty's explicit rules and compliance with the treaty's objective.[3] It is, however, difficult to assess compliance with the "spirit" of an agreement, since this evaluation can be quite subjective. The third term, *enforcement*, indicates the methods that are available to force states not only to implement but also to comply with treaty obligations. Whereas compliance and implementation concern the actions of the states themselves, *effectiveness*, as the term indicates, is more concerned with the effect of the treaty as a whole. *Effectiveness* addresses the question of whether a treaty that is correctly complied with actually achieves its stated objectives, or whether the treaty actually helped to reach the environmental goal for which it was designed.

The terms *compliance* and *effectiveness* are often used interchangeably but, in fact, have very distinct meanings. Compliance is in most cases a condition for effectiveness, if by effectiveness we mean the reaching of the treaty's goals. If a treaty is complied with, however, this does not automatically signify that it is effective in reaching the environmental goal for which it was originally designed. Effectiveness also depends on the actual treaty design, the instruments and goals contained in the treaty, as well as other external factors, such as a changing political situation or even changing environmental conditions. The Kyoto Protocol is an example: even if states fully comply with the requirements of that treaty, the protocol is still insufficient to stop climate change from occurring. Hence, compliance is only a proxy for effectiveness; greater compliance will usually lead to environmental improvement, but whether this is actually the case will to a large extent depend upon the contents of the treaty. One could even imagine a treaty that is so badly drafted that noncompliance would even contribute to its effectiveness. For example, this ironic result could be reached in a treaty that on paper protects the environment (or potential victims) but that, in fact, protects industrial operators, for example, by introducing financial caps on their liability. One could argue that potential victims would be better off with noncompliance, but this is obviously true only in cases where special interests (not primarily environmental concerns) dictated the contents of the treaty.

We will concentrate here on the issue of compliance as a requirement for an effective treaty. This issue has received increasing attention in scholarly writing and in practice since the mid-1990s. Increased attention has led to the development of a new approach to the compliance issue. The traditional view of compliance was very much connected to the principle of sovereignty of states. According to this principle, states are sovereign actors in the international arena, meaning that they are free to act as they find necessary, unrestricted by any external authority or rules. Based on this principle, one tended to believe that governments therefore accepted only those international treaties that were in their own interest. A breach of these treaties was thus seen as unlikely. If a state was in breach of its treaty obligations, it was usually considered to be intentional. Enforcement measures were thus often limited and were regarded as severe actions. Examples of these enforcement measures are procedures where states can file an official complaint against the violating state or impose trade sanctions. Because of the gravity of these sanctions, however, they are rarely applied in practice. Even in the European context, direct complaints of one state against another are still highly exceptional.[4]

The traditional view of compliance problems is being abandoned in recent scholarly writings. This change goes hand in hand with the new approach to sovereignty. Some argue that states are no longer seen as completely sovereign entities but are willing to accept limits on their original sovereign rights for the benefit of the environment, future generations, or the international community as a whole.[5] The international community is increasingly organized in *regimes*.[6] These regimes consist of a framework with a relatively well-developed set of rules and norms concerning a specific subject. The development of regimes can be placed between the traditional concept of sovereignty, leaving the states unbound, and a comprehensive world order, placing the states within a new world governance. Examples of important regimes are the climate change regime, constructed around the FCCC and its Kyoto Protocol (the latter is not yet in force), and the international trade regime, based on the agreements concluded under the World Trade Organization (WTO). With the development of these regimes, "sovereignty no longer consists in the freedom of states to act independently, in their perceived self-interest, but in membership in reasonably good standing in the regimes that make up the substance of international life."[7] States' interests are increasingly determined by their membership in, as well as good reputation under, these regimes.

The new approach tries to place compliance problems in this increasingly complicated international context, with a multitude of regimes, interdependent actors, and different interests and obligations. Within this new context many factors can lead countries to conclude treaties. These factors also affect the states' willingness and, more important, their ability to comply with the obligations. In this more complex perception of compliance, the actors at the international level can no longer be seen as utilitarian decision makers weighing the benefits and costs of compliance. The compliance record of states is influenced by a large number of factors, in which the willful desire to violate rules plays only a minor role. Often it is practical obstacles, outside the direct will or control of states, that make compliance difficult.

This new concept of compliance also necessitates new solutions to problems. The traditional sanction mechanisms, based on the notion that states intentionally do not comply, have proven largely ineffective. Moreover, some of these are now often unlawful under other international arrangements. The use of military action is strictly regulated under international law, although states obviously observe such regulations unevenly, and force is now allowed in a legal sense in a limited number of situations. Certainly it is not seen as a legally appropriate or practical method of seeking compliance with environmental treaties.[8] Economic sanctions have become more difficult to apply since the development of an increasingly comprehensive international trade regime. It is now necessary to take into account the actual abilities of states to comply, and sanctions for noncompliance need to be developed that fit within the new international regimes. Solutions for compliance problems need to be based more on what is referred to as a "managerial approach" rather than on a more traditional "enforcement approach."[9]

Sources of Compliance and Noncompliance

The following section will address several factors that may affect compliance with environmental agreements and possible sources of noncompliance.

Regime Rules

The regime rules refer to the actual contents of the treaty that the parties have signed. These rules define the behavior that is required of the participating states under the terms of the treaty. The regime rules are directly related to the activity that the environmental accord is supposed to regulate. Even during the negotiations, when the primary rules are defined, the degree of treaty compliance can be determined to a large extent.

A first important aspect of the design of the regime rule system relates to whether it requires any behavioral change, what the costs of this change will be, and by whom this behavioral change is required. It is easier to achieve compliance if the degree of behavioral change and the costs of this change are low. It is therefore argued, for instance, that it might be harder to achieve compliance with the Kyoto Protocol than with the Montreal Protocol, since more people and industries must make bigger behavioral changes. The Montreal Protocol mainly requires behavioral changes by the producers and corporate users of a limited number of very important but replaceable chemicals. The greenhouse gas emission reduction targets in the Kyoto Protocol, however, require larger-scale behavioral changes, not only by industry but also by individuals, particularly with respect to the production and consumption of energy.[10]

In a number of cases treaty rules require no change in behavior of the industry in a specific country. This is often the case when industry is already meeting a specific pollution standard (for example, emissions). Those industries may even lobby in favor of treaties that will impose on their foreign competitors the standards that domestic industries already have to comply with at the national level.[11] In those cases the industries already meeting the specific standard will obviously readily comply, since the treaty merely erects a barrier to entry for the foreign competitors.

In some cases the treaties are clearly in the interest of industry for other reasons. One example is the treaties relating to liability for nuclear accidents and oil pollution. On paper these treaties serve the interests of victims, but, in fact, the contents are often such that the liability of operators is limited (for example, through financial caps). The nuclear liability conventions that originated in the late 1950s came into being as a reaction to the growing nuclear industry's fear of unlimited liability. Hence, compliance with the conventions, which included limited liability of nuclear operators, was relatively high.[12]

The amount of detail or specificity in a treaty may affect future compliance. States can facilitate their own compliance by negotiating vague and ambiguous rules. Examples include agreeing to provisions that on paper seem to be in the environmental interest but are sufficiently vague to allow business as usual. However, primary rules can often increase compliance through greater specificity. Specific obligations make compliance easier by reducing the uncertainty about what states need to do to comply. Specific treaty language will also remove the possibility of the excuse of inadvertence and misinterpretation in case of noncompliance. Moreover, the advantage of conventions with relatively precise obligations (such as the Montreal Protocol) is that it is easier to judge whether states do, in fact, comply. If the obligations are vaguer, assessing implementation and compliance becomes more difficult.

One obvious remedy for inadvertence as a source of noncompliance is, therefore, to draft specific, detailed obligations. These, together with an information campaign, can at least prevent states from justifying noncompliance on the basis of a lack of information or clarity with respect to their obligations. A general formulation of the obligations may, however, be unavoidable in some cases simply because political consensus may not support more precision. Article 4(2)(a) of the FCCC is an example of diplomatically formulated "obligations." The article leaves unclear whether there is any specific obligation at all.[13]

One source of noncompliance may be the incapacity of states to fulfill the treaty obligations due to a lack of resources or technological abilities. When these problems are recognized during the drafting stage, noncompliance may be prevented by designing the primary rules in such a manner that the differing capacities of states are taken into account. Treaty obligations can be differentiated, based on the varying capacities of states, or resources or technologies can be transferred. This is, again, an example of a managerial approach; instead of blunt sanctions, instruments are developed in the treaty design stage that take into account the varying capacities and thus prevent noncompliance.

The idea of differentiated standards according to a state's capacities is predominant in the FCCC and its Kyoto Protocol. This treaty regime places its signatory states in different categories, imposing different obligations for each group. All signatory states commit themselves to the general obligations, such as developing national greenhouse gas inventories. Under the FCCC, only the developed states and states in transition that are listed in Annex I of the FCCC are required to stabilize their carbon dioxide emissions. Under the Kyoto Protocol, only the developed states and states in transition that are listed in Annex B of the protocol are required to limit their greenhouse gas emissions in accordance with the targets contained in that Annex. Annex II of the FCCC lists the developed countries that additionally need to provide financial resources to facilitate compliance by developing countries.[14] The transfer of funds from developed to developing states can also be observed in other treaties. The Montreal Protocol, for instance, provides a framework within which financial support as well as technical assistance is provided. The EU uses the instrument of structural funds to promote economic and social development of disadvantaged regions within the EU.

A new concept in the area of climate change, which also takes into account differing abilities of states, is the use of "flexible mechanisms." These mechanisms allow developed countries to meet their emission limitation targets through buying "emission rights" from countries in which the marginal costs of emission reduction are lower, thus reducing the costs of compliance. The Kyoto Protocol's flexible mechanisms are Joint Implementation (JI), the Clean Development Mechanism (CDM), and International Emissions Trading (IET). The CDM is the most interesting of these mechanisms; it allows developed countries to invest in emission reduction projects in a developing country and in return receive emission rights that can be used to comply with their emission limitation obligations. A well-implemented CDM project can thus help provide financial aid and technologies to developing countries and hence also help remedy capacity problems.[15]

The only problem with these various inducements is that they are vulnerable to "moral hazard." Moral hazard refers to the fact that incentives for the prevention of emissions may be diluted if states are subsidized through financial or technological transfers. States may indeed misrepresent their abilities in order to have others pay for their compliance costs. The approach of using differentiated standards and financial and technological transfers is the basis of the more comprehensive noncompliance response systems that we will discuss below (see box on the Montreal Protocol as an example of the managerial approach).

Reporting and Information

The likelihood of compliance will also depend upon informational issues. Information plays an important role at several stages. First, accurate information on the environmental risks increases the chances of adopting a treaty on the specific subject and also the likelihood of compliance. Second, information, through monitoring or reporting systems, serves to increase the transparency of the implementation and compliance records of states.

With regard to the first factor, it is broadly assumed that the more information there is about an environmental issue, the more effective implementation and compliance will be.[16] This understanding is rather straightforward: the clearer the presentation of the activities and risks that are the subject of the treaty, the easier it will be to build political pressure (through, among others, NGOs) via public opinion to induce compliance. One of the reasons that the swift adoption of the Montreal Protocol came as a surprise to the international community was that it occurred in a time of still important scientific uncertainties about the causes and effects of the changing ozone layer.[17] These uncertainties are still significantly influencing the negotiations concerning climate change. The scientific reports of the Intergovernmental Panel on Climate Change (IPCC) play an important role in forming international consensus about the problem.[18]

With regard to the second factor, information increases the transparency of the implementation and compliance records of states. If it is known that a state does not comply, international and domestic groups can take actions aimed at improving a state's compliance. Transparency with respect to the compliance record will to a large extent depend upon the complexity of the issue covered by the treaty as well as the democratic character of the complying state. Transparency can lead to public pressure to increase compliance. In this respect, one can cite the actions of NGOs to identify noncompliance, thereby giving incentives for compliance without a need for formal sanctions. Transparency is considered an almost universal element of compliance management strategy. Indeed, transparency in the form of "naming and shaming" is increasingly being used as a sanction for noncompliance, building on the desire of states and companies to satisfy an environmentally aware electorate, consumers, and shareholders.

Transparency can be achieved through an effective compliance information system that is laid down in the treaty. To a large extent, treaties rely on self-reporting by states. As noted above, in a regime system with often delicate political links and pressures, the "status" of a state is often very important. States are generally careful about "losing face" with other states and their own population. This fear of losing face has traditionally been used in many treaties, including those outside the environmental field, by imposing a requirement that the state report on its compliance with the treaty. This report would allow other states and citizens to hold it accountable for its compliance record. Although reporting procedures can be found in most environmental treaties, they are often vaguely formulated, and the reports are poorly drafted. Hence, the reporting procedure is often criticized for its "weak" character and the absence of sanctions in case of noncompliance with the reporting requirements.

Self-reporting is also criticized because it may lead to self-incrimination. If states take this duty seriously, they should report their own noncompliance.

The hesitancy of states to incriminate themselves may be one of the reasons why the reporting requirements of environmental treaties are often violated. Moreover, governments, particularly of smaller states, are sometimes overburdened with administrative tasks, and filing reports is seen as yet another burden. Reporting can also be difficult for developing countries that often lack both financial resources and the capacity to comply with detailed reporting obligations. Reporting by states is, therefore, a first step, but obviously no guarantee of compliance.[19]

Compliance can be improved through monitoring by an independent third party. The likelihood of compliance will to a large extent be influenced by the treaty's provisions for effective monitoring. This in turn depends on the contents of the primary rules. The Montreal Protocol, for instance, regulated the production rather than the consumption of chlorofluorocarbons (CFCs) because it is easier to monitor a few producers rather than thousands of con-

---

The Montreal Protocol . . .

The approach to international environmental treaty design has changed in the past decades, mainly because of the new, more realistic "managerial" approach. Prime examples of this new approach are the Vienna Convention for the Protection of the Ozone Layer and, more important, its subsequent Montreal Protocol on Substances that Deplete the Ozone Layer, adopted under this Convention.

The Vienna Convention was adopted in 1985. It did not contain any substantive commitments for the states but provided for a general framework, including the possibility of adopting protocols in the Conference of the Parties, the main institution set up under the Convention. Only two years after the adoption of the Convention, the 1987 Montreal Protocol on Substances that Deplete the Ozone Layer was adopted. The Vienna Convention and, more particularly, its Montreal Protocol surprised the international community by their swift adoption, their specific goals, their effectiveness, and the large number of states that have become parties to them (more than 180 as of November 2003). One of the main reasons given for this effectiveness is the design of the treaty system, which has several "modern" characteristics that make it very suitable for dealing with environmental problems in the current international context. In many of the more recent international environmental treaties the Vienna/Montreal system is used as a model, largely because of the flexibility of its primary rule system.

The Vienna Convention establishes the Conference of the Parties (Article 6), which is to meet "at regular intervals," in practice every three to four years. The Montreal Protocol adds a Meeting of the Parties. Montreal protocol meetings are now held annually to discuss implementation of the commitments and possible improvements to or adoption of new commitments. They are organized by the Ozone Secretariat, set up under Article 7 of the Vienna Convention and Article 12 of the Montreal Protocol. The regular convening of the Meeting of the Parties has proven very useful in keeping the treaty objectives on the political agenda and has ensured a continuous updating of its goals and standards. This updating was made possible by the framework structure chosen by the Vienna Convention. Although not a new structure (it was also used in the 1979 UN-ECE Convention on Long-Range

sumers. Some treaties, such as those on nuclear weapons, allow on-site monitoring. This obviously is one of the most effective instruments to control whether states not only formally adopt legislation implementing a treaty but also comply with the contents. On-site monitoring is, however, still heavily debated, since it constitutes an important infringement on state sovereignty.

Even in the EU, on-site monitoring by a European authority of member state violations of environmental directives is still not used. The compliance record will inevitably depend upon the ability to monitor violations. This brought Gro Harlem Brundtland, the Norwegian prime minister and chair of the World Commission on Environment and Development, to recommend the establishment of "an international authority with the power to verify actual emission and to react with legal measures if there are violations of the rules" in order to ensure compliance with carbon dioxide emission targets.[20]

. . . A "Managerial" Primary Rule System

Transboundary Air Pollution), it has been particularly effective. Whereas the Vienna Convention does no more than establish the framework for further negotiations, the real commitments are laid down in the Montreal Protocol—the first and, to date, only protocol adopted under this Convention. The provisions of the Montreal Protocol are regularly updated by means of amendments. In its brief existence, the Montreal Protocol has already seen five amendments and adjustments (in 1990, 1992, 1995, 1997, and 1999). This shows how compliance is likely to be influenced in the treaty design stage by creating a primary rule system that can develop over time, responding to evolving science and the capacity to deal with environmental problems.

The Montreal Protocol also provides an example of how the individual capacities of states may determine their willingness to accept treaty obligations in the first place. India and China would not become parties to the Montreal Protocol until the agreement about compensatory financing had been adopted at the London meeting in 1990. This agreement provided for financial support to developing states in order to allow them to become parties to the protocol and be financially capable of complying with its obligations.

Under the Montreal Protocol, various instruments have been developed to remedy financial incapacity. A Multilateral Fund was set up (Article 10) to provide financial assistance. The fund's implementing agencies—the International Bank for Reconstruction and Development (World Bank), the United Nations Environment Programme, and the United Nations Development Programme—have drawn up "country programmes" and "country studies" that offer financial support, assistance, and training. Furthermore, the Montreal Protocol provides for the transfer of technology under its Article 10A. On the basis of this article, all states party to the protocol "shall take every practicable step" to ensure that "the best available, environmentally safe substitutes and related technologies are expeditiously transferred" to developing countries (as defined in Article 5[1] of the protocol) and that those transfers "occur under fair and most favourable conditions."

The problems with reporting procedures have led to the development of *compliance information systems.*[21] These systems contain elaborate procedures for the provision of information by member states, the possible review of this information by independent experts, and the availability of this information to the general public. By developing a more elaborate and transparent system for the provision of information on the compliance of member states, their accountability automatically increases.

For example, the FCCC contains, in Articles 4 and 12, elaborate provisions concerning the communication by member states of their implementation of the Convention. Although the word *reporting* is avoided in the context of the Convention—replaced by the word *communicate*—these communications have the character of national reports. The first FCCC Conference of the Parties (COP-1), in 1995, promulgated the first guidelines for preparation of national communications, and, more important, procedures were adopted for the in-depth review of individual reports from developed countries by teams of experts. Between 2001 and 2003, most developed countries submitted their third national communications, all of which have been subjected to an in-depth review. Although written in "non-confrontational language," the in-depth review procedure does provide an important impetus for member states to increase their efforts to comply. All national communications and the in-depth reviews are collected by the FCCC Secretariat in Bonn, Germany. Under Article 12(10) of the FCCC, the Secretariat makes these communications and their in-depth reviews publicly available. The reports may also be accessed at the Secretariat's Web site (http://www.unfcc.int). Under the Kyoto Protocol, this reporting procedure will be further strengthened, with additional reporting requirements and a more rigorous review procedure, the results of which feed into the protocol's noncompliance procedure.

This increased attention to information systems and reporting procedures is part of the transformation from an enforcement approach to a managerial approach to compliance. Traditionally, the incentives for states to report their own noncompliance were low, since such an admission could lead only to "bad news," such as the imposition of sanctions. The situation totally changes, however, when noncompliance is not necessarily considered the intentional act of a sovereign state but may be due, for example, to incapacity. In that case, reporting the problem may lead other partners in the regime to look for remedies to overcome the difficulty, for example, through a transfer of finances or technology. In this managerial approach, reporting noncompliance should not be threatening but may well be in the state's interest. The desired result of this new approach is that in the end a higher compliance record is achieved than with traditional enforcement methods. Thus the reporting of noncompliance under the Montreal Protocol leads the Implementation Committee to investigate the possibilities of financial and technical assistance instead of threatening with sanctions.

Country Characteristics

The characteristics of the parties involved in negotiating and adopting international environmental treaties, that is, the states concerned, will have an impact on the likelihood of treaty adoption; in addition, they will have considerable influence on the probability of compliance.

There may be many reasons why states sign treaties but nevertheless do not comply. States may sign an agreement because of international pressure or to serve domestic interests. Domestic interests, however, may also oppose compliance. Hence, it may well be in the states' interest to sign the agreement but not comply. Moreover, compliance with international environmental agreements is seldom a black or white situation: states may view most provisions of a treaty in their interest, complying with those provisions but violating a few others.

Other factors that may play a role include the cultural traditions, political system, administrative capacities of the country concerned, and economic factors. Compliance may also be influenced by the strength of nongovernmental organizations (NGOs), an issue that will be discussed below.

An important factor is whether a country has a democratic form of government. Many features of democratic governments contribute to improved implementation and compliance. There may be more transparency and hence easier monitoring by citizens who can exert pressure to improve the implementation record. Also, NGOs generally have more freedom to operate in democratic countries. A considerable role can also be played by individuals, such as the heads of state. In many cases the personal enthusiasm of a particular head of state has facilitated compliance, usually during the treaty negotiating process.[22]

As was indicated above, compliance may also fail because of incapacity. This could be due to the country's lack of administrative capacity to implement the treaty, which in turn may have to do, for example, with the level of education and training of the bureaucrats. The level of administrative capacity is also dependent upon economic resources. In addition, compliance with treaties sometimes requires investment in technologies that countries with fewer resources simply lack.

Number of States and the "International Environment"

The greater the number of countries that have ratified an accord, and the greater the extent of their implementation and compliance, the greater is the probability of compliance by any individual country. Noncompliance would then run counter to international public opinion.[23] There is also a relationship between the area to be regulated in the environmental treaty and the number of countries that can be expected to comply. For example, the international whaling commission faces a trade-off between, on the one hand, maintaining a moratorium on commercial whaling in a treaty that fewer countries have been willing to sign, or, on the other hand, allowing some commercial whaling in order to keep a larger number of countries within the scope of the treaty and thus achieve a higher compliance record.[24] Having a large number of countries accept the contents of a treaty comes at a price, and it may lead to a lowering of the standard to be achieved.

The general "international environment" will have an influence on the willingness of a country to engage in the treaty obligations and on the subsequent compliance record as well. This can be analyzed in terms of the problems of "free riding" and "prisoners' dilemma." [25] Free riding refers to the fact that individual states may hope that others will take the necessary measures to reduce the sources of a transboundary pollution problem, thus "free riding" on their efforts. The game-theoretical "prisoners' dilemma" in this context refers to the fact that although mutual compliance may be in the interest of all states in order, for example, to reduce transboundary industrial pollution, the absence of enforcement may lead all parties to believe that they can violate. Because of these problems, enforcement was traditionally advocated to guarantee compliance.

Compliance also depends on the distribution of power among nations, which can influence individual states' compliance strategies. A dominant state, perceiving sufficient benefits from complying, may force compliance by other, weaker states.[26] In those cases compliance does not even require explicit enforcement. Obviously, the division of power between states may change, which will also produce changes in the incentives to comply.[27]

States sign numerous international treaties. Negotiations on treaties and compliance often involve situations in which states will encounter each other repeatedly in the context of various treaties (often referred to as "repeat player games"); such multiple encounters may have a beneficial influence on compliance. Thus the fear of free riding can be overcome if the record of compliance is related to potential benefits for states in existing and future international agreements.[28] In other words, states may comply because future agreements with the same partner states will be possible if they have an acceptable compliance record.

This "international environment" perspective underscores the point made in the "Theory of Compliance" section above that states increasingly belong to various regimes, which engage them in a repeat player game. Hence, the incentives to comply may emerge from these regimes, reducing the need for formal enforcement of one particular treaty.

Role of NGOs

NGO activity can beneficially influence the compliance record of a country in various ways.[29] International environmental NGOs may influence international public opinion, shaping the agenda that determines the issues to be dealt with in a treaty. For instance, activities of environmental NGOs contributed, through increasing pressure on the international community, to the agreement on the Framework Convention on Climate

Change, leading to the adoption of the Kyoto Protocol in December 1997. Once a treaty has come into being, NGOs can play a crucial role in ensuring compliance. As watchdogs, they can pressure their governments to uphold the key provisions of specific regimes. This so-called bottom-up approach to compliance is increasingly stressed in the literature.[30] The role of NGOs here also illustrates that their actions can lead to what is referred to as "compliance as self-interest," or at least not treaty-induced. Through pressure by environmental groups, public opinion may be influenced in such a manner that the country views the costs of a potential violation of treaty provisions as prohibitively high.[31]

Finally, NGOs can also provide information about activities that are addressed in international environmental treaties. Greenpeace, for instance, is an important source of information about ocean dumping.[32] Hence, NGO activity may foster transparency both at the negotiating and at the implementation and compliance stages.

These factors generally merit the conclusion that stronger and more active NGOs help increase the probability of compliance.

Responses to Noncompliance

As we have discussed, traditional treaty mechanisms for noncompliance were restricted to adversarial dispute settlement procedures (DSPs). These procedures, used generally under international environmental law, mostly involve a sequence of diplomatic and legal means of dispute settlement. Diplomatic settlement procedures usually involve negotiation and consultation in a first instance. If negotiation and consultation do not lead to a solution, some form of mediation or conciliation is often prescribed. This involves third parties or international institutions. In case of deeper conflicts, parties often can have recourse to legal means of dispute settlement, either arbitration or the International Court of Justice. In July 1993 the International Court of Justice set up a special chamber for environmental matters.[33]

This standard sequence of dispute resolution—negotiation, mediation, and finally arbitration or submission to the International Court of Justice— can still be found in more recent treaties, such as the Vienna Convention for the Protection of the Ozone Layer and the FCCC. Article 11 of the Vienna Convention prescribes negotiation as the first means of dispute resolution (paragraph 1). If this fails, parties must seek mediation by a third party (paragraph 2). As an ultimate remedy, arbitration or submission to the International Court of Justice, or in absence of agreement over this remedy a conciliation committee, is prescribed (paragraphs 3– 5). Article 14 of the FCCC and Article 19 of the Kyoto Protocol contain similar wording.

The number of cases brought under dispute settlement proceedings is still very limited, especially considering the compliance problems with most environmental treaties. The International Court of Justice has so far never dealt with a purely environmental conflict.[34] Conflicts under dispute settlement proceedings mostly involve either trade relationships or territorial disputes. One of the reasons for the limited use of dispute settlement instruments is that these procedures are characterized by an adversarial relationship between the parties, so they are only used as a last resort. States are rarely willing to risk their relationship with other sovereign international actors by openly challenging them. As stated above, even in a close community of states such as the EU, the state complaints procedure under Article 227 of the treaty establishing the European Community (EC Treaty) has rarely been used. Not only are traditional dispute settlement procedures rarely used, they are also considered less effective and appropriate in environmental treaties. The result of noncompliance with environmental treaties is often damage to the global commons in general, affecting all states rather than one or several well-identified parties.

The ineffectiveness of dispute settlement proceedings in international environmental agreements has led to the development of a new system for responding to noncompliance, called noncompliance procedures (NCPs). Such procedures, rather than "punishing" noncompliance, are aimed at finding ways to facilitate compliance by the state that is in breach of its obligations. They provide a political framework for "amicable" responses to noncompliance that cannot be considered "wrongful." This tendency to use NCPs reflects the new managerial approach, which no longer assumes that noncompliance is the result of a willful desire to violate.

One of the consequences of shifting from an adversarial approach to a more managerial approach is that sanctions play only a minor role in the noncompliance response system. Three categories of sanctions can be distinguished: treaty-based sanctions, membership sanctions, and unilateral sanctions.[35] The latter category of unilateral sanctions is now severely restricted under international law. As discussed above, resort to the use of military force is exceptional. Trade sanctions are increasingly difficult to invoke under the rapidly developing international trade regimes. Treaty-based sanctions have not proven very popular, which can be explained by the political difficulties involved in the use of such a system. The European Union may, however, be an exception to this. Since November 1993, the European Commission (which supervises the application of the EC Treaty) has had the competence to ask for the imposition of a financial penalty upon a member state that is in breach of its obligations (Article 228 of the EC Treaty). The commission has initiated a number of cases in which it has asked that a penalty be imposed on a member state. Although such a penalty has been imposed in only one instance,[36] this provision has had an important preventive effect, as member states now remedy their violation before the final court decision.

Sanctions against states party to an international treaty, including expulsion or suspension of rights and privileges, are also not considered an effective response in the case of noncompliance with an environmental treaty, since one of the aims of these treaties is to achieve global membership. (See the box on noncompliance procedures of the Montreal Protocol.)

Toward Comprehensive Noncompliance Response Systems

In this chapter we have given an overview of the new approaches to compliance with international environmental treaties that have been developed since the beginning of the 1990s. We have observed a clear shift from the "old" approach, including dispute settlement proceedings and sanctions in treaties, to the "managerial" approach, which tries to use a more comprehensive system of different methods for solving compliance problems. Increasingly, more recent treaties have included a comprehensive combination of different instruments for responding to noncompliance. These systems, also referred to as comprehensive

---

Noncompliance Procedures:
The Montreal Protocol and the Kyoto Protocol

The more recent environmental treaties have new noncompliance procedures, often side by side with the traditional dispute settlement procedures. A prime example of a well-functioning noncompliance procedure is the one set up under Article 8 of the Montreal Protocol. This article states that the parties to the protocol "shall consider and approve procedures and institutional mechanisms for determining noncompliance with the provisions of this Protocol and for treatment of Parties found to be in noncompliance."

At the Copenhagen meeting in November 1992 the Meeting of the Parties adopted the procedure under this article. An Implementation Committee was set up, consisting of ten representatives elected by the Meeting of the Parties, based on equitable geographical distribution. Although under the noncompliance procedure parties can also submit reservations regarding another party's implementation of its obligations under the protocol, this adversarial action has in practice not become the main function of the procedure. The focus has instead been on the nonadversarial functions. The procedure allows states, when they believe they are unable to comply with their obligations, to report this inability to the Secretariat and the Implementation Committee. The Implementation Committee also discusses the general quality and reliability of the data contained in the member states' reports. The Implementation Committee, meeting three to four times a year, has, in fact, assumed a very active role in improving the quality and reliability of the data reported by the member states and, in a cooperative sphere, has sought solutions for parties with administrative, structural, and financial difficulties.

The noncompliance procedure under the Montreal Protocol has served as an important source of inspiration for the development of the compliance regime under the Kyoto Protocol. This regime, which was finalized at the FCCC meeting in Marrakesh in 2001 (COP-7), will have both a facilitative and an enforcement branch. The enforcement branch will determine whether a country has met its emissions target and as a result of this determination apply the consequences for non-compliance that were agreed between countries at COP-7 if this is not the case. The mandate of the facilitative branch is based on the nonadversarial role that the Compliance Committee of the Montreal Protocol has assumed in practice. The facilitative branch will have the task of assisting all countries in their implementation of the protocol.[a]

---

[a] See Xueman Wang and Glenn Wiser, "The Implementation and Compliance Regimes under the Climate Change Convention and Its Kyoto Protocol," *RECIEL* 11, no.2 (2002): 181–198.

noncompliance response systems, contain not only methods to sanction violations but also, and perhaps more importantly, methods to facilitate compliance,
improve transparency and reporting procedures, and prevent violations.[37]

The various capacities of states can be taken into account in the design of
the primary rule system by allowing financial or technology transfer mechanisms. These differing capacities can also be taken into account in the noncompliance response system. The fact that self-reporting of noncompliance
should not immediately result in "negative" sanctions but can lead to actual
support to remedy incapacity can, in turn, also increase the reporting record.
Although the managerial approach is proving very successful in treaties such
as the Vienna Convention and the Montreal Protocol, one should not forget
that we are only at the beginning of new efforts to find solutions to compliance problems. The flexible mechanisms under the Kyoto Protocol, for
instance, are still to be tested. In many other areas it remains difficult to reach
any international consensus at all on the protection of our global environment.

International environmental law is increasingly moving from a phase in
which the emphasis was on the adoption of standards to one in which the
focus is on the implementation of and actual compliance with these standards. One should not forget, however, that it is especially in the phase of
adoption that a well-designed noncompliance response system can prove
decisive in getting states to agree to new commitments.

Notes

1. United Kingdom, House of Lords, Select Committee on the European Communities, "Implementation and Enforcement of Environmental Legislation," Session
   1991–1992, 9th report, HL paper 53-I, March 10, 1992, sec. 39.
2. Harold K. Jacobson and Edith Brown Weiss, "Strengthening Compliance with
   International Environmental Accords: Preliminary Observations, from a Collaborative Project," *Global Governance* 1 (1995): 119–148. The authors rightly point to the
   fact that there are very few studies of compliance with international environmental
   treaties and even fewer studies that focus on factors at the national level that affect
   compliance. Their cross-treaty and cross-country evaluation of compliance is an
   important exception. See also Ronald B. Mitchell, "Compliance Theory: An
   Overview," in *Improving Compliance with International Environmental Law,* ed.
   James Cameron, Jacob Werksman, and Peter Roderick (London: Earthscan, 1996),
   3–28; and David G. Victor, Kal Raustiala, and Eugene B. Skolnikoff, eds., *The
   Implementation and Effectiveness of International Environmental Commitments: Theory
   and Practice* (Cambridge: MIT Press, 1998).
3. Jacobson and Brown Weiss, "Strengthening Compliance," 124.
4. Article 227 of the treaty establishing the European Community, one of the treaties
   forming the basis of the EU, contains the possibility of one or more member states
   bringing another member state before the European Court of Justice. Since the
   founding of the European Community in 1958, this procedure has been used only
   four times. One example is the Court's judgment in the fisheries conflict between
   France and the United Kingdom (Case 141/78). In this case the UK was held to have
   breached EC law when searching a French trawler and convicting its master.
5. This new idea is probably best formulated by Abraham Chayes and Antonia Handler-
   Chayes, *The New Sovereignty: Compliance with International Regulatory Agreements*
   (Cambridge: Harvard University Press, 1995); see especially chap. 1.

6. For a review of the early literature on regimes, see Marc A. Levy, Oran R. Young, and Michael Zürn, "The Study of International Regimes," *European Journal of International Relations* (1995): 267–330. See also Oran Young, ed., *The Effectiveness of International Environmental Regimes* (Cambridge: MIT Press, 1999).

7. Chayes and Handler-Chayes, *New Sovereignty*, 27.

8. Articles 2 (3) and 2 (4), in combination with Articles 42 and 51 of the UN Treaty.

9. Chayes and Handler-Chayes, *New Sovereignty*, 22–28.

10. For a comparison of these two cases, see David Downie, "Road Map or False Trail: Evaluating the Precedence of the Ozone Regime as Model and Strategy for Global Climate Change," *International Environmental Affairs* 7, no. 4 (fall 1995): 321–345.

11. Examples of this can be found in European environmental law. See Michael Faure and Jürgen Lefevere, "The Draft Directive on Integrated Pollution Prevention and Control: An Economic Perspective," *European Environmental Law Review* 5 (April 1996): 112–122.

12. See, with respect to nuclear accidents, Organization for Economic Cooperation and Development, *Liability and Compensation for Nuclear Damage: An International Overview* (Paris: OECD, 1994); Michael Faure and Göran Skogh, "Compensation for Damages Caused by Nuclear Accidents: A Convention as Insurance," *Geneva Papers on Risk and Insurance* 17 (October 1992): 499–513; J. Deprimoz, "Regime juridique des assurances contre les risques nucléaires," *JurisClasseur* 555 (1995): 1; with respect to civil liability for marine oil pollution, see Michael Faure and Günter Heine, "The Insurance of Fines: The Case of Oil Pollution," *Geneva Papers on Risk and Insurance* 17 (January 1991), 39–58; and for recent developments, see E. H. P. Brans, "Liability for Ecological Damage under the 1992 Protocols to the Civil Liability Convention and the Fund Convention and the Oil Pollution Act of 1990," *Tijdschrift voor Milieuaansprakelijkheid* 94, nos. 3, 4 (1994): 61–67 and 85–91.

13. "The developed country Parties and other Parties included in Annex I commit themselves specifically as provided for in the following: (a) Each of these Parties shall adopt national policies and take corresponding measures on the mitigation of climate change, by limiting its anthropogenic emissions of greenhouse gases and protecting and enhancing its greenhouse gas sinks and reservoirs. These policies and measures will demonstrate that developed countries are taking the lead in modifying longer-term trends in anthropogenic emissions consistent with the objective of the Convention, recognizing that the return by the end of the present decade to earlier levels of anthropogenic emissions of carbon dioxide and other greenhouse gases not controlled by the Montreal Protocol would contribute to such modification, and taking into account the differences in these Parties' starting points and approaches, economic structures and resource bases, the need to maintain strong and sustainable economic growth, available technologies and other individual circumstances, as well as the need for equitable and appropriate contributions by each of these Parties to the global effort regarding that objective. These Parties may implement such policies and measures Jointly with other Parties and may assist other Parties in contributing to the achievement of the objective of the Convention."

14. For details, see Jacob Werksman, "Designing a Compliance System for the UN Framework Convention on Climate Change," in Cameron, Werksman and Roderick, *Improving Compliance with International Environmental Law*, 85–112; and see Philippe Sands, *Principles of International Environmental Law*, vol. 1, *Frameworks, Standards and Implementation* (Manchester, England: Manchester University Press, 1995), 217–280.

15. For a more in-depth background on the Kyoto Protocol mechanisms, see Sebastian Oberthür and Hermann Ott, *The Kyoto Protocol: International Climate Policy for the 21st Century* (Berlin: Springer, 1999).

16. Jacobson and Brown Weiss, "Strengthening Compliance," 126.

17. Richard Benedick, *Ozone Diplomacy, New Directions in Safeguarding the Planet* (Cambridge: Harvard University Press, 1998); Benedick describes this process of decision making under scientific uncertainty.
18. The IPCC published its Third Assessment Report in 2001. This report is available from the IPCC's Web site: http://www.ipcc.ch.
19. Several varieties of reporting and data collection are discussed by Chayes and Handler-Chayes, *New Sovereignty*, 154–173.
20. Gro Harlem Brundtland, "The Road from Rio," *Technology Review* 96 (1993): 63.
21. Mitchell, "Compliance Theory," 14; and Lynne M. Jurgielewicz, *Global Environmental Change and International Law* (Lanham, Md.: University Press of America, 1996), 113.
22. Jacobson and Brown Weiss, "Strengthening Compliance," cite the important role of the Brazilian president Fernando Collor in the UNCED conference (142). President Bill Clinton played an important role in Kyoto in December 1997, contributing to the adoption of the Kyoto Protocol.
23. Ibid., 129.
24. Mitchell, "Compliance Theory," 24.
25. Jacobson and Brown Weiss, "Strengthening Compliance," 143; and Oran Young, *International Governance: Protecting the Environment in a Stateless Society* (Ithaca, N.Y.: Cornell University Press, 1994), 110–115.
26. Young, *International Governance*, 37–39.
27. Mitchell, "Compliance Theory," 15.
28. Ibid., 11.
29. For a general discussion of the role of NGOs in international environmental law, see The Foundation for International Environmental Law and Development (FIELD) and Ecologic, *Participation of Non-Governmental Organisations in International Environmental Governance: Legal Basis and Practical Experience* (German Umweltbundesamt, June 2002), available from the Web site http://www.field.org.uk/tisd_11.php. See also Chayes and Handler-Chayes, *New Sovereignty*, 250–270. See also chapter 5, "The Role of Environmental NGOs in International Regimes," in this book.
30. See, for example, James Cameron, "Compliance, Citizens and NGO's," in Cameron, Werksman, and Roderick, *Improving Compliance with International Environmental Law*, 29–42, and, more particularly, see the book review by Oran R. Young in *International Environmental Affairs* 9 (winter 1997): 84.
31. Mitchell, "Compliance Theory," 9.
32. For further details, see Jacobson and Brown Weiss, "Strengthening Compliance," 129 and 140–142.
33. Patricia Birnie and Alan Boyle, *International Law and the Environment* (Oxford: Oxford University Press, 2002), 224–226.
34. A recent example of a case that does not explicitly deal with environmental issues, but one in which the environment plays an important role, is the one concerning the Gabcikovo-Nagymaros Dam on the Danube River, on which the International Court of Justice pronounced judgment on September 25, 1997.
35. Chayes and Handler-Chayes, *New Sovereignty*, 30.
36. *Commission v. Greece* (Case C387/97).
37. Mitchell, "Compliance Theory," 14; Chayes and Handler-Chayes, *New Sovereignty*, 25; Werksman, "Designing a Compliance System," 115–116.

PART III. IMPLEMENTING GLOBAL POLICY: CASES AND CONTROVERSIES IN SUSTAINABLE DEVELOPMENT

10

Understanding United States Unilateralism: Domestic Sources of U.S. International Environmental Policy

Elizabeth R. DeSombre

If we are to err in designing measures to protect the ozone layer, let us, conscious of our responsibility to future generations, err on the side of caution.

Richard Benedick, head U.S. negotiator, Montreal Protocol[1]

We must be very careful not to take actions that could harm consumers. . . . This is especially true given the incomplete state of scientific knowledge on the causes of, and solutions to, global climate change.

President George W. Bush, in a letter to Senator Charles Hagel[2]

The United Nations Conference on Environment and Development, held in Rio de Janeiro in 1992, is often considered an important turning point for the United States' pattern of nonparticipation in international environmental politics. Of the two binding agreements signed there, the United States signed but refused to ratify the Convention on Biological Diversity (and has not signed its Biosafety Protocol), and signed and ratified the United Nations Framework Convention on Climate Change (UNFCCC) but refused to ratify the Kyoto Protocol to that agreement, negotiated later, which contained actual abatement obligations. This latter process gained the United States notoriety, as U.S. president George W. Bush indicated a desire to "unsign" the agreement.[3] U.S. unwillingness to participate delayed the protocol's entry into force and weakened the agreement, since without the United States it needed the participation of almost all industrialized countries, many of which also refused to go along until their obligations were made more flexible and less onerous.

Refusal by the United States to participate in important international environmental agreements did not begin in 1992, however. Its lack of ratification of the Basel Convention on the Control of Transboundary Movements of Hazardous Wastes and Their Disposal (1989) and of related treaties on transborder movement of other toxic materials suggests that the

181

United States managed to avoid important global environmental obligations before Rio. (Its public and sudden refusal to ratify the United Nations Convention on the Law of the Sea [1982], at least partially for reasons relating to how it addressed access to resources of the deep seabed, extends this pattern farther back in time.) The recent unilateral behavior of the United States is not restricted to issues of environmental cooperation. Apart from broader difficulties with the United Nations over Iraq, the United States has refused to join the International Criminal Court, to sign the Convention on the Prohibition of the Use, Stockpiling, Production and Transfer of Anti-Personnel Mines and on Their Destruction (1997), or to ratify the Comprehensive Test Ban Treaty (1996), to name just a few recent issues.

The recent unwillingness of the United States to lead—and often even to join—efforts at multilateral environmental cooperation in the post–cold war world thus seems overdetermined: it is neither an entirely new phenomenon nor one restricted to environmental issues. It is an essential trend to recognize, however, especially given a U.S. history of strong domestic environmental action, previous leadership on global environmental issues, and the U.S. contribution to global environmental problems. When does the United States lead in addressing global environmental problems, and when does it refuse even to go along?

This chapter examines the U.S. pattern of participation in or avoidance of multilateral environmental cooperation. It examines whether U.S. actions can be explained by the country's broader characteristics, its ideological goals, the degree of uncertainty about environmental problems, the ecological vulnerability of the United States, the costs of taking action, or the domestic political power of industrialized actors likely to bear those costs.

Ultimately, the most promising explanation for the pattern of U.S. unilateralism on international environmental issues involves characteristics of the domestic political system and the way in which national policy-making relates to international negotiations. The issues on which the United States leads internationally are those it has previously regulated domestically. The intersection between domestic politics and international relations can go a long way toward explaining what we see, and what we should expect, from U.S. environmental leadership. It also explains why, despite the particularly unilateralist bent of the George W. Bush administration, the actions and the party of the president matter much less than the regulatory processes undertaken by Congress in providing an understanding of U.S. environmental leadership or the lack thereof. If we want to understand what the United States has chosen to pursue or avoid internationally in terms of environmental policy, we need to look at what it has regulated or shunned domestically.

U.S. Environmental Leadership

The United States has traditionally been among the countries with the strictest environmental regulations on the domestic level and has often been a leader internationally on environmental issues. It has a reputation for "taking environmental treaties seriously," [4] suggesting that when it does participate in multilateral environmental efforts, it tends to implement the relevant provisions domestically and comply with the obligations of the treaties. Moreover, it has been the driving force behind the negotiations to address a number of international environmental problems. This leadership can be seen in the context of U.S. actions to protect endangered species internationally and to protect the atmosphere from substances that deplete the ozone layer.

Endangered Species

The United States was one of the principal proponents of international action to protect endangered species, beginning in 1900 with the Lacey Act, which prohibited trafficking in animals taken illegally in their country of origin as well as those killed in violation of any U.S. or international law.[5] Domestically the U.S. Endangered Species Act (and its predecessors) restricted the taking, importing, exporting, or selling of species listed as endangered and adopted a variety of increasingly strict regulations to protect species wherever they were found. Early versions of this legislation also called on the United States to negotiate binding international agreements to protect endangered species worldwide.[6] The United States followed this concern by working for international protection of endangered species via the Convention on International Trade in Endangered Species of Wild Fauna and Flora (CITES) (1973). U.S. participation was important in other early international negotiations to address endangered species, such as the Ramsar Convention on Wetlands of International Importance Especially as Waterfowl Habitat (1972) and in the creation of a moratorium on commercial whaling—agreed to in 1982 and in effect beginning in the 1985–1986 whaling season—under the International Convention for the Regulation of Whaling (1949).[7]

Ozone Depletion

U.S. leadership on global atmospheric issues was evident in its response to ozone depletion. U.S. involvement with this issue stemmed from scientific research undertaken in the early 1960s to ascertain whether a planned fleet of supersonic aircraft would harm the ozone layer. Much of the other early scientific work on sources of possible harm to the ozone layer also took place in the United States.[8] The United States also took the lead in domestic regulation, including in the 1977 Clean Air Act amendments the requirement that U.S. industry phase out use of chlorofluorocarbons (the main substances implicated in ozone depletion) in nonessential aerosols, beginning in 1978.[9] The United States hosted the 1977 International Conference on the Ozone Layer, the first intergovernmental discussion of the problem of ozone depletion, which produced the World Plan of Action on the Ozone Layer.

Although the United States resisted meaningful international regulation during the period shortly following that conference, by the early 1980s it had joined with the Nordic countries, Austria, Canada, and Switzerland in support of deep cuts in international production and use of ozone-depleting substances. This coalition supported such measures in the negotiation of the 1985 Vienna Convention for the Protection of the Ozone Layer. But staunch opposition from European countries, which had not yet taken any action to regulate their domestic production of ozone-depleting substances, resulted in a framework treaty that simply supported the principle of ozone-layer protection without requiring substantive abatement obligations.

The United States came out as a clear leader, however, in the negotiations for binding reductions of emissions of ozone-depleting substances that resulted in the 1987 Montreal Protocol on Substances that Deplete the Ozone Layer. U.S. proposals began with a freeze on the use of harmful substances and then suggested a range of further reductions. Along with its negotiating partners (and against the European Community), the United States also insisted that all known ozone-depleting substances be regulated under the protocol. In addition, several bills introduced in Congress in 1987 would have prohibited imports of ozone-depleting substances and products that contained them or were made from them if the exporting countries did not adopt domestic measures to protect the ozone layer. (This legislation was abandoned when the protocol was successfully negotiated.)[10]

Lack of Leadership

More recent U.S. refusals to ratify the major international initiatives to address global issues such as climate change and biodiversity protection suggest that the United States is often unwilling to exercise leadership or even participate in some multilateral environmental efforts. In addition to these two issues, it is useful to examine U.S. refusals (some earlier than the Rio conference) to accept a variety of efforts to regulate the international movement of hazardous chemicals and waste.

Climate Change

The U.S. position on global efforts to mitigate climate change (global warming) is the most obvious evidence of the country's recalcitrance. The United States participated in the negotiation of the United Nations Framework Convention on Climate Change, signed at the Earth Summit in Rio in 1992. Its main goals for the negotiation, however, were to avoid the creation of binding targets and timetables for reduction of greenhouse gas emissions (which European states were willing to negotiate) and to ensure that all major greenhouse gases (rather than just CO_2) be included in any agreement. The U.S. goals were accepted by the other major negotiators because they did not want to create an agreement without U.S. participation.[11] The Convention nevertheless lays out a potentially important set of principles that member states accept by ratification. The agreement's objective is to stabilize atmospheric greenhouse gas concentrations "at a level that would prevent dangerous anthropogenic interference with the climate system," though that level is not specified. The agreement acknowledges the use of the precautionary principle, indicating that lack of full certainty is not to be used to postpone taking action to address the issue, and specifies that "the developed country Parties should take the lead in combating climate change and the adverse effects thereof." [12] The Senate ratified this agreement quickly,[13] and the United States has lived up to its implementation obligations by reporting on its emissions and policies pertaining to climate change.

U.S. interaction with the Kyoto Protocol—the agreement that requires cuts in emissions of greenhouse gases from developed country parties—has been less productive from the perspective of international environmental cooperation. The United States did take part in the negotiation of the agreement. Tim Wirth, the U.S. undersecretary of state for global affairs, suggested during negotiations in 1996 that "a realistic, verifiable, and medium-term emissions target" should be set, making the United States the first major UNFCCC party to call for binding reductions.[14] In general, the United States advocated in the negotiation process that the greatest degree of flexibility (from trade in emissions, joint implementation, and the counting of "sinks" for greenhouse gases) be included, and most of these issues were written into the agreement largely the way the United States wanted. The one exception was the actual abatement obligations. U.S. president Clinton originally set the U.S. negotiating position at a freeze at 1990 emissions levels by 2008. In the agreement as negotiated in Kyoto, the United States was persuaded to accept a greenhouse gas emissions reduction of 7 percent below 1990 levels.[15]

Several months before the final negotiation at which the agreement was to be signed, the U.S. Senate passed what came to be known as the Byrd-Hagel resolution. It indicated the Senate's intention not to ratify any agreement that would require abatement obligations from industrialized countries unless it simultaneously "mandates new specific scheduled commitments to limit or reduce greenhouse gas emissions for developing country parties within the same compliance period." This resolution passed by a vote of 95–0.[16] The Senate's resolution did not succeed in influencing the agreement's treatment of developing countries, as the entire Kyoto negotiation process had been premised on a lack of specific abatement obligations for developing countries in the first commitment period. It did, however, ensure that the Clinton administration, despite having signed the agreement, could not realistically submit it to the Senate for ratification.

Congress has also influenced the extent and content of domestic U.S. action in the absence of the Kyoto Protocol. One congressional approach was to craft provisions that would have encouraged voluntary emissions reductions by granting credit to industries that early on undertook reductions in the event that later policies required them. In the absence of such policies, those who took early action might have more difficulty than their competitors in further increasing their energy efficiency if specific U.S. policies were passed. Several similar bills for this purpose were introduced in the 105th and 106th Congress but were defeated. Though some argued that these efforts were not strong enough to address the climate problem, the real opposition came from those who opposed any legislative measures to encourage the reduction of greenhouse gas emissions. Former presidential candidate Jack Kemp, for example, argued in opposition to these measures that we must "guard against a milder version of the Kyoto treaty that would serve the same purpose, offering concessions to companies that would acquiesce in creating the biggest global regulatory regime yet conceived." [17]

In reaction to efforts to encourage voluntary measures, other members of Congress introduced bills to forbid any action on climate change. Representative David McIntosh, R-Ind., proposed H.R. 2221, which would not only have prohibited the use of federal funds for advocating, developing, or implementing early credit systems for voluntary emissions reductions but would also have mandated that federal funds not be used "to propose or issue rules, regulations, decrees, or orders or for programs designed to implement, or in preparation to implement, the Kyoto Protocol" before the Senate ratified the agreement. While this legislation did not pass, it inhibited the creation of new policies to give credit for voluntary measures.[18] A more successful effort came from attaching a legislative rider to appropriations bills in 2000 and 2001. Representative Joseph Knollenberg, R-Mich., inserted language into these bills prohibiting the government from undertaking any action that would contribute to meeting the goals of the Kyoto Protocol before it had been ratified by the Senate.[19]

More recent efforts, however, have resulted in congressional proposals that the United States take domestic action, outside the Kyoto framework, to address its emissions of greenhouse gases. Senators Joseph Lieberman, D-Conn., and John McCain, R-Ariz., for example, introduced legislation in 2003 that would create a cap-and-trade system for greenhouse gases in the United States, with the objective of returning U.S. emissions by 2010 to what they had been in 2000.[20] As of early 2004, these efforts have garnered little support, leaving the United States without any government-supported emissions reduction plan and slim chances of supporting existing international measures.

At the same time, President George W. Bush accepted the need to address climate change in some way, even if it is not via the Kyoto Protocol. In 2003 he proposed reducing U.S. greenhouse gas intensity—decreasing the amount of greenhouse gas emissions required to produce a unit of GDP—by 18 percent by the next decade. And even without congressional authorization for voluntary initiatives, some industry actors are starting to reduce these emissions. The Energy Information Administration reported that, in 2001, 228 U.S. companies undertook more than 1,700 projects to reduce or sequester greenhouse gas emissions, amounting to more than 4 percent of total U.S. greenhouse gas emissions.[21] Perhaps the most innovative voluntary approach is the creation of the Chicago Climate Exchange, founded by thirteen major companies and the city of Chicago in 2003. These members, including DuPont, Ford, International Paper, and Motorola, have pledged to reduce their greenhouse gas emissions by 1 percent each year until 2006. The exchange allows members to sell emissions credits if they exceed that goal and to buy them if that is the easiest way to reach the goal.[22] The U.S. industries that have worked to change their behavior to reduce emissions of greenhouse gases, despite the lack of a requirement or even a set of government-induced incentives to do so, have concluded that it is in their interest to address this issue, most likely because they see the inevitability of obligations to address climate change.

It is certainly true that climate change provides an unusually difficult case for U.S. leadership; its emissions of greenhouse gases, both absolutely and on a per capita basis, are far higher than those of any other state. Certain demographic characteristics contribute to this high level of emissions, such as the large size of the country and the long distances people travel (particularly those without access to public transportation). The country's large size makes possible a number of individual choices, not only about commuting but also about the size and number of residential housing units, which increase greenhouse gas emissions. A tradition of low gasoline prices and easy access to fossil fuels has increased reliance on individual transportation and discouraged fuel efficiency and alternative energy generation. But the level of U.S. unwillingness to entertain domestic or international efforts to mitigate climate change, in conjunction with evidence of voluntary behavior on the part of industry, especially in the context of other reluctant environmental leadership, needs to be explained.

Biodiversity

The other main issue initiated at the 1992 Earth Summit in Rio on which the United States has resisted international action is biodiversity. In keeping with its history of concern about the protection of species, the United States helped launch the initial negotiations in the late 1980s. It became apprehensive, however, at the direction of the negotiations. In particular, the United States feared that the resulting treaty would require strengthening the U.S. Endangered Species Act and the conservation of wetlands, both of which the George H. W. Bush administration was trying to weaken. The United States was also concerned about the principle, favored by developing countries, of the equitable sharing of the benefits of biodiversity. This principle, as well as other fears about inadequate protection for intellectual property rights under the treaty, was of concern to the biotechnology and pharmaceutical industries within the United States. It was in response to these concerns that all references to "biosafety" (or efforts to limit the trade in genetically modified organisms) were omitted in the negotiated draft. [23] The United States announced, however, before the Rio conference, that it would not sign the Convention on Biological Diversity (CBD), even in this weakened form. President Bush indicated, in particular, that he was concerned about the treaty's possible impact on jobs in the United States.[24]

After Clinton was elected president at the end of 1992, a group of non-governmental organizations and biotechnology and pharmaceutical firms met on their own initiative for several months to determine whether there could be advantages to U.S. participation in the treaty.[25] This group eventually proposed that the United States sign the agreement but issue an interpretive statement providing its understanding of its obligations under the treaty. In particular, this group, which included major firms such as Merck and Genentech, concluded that the treaty would not create major economic difficulties in the near term, and that participating in the process might be better for the United States than remaining outside of it. At the same time, the United States conducted an interagency review that determined that the treaty could be implemented within the existing legal framework.[26] President Clinton signed the CBD in 1993 and sent it to the Senate for ratification, along with a letter of submittal that incorporated the interpretive language indicating that the treaty would not endanger essential patent protection or harm research or innovation by industry.

Ratification did not follow, however. Despite a vote of 16–3 by the Senate Committee on Foreign Relations in support of the treaty, a vote was not taken in the Senate in either 1993 or 1994, presumably because the Senate majority leader (George Mitchell, D-Maine) ascertained that the two-thirds majority needed for approval would not materialize. By the time the issue would have been considered in 1993, thirty-five Republican senators (one more than required to block ratification) had come out against the treaty. The reasons given for opposition were varied, including claims that the text was too vague; the treaty was unnecessary; it would hamper U.S. business interests or would commit the United States to transfers of funding and technology to developing countries.[27] With more recent Republican majorities in the Senate, the issue of ratification has not even been considered. The lack of ratification by the United States has reduced its role to that of an observer at Meetings of the Parties (although an observer whose interests are nevertheless influential) and in the negotiation of the protocol to the Convention.

Trade in Hazardous Wastes

The United States generates the overwhelming majority of hazardous wastes in the world, though much of it is disposed of within U.S. borders. Nevertheless, the approximately 1 percent of U.S. hazardous wastes that is traded marks it as a higher exporter of wastes, in terms of actual volume, than many other major countries.[28] The United States has signed, but refrained from ratifying, the main treaty to address trade in hazardous wastes, the Basel Convention on the Control of Transboundary Movements of Hazardous Wastes and Their Disposal (1989).

The United States was involved in the negotiation of the Basel Convention and used its role to weaken the proposed agreement. The treaty negotiation was an effort to make formal a set of nonbinding guidelines created by the United Nations Environment Programme (UNEP) governing council in 1987. Many states that were the recipients of hazardous wastes wanted the new binding agreement to go further and actually ban trade in hazardous wastes; concurrent discussions outside of the specific negotiations indicated that many European states were sympathetic to a stronger regulatory framework. The United States, however, served as the center of a coalition of developed states that refused to participate if such stringent regulations were enacted. As a result, the eventual treaty created a system that required states to be notified (and given the opportunity to refuse) before hazardous wastes were sent to them. It also included an agreement that hazardous wastes had to be disposed of in a manner that was environmentally sound, although that term was not defined.

The United States signed the agreement but did not immediately send it to the Senate for ratification. President Clinton announced his intention to submit the treaty for ratification in 1998, but it has still not been ratified. One of the difficulties for the United States in terms of contemplating implementation of this agreement is that the definition of hazardous waste under the Basel Convention is broader than under current U.S. domestic regulation, and industry groups oppose expanding current regulations.[29] Although the United States has reasonably strong existing controls on how it deals with hazardous wastes, these measures are in a different format (and thus regulate a somewhat different list of substances) than would be required under the Basel agreement.

In addition, the United States actively opposes an amendment to the Convention, referred to as the Basel Ban, which would end all such trade between rich and poor countries. During the negotiations on the ban the United States made a clear effort to defeat it, even though, as a non-party to the treaty, its direct forms of influence were limited. It nevertheless worked hard to convince individual states to take leadership positions opposing the ban and allocated funding for international meetings to help persuade others of its possible negative ramifications.[30] The ban ultimately was negotiated in the form of an amendment to the Convention, but it has experienced delays in entering into force. Some environmental nongovernmental organizations now actually discourage U.S. ratification of Basel if, as seems inevitable, it would happen without simultaneous ratification of the Ban amendment.[31] They fear that U.S. ratification of the agreement without the ban would allow the United States to work to undermine the ban and enable it to trade with other Basel members that have not accepted the ban.

The United States has also been slow to take action on two other treaties on toxic substances—the Stockholm Convention on Persistent Organic Pollutants (2001) and the Rotterdam Convention on the Prior Informed Consent Procedure for Certain Hazardous Chemicals and Pesticides in International Trade (1998) (see Chapter 7 for further discussion). Although President George W. Bush signed the Stockholm Convention and indicated an interest in ratifying it, the ratification process has been held up because some members of the Senate have expressed concern about the process that would be used to identify and potentially restrict additional chemicals under the treaty.

In the negotiations on what became the Rotterdam Convention, moving from a voluntary "prior informed consent" procedure to one that was mandatory for trade in hazardous chemicals and pesticides, the United States supported a proposal that increased the difficulty of including a chemical on the list. In place of a system where any chemical banned in one country would immediately trigger a PIC procedure, the chemical would need to be banned in two different countries representing two different regions, thereby preventing a chemical banned only in European countries from making the list.[32] Despite the inclusion of this U.S.-supported measure in the final version of the treaty, the United States has not ratified this agreement.

Understanding Unilateralism

What explains the variety of U.S. actions? In an examination of only the specific cases discussed here, several possible conclusions emerge about the determinants of U.S. international environmental leadership. These include a consistent ideological approach to international regulation or other elements of U.S. exceptionalism (including a general suspicion of multilateralism), the issue of uncertainty, the severity of the environmental problem for the United States, and the degree to which U.S. industry is impacted by proposed regulations. Certainly an underlying hypothesis is that the United States has become more unilateral in its actions in recent years, although this is not a sufficient explanation; one can point to earlier strong rejection of multilateral cooperation on environmental issues (such as the deep seabed issues in the Law of the Sea), as well as relatively recent U.S. willingness to cooperate on increasingly strict protection of the ozone layer. But to the extent that recent behavior indicates a trend, ascertaining the reasons behind this trend is nonetheless important.

Before examining a more specifically environmental hypothesis, it is worth exploring the possibility that there is a normative unity to the environmental goals the United States pursues or avoids internationally. There appear to be some ideological consistencies in the international environmental issues in which the United States has avoided serious international participation. Harold Jacobson argues that what the UNCBD, the Kyoto Protocol, and the Law of the Sea (three of the major international agreements that the United States has refused to ratify) have in common are specific provisions for redistributing the benefits of cooperation to developing countries.[33] The Kyoto Protocol eschews abatement obligations for developing countries but includes the promise of funding and technology transfer to them. The CBD requires that the profits and results from biotechnology development be shared with those states from which the biodiversity resources were obtained. The Law of the Sea created a deep seabed mining regime in which the benefits of such mining would explicitly be redistributed to developing countries.

Objections to these provisions were stated as the major impediments to U.S. participation in the agreements. These types of policies represent the approaches pursued by developing countries under the rubric of the "New International Economic Order" in the 1970s and 1980s. It is particularly telling that the United States participated actively in the negotiation of all of these agreements and, in the case of the Law of the Sea and the CBD, explicitly attempted to exclude these redistributive measures but failed. The analysis breaks down partly in the context of the Kyoto Protocol, however, since the United States did not actively push for developing country obligations. And, as Jacobson points out, the flexibility mechanisms the United States supported so strongly for the Kyoto Protocol would likely result in some level of income redistribution to developing countries;[34] developing countries would be able to receive funding for undertaking action that reduces global emissions of greenhouse gases. Moreover, other international agreements the United States has avoided, such as the Basel Convention, do not contain these redistributive elements, and some that the United States has joined do contain them, such as the Montreal Protocol (under which the United States is the largest contributor of funding). If ideology does not explain recalcitrance, what does?

A related explanation points to the general U.S. reluctance to accept international norms on a wide range of issues, from human rights to international security, with environment just one additional manifestation of this approach. Some identify this issue as "exceptionalism," focusing particularly on the idea of cultural relativism.[35] If the United States is indeed exceptional, its reluctance to take on unnecessary foreign entanglements may be one side effect of this phenomenon. A related issue is the possibility that the United States, as the most powerful state internationally in the post–cold war era, knows that it does not need international cooperation to guard its interests. However, this seems an unlikely explanation for issues concerning the global environmental commons, as states cannot protect themselves unilaterally. In any case, as Andrew Moravcsik points out, identifying exceptionalism, even where relevant, does not explain it.[36]

When the United States chooses not to take action on a given environmental issue such as global climate change, uncertainty is often given as a reason for inaction. U.S. reticence on climate change frequently mentions incomplete knowledge. On the face of it, this explanation for U.S. behavior seems implausible. Though genuine uncertainty may exist on many of these issues, the United States was willing to act in the face of uncertainty on ozone depletion, and few would argue that U.S. inaction on biodiversity can be primarily attributed to lack of information. Moreover, other states have access to the same degree of information on these issues that the United States has, yet make different decisions about how to act internationally. That may not damn this explanation; some have suggested that the United States handles uncertainty in the political process in ways that may be different from other states.

In particular, the United States has a different approach to risk than others do. Sheila Jasanoff has compared the different ways that states approach risk on the domestic level and notes that the European policy process is more cautious about accepting risk than that of the United States.[37] This finding would not seem to explain U.S. reluctance on the international level on issues pertaining to risk (such as climate change and biodiversity or biosafety), especially when the main proponents of international cooperation on these issues are European states. Jasanoff addresses this issue with respect to U.S. responses to climate change, suggesting that because the scientific community in the country does not have a clear hierarchy, when there are political actors that profit from avoiding action, they can make use of existing uncertainty, implicitly painting the taking of action as riskier than doing nothing. Lawrence Susskind argues that the United States uses scientific evidence to support preferred international action, but "when we prefer to take a different political course we attack the available data as insufficient regardless of the strength of the worldwide scientific consensus." [38] In this context, uncertainty is an excuse but not an explanation.

A common explanation for the leadership behavior of states on environmental problems is the extent to which states are likely to be harmed by them. Detlef Sprinz and Tapani Vaahtoranta argue that "the worse the state of the environment, the greater the incentives to reduce the ecological vulnerability of a state." [39] They suggest that states will be "leaders" on international environmental issues when they are particularly affected by the issue environmentally but will either resist action or simply go along when their ecological vulnerability is low. It is true that the United States is less likely to be harmed by issues such as climate change or biodiversity loss than are states that are more generally dependent on land-based resources and less able to adapt to environmental change. However, a simple comparison of U.S. vulnerability on even the issues addressed here does not explain why the United States was more willing to act on ozone depletion than on climate change (the latter certainly has a bigger environmental and economic impact on the country than the former), or less willing to act on biodiversity protection than on trade in endangered species.

Another plausible interpretation of U.S. decisions on environmental issues is that it depends on the extent to which domestic industry bears a cost from taking action to address the issue. Sprinz and Vaahtoranta also posit that the costs of abatement play an important role in determining the extent of state leadership on the international level. Although they examine cases where restricting emissions is the abatement cost, it could be argued that the predicted costs of international action on an issue more broadly can play an important role in determining what a state—in this instance, the United States—will choose to undertake internationally.

This logic fits well with anecdotal evidence and theories about the particularly important role U.S. businesses play in politics within the country. It also appears consistent with U.S. avoidance of action on climate change. Sebastian Oberthür and Hermann Ott argue that the U.S. position on climate change can be understood on the basis of the status of the United States as the world's largest producer of coal, oil, and gas.[40] While estimates of the cost to the United States of implementing the Kyoto Protocol vary widely (and have some correlation with the political position of those making the estimates), it is clear that addressing climate change could impose great cost and disruption, at least initially, on the U.S. way of life. A Department of Energy report comparing studies predicting the costs of implementing Kyoto obligations (though not accounting for emissions trading or other flexibility mechanisms) found estimates ranging from $91 billion to $311 billion.[41] (It is also worth noting that the energy intensity of the U.S. economy[42] provides additional opportunities for behavior change not available to other states.)

On the other hand, a straight comparison of the costliness of regulatory action does not predict the U.S. pattern of international leadership on environmental issues. While some in the U.S. biotechnology and pharmaceutical industries feared the economic cost of the Convention on Biological Diversity and urged President George H. W. Bush not to sign it, other similar industries had determined within the space of the year that the economic costs would not be large. Similarly, U.S. action on ozone depletion was likely to be at least as costly (and these costs were more clearly known in advance) as the potential cost of protecting biodiversity. And if one considers the cost to the United States of implementing the provisions of CITES, which includes a set of border controls that would otherwise not be required, they are likewise larger than might have been the case for biodiversity.

A related view is that what matters is the political power of industry within the United States on a given issue. Even if the cost to the country as a whole of an abatement measure for a given environmental problem is not enormous (or is not the main basis on which decisions about international action are made), the cost to the industry that has to adapt is meaningful to that industry. The extent of its influence on the U.S. political process may then have an impact on the willingness of the United States to take a stand internationally. Detlef Sprinz and Martin Weiß argue that industry opposition to the reduction of greenhouse gas emissions had a disproportionate impact on the U.S. negotiating process on the UNFCCC.[43] We would need to come up with a more sophisticated explanation, however, for what causes this disproportionate impact on policymaking and how to generalize when and how it will affect U.S. international environmental actions.

Domestic Politics and International Unilateralism

A more nuanced view of the extent to which U.S. industry will be able to marshal domestic political efforts to avoid international commitments would focus on specific aspects of the domestic political process that allow those opposing international environmental leadership to have influence. One argument made on a different issue is that the United States has a set of decentralized political institutions that "empower small veto groups."[44] Peter Cowhey has suggested that "national politicians have been unlikely to accept any global regime that fails to reinforce the preferred domestic regime." [45] Kal Raustiala points out that states rarely create completely new domestic regulatory structures to address international issues, relying instead on existing institutional structures domestically. That observation suggests that how domestic institutions are structured "influences what can be implemented, and often what is negotiated." [46] This explanation may help us identify either domestic structural determinants of U.S. global environmental leadership or simply content-based approaches to evaluating the likelihood of eventual U.S. international action on an issue.

The United States has an admirable tradition of accepting only those international environmental obligations that it intends to comply with—unlike some states, including the European Union, that are more likely to see commitments as goals. Other states (such as the former Soviet Union) frequently accept obligations they have no intention of complying with or know they will be incapable of fulfilling in the near future.[47] This propensity may influence the degree to which the United States is willing to take on obligations, limiting commitment to those it intends to comply with. Structural constraints only serve to magnify this tendency.

Structurally, the separation of powers between the executive and legislative branches of government and the constitutional requirement that the Senate must ratify treaties by a two-thirds majority can be seen as hindering international environmental action under certain circumstances. Although most countries have a domestic ratification process for treaties, the U.S. barrier is doubly high; it requires not only approval of the president but also a supermajority vote in the Senate, which is a separate branch of government. Many other advanced industrialized democracies operate under parliamentary systems in which the head of government is a member of the majority (or largest) party, and thus treaties submitted to the parliament for ratification by the prime minister are likely to be accepted. Some have noted that the willingness of Congress to reassert its control over foreign policy increased in the post–cold war era, when the need for strong executive leadership lessened.[48] According to this explanation, the two branches of government may be at odds about what a policy should be, resulting in a situation in which the president pushes an international approach that Congress refuses to go along with. The Senate is particularly prone to economic pressure from special interest groups. Each state is represented by two senators concerned about the issues that matter to their particular state to a greater degree than those that affect the country as a whole. This focus is an avenue for industry's impact. This difference, however, may serve to explain increased U.S. reluctance on international environmental issues compared with other major industrialized states, but it cannot explain the various degrees of U.S. unilateralism on different environmental issues.

What is possible, however, is that the role of the Senate intersects with some characteristics of environmental issues to influence the likelihood of U.S. international leadership on a given issue. The Senate's consideration and adoption of the Byrd-Hagel resolution indicates the importance of the congressional role in addressing international environmental policy. The Senate took up this issue on its own, not only without direction from the executive branch but without making President Clinton aware, until the last minute, that such a debate would happen. At that point the White House could not hope to stop the adoption of the resolution and simply tried to moderate its language.[49] Senator Robert Byrd represents West Virginia, a major coal producer, and Senator Charles Hagel represents Nebraska, where agriculture, the most important economic sector, is highly mechanized and thus sensitive to the price of oil.[50]

What brings these explanations together is the process of domestic congressional regulation. One notable consistency in U.S. international environmental leadership is the extent to which the United States had already undertaken domestic regulatory action at the point at which such action was being pushed internationally. Harold Jacobson provides a telling description of the wave of U.S. multilateral environmental diplomacy in the 1970s: "[A]s soon as U.S. legislation designed to protect and enhance the environment was in place, the United States typically proposed that multilateral treaties be negotiated to achieve the same objective." [51] Note, for example, that a major concern in the U.S. decision about whether to sign or ratify the CBD was whether it could be implemented within the existing legal framework protecting endangered species and land resources. This understanding helps explain U.S. reluctance on climate change particularly well; the United States has no preexisting policy on domestic climate change mitigation and has traditionally rejected any sort of tax on energy. This reluctance has been particularly demonstrated in Congress. For example, the possibility that future expansion of the Stockholm Convention on Persistent Organic Pollutants could call for restricting or eliminating chemicals that the United States has not already banned domestically is a particular sticking point in the effort at Senate ratification.

This does not imply that U.S. industry is always cheerful about adopting international environmental regulations, but it does suggest that the existence of previous regulations on the domestic industry changes its interests internationally. The example of ozone depletion, a potentially costly regulatory issue with a reasonably high degree of uncertainty at the time of international regulation, is illustrative. The history of U.S. regulatory efforts in this area shows that producers and large consumers of CFCs fought initial regulatory efforts (and invoked scientific uncertainty as well as industrial cost as arguments against regulation), but industry eventually acquiesced to international regulation. The process began domestically, when consumer purchasing habits and pressure from domestic environmental organizations persuaded Congress to include a ban on CFCs in nonessential aerosols in the 1977 Clean Air Act amendments. That regulation, which the main producers of CFCs fought from the beginning (and attempted to get repealed after it had passed),[52] put CFC producers and consumers on notice that they would have to come up with alternatives for at least some of their activities. It also fundamentally changed their incentive structure (especially when they realized that increasingly severe domestic regulations were likely). They were then more likely to support international controls on CFCs, so that foreign industries with which they competed internationally would have to be bound by the same costly restrictions.

Conclusion

It is true that United States leadership (or even level of participation) in international environmental agreements has been mixed, and even can be seen as having declined in the last decade and a half. To attribute this trend simply to U.S. unilateral urges misses the opportunity to understand when and why the United States is more or less likely to lead internationally on environmental issues. Within a domestic framework that can make international participation difficult, it is nevertheless possible for the United States to exercise international leadership. It tends to do so on issues it has already addressed domestically, and where the form of the domestic regulation fits the format of the international regulation being considered. Under those circumstances, domestic opposition to international action is muted or even avoided. Domestic industries, which have disproportionate influence on the senators who have to vote for ratification of any international agreements, may not be additionally disadvantaged by new international regulations that mirror existing domestic ones, or they may even welcome regulations that restrict the actions of their international competitors.

The United States took an early lead in the domestic regulation of many environmental hazards in the 1960s and 1970s, and those regulations laid the groundwork for many international efforts to deal with the global aspects of these problems. It is thus no surprise that the United States would be both willing and able to lead globally in addressing them. To the extent that the United States has more recently ceased to be a domestic innovator on environmental policy in many issue areas, it is also no surprise that the country resists international action on newer international environmental issues. Although issues such as scientific uncertainty, the environmental problem's effect on the United States, or the costliness of regulatory solutions certainly contribute to the difficulty of international regulation, they may be particularly important at the level of domestic regulation. Those who would prefer that the United States lead internationally should perhaps focus their efforts on creating the domestic regulations that give it the incentive to do so.

The issue is rarely so clear-cut, however, and the links between domestic and international action are becoming more porous. The case of climate change particularly bears watching, as U.S. domestic industries are in some instances becoming the major proponents of U.S. action on climate change or are undertaking meaningful voluntary steps themselves to address the problem. The pattern we have traditionally seen, of U.S. action following only after domestic regulation, may be changing due to the more diffuse and complex environmental issues that are appearing on the international agenda. It may come to pass that U.S. domestic action on such issues as climate change happens in reverse, pushed by industry impacted by international regulation.

Notes

1. Quoted in Richard Benedick, *Ozone Diplomacy: New Directions in Safeguarding the Planet* (Cambridge: Harvard University Press, 1998), 4.
2. Julian Borger and Ian Black, "Bush Drops Pledge on Cutting CO_2," *Guardian*, March 15, 2001, 15.
3. Eric Planin, "U.S. Aims to Pull Out of Warming Treaty," *Washington Post*, March 28, 2001, A1. There is no provision under international law to "unsign" an agreement that has been signed, and withdrawal is possible only by a state bound by the treaty once it has entered into force.
4. Michael J. Glennon and Alison L. Stewart, "The United States: Taking Environmental Treaties Seriously," in *Engaging Countries*, ed. Edith Brown Weiss and Harold K. Jacobson (Cambridge: MIT Press, 1998), 197–213.
5. 16 U.S.C. 3372(a)(1)(1988).
6. The Endangered Species Conservation Act of 1969 called on the United States to seek "the signing of a binding international convention on the conservation of endangered species." P.L. 91-135 (Section 5).
7. It should be noted, however, that the United States is not a participant in the Bonn Convention on the Conservation of Migratory Species of Wild Animals (1979).
8. William C. Clark et al., "Acid Rain, Ozone Depletion, and Climate Change: An Historical Overview," in Social Learning Group, *Learning to Manage Global Environmental Risks*, vol. 1 (Cambridge: MIT Press, 2001), 35.
9. 43 *Federal Register* 11301; 43 *Federal Register* 11318.
10. Elizabeth R. DeSombre, *Domestic Sources of International Environmental Policy: Industry, Environmentalists, and U.S. Power* (Cambridge: MIT Press, 2000), 94.
11. William A. Nitze, "A Failure of Presidential Leadership," in *Negotiating Climate Change*, ed. Irving M. Mintzer and J. A. Leonard (Cambridge, England: Cambridge University Press, 1994), 188.
12. United Nations Framework Convention on Climate Change (1992), Articles 2 and 3.
13. U.S. Congress, Senate, 102d Cong., 2d sess. *Senate Congressional Record*, daily ed. October 1992, S.17, 156.
14. Michael Grubb with Christiaan Vrolijk and Duncan Brack, *The Kyoto Protocol* (London: Royal Institute of International Affairs, 1999), 54.
15. Kyoto Protocol (1997), Annex B.
16. U.S. Congress, Senate, 105th Cong., 1st sess. *Congressional Record*, daily ed. July 27, 1997, S8113–8138.
17. Jack Kemp and Fred L. Smith, Jr., "Beware of the Kyoto Compromise," *New York Times*, January 13, 1999, A19.
18. Kai S. Anderson, "The Climate Policy Debate in the U.S. Congress," in *Climate Change Policy*, ed. Stephen H. Schneider, Armin Rosencranz, and John O. Niles (Washington, D.C.: Island Press, 2002), 243.
19. Ibid., 244.
20. Joseph I. Lieberman and John McCain, "Tap U.S. Innovation to Ease Global Warming," *U.S. Department of State International Information Programs*, January 8, 2003; available at http://usinfo.state.gov/topical/global/climate/03010801.htm (accessed on April 1, 2003).
21. Jim Fuller, "U.S. Companies and States Launch Initiatives to Combat Climate Change," *U.S. Department of State International Information Programs;* available at http://usinfo.state.gov/topical/global/climate/03033101.htm (accessed on April 1, 2003).
22. Peter Behr and Eric Pianin, "Firms Start Trading Program for Greenhouse-Gas Emissions," *Washington Post*, January 17, 2003, A14.

23. Kal Raustiala, "The Domestic Politics of Global Biodiversity Protection in the United Kingdom and United States," in *The Internationalization of Environmental Protection,* ed. Miranda A. Schreurs and Elizabeth C. Economy (Cambridge, England: Cambridge University Press, 1997), 42–73. These were later included in a separate protocol.

24. Ann Devroy, "President Affirms Biodiversity Stance; Citing Jobs, Bush Firmly Rejects Treaty," *Washington Post,* June 8, 1992, A1.

25. Kal Raustiala, "Domestic Institutions and International Regulatory Cooperation: Comparative Responses to the Convention on Biological Diversity," *World Politics* 49, no. 4 (1997): 482–509.

26. Raustiala, "Domestic Politics," and Raustiala, "Domestic Institutions and International Regulatory Cooperation."

27. Robert L. Paarlberg, "Earth in Abeyance, Explaining Weak Leadership in U.S. International Environmental Policy," in *Eagle Adrift: American Foreign Policy at the End of the Century,* ed. Robert J. Lieber (New York: Longman, 1997), 135–160.

28. Marian A. L. Miller, *The Third World in Global Environmental Politics* (Boulder, Colo.: Lynne Rienner, 1995), 87–88.

29. Kate O'Neill, "Hazardous Waste Disposal," *Foreign Policy in Focus* 4, no. 1 (January 1999); available at http://www.fpif.org (accessed on April 29, 2003).

30. Jim Puckett, "The Basel Ban: A Triumph Over Business-As-Usual"; available at http://www.ban.org/about_basel_ban/jims_article.html (accessed on May 8, 2003).

31. See, for instance, the Basel Action Network: http://www.ban.org.

32. Kristin S. Schafer, "Global Toxics Treaties: U.S. Leadership Opportunity Slips Away," *Foreign Policy in Focus* 7, no. 11 (September 2002); available at http://www.fpif.org (accessed on May 7, 2003).

33. Harold K. Jacobson, "Climate Change, Unilateralism, Realism, and Two-Level Games," in *Multilateralism and U.S. Foreign Policy: Ambivalent Engagement,* ed. Shepard Forman and Stewart Patrick (Boulder, Colo.: Lynne Rienner, 2002), 428.

34. Ibid., 428.

35. David Forsythe, *The Internationalization of Human Rights* (Lexington, Mass.: Lexington Books, 1991).

36. Andrew Moravcsik, "Why Is U.S. Human Rights Policy So Unilateralist?" in Forman and Patrick, *Multilateralism and U.S. Foreign Policy: Ambivalent Engagement,* 435–476.

37. Sheila Jasanoff, "American Exceptionalism and the Political Acknowledgment of Risk," *Daedalus* 19, no. 4 (fall 1990): 395–406.

38. Lawrence E. Susskind, *Environmental Diplomacy: Negotiating More Effective Global Agreements* (Oxford: Oxford University Press, 1994), 65.

39. Detlef Sprinz and Tapani Vaahtoranta, "The Interest-Based Explanation of International Environmental Policy," *International Organization* 48, no. 1 (winter 1998): 77–105.

40. Sebastian Oberthür and Hermann E. Ott, *The Kyoto Protocol* (New York: Springer, 1999), 18.

41. Department of Energy, "Comparing the Cost Estimates for the Kyoto Protocol," Report No. SR/OIA/98-03 (1998); available at http://www.eia.doe.gov/oiaf/kyoto/cost.html (accessed on April 10, 2003).

42. For a discussion of energy intensity, see chap. 13.

43. Detlef Sprinz and Martin Weiß, "Domestic Politics and Global Climate Policy," in *International Relations and Global Climate Change,* ed. Urs Luterbacher and Detlef F. Sprinz (Cambridge: MIT Press, 2001), 67–94.

44. Andrew Moravcsik lists this as one of the four characteristics he sees as explaining U.S. unilateralism on international human rights issues. Moravcsik, "Why Is U.S. Human Rights Policy So Unilateralist?"

45. Peter F. Cowhey, "International Telecommunications Regime: The Political Roots of Regimes for High Technology," *International Organization* 44 (spring 1990): 171.

46. Raustiala, "Domestic Institutions," 487.

47. See, generally, Edith Brown Weiss and Harold K. Jacobson, eds., *Engaging Countries: Strengthening Compliance with International Environmental Accords* (Cambridge: MIT Press, 1998).
48. Stewart Patrick, "Multilateralism and Its Discontents: The Causes and Consequences of U.S. Ambivalence," in Forman and Patrick, *Multilateralism and U.S. Foreign Policy: Ambivalent Engagement,* 1–44.
49. Jacobson, "Climate Change, Unilateralism, Realism, and Two-Level Games," 442.
50. Ibid., 442.
51. Ibid., 415.
52. The main industry lobbying group, the Alliance for Responsible CFC Policy, did such things as draft legislation to be introduced into Congress to limit the EPA's ability to regulate ozone-depleting substances. "Congress Debates Depletion of Ozone in the Stratosphere," *Christian Science Monitor,* October 14, 1982, 19.

11

The European Union as an Environmental Governance System

Regina S. Axelrod, Norman J. Vig, and Miranda A. Schreurs

The creation of the European Union (EU) has transformed western Europe. The addition of ten new member states on May 1, 2004, advances the political integration of Europe even further. The objective of establishing a common internal economic market has contributed to the openness of national borders and the harmonization of many policies once in the exclusive domain of individual member states. The EU also has established some of the strongest and most innovative environmental protection measures in the world and has increasingly taken the lead on international environmental issues such as global warming. In principle, environmental protection now enjoys equal weight with economic development in EU policymaking.

Political will and public support have been the keys to EU success in approaching the environment from an integrated perspective. First, the legal foundations have been firmly established so that the EU has an unchallenged right to protect the environment. Second, all states recognize that without common environmental policies, barriers to free trade develop. Third, political, economic, and geographic diversity have challenged policymakers to develop innovative strategies for overcoming differences and sharing burdens equitably.

The EU is therefore an important model to study, both as the most advanced regional organization of states and as a comprehensive environmental policy regime. But the EU also has become an important actor in global environmental diplomacy. In addition to individual member states, the EU is a party to most international conventions negotiated in the 1990s.[1] Since the 1992 United Nations Conference on Environment and Development, the EU has played a leading role in pushing the United States and other nations to adopt more stringent environmental agreements on matters such as climate change. As a result of enlargement, the EU will play a role in shaping environmental policy from the Baltic to the Aegean. New member states are required to transpose into their national systems the entire body of EU laws, regulations, and directives, known as the *acquis communautaire*. The chapter for the environment in the *acquis communautaire* is known as the *environmental acquis*. The EU will face a number of important problems and opportunities as it becomes a larger and more integrated governance system. This chapter explores the history, institutions, current environmental policies, and future challenges of this unique organization.

The Political Origins of the European
Union and Environmental Policy

The quest for political and economic union in Europe has its origins in the 1920s and 1930s, when it was recognized that some kind of supranational organization was needed to avoid brutal competition, protectionism, and war. But it was the experience of World War II that convinced statesmen to seek a new type of unity. U.S. economic assistance under the postwar Marshall Plan also called for regional cooperation.

The first step toward building a more integrated Europe was the formation of the European Coal and Steel Community (ECSC). The idea of French economic planner Jean Monnet and foreign minister Robert Schumann, the ECSC was created by the Treaty of Paris on April 18, 1951. The original members were Belgium, France, Germany, Italy, Luxembourg, and the Netherlands. Its economic goal was to pool the production of coal and steel for the benefit of all six countries. Its other purpose was to lock Germany politically and economically into a stable partnership with western Europe.

Other cooperative activities were slow to develop, but in June 1955 the six ECSC members decided to move toward closer economic integration. They saw a European free trade area or "common market" as a means to increase industrial and agricultural exports, to redistribute resources to economically depressed areas, and to encourage travel among countries. The result was the 1957 Treaty of Rome, which established the European Economic Community (EEC) and the European Atomic Energy Authority (Euratom). In the 1970s Denmark, Ireland, and the United Kingdom joined the EEC, and Greece, Portugal, and Spain followed suit by 1986. Austria, Finland, and Sweden became full members in 1995, bringing the membership to fifteen.[2] In 2004 the membership of the EU expanded to twenty-five, with the accession of Cyprus, the Czech Republic, Estonia, Hungary, Latvia, Lithuania, Malta, Poland, the Slovak Republic, and Slovenia. Bulgaria and Romania will be candidates for accession at a later date.[3]

The Treaty of Rome contained no explicit provisions for protection of the environment. EEC policy on the environment dates from the 1972 Paris summit of the Community's heads of state and government, which was inspired in part by the United Nations Conference on the Human Environment held earlier that year in Stockholm. Under Article 235 of the Treaty of Rome, which permits legislation in new areas if consistent with EEC objectives, the summit proposed the creation of an Environmental Action Programme, in effect adding an environmental agenda to the Treaty of Rome.

Over the next dozen years, the EEC adopted three environmental action plans (for 1973–1976, 1977–1981, and 1982–1986, respectively) and enacted more than twenty major environmental directives covering air and water pollution, waste management, noise reduction, protection of endangered flora and fauna, environmental impact assessment, and other topics. It took most of these actions first under Article 235 of the Treaty of Rome and later under Article 100a (added to the treaty by Article 18 of the Single European

Act), which authorizes actions that directly affect "the establishment or functioning of the common market." The motivation for these laws was to avoid trade distortions caused by different environmental standards while dealing with problems that were inherently transboundary in nature.[4]

The next milestone in the development of the treaties was the Single European Act of 1986, which accelerated the integration process by calling for establishment of a single internal economic market by the end of 1992. Equally important, the act added a new section to the Treaty of Rome that formally defined the goals and procedures of EEC environmental policies and called for "balanced growth" by integrating environmental policy into all other areas of decision making. These goals and procedures can be found in Articles 174, 175, and 176 of the Consolidated Version of the Treaty Establishing the European Community (Consolidated Treaty), which was published in 2002. The volume of new environmental legislation reached a peak during the 1987–1992 period.

The Maastricht Treaty (also called the Treaty on European Union), which entered into force in 1993, advocated closer political and monetary union, including development of a common European currency. The euro was put into circulation by twelve member states in January 2002. The Maastricht Treaty also created two new "pillars"—to promote common foreign and security policies and cooperation in justice and home affairs—that, together with the first pillar, the European Community (EC, until this time called the EEC), now form the EU. The ability of the EU to forge a common foreign and security policy has been sorely tested in relation to both Kosovo and Iraq. It has been more successful in the environmental realm.

In addition, the treaty further strengthened the legal basis and procedures for environmental policymaking. This trend was continued with revisions made by the Treaty of Amsterdam in June 1997. Article 3d of the Amsterdam Treaty (which became Article 6 of the Consolidated Treaty) states explicitly that "environmental protection requirements must be integrated into the definition and implementation of Community policies and activities . . . in particular with a view to promoting sustainable development."[5]

Expansion of the EU was addressed by the Treaty of Nice, which came into effect on February 1, 2003. Although the treaty deals primarily with the effects of enlargement on EU institutions, it also reaffirms the Union's commitment to environmental policy. At the December 2000 Nice conference that led to the treaty's formation, a declaration was adopted affirming member states' determination "to see the European Union play a leading role in promoting environmental protection in the Union and in international efforts promoting the same objective at the global level."[6] Further changes are likely in the future, especially if a constitution is eventually agreed upon.[7]

The EU has created the most comprehensive regional environmental protection regime in the world. Although scholars still debate whether the EU is primarily an "intergovernmental" organization dominated by the interests of individual member states or a "functional" regime that represents common transnational interests and actors, it is increasingly regarded as a "multi-level governance structure" in environmental policy.[8]

EU Institutions and Policymaking Processes

Institutions

The EU's primary institutions are the European Council and the Council of Ministers, the European Commission, the European Parliament, and the European Court of Justice (ECJ). There are also fifteen secondary agencies, including the European Environment Agency (EEA).[9]

The European Council and the Council of Ministers are often simply called "the council." Technically, when the heads of government meet, which they must do at least twice a year, it is known as the European Council or "summit." Broad policy directions are set at these summits. More specific policy decisions are made in meetings of the relevant Council of Ministers. Thus, for example, environmental decisions are reached by the Council of Environment Ministers, which as the name suggests is made up of member states' environment ministers. The presidency of the council rotates among the member states every six months, and the country in charge can shape the agenda of all council meetings. The council is the most important EU body because it must approve all legislation. Its directives must be adopted by the individual member states and incorporated into national law within a specified period of time, usually two years. The EU can enact regulations that automatically apply to the states, but they are less common. The council also makes decisions on international treaties and agreements. In general, the council's actions reflect the national interests of the states. The Single European Act introduced qualified majority voting on some environmental matters. This is a special procedure that gives greater weight to states with large populations but protects smaller states by requiring a majority of votes (71 percent) for a measure to pass. The Treaty of Nice assigned new voting weights to member states but kept the 71 percent rule. It also extended qualified majority voting to thirty other areas.

The European Commission is a body of commissioners (and their staffs) who head twenty-three directorates-general (DGs). With enlargement, the number of commissioners is to be kept below twenty-seven. DG XI, now called the Environmental Directorate, is responsible for the environment, nuclear safety, and civil protection. The commission's task is to initiate EU legislation and to oversee its implementation by member states. The Treaties of Amsterdam and Nice strengthened substantially the powers of the commission president. Romano Prodi has held this position since 1999. A multinational bureaucracy of somewhat less than 20,000 serves the commission and its directorates in Brussels.[10]

The European Parliament, in contrast, is elected directly by voters in each country and tends to reflect the diverse interests of political parties and groupings across Europe. The Treaty of Nice restricts the number of parliamentarians in the enlarged EU to a maximum of 732. The parliament holds plenary sessions in Strasbourg, France, but much of its staff is in Luxembourg, and most of its committee meetings are held in Brussels. Draft legislation from the commission is submitted to the parliament, which can either accept the draft as is or propose amendments. The parliament also must approve the commission budget and EU treaties, and it votes on the appointment of the president and commissioners.[11]

The European Parliament is not regarded as a true legislature because it cannot initiate measures. However, the Maastricht Treaty allows a majority of members to request that the commission develop a proposal if it concerns implementation of the treaty, and parliament committees also can informally influence policy formation in other ways. Under the Amsterdam Treaty revisions, a "co-decision" procedure was extended to many more areas of environmental legislation; if the parliament does not agree with the council position after a second reading, a conciliation committee is formed to resolve differences. If agreement still cannot be reached, the parliament can reject the proposal by majority vote, giving it a de facto veto. The new procedure has increased the parliament's role in policymaking, resulting in more transparent decision making and reducing the so-called democratic deficit.

The European Court of Justice, located in Luxembourg, considers cases brought before it by the commission, the council, or member states concerning the application of EU treaties. ECJ decisions are binding on member states, but the ECJ must depend on national courts to carry them out, making enforcement difficult. Under the Maastricht Treaty, the ECJ can levy fines on member states that fail to comply with its decisions. The ECJ also has made it easier for citizens to enforce their EU rights in national courts.[12]

Some ECJ decisions have helped define the rights of member states to enact environmental legislation that may violate EU treaty provisions prohibiting restraints of trade. For example, in the 1988 Danish bottle case, the ECJ upheld Denmark's law requiring the use of returnable bottles for beer and soft drinks on the grounds that its environmental benefits were sufficient to justify a minor restraint on trade.[13] Like courts in the United States, the ECJ is emerging as an important policymaker in balancing economic and environmental interests. Significantly, the *acquis communautaire* includes the judgments passed by the ECJ.

The European Environment Agency, approved in 1990, was established in 1994 in Copenhagen after a long battle over its location. Although it does not have the regulatory and enforcement powers of the Environmental Protection Agency in the United States, the EEA is becoming an important actor in EU policymaking. Its membership includes, in addition to the EU member states, the three European Economic Area states (Iceland, Norway, and Liechtenstein) and Bulgaria, Romania, and Turkey. Its mission is to compile a scientific database on environmental conditions in Europe and develop analytical models for understanding environmental processes and improving decision making. It collects and distributes data through the European Environment Information and Observation Network (EIONET), which consists of about 300 environmental bodies, agencies, and research centers.[14]

The Policy Process

Policymaking within the EU is more "political" than a description of the institutions might suggest.[15] Because the EU is a fluid and developing institution, policymaking is complicated by uncertainty over roles, powers, and decision rules. As we have seen, the council, commission, and parliament perform functions different from those of the three branches of the U.S. government.

The commission and the parliament can be viewed as supranational bodies, whereas the council remains essentially intergovernmental. The commissioners and their staffs are international civil servants who are not supposed to serve any national interest; therefore, the commission's proposed legislation tends to favor greater "harmonization" of European policies. Parliament also tends to favor stronger EU policies, especially in fields such as environmental and consumer protection that are popular with the electorate. The council, in contrast, is usually more cautious because of its sensitivity to national political interests and the costs of implementing EU policies (which largely devolve on national governments). The council is more likely to invoke the principle of *subsidiarity*, under which actions are to be taken at the EU level only if they cannot be carried out more efficiently at the national or local level.[16]

Conflicts of interest among the states are evident in the council. In the past, a fluid coalition of Denmark, Germany, and the Netherlands pushed the hardest for environmental protection. These "green" countries often had higher regulatory standards than the EU and tried to get the EU to adopt these standards—a process that has been called "regulatory competition." [17] For example, Germany was influential in proposing tough air pollution controls on large combustion plants, while the Netherlands convinced the council to adopt its high standards for small car and truck emissions. More recently, Austria, Finland, and Sweden have joined Denmark and the Netherlands as the environmental leaders, with Germany taking a somewhat more cautious position because of economic difficulties at home.[18] At the other end of the spectrum, the poorer countries, such as Greece, Ireland, Portugal, and Spain, have been more reluctant to carry out EU environmental policies, while Belgium, the United Kingdom, France, Italy, and Luxembourg tend to fall in between. One of the principal challenges facing the EU has been to find ways of accommodating different levels of environmental commitment and regulatory capacity without weakening ultimate goals. This will become an even bigger challenge because of the accession of the central and eastern European states, which are much poorer and have far less experience with environmental protection programs than the older member states.

Lobbying by private interests is also omnipresent in the EU.[19] Industry is very concerned about the impact of new environmental legislation on competitiveness and maintains an army of lawyers in Brussels. Both the commission directorates and parliamentary committees regularly consult such interests, which tend to represent the largest companies and trade associations. Environmental, consumer, and other public interest groups also have representation. An umbrella organization in Brussels, the European Environmental Bureau, represents over 140 environmental organizations from the EU, accession states, and some neighboring countries.[20] It closely monitors DG XI and tries to influence proposed legislation. Other international environmental nongovernmental organizations (NGOs), such as the Worldwide Fund for Nature and Greenpeace, also lobby intensely and are regarded as among the most effective pressure groups.[21] A broad range of stakeholders and policy networks influence the EU policy process at all levels.

Environmental policy is closely related to other issues such as economic competition, taxation, research and development, energy, agriculture, and transportation.[22] Effective policymaking therefore requires interaction and cooperation among many EU directorates and parliamentary committees. For example, the development of efficiency standards for electrical appliances involved a working group of members from the environment and energy directorates. The divergent perspectives of these directorates often lead to different policy preferences. The requirement introduced by Article 3d of the Amsterdam Treaty that environmental protection must be integrated into all fields of EU policy gives weight to the issue. As relatively new and understaffed, however, the environment directorate is often in a weak position in negotiating with its counterparts, especially the leading economic directorates for industry and trade. Final policy resolution by the commission and council usually involves extensive political compromise, which sometimes takes the form of "side payments." For example, in an effort to gain approval for an overall EU target for reducing carbon dioxide, a burden-sharing plan was worked out, under which some states agreed to exceed EU targets so that other states would have lower burdens to meet. Such differentiated obligations, along with "derogations" allowing some countries more time to comply with EU directives, are creating a "multispeed" Europe despite efforts to integrate and harmonize policies.

Harmonization of Environmental Standards

One general rationale for creating common environmental policies and "harmonizing" standards across member states has been to level the economic playing field. A danger associated with this, however, is that the lowest common denominator will prevail and, in the case of environmental standards, result in community norms that are considerably weaker than those of the leading states. To mitigate this problem, the Single European Act added to the Treaty of Rome three new articles: 130r, 130s, and 130t. These are now articles 174, 175, and 176, respectively, of the Consolidated Treaty. Article 174 guarantees that the EU will take action for "preserving, protecting, and improving the quality of the environment, protecting human health, prudent and rational utilization of natural resources, and promoting measures at (the) international level to deal with regional or worldwide environmental problems." Article 175 allows the council to decide which measures can be decided by qualified majority voting. Article 176 specifies that protective measures taken at the community level "shall not prevent any Member State from maintaining or introducing more stringent protective measures" so long as these measures are compatible with treaty law.[23]

Lead states are able to retain higher environmental standards than other countries so long as the commission or the ECJ does not find them in violation of other treaty rules. For example, half of the EU 15 introduced national carbon taxes (Denmark, Finland, Germany, Italy, the Netherlands, Sweden, and the United Kingdom). Naturally, they would rather bring the EU norms up to their level so they are not at a competitive economic disadvantage.[24]

The Maastricht Treaty allowed most environmental legislation to be enacted by a qualified majority in the council, whereas previously unanimity was normally required. In an offsetting provision, the treaty placed greater emphasis on the principle of subsidiarity, under which actions should be taken by the member states unless the objectives can be better achieved through EU actions. Since 1992 some states have used this principle as a rationale to challenge some community-wide environmental legislation. The Amsterdam Treaty did not alter the provisions on majority voting and failed to clarify the meaning of subsidiarity, leaving this conflict unresolved. Effective implementation of subsidiarity also has been a matter of debate in the discussions of a European constitution.

The Sixth Environmental Action Programme

As noted, since 1972 the commission has developed environmental action programmes to guide its activities for a multiyear period. Although these programs are not legally binding, they have had substantial influence on policy development at the EU level and among member states. The Fifth Environmental Action Programme, "Towards Sustainability," focused on the need to integrate environment into other economic and sectoral policies. In line with this, the commission's "Communication on Environment and Employment," issued in November 1997, spelled out for the first time how environmental protection and job creation can be mutually reinforcing.[25] The Sixth Programme, "Environment 2010, Our Future, Our Choice," continues this theme. It calls for the EC to integrate environmental concerns into all its policies and to promote sustainable development within the enlarged Community. The programme is based on "the polluter pays principle, the precautionary principle and preventive action, and the principle of rectification of pollution at source." Its four priority areas are: climate change, nature and biodiversity, environment and health, and natural resources and waste. Progress in achieving goals is to be measured in relation to targets and timetables covering a ten-year period.

The programme also places great importance on the achievement of sustainable development in the accession countries through implementation of the environmental *acquis,* promotion of the transfer of clean technologies, exchange of information, and promotion of civil society. In responding to criticism that the Community needs to do more to fulfill its own environmental goals, the programme encourages greater emphasis on effective implementation.[26]

Legislative Action

The EU has more than 200 pieces of environmental legislation in force.[27] Most of this legislation was enacted during the 1970s and 1980s to address the major sources of pollution. Since 1992 there has been a marked slowdown in the passage of legislation. One reason for this is that the principle of subsidiarity was elevated to a prominent place in the Maastricht Treaty to gain the support of several states that were reluctant to move toward further economic integration. According to Article 5 of the Consolidated Treaty, the EU can take action only "if and in so far as the objectives of the proposed action cannot be sufficiently achieved by the Member States and can therefore, by reason of the scale or effects of the proposed action, be better achieved by the Community." [28] Although the exact meaning of this wording is unclear, one consequence is that the commission has been more cautious in proposing new regulations and directives since 1992. Another is that there has been substantially increased pressure from industry and from some governments for deregulation or at least greater flexibility in the design and implementation of policies. Sluggish economic growth and high unemployment have made pivotal states such as Germany and France more reluctant to impose new costs on industry. Finally, there is growing acceptance of the need to work to integrate environmental policies into existing sectoral policies.

The EU has shifted its emphasis toward consolidation of existing policies, improving implementation and enforcement, and promoting more integrated decision making before extending regulation in new areas. The EU has also taken on more of a global environmental leadership role. It has taken a relatively aggressive stance on certain global issues, championing the Kyoto Protocol on climate change despite U.S. opposition to the agreement and differing with the United States in agricultural trade negotiations on the issue of the safety of genetically modified organisms.[29]

Regulations, Directives, and Framework Directives

Legislation in the EU can take the form of either regulations or directives. Regulations are directly binding on member states and require no further legislation at the national level; they are used when technical standardization is necessary. Directives are more commonly used for environmental regulation.

There have been some efforts to establish new directives. In November 2000, for example, the commission adopted a Green Paper on Security of the Energy Supply, which raises issues regarding the position of nuclear energy vis-à-vis other energy sources in lieu of concerns about meeting goals for reduction of greenhouse gas emissions, on the one hand, and concerns about aging nuclear power plants on the other. Since December 2001 the council has requested regular reports on nuclear safety, and in December 2002 the ECJ confirmed in a judgment that the Community has the authority to legislate in relation to nuclear safety. In January 2003 the commission adopted two proposals for directives for a Community approach to issues of nuclear plant safety and radioactive waste disposal.[30]

Much of the commission's work in the past decade, however, has been focused on consolidating existing directives with the establishment of framework directives. Under Article 249 of the Consolidated Treaty, directives "shall be binding, as to the result to be achieved, upon each Member State . . . but shall leave to the national authorities the choice of form and methods." [31] This means that directives must be transposed into national law—each country must pass or amend legislation to achieve the stated objectives. This allows states to adapt EU policies to their particular legal and administrative traditions, but "choice of form and methods" gives states considerable discretion in deciding how to achieve EU policy goals. The result has been wide variations among countries in the implementation of EU environmental laws and severe difficulties in monitoring and assessing progress toward common goals.

Framework directives attempt to deal with this problem by establishing comprehensive long-term environmental quality goals and standards that can be used to measure progress across a wide range of specific policy instruments and actions. They provide a mechanism for consolidating, integrating, and simplifying related pieces of legislation (for example, separate directives on drinking water, bathing water, and protection of shellfish) to encourage more comprehensive and efficient management of resources. While allowing countries greater flexibility in pursuing these goals, they can also serve as a catalyst to force states to adopt a more integrated approach to environmental protection. Finally, an explicit purpose of the new directives is to increase "transparency" in environmental regulation by ensuring public access to information in a timely fashion.

Despite these laudable objectives, many environmental groups and members of parliament fear that the trend toward more general framework directives will result in a weakening of existing environmental controls. They are concerned that minimum standards may be set too low and that EU enforcement will become even more difficult than it already is. Therefore, in the process of reviewing the directives drafted by the commission, the parliament has adopted the role of preventing any weakening of existing environmental controls.

In addition to numerous directives addressing such matters as environmental impact assessment, nature protection, chemicals in the environment, and genetically modified organisms, there are now environmental framework directives addressing air quality, integrated pollution prevention and control, waste, and water quality.

Integrated Pollution Prevention and Control. The Integrated Pollution Prevention and Control Directive (96/61/EC), issued in 1996, is intended to provide much of the operational foundation for the other directives because it imposes common requirements for issuing permits to large industrial sources of pollution throughout the EU. Member states must require all new and existing facilities to obtain operating permits that ensure that all appropriate measures are taken to prevent or minimize pollution of the air, water, and land. The directive calls for use of both environmental quality and emission standards (the "combined approach"), which accommodates different national systems; for example, the British rely on ambient quality standards, but the Germans insist on strict emission limits. Emission standards are to be based on the "best available techniques," but state authorities are given discretion to determine specific technologies appropriate to local conditions. However, the directive reserves the council's right to set community-wide emission limit values for certain categories of installations and pollutants if necessary.

The larger significance of the directive is that states are encouraged to take a comprehensive, integrated approach to pollution reduction at the source, including waste minimization, efficient use of energy, and protection of soil and groundwater as well as surface waters and air. This approach is in line with the shift evident in Europe from end-of-the-pipe controls to pollution prevention; more integrated, long-term environmental management; and greater flexibility in the use of policy instruments. The subsequent air and water directives are designed to consolidate existing legislation and provide a legal framework for integrating policy across these media.

Ambient Air Quality and Auto Emissions Standards. EU legislation to protect air quality goes back to 1970, when the first directive to regulate emissions from automobiles was passed (70/220/EEC). Since then, the Council of Ministers has enacted more than thirty directives on air pollution covering, among other things, diesel engine emissions, the lead and sulfur content of fuels, and emissions from large industrial facilities, power plants, and waste incinerators. Ambient air quality standards also have been set for sulfur dioxide, nitrogen dioxide, particulates, and lead; and regulations to limit chlorofluorocarbons (CFCs) and other ozone-depleting gases have been implemented under the Montreal Protocol. Europe generally followed the lead of the United States in setting these standards but lagged somewhat behind, for example, in not requiring the installation of catalytic converters in cars until 1991. Air pollution has become a severe problem in many European cities; however, methods for measuring, assessing, and reporting air quality data have varied greatly from country to country, making it difficult to apply common standards.

The commission proposed a new air quality framework directive in July 1994, which was adopted by the council in September 1996. The primary goals of the directive are to "define and establish objectives for ambient air quality in the Community designed to avoid, prevent or reduce harmful effects on human health and the environment as a whole" and to "assess the ambient air quality in member states on the basis of common methods and criteria." [32] Additionally, three "daughter directives" have been drafted by expert working groups that set limit values for nitrogen oxides, sulfur dioxide, lead, particulate matter, carbon monoxide, benzene, and ozone. Public release of this information is also required. A fourth daughter directive is under development.[33]

At the same time, the commission has developed separate legislation to further reduce acid precipitation (primarily from sulfur dioxide and nitrogen dioxide) and to cut pollution from vehicles. Increasingly, stakeholders are being brought into the decision-making process. In 1993 the Energy, Industry and Environment commissioners jointly launched the Auto-Oil Programme (AOP), inviting auto manufacturing and petroleum industries to participate in the development of a plan for meeting EU-wide air quality standards. Both industries felt that they were being disproportionately burdened in efforts to reduce traffic-related emissions. The AOP involved an intense series of negotiations and scientific studies that led to a commission proposal in 1996 to regulate the content of fuels and set far more stringent emission limits on new cars. However, the proposal received strong protests from manufacturers (for being too expensive) as well as from environmentalists (for not being strict enough).[34] The decision-making process was also criticized for failing to include other stakeholders.

One of the major points of contention was whether the higher standards set for 2005 would be voluntary, as the commission proposed, or mandatory. Germany, the Netherlands, and the Nordic countries supported tighter exhaust standards, while countries such as France, Italy, and Spain opposed mandatory controls.[35] The parliament largely sided with the former states, passing more than 200 amendments in early 1997 that would further tighten and make mandatory the emission controls for 2005, while offering additional time to the poorer southern states to meet the fuel standards.[36] Then in June 1998 the council and the parliament reached a compromise agreement on the first Auto Oil Directive that mandates a 70 percent reduction in tail pipe emissions by 2005.[37]

A second stage of the program (Auto-Oil Programme II) was launched in 1997. In addition to the auto and petroleum industries, local authorities, member states, and nongovernmental organization representatives were invited to join in the work of this program. AOP II assessed the applicability of the standards set for 2005, considered further standards for fuels and motorcycles, and proposed nontechnical and local measures for the implementation of emissions reductions. Also proposed was the increased use of taxation and other fiscal measures to alter consumer behavior. The AOP II decision-making process was more inclusive of different viewpoints and thus has helped pave the way for multi-stakeholder assessments of measures in other policy areas as well.[38]

Building on the success of the AOPs, for example, in May 2001 the commission established the Clean Air for Europe (CAFE) Programme. It uses the multi-stakeholder approach in assessing measures to address particulate matter, tropospheric ozone, acidification, eutrophication, and damage to cultural heritage.[39]

Water Resources Management. EU water quality has been protected since 1975 by directives covering drinking and bathing water, fish and shellfish, groundwater, urban waste water, and protection against nitrates from fertilizers and various dangerous chemicals. Other policies covered pollution of European seas and rivers under various international maritime conventions and agreements. A new drinking water directive was adopted in 1998.

In February 1996 the commission called for a water framework directive that, like the air framework, would establish broad guidelines for the protection and management of all freshwater resources. In October 2000 the EU Water Framework Directive (Directive 2000/60/EC), which replaced seven existing directives, was finally adopted after years of sometimes tense discussion and debate. The directive is based on a river basin management approach, with the idea that water quality can best be protected if an entire ecological system's pollution problems are dealt with in an integrated fashion combining emission limits and quality standards. States were to have transposed the directive into national policy by 2003. In the coming years, they are to conduct studies of the characteristics of river basins, establish a monitoring network, finalize their river basin management plans, and introduce pricing policies. The ultimate goal is to obtain "good status" for water quality throughout the EU by 2015.[40]

Proposal for an Environmental Liability Directive. The White Paper on Environmental Liability, issued in February 2000, called for the establishment of a Framework Directive on Environmental Liability that would introduce the possibility of NGOs bringing suits for environmental harms.[41] The subsequently proposed EU Environmental Liability Directive, however, dropped this provision in favor of a system that focuses on environmental restoration and cost recovery.[42]

Other Legislation

The EU has enacted legislation on many other aspects of environmental protection, including environmental impact assessment, control of chemicals and other dangerous substances, hazardous waste transfer and management, development of renewable energy, and protection of forests, wildlife, and biodiversity. Space does not permit analysis of all of these policies, many of which continue to undergo amendment and revision. The following section briefly examines two areas in which the EU has tried to take the lead: packaging reduction and eco-labeling. In both cases individual states had begun to adopt national legislation that threatened to create barriers to trade, which could trigger action by the European Commission.

Packaging and Recycling. Beginning in the 1970s, a number of European countries began to enact laws to reduce the volume of solid waste by requiring the use of returnable beverage containers, encouraging recycling of materials, and limiting waste in packaging. Denmark led the way by banning the use of aluminum cans and requiring that beer and soft drinks be sold in reusable bottles. Denmark's action eventually led to the seminal ruling by the ECJ in 1988 that such restrictions on trade may be justified on environmental grounds, provided that they do not unfairly discriminate in favor of domestic producers. Other countries have since passed legislation mandating the reduction or recycling of certain materials, including packaging. In 1991 Germany gained international attention for its novel packaging ordinance (*Verpackungsverordnung*), which required retail stores to take back all used packaging materials from consumers and process them. The ordinance allowed business and industry to set up a private collection system (the green dot system) on condition that it could meet ambitious recycling targets for various materials; otherwise a mandatory deposit would be levied on the sale of relevant products. The Netherlands also established an ambitious recycling program that required industry to reduce its volume of packaging by 2000.[43]

The EC had adopted a directive on beverage containers in 1985, but in the wake of the German and Dutch laws and the Danish bottle decision it was moved to draft a packaging directive that would accommodate recycling of other materials while preventing the development of potential trade restrictions. After much haggling over German and Dutch approaches mandating higher recycling targets and a coalition led by the United Kingdom that objected to such rigid quotas, a compromise was reached that lowered the mandatory targets to 50 percent recovery, 25 percent overall recycling, and 15 percent minimum recycling for each material. While states were allowed to exceed these targets, Germany's experience suggested that too high recovery rates could lead to excessive accumulation and export of waste materials because of inadequate processing capacity. Therefore, the final EU packaging and packaging waste directive (94/62/EC), passed in 1994, also set "maximum recovery" rates of 65 percent and recycling rates of 45 percent, over the objections of Denmark, Germany, and the Netherlands. According to some analysts, this compromise illustrates that the establishment of an integrated market still takes precedence over environmental protection.[44] It is noteworthy, however, that despite industry opposition, the commission presented a proposal to amend the 1994 directive in December 2001. The proposal set new targets for recovery and recycling to be met by midsummer 2006 for all pre-enlargement member states except Greece, Ireland, and Portugal, which were given three additional years to meet the targets. The proposal, which through a co-decision procedure was approved by the parliament on September 3, 2002, requires overall recovery and recycling targets of between 60 to 65 percent and 55 to 70 percent, respectively.[45]

In February 2001 the commission adopted a Green Paper presenting ideas for strengthening product-focused environmental policies. Two years later the commission held meetings with stakeholders in order to evaluate the implementation of the directive and to assess ways to reduce packaging and encourage reuse of packaging.[46] The commission also is currently studying the possibility of introducing an Integrated Product Policy (IPP) that would address the entire life cycle of a product and its environmental impacts, an approach that is consistent with promoting sustainable development.[47]

Eco-Labeling. Another approach to limiting waste and environmental damage generally is to encourage consumers to purchase more ecologically benign products by providing better information. Germany had introduced an eco-labeling system, and several other countries were planning to do so when in 1990 the council asked the commission to prepare a regulation establishing criteria for an EC labeling scheme. The initial criteria used for granting a "green" label took into account the environmental impact of the product throughout its entire life cycle, including the materials used, manufacturing technologies, health and safety of workers, and ultimate disposal costs. Under the council regulation (92/880/EEC) of March 23, 1992, member states were authorized to appoint a competent body to award the EC eco-label to manufacturers or importers whose products met the criteria. Participation by industry was voluntary, but it was hoped that consumer demand for "green" products would drive producers to compete for the label (symbolized by a flower) by designing better products.

In July 2000 a revised eco-labeling regulation (1980/2000/EC) was passed. It authorizes a new EU Eco-Labeling Board, consisting of eco-labeling bodies in each member state, consumer groups, environmental NGOs, trade unions, industry, and small and medium-sized enterprises, to jointly develop eco-label criteria for different product groups. There are now nineteen product groups, ranging from furniture and household appliances to electrical equipment and bedding. Consumers can learn about products bearing the eco-label on the eco-label catalogue Web site.[48] National eco-labeling bodies remain in charge of implementing the system.

Major Challenges Facing the European Union

Implementation of Environmental Laws

As the examples suggest, the success of the EU commitment to environmental protection depends on the extent to which member states transpose EU law into national law. However, they must also apply and enforce the law in practice.[49] Although there are few thorough analyses of EU treaty compliance and enforcement to date, scattered studies indicate that the record is uneven and that in some areas implementation may be deteriorating.[50]

The European Commission monitors policy implementation and seeks to detect violations of EU law, but it has no authority to investigate or inspect specific facilities. In 2001 the commission brought seventy-one environmental cases before the ECJ, an increase of approximately 40 percent over the previous year. Environmental cases represented one-third of all infringement cases and complaints. The reasons for the growing number of complaints include greater awareness on the part of citizens that they can bring complaints to the commission, greater environmental awareness, the commission's monitoring of national conformity to EU law, the lack of adequate institutions at the national level, and the complexity of EU directives and regulations. The rate of alleged violations varies greatly among states: in 2001 France and Italy both had twenty-two infringement cases referred to the ECJ, compared with five for the Netherlands and two for Denmark.[51]

The EU has some legal enforcement mechanisms at its disposal. Citizens, local authorities, businesses, or interest groups have the right to lodge complaints on the inadequate application or transposition of EU law directly before the commission. Once a complaint has been brought, efforts are made to mediate the dispute or to informally persuade the national government to take appropriate action. If a party is found to be in violation of EU law, the commission can issue a formal notice to the state. If all else fails, an infringement case can be brought before the ECJ to force compliance. However, resolution of cases can take many years, and even if a government is found guilty, compliance is not automatic. Article 171 of the Maastricht Treaty allows the ECJ to levy financial penalties on states that fail to carry out its decisions, but the ECJ has only recently begun to use this power. As part of the trend in the EU to increase transparency, as of January 2001 formal notices to refer cases to the ECJ and to terminate cases are published on the secretariat-general's Web site.[52]

Some of the variation in compliance among states is related to different levels of awareness of citizens and interest groups.[53] Some states may have proportionately more complaints lodged because their citizens are more alert, informed, and able to bring matters to the attention of the EU. But differential enforcement is also the result of variations in the budgets and other resources of governments to carry out EU mandates. Because states choose their own means of compliance, differences are inevitable in the instruments used and in the severity of penalties levied against violators.[54] For example, the ECJ found Italy guilty of nontransposition and noncompliance with an EU directive on protection of wild birds (86/411/EEC) and fined the government. In another example, the ECJ censured France for failing to comply with EU directives on air pollution. As a consequence, France incorporated the directives directly into its laws.[55]

A growing volume of such cases has led to calls in the parliament and elsewhere for an EU inspectorate, possibly under auspices of the EEA. However, states have resisted any such extension of supranational powers, and its establishment does not appear likely. The commission instead works with an informal network of national environmental officials, known as the Implementation and Enforcement of EU Environmental Law (Impel) network.[56] In October 1996 the commission also issued a communication on implementation, which proposed guidelines for states to follow in carrying out inspections, handling public complaints about legal enforcement, and guaranteeing access by NGOs to national courts.[57]

The commission is interested in the introduction of a standard clause on sanctions that would require national governments to enforce effective penalties and sanctions for noncompliance of environmental laws. To date, however, the commission has failed to win adequate support for this or even for a comprehensive review of fines and penalties as they are used by various member states.[58]

New Instruments and Approaches

In part because of the ineffectiveness of some existing legislation but also because of looming new problems that will require different regulatory approaches, the Fifth Environmental Action Programme called for broadening the range of instruments for attaining sustainable development. The Sixth Environmental Action Programme has continued this theme, calling for the active involvement of all sectors of society, and has issued a user-friendly publication, *Our Future, Our Choice.*

There is growing interest in the EU in market-based instruments (including taxes and economic incentives, environmental auditing, and voluntary agreements), horizontal supporting instruments (research, information, and education), and new financial support mechanisms.[59] Such new approaches are now widely advocated to improve the economic efficiency of regulation and to involve all sectors of society in "shared responsibility" for the environment. As the costs of environmental regulation rise, they are also supported (at least in theory) by business and industry as an alternative to traditional "command and control" regulation.

Several countries in northern Europe have enacted extensive "green" taxes to promote waste reduction and energy saving.[60] Although the EU does not have the legal competence to impose new taxes directly, it can encourage states to do so on a coordinated or harmonized basis; for example, the European Commission issued a communication in early 1997 setting out guidelines for such taxes.[61] The environmental tax base as a share of the total EU tax base is on the rise. It went from 5.87 percent in 1980 to 6.17 percent in 1990 and 6.71 percent in 1997. Ninety-five percent of this comes from taxes on energy and transport but less than 5 percent from taxes on emissions, chemical substances, waste products, and natural resources.[62]

Particularly as a reaction to concerns about how to meet reductions in greenhouse gas emissions under the Kyoto Protocol, the EU has moved rapidly in recent years to adopt new policy instruments. We comment briefly on four: energy taxes, emissions trading, renewable energy portfolios, and voluntary industry agreements.

Energy Taxes. Concern over global climate change due to the accumulation of carbon dioxide and other greenhouse gases in the atmosphere has been particularly strong in Europe and has led to a search for effective means of reducing dependence on fossil fuels. For many years, the commission sought to win acceptance of the idea of a carbon tax and made numerous proposals to this effect, but to no avail. In 1997 the commission for a third time proposed the establishment of a directive on energy taxation. The plan would have extended the existing harmonized excise tax duties on mineral oils to coal, natural gas, and electricity, while allowing national governments to offer rebates for environmentally friendly forms of energy production. In the spring of 2003, EU finance ministers finally agreed on a watered-down version of the commission's proposal. They called for a directive on minimum rates of energy taxation to curb the use of fossil fuels and encourage sustainable transport.

Emissions Trading. The idea of a carbon emissions trading scheme was originally proposed by the United States during the negotiations leading to the Kyoto Protocol but was initially strongly resisted by the EU. After the Bush administration announced it would withdraw from the Kyoto Protocol in the spring of 2001, however, the EU unanimously resolved to move forward in trying to put the agreement into force even without the United States and began to look more positively at emissions trading schemes.

Under the Kyoto Protocol, the EU agreed to reduce its combined emissions of greenhouse gases (including carbon dioxide) by 8 percent of 1990 levels by 2008–2012. Under an internal burden-sharing arrangement, countries such as Germany and the United Kingdom are required to reduce their emissions by substantial amounts, while countries such as Greece, Spain, and Portugal are allowed to increase emissions. A report issued by the EEA found that, as of 2000, the EU as a whole had met its interim goal of stabilizing carbon dioxide emissions by 2000, but that some member states were behind in meeting their respective reduction targets. Steep cuts in emissions in Germany and the United Kingdom largely explain the stabilization of emissions within the EU. The report went on to note that if the EU is to meet its 8 percent reduction target, other measures, such as emissions trading, are necessary.[63]

In October 2001 the commission proposed a greenhouse gas emissions trading scheme to the parliament and the council. Modeled on the successful sulfur dioxide emissions trading system employed in the United States, the EU scheme will be the first international trading system in the world. It is to come into effect in 2005 and will cover the member states of the EU as well as members of the EEA. It will establish absolute limits on emissions of carbon dioxide and then set up a system allowing installations to trade emission allowances. For example, if a firm wants to expand and thus pollute more, it will have to buy more emission allowances. Firms that can reduce their emissions at relatively low cost will have an incentive to do so and to sell off their allowances.[64] This kind of scheme may in fact work well in the EU, where there is a long history of burden sharing, an underpinning for voluntary agreements.

Renewable Energy. Another policy measure that has been proposed to reduce greenhouse gas emissions is the Directive on the Promotion of Electricity from Renewable Energy Sources. The directive obliges member states to ensure access to the grid of renewable energy sources and sets a goal of 12 percent of all electricity being produced from renewable energy by 2010.[65] The remarkable growth of wind energy in the EU suggests strong public interest in promoting renewable energy.

Voluntary Agreements. Yet another innovative strategy calls for voluntary agreements between government and industrial sectors or individual companies to pursue pollution prevention and sustainable development. Such agreements or "covenants" have been a central feature of Dutch planning and were endorsed in the Fifth Environmental Action Programme. The idea is that voluntary cooperation can supplement (but not replace) legal obligations in many sectors in setting and achieving goals and can at times be more cost efficient.[66] Examples are industry agreements in Denmark on the phasing out of organic solvents used in paints and varnishes; in Belgium on elimination of CFCs; and on waste management and improving energy efficiency in several states. While such agreements can improve communication and cooperation between regulated industries and governments, environmental groups have been skeptical of them on the grounds that they may not be transparent and may amount to a form of backdoor "deregulation" that allows companies to circumvent existing laws. Nevertheless, their use is becoming increasingly common.

The commission issued a communication on voluntary agreements in late 1996 that attempted to clarify the legal and other considerations that should guide such agreements. Under these guidelines, agreements must take contractual form, be published and open to the public, have quantified objectives and deadlines, and be monitored, with performance reported to competent authorities. When appropriate, they may include sanctions for nonfulfillment. When the agreements are used to implement EU policy, the commission must be notified of all details and will then scrutinize them for conformity with Community law and certify their transparency and credibility.[67] In some cases the commission also makes voluntary agreements directly with industry. For example, in 1997 and 1998 the commission conducted negotiations with the European auto manufacturing association on reduction of carbon dioxide emissions of future models, leading to a voluntary agreement to cut emissions of new cars by about one-quarter by 2008. This agreement was accepted by the Council of Ministers in October 1998, eliminating the need for new legislation in this area.

In June 2002 the commission published an Action Plan on Simplifying and Improving the Regulatory Environment, which endorses the use of voluntary agreements at the European level as well. Whereas the 1996 communiqué dealt only with voluntary agreements at the national level, the Action Plan outlines how voluntary agreements can be used at the EU level as a means of achieving the Sixth Environmental Action Programme's goal of improving the effectiveness and efficiency of implementation.[68]

Enlargement

Perhaps the greatest challenge to EU environmental policy of the future will be to bring the ten new member states up to existing pollution standards. Under the treaty, all new members of the EU must comply with the full *acquis communautaire*, including all environmental directives and regulations. The EU increasingly shies away from giving concrete estimates of the cost of bringing the accession countries into compliance with the *acquis*. It is, however, possible to ascertain costs to date. For the 1990–2003 period, close to 20 billion euros were expended in the accession countries. The amount committed for the 2004–2006 period is 49.5 billion euros, most of which are for agriculture and structural operations.[69] As the environmental *acquis* is just one of many chapters of the *acquis communautaire* that accession countries must meet, the competition among programs for limited financial resources is likely to be great.

The central and eastern European countries have far higher levels of pollution than western European countries because of the lax environmental standards under their former communist governments. In addition to outdated coal-burning power plants and factories, several of these countries rely heavily on Soviet-designed nuclear plants that pose substantial safety risks. Although some of the worst facilities have been closed down, safety concerns remain. Many of the accession countries lack adequate sewerage and waste disposal systems. Estimates of meeting the environmental *acquis* for the ten accession countries typically range from 80 to 120 billion euros, or approximately 10 billion euros annually. While these figures are fraught with uncertainty, the cost of coming into compliance will certainly place a great strain on national budgets. Nevertheless, there are benefits to be accrued from compliance in terms of a reduction in the hidden costs to the economy of pollution and human health problems.[70] A World Bank report also suggests the potential for reducing the costs of coming into compliance through effective planning and use of innovative policy measures.[71]

The EU's Agenda 2000 recognizes that there is a strong possibility that the new members will enter the EU with compliance levels well below even the worst current offenders, but emphasizes the importance of working toward the long-term improvement of environmental conditions, especially air and water quality. Cooperation at all levels, including both public and private financing, will be necessary to assist the accession countries in transposing, interpreting, and implementing the environmental *acquis*.

Conclusion

The EU is at a critical stage in its evolution because of the further "deepening" of integration through the new monetary union and the largest "widening" in its history.[72] Without question, the EU has made great strides toward environmental protection over the past quarter-century, but it has also entered a transition phase in this policy area. After two decades of imposing increasingly detailed environmental directives and regulations from Brussels, the EU has begun to revise its approach since adoption of the Maastricht Treaty in 1992 and its emphasis on the principle of subsidiarity. Member states have pressed for greater freedom in implementing EU legislation while supporting the general principles of sustainable development. The European Commission has responded by turning toward the use of broader framework directives that set long-term environmental goals while allowing more flexibility in the choice of means to achieve them; it also has encouraged the introduction of new policy instruments at both the national and EU levels to improve environmental performance and cost-effectiveness. At the same time it has backed the Kyoto Protocol over U.S. opposition and is developing the world's first international carbon dioxide emissions trading scheme.

Despite these accomplishments, the EU faces daunting challenges both in extending its policies eastward and in maintaining its standards in the member states. Economic stagnation and high levels of unemployment have dampened public and government enthusiasm for increased environmental protection. Implementation of EU environmental laws at the national level leaves much to be desired, and there is still a large gap between the northern "green" states (including the three members that joined in 1995) and the less wealthy southern countries. The addition of the ten primarily central and eastern European states, which are economically farther behind the western European states, threatens to shift the balance of power toward the laggards. On the other hand, from a global perspective, enlargement of the EU to include these countries could improve conditions in the region as a whole if the new members can be convinced to significantly raise their standards.

Within the EU generally, sustainable development will require much greater integration of environmental perspectives into other policy areas such as energy, transportation, agriculture, and tourism.[73] Article 6 of the Consolidated Treaty legally obligates all EU bodies and member states to pursue such integrated sustainable development strategies. The real test of the EU governance system therefore still lies ahead.

Notes

The authors wish to thank Nicolas Colaninno of the EU Delegation to the United Nations and Rita Edwards, librarian at Adelphi University, for assistance in securing documentary resources. Regina Axelrod is indebted to the EU Commission, Directorate-General XI, Economic Analysis Unit, for the opportunity to work with them in November 1997. Norman Vig would like to thank the Institute for Transnational Legal Research of Maastricht University for use of its facilities. Miranda Schreurs wishes to thank Vincent Fruchart for his comments.

1. The EU negotiates on behalf of the member states insofar as they are in agreement and is a signatory to most recent conventions, but it does not have exclusive jurisdiction. Individual member states can sign separately, as a member of the EU, or both. See Angela Liberatore, "The European Union: Bridging Domestic and International Environmental Policy-Making," in *The Internationalization of Environmental Protection*, ed. Miranda A. Schreurs and Elizabeth C. Economy (Cambridge: Cambridge University Press, 1997), 204–206.

2. On the general history and development of the EC/EU, see Clifford Hackett, *Cautious Revolution: The European Community Arrives*, rev. ed. (New York: Praeger, 1996); Desmond Dinan, *Ever Closer Union? An Introduction to the European Community* (Boulder, Colo.: Lynne Rienner, 1994); David M. Wood and Birol A. Yesilada, *The Emerging European Union* (White Plains, N.Y.: Longman, 1996); Neill Nugent, *The Government and Politics of the European Union* (Durham, N.C.: Duke University

Press, 2003); Michelle Cini, ed., *European Union Politics* (Oxford: Oxford University Press, 2003).

3. See European Council, "Presidency Conclusions, Copenhagen European Council, 12 and 13 December 2002," press release, 13/12/2002, Nr: 400/02.

4. For a summary of the programs, see Stanley P. Johnson and Guy Corcelle, *The Environmental Policy of the European Communities,* 2d ed. (London: Kluwer Law International, 1995); and David Judge, ed., *A Green Dimension for the European Community* (London: Frank Cass, 1993). See also John McCormick, *Environmental Policy in the European Union* (Basingstroke, U.K: Palgrave, 2001).

5. For the Consolidated Treaty, see http://europa.eu.int/eur-lex/en/treaties/dat/EC_consol.html.

6. See "Treaty of Nice Amending the Treaty on European Union, The Treaties Establishing the European Communities and Certain Related Acts," 2001/C 80/01, Official Journal of the European Communities, 10.3.2001; available at http://europa.eu.int/eur-lex/en/treaties/dat/nice_treaty_en.pdf.

7. The European Convention, The Secretariat, "Draft Treaty Establishing a Constitution for Europe, CONV 850/03," (Brussels, July 18, 2003). The changes to the draft treaty, agreed upon in June 2004, can be found in "Conference of the Representatives of the Governments of the Member States," CIG 85104, PRESID 27 (Brussels, June 18, 2004). All member states must ratify the Constitution for it to go into force.

8. See, for example, Albert Weale et al., *Environmental Governance in Europe: An Ever Closer Union?* (Oxford: Oxford University Press, 2002); Andrew Jordan, ed., *Environmental Policy in the European Union* (London: Earthscan, 2002); Gary Marks et al., *Governance in the European Union* (London: Sage Publications, 1996); and Alan W. Cafruny and Carl Lankowski, eds., *Europe's Ambiguous Unity: Conflict and Consensus in the Post-Maastricht Era* (Boulder, Colo.: Lynne Rienner, 1997).

9. A useful introduction to the institutions of the EU is Nugent, *The Government and Politics of the European Union.*

10. Michelle Cini, *The European Commission* (Manchester: Manchester University Press, 1996); Geoffrey Edwards and David Spence, eds., *The European Commission,* 2d ed. (London: Catermill, 1997).

11. Richard Corbett, Francis Jacobs, and Michael Shackleton, *The European Parliament,* 3d ed. (London: Catermill, 1995); and Martin Westlake, *A Modern Guide to the European Parliament* (London: Pinter, 1994). On the role of political parties, see Simon Hix and Christopher Lord, *Political Parties in the European Union* (New York: St. Martin's, 1997).

12. L. Neville Brown and Tom Kennedy, *The Court of Justice of the European Communities,* 4th ed. (London: Sweet and Maxwell, 1994); Han Somsen, ed., *Protecting the European Environment: Enforcing EC Environmental Law* (London: Blackstone Press, 1996).

13. "Commission of the European Communities v. Kingdom of Denmark—Case 302/86," *Report of Cases Before the Court,* vol. 8 (Luxembourg: Office for Official Publications of the European Communities, 1988).

14. See the EEA at http://org.eea.eu.int.

15. See, for example, Jeremy J. Richardson, ed., *European Union: Power and Policy-Making* (London: Routledge, 1996); Helen Wallace and William Wallace, *Policy-Making in the European Union* (Oxford: Oxford University Press, 1996); Stephen George, *Politics and Policy in the European Community* (Oxford: Oxford University Press, 1991); and Carolyn Rhodes and Sonia Mazey, eds., *The State of the European Union, Building a European Polity?*, vol. 3 (Boulder, Colo.: Lynne Rienner, 1995).

16. See Regina S. Axelrod, "Subsidiarity and Environmental Policy in the European Community," *International Environmental Affairs* 6 (spring 1994): 115–132.

17. Adrienne Héritier et al., *Ringing the Changes in Europe: Regulatory Competition and Transformation of the State: Britain, France, Germany* (Berlin and New York: Walter de Gruyter, 1996).

18. Mikael Skou Andersen and Duncan Liefferink, eds., *European Environmental Policy: The Pioneers* (Manchester, England: Manchester University Press, 1997); and D. Liefferink and M. S. Andersen, "Strategies of the 'Green' Member States in EU Environmental Policy-Making," *Journal of European Public Policy-Making* 5 (June 1998): 254–270.

19. Sonia Mazey and Jeremy Richardson, eds., *Lobbying in the European Community* (Oxford: Oxford University Press, 1993); Sonia Mazey and Jeremy Richardson, "The Logic of Organisation: Interest Groups," in Richardson, *European Union.*

20. See the European Environment Bureau, http://www.eeb.org/Index.htm.

21. "Pressure Groups Become a Political Force," *European Voice,* June 11–17, 1998.

22. See Andrea Lenschow, ed., *Environmental Policy Integration: Greening Sectoral Policies in Europe* (London: Earthscan, 2002).

23. See http://europa.eu.int/eur-lex/en/treaties/dat/EC_consol.html.

24. European Environment Agency, "Environmental Signals 2002," Environmental Assessment Report no. 9, Copenhagen, European Environment Agency, May 14, 2002, 127.

25. Commission of the European Communities, *Communication on Environment and Employment,* COM (97) 592 Final (Brussels, November 18, 1997).

26. "Decision No. 1600/2002/EC of the European Parliament and of the Council of 22 July 2002 laying down the Sixth Community Environmental Action Programme," Official Journal of the European Communities, L242/1 vol. 45, September 10, 2002.

27. Johnson and Corcelle cite as many as 400 acts in *Environmental Policy of the European Communities;* see also Sevine Ercmann, *Pollution Control in the European Community: Guide to the EC Texts and Their Implementation by the Member States* (London: Kluwer Law International, 1996).

28. See http://europa.eu.int/eur-lex/en/treaties/dat/C_2002325EN.003301.html.

29. See Norman J. Vig and Michael Faure, eds., *Green Giants? Environmental Policies of the United States and the European Union* (Cambridge: MIT Press, 2004).

30. See http://europa.eu.int/rapid/start/cgi/guesten.ksh?p_action.gettxt=gt&doc=IP/03/132/O/Rapid&lg=EN&display=.

31. See http://europa.eu.int/eur-lex/en/treaties/dat/EC_consol.html.

32. *Council Directive 96/62/EC of 27 September 1996 on Ambient Air Quality and Assessment,* Article 1.

33. See the European Commission, http://europa.eu.int/comm/environment/air/ambient.htm.

34. "Outcry Over Plan for Car Emissions," *European Voice,* May 30–June 6, 1996.

35. "Battle Lines Drawn for Confrontation Over Car Emissions," *European Voice,* January 30–February 5, 1997.

36. "MEPs Take Hard Line on Car Emissions," *European Voice,* May 29–June 4, 1997; "Delays Hinder Progress of 'Auto-Oil' Deal," *European Voice,* July 3–9, 1997.

37. Press release, "Auto-Oil Programme Is on the Road" (Parliament-Council Conciliation Committee), General Secretariat of the Council of the European Union, 9924–98 (PRESS 230) (Brussels, June 29, 1998).

38. Frazer Goodwin, "Controlling Traffic Pollution and the Auto Oil Programme," European Federation for Transport and the Environment, T&E 99/8.

39. See http://europa.eu.int/scadplus/leg/en/lvb/128026.htm.

40. "Directive 2000/60/EC of the European Parliament and of the Council of 23 October 2000," Official Journal L 327, 22/12/2000, pp. 0001–0073. See also http://europa.eu.int/comm/environment/water/index_en.html.

41. Commission of the European Communities, "White Paper on Environmental Liability", COM (2000) 66 (Brussels, February 9, 2000).

42. Timothy Swanson and Andreas Kontoleon, "What Future for Environmental Liability? The Use of Liability Systems for Environmental Regulation in the Courtrooms of the US and the EU," in Vig and Faure, *Environmental Policies of the United States and the European Union.*

43. Markus Haverland, "Convergence of National Governance under European Integration? The Case of Packaging Waste" (paper presented at the Fifth Biennial Conference of the European Community Studies Association, Seattle, May 29–June 1, 1997).
44. Thomas Gehring, "Governing in Nested Institutions: Environmental Policy in the European Union and the Case of Packaging Waste," *Journal of European Public Policy* 4 (September 1997): 337–354.
45. Commission of the European Communities, "Proposal for a Directive of the European Parliament and of the Council Amending Directive 94/62/EC," COM (2001) 729-Final, Official Journal C 103, April, 30, 2002. See also http://europa.eu.int/ scadplus/leg/en/lvb/121207.htm.
46. See http://europa.eu.int/comm/environment/waste/events_packaging_270303.htm.
47. Commission of the European Communities, "Green Paper on Integrated Product Policy," COM (2001) 68 Final (Brussels, February 7, 2001).
48. See www.eco-label.com.
49. See Peter M. Haas, "Compliance with EU Directives: Insights from International Relations and Comparative Politics," *Journal of European Public Policy* 5 (March 1998): 17–37.
50. Alberta Sbragia, "Environmental Policy in the European Community: The Problem of Implementation in Comparative Perspective," in *Towards a Transatlantic Environmental Policy* (Washington, D.C.: European Institute, 1991); Jeremy Richardson, "Eroding EU Policies: Implementation Gaps, Cheating and Re-Steering," in Richardson, *European Union;* Wyn Grant, Duncan Matthews, and Peter Newell, *The Effectiveness of European Union Environmental Policy* (London: Macmillan, 2000).
51. Commission of the European Communities, *Nineteenth Annual Report on Monitoring the Application of Community Law (2001),* COM (2002) 324 Final (Brussels, June 28, 2002).
52. See http://europa.eu.int/comm/secretariat_general/sgb/droit_com/index_en.htm# infractions.
53. See also Tanja A. Börzel, *Leaders and Laggards in European Environmental Policy* (Cambridge: Cambridge University Press, 2003).
54. See also Jonathan Golub, ed., *New Instruments for Environmental Policy in the EU* (London: Routledge, 1998), and Matthieu Glachant, ed., *Implementing European Environmental Policy* (Cheltenham, England: Edward Elgar, 2001).
55. *Europe Energy,* no. 367, November 15, 1991, 1, 7.
56. "Inspectors Agree to Expanded Enforcement Role," *ENDS Environment Daily,* May 20, 1997.
57. Commission of the European Communities, *Implementing Community Environmental Law,* COM (96) 500 (Brussels, October 22, 1996).
58. See http://europa.eu.int/comm/environment/env-act5/chapt6.htm.
59. Commission of the European Communities, *Toward Sustainability,* (Brussels: Commission of the European Communities, 1992) chap. 7.
60. Mikael Skou Andersen, *Governance by Green Taxes: Making Pollution Prevention Pay* (Manchester: Manchester University Press, 1994); Timothy O'Riordan, ed., *Ecotaxation* (London: Earthscan, 1997).
61. Commission of the European Communities, *Environmental Taxes and Charges in the Single Market,* COM (97) 9 (Brussels, January 29, 1997).
62. European Environment Agency, "Environmental Taxes Gaining Importance in EU Member Countries," press release, Copenhagen, January 20, 2000.
63. European Environment Agency, "Greenhouse Gas Emissions Trends and Projections in Europe," *Environmental Issue Report,* no. 33 (Copenhagen: European Environment Agency, 2002).
64. Commission of the European Communities, "Proposal for a Directive of the European Parliament and of the Council establishing a scheme for greenhouse gas emission allowances trading within the Community and amending Council Directive 96/61/EC," COM (2001) 581 Final; 2001/0245 (COD) (Brussels, October 23, 2001).

65. See Commission of the European Communities, "Proposal for a Directive on the Promotion of electricity produced from renewable energy sources in the electricity market" COM (2000) 0884 Final, and Commission of the European Communities, "Communication from the Commission to the Council, the European Parliament, and the Economic and Social Committee of the Regions on the implementation of the Community Strategy and Action Plan on Renewable Energy Sources (1998–2000)," COM (2001) 69 Final (Brussels, February 16, 2001).

66. "Voluntary" agreements are seldom entirely voluntary and may be a tool for enforcing existing regulations. See Duncan Liefferink and Arthur P. J. Mol, "Voluntary Agreements as a Form of Deregulation?" in *Deregulation in the European Union: Environmental Perspectives*, ed. Ute Collier (London: Routledge, 1998).

67. Commission of the European Communities, "Communication from the Commission to the Council and the European Parliament on Environmental Agreements," COM (96) 561 Final (Brussels, November 27, 1996).

68. Commission of the European Communities, *Action Plan on Simplifying and Improving the Regulatory Environment*, COM (2002) 278 Final (Brussels, June 5, 2002).

69. See http://europa.eu.int/com/enlargement/faq/faq2.htm#22.

70. See EcoTec Research and Consulting Limited, "The Benefits of Compliance with the Environmental Acquis," DGENV Contract: Environmental Policy in the Applicant Countries and their Preparation for Accession. Service Contract B7-8110/2000/159960/MAR/H1, Final Report, Executive Summary, July 2001, C/1849/PtB.

71. World Bank, "Meeting the Environmental Acquis: Cost Estimates for Accession Countries," (Washington, D.C.: 2002); available at http://europa.eu.int/comm/environment/enlarg/pdf/benefit_xsum.pdf.

72. See Pierre-Henri Laurent and Marc Maresceau, eds., *The State of the European Union, Deepening and Widening*, vol. 4 (Boulder, Colo.: Lynne Rienner, 1998).

73. See Lenschow, *Environmental Policy Integration: Greening Sectoral Policies in Europe*.

12

The View from the South:
Developing Countries in
Global Environmental Politics

Adil Najam

This chapter examines the collective behavior of developing countries in global environmental politics. In the now burgeoning literature on global environmental politics there is no single aspect whose importance is acknowledged as consistently, but treated as casually, even shabbily, as the role of developing countries. Although very good work has been produced on the behavior of specific developing countries with regard to particular environmental issues, there is little analysis of how this group of countries—often referred to as the South or the third world—tends to behave collectively in global environmental politics, or even if it makes sense to talk about this group of countries as a collective.

Of course, it would be wrong to suggest that developing countries are a monolithic or entirely united bloc. Indeed, individual developing countries often differ, and sometimes bicker, on particular environmental issues. However, despite such specific differences, there is a generally acknowledged and easily identifiable sense of shared identity and common purpose among the developing countries of the South.

This chapter explores the nature of this shared identity and common purpose and how it manifests itself in global environmental politics. Its four sections will (a) outline a historical and conceptual understanding of "Southness"; (b) highlight the motivations and aspirations that developing countries have invested in global environmental politics; (c) review the experience of the developing countries in key aspects of this politics since the UN Conference on Environment and Development (UNCED)—also known as the Earth Summit—held in Rio de Janeiro in 1992; and (d) explain why developing countries harbor a certain sense of frustration with global environmental politics. A core argument of the chapter is that the South's current desire for what could be described as a New International *Environmental* Order stems from the same hopes and fears that had prompted its call in the 1970s for a New International *Economic* Order.

Understanding the Collective South

Over the last decade and a half, the term "South" has once again become a descriptor of choice for the set of nations variously referred to as developing countries, less developed countries, underdeveloped countries, or the third world. Especially in the context of global negotiations—and even more so in global environmental negotiations—these countries often choose, and sometimes demand, to be referred to as the South. This is more than a matter of semantics. The term reflects a certain aspect of their collective identity and their desire to negotiate as a collective.[1]

The term, and its use in the concept of the North-South divide, was a staple of scholarly and populist political discourse during the 1970s, particularly as a rallying cry in the demand by developing countries for a New International Economic Order (NIEO).[2] After having spent most of the 1980s in hibernation, the phrase again gained currency during the 1990s. In particular, the term's wide use by governments, nongovernmental organizations, the media, and officials during the Rio conference in 1992 revitalized it in popular environmental contexts.

Writing in the 1980s, the then secretary general of the Organization for Economic Cooperation and Development (OECD) pointed out that the North-South concept, "like all powerful ideas . . . has the virtue of grand simplicity" and described it as a divide between the developed countries of the North, which have "advanced or relatively advanced income levels and social conditions and a more or less completed process of national integration," and the developing countries of the South, "where the development process is still very much in train, where dual economies and dual societies are characteristic, and where, in many cases, hunger and poverty remain the dominant way of life for millions of people."[3] This still popular view of the North-South divide as a binary distinction between haves and have-nots is a powerful, and not untrue, way of understanding the concept—so long as one remembers that the South seeks not simply economic development but also a say in the political decisions affecting its destiny.[4] The 1990 South Commission Report defined the term in a decidedly more political context by talking not merely about economic poverty but also the "poverty of influence."[5] For the commission, the defining feature of the South is not just its economic weakness but also its political dependence. The self-definition of the South, therefore, is a definition of exclusion: these countries believe that they have been bypassed and view themselves as existing on the periphery. To redress what they consider to be an imbalance of influence, the developing countries have sought the vehicle of global negotiations, often referred to as the North-South dialogue.[6]

There are, of course, some who believe that events have made the concept of the South largely irrelevant or inaccurate. For example, a 1994 headline in the *New York Times* proclaimed, "The 'Third World' Is Dead."[7] Such unwarranted obituaries have been, and remain, an enduring feature of the collective's decidedly rocky history. For those who define the third world, or the South, solely in terms of cold war polarizations, the conclusion is obvious: the emergence of Southern unity, they insist, was a result of cold war politics; now that the cold war is dead, the alliance should also be buried.[8]

Yet at the simplest and most pragmatic level, what Roger Hansen had to say about the validity of North-South thinking twenty-five years ago seems equally valid today: "If over [130] developing countries time and again, in forum after forum, act as a diplomatic unit, they would seem to merit analysis as a potential actor of major importance in the international system."[9] At a deeper level of analysis, it is important to remember that for many of these countries, the desire for unity in the face of an international order that they believe continues to place them at a systemic disadvantage still outweighs the internal diversity or differences. Most importantly, even if some Northern observers consider the South's agenda of the 1970s "discredited,"[10] it remains unfinished business for much of the South and a goal believed to be well worth pursuing.[11]

A sense of new vulnerabilities, the persistent pangs of an unfinished agenda, and the opportunity to renew a North-South dialogue under environmental auspices has served as a rallying point, translated into a renewed assertiveness by the South, especially around the broad issue of sustainable development.[12] The reinvigoration that the South seems to have enjoyed during and since the 1992 Earth Summit and the prominence regained as a relatively cohesive negotiating collective took many by surprise. After all, it was not illogical to conclude that long-standing economic, political, and geographic differences within the South could only be compounded by subsequent environmental differences. And indeed, at many turns during the 1992 Earth Summit, and in global negotiations since then, differences within the developing countries of the Group of 77 (G-77) have led to apparent fractures and frictions in the collective. For example, in the climate change negotiations the influential oil-producing (and comparatively wealthy) members of the G-77 have had a significantly different agenda than the G-77 members who belong to the Alliance of Small Island States (AOSIS) and other coastal nations with far lower income levels who face serious threats from a possible rise in the sea level.[13] Negotiations on the Biosafety Protocol to the Biodiversity Convention saw developing countries take significantly different positions based on their trade priorities.[14] In the negotiations on desertification, a dispute between African and non-African members nearly brought G-77 coordination to a halt.[15]

However, even when developing countries have different priorities on specific issues in global negotiations—something that should not be surprising—they almost always have chosen to pursue these interests within the framework of the Southern collective. The collective has remained remarkably resilient in the face of conditions that could have predicated disintegration. Analysts trace this to a common view of the nature of environmental issues and their placement within a North-South framework, which suggests that the collective South will continue to play an important role in future global environmental politics. As Porter, Brown, and Chasek note, "Despite growing disparities among the developing countries between rapidly industrializing countries such as China, India, Malaysia, and Brazil, and debt-ridden countries that have experienced little or no growth since the 1980s, such as most of sub-Saharan Africa, Vietnam, Myanmar, and Nicaragua, developing countries share a common view of the relationship between global environmental issues and North-South economic relations."[16]

Institutionally, the South consists of two distinct organizations—the Non-Aligned Movement (NAM) and the Group of 77—which have played different but complementary roles in furthering the Southern agenda. As Sauvant has noted, "While the Non-Aligned Countries [have] played a key role in making the development issue a priority item of the international agenda, the Group of 77 has become the principal organ of the Third World through which the concrete actions . . . are negotiated within the framework of the United Nations system."[17] An instrument of political summitry, the hundred-plus members of NAM meet every three years at the summit level to renew (or redefine) their vows. Meetings of foreign ministers are held every eighteen months. Operating through ministerial committees, NAM has no permanent institutional infrastructure to manage its activities between these meetings. On environmental issues, NAM has made some—but relatively few—declaratory statements of aspiration, and it is the G-77 that remains the collective voice of the developing countries in global environmental politics.

The Group of 77 has been described by Julius Nyerere, former president of Tanzania, as the "trade union of the poor."[18] It functions as the negotiating arm of the developing country collective during global negotiations. The G-77 describes its goal as "provid[ing] the means for the developing world to articulate and promote its collective economic interests and enhance its joint negotiating capacity on all major North-South international economic issues in the United Nations system, and promote economic and technical cooperation among developing countries."[19] Although the G-77 emerged around the same time as NAM, it has distinctive origins and, unlike NAM, was born within—and was primarily a result of—the changing composition of the United Nations in the 1960s. Starting as a temporary caucus of seventy-seven developing countries, it has now grown into an ad hoc but quasi-permanent negotiating caucus of 132 members, plus China, which has the status of associate member but plays an influential role in the collective (see Figure 12-1).

One of the main historical achievements of the G-77 was its role as chief negotiator for Southern demands for a New International Economic Order. Although the NIEO never achieved its goals, the G-77 has remained a negotiation collective and has exerted influence in agenda setting within various UN forums. It enjoyed particular successes in shaping final compromises during the 1992 Earth Summit and in a series of subsequent global environmental negotiations.[20]

Annual ministerial meetings, convened at the beginning of the regular sessions of the UN General Assembly, serve as the major decision-making body for the G-77. Special ministerial meetings are periodically called to focus on particular issues or to prepare for important global negotiations. G-77 hubs have sprung up in New York, Geneva, Rome, Vienna, Paris, Nairobi, and

Figure 12-1 The Group of 77 plus China

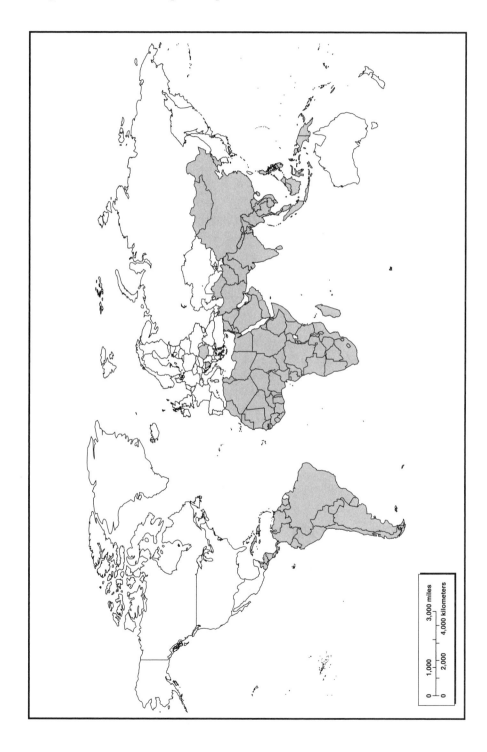

Washington, where various international organizations are based. In addition, G-77 caucuses are active in most international negotiations, where they adopt joint bargaining positions and strategies. The G-77 chairmanship rotates on an annual basis among its three regional subgroups—Asia, Africa, and Latin America—and the delegation from the chairperson's country serves as the designated spokesperson for the entire caucus in all negotiations during that year. Although the South has emerged as a stable and resilient collective in global environmental politics, it has often been forced to adopt lowest common denominator positions because of the impulse for risk reduction, low expectations, assumed habits of collaboration wrought out of a long history, and the need to herd a large and differentiated collective in the face of chronic resource constraints and no management effort. This has limited the G-77's ability to negotiate effectively for the shared goals of the collective or the differentiated interests of its members. The unity of the G-77, while not insignificant, is forever tentative; it is a unity that the G-77 stumbled into—a unity that it has learned to stumble into.

Southern Motivations in Global Environmental Politics

The timing of the 1992 Earth Summit was opportune for the South. The UNCED preparatory process coincided with the withering away of cold war politics. The end of the cold war not only instilled a sense of new vulnerabilities in the developing world but also provided the motivation for revitalizing the collective South. At the same time, Rio offered an opportunity to engage the North in a new dialogue. UNCED gave the South a forum, an issue, and an audience that it had been denied since the 1970s. The South—represented by an energetic G-77—succeeded not only in reopening the North-South dialogue but also effectively made it the focus of the Rio conference. Ultimately, the achievements at Rio and its legacy did not match the South's exaggerated hopes.[21] However, it is also true that Rio and subsequent global negotiations provided the South with opportunities to influence the global environmental agenda, particularly within the context of sustainable development.

A close examination of the goals and actions of developing countries during global environmental negotiations suggests that the South currently seeks what can be described as a New International *Environmental* Order (NIEnvO) and that this goal stems from the same concerns and ambitions that had prompted its call for a New International *Economic* Order in the 1970s.[22] Roger Hansen defined the original NIEO debate as a conflict over "conceptions about the management of society."[23] Rallying its newfound unity and negotiating as a tight bloc, the G-77 gained a major victory when a 1974 special session of the United Nations General Assembly legitimized the South's demand for the creation of a New International Economic Order by passing a resolution to that effect and drawing up a plan of action. However, the optimism reflected in the UN resolution proved misplaced, and the differences persisted—North accusing South of being confrontational, and South blaming North for perpetuating an unjust order. By the 1980s it was obvious that the momentum had been lost, and as Mahbub-ul-Haq put it, "North-South negotiations [had] deteriorated to a ritual and a skillful exercise in *non*-dialogue."[24] In subsequent years, as the North's perception of the economic importance of natural resources in the South (particularly mineral and agricultural products) diminished, so did the perceived leverage enjoyed by the G-77. The NIEO agenda rapidly receded from world attention, as did discussions about North-South dialogue. It wasn't until the Earth Summit in 1992 that the relevance of and need for North-South negotiations once again became the subject of broad academic, policy, and even public discussion.

One should note, however, that the environmental issue as an exemplar of the North-South divide actually predates Rio by at least twenty years. It is, in fact, striking that the vast literature on the history of the North-South conflict, as well as the now bulky scholarship on international environmental politics, treats the role of developing countries in the United Nations Conference on the Human Environment (UNCHE), held in Stockholm in 1972, as a mere footnote. In fact, UNCHE was one of the first global forums at which the South consciously negotiated as a unified collective and adopted many of the very same substantive arguments and negotiation strategies that were soon to become the hallmark of the NIEO debates.[25]

From the very beginning, many developing countries perceived environmental concerns as a distinctively North-South issue and, in some cases, as an effort to sabotage the South's developmental aspirations. The intellectual leadership of the South very poignantly set out to redefine the environmental issue area in a decidedly North-South context. The most telling example was the so-called 1971 Founex Report, produced by a distinguished group of Southern intellectuals as part of the UNCHE preparatory process.[26] The tone and substance of the report foreshadowed, nearly exactly, what was soon to become the rhetoric of the South not only during the NIEO debates in the early 1970s but also during UNCED in 1992 and in other major environmental forums before and since then. The Founex Report, one of the most authentic and articulate enunciations of the South's collective interests on issues of environment and development, provides critical testimony that (1) these interests have remained unchanged over time; (2) they are the same interests that informed the NIEO ideology; and (3) these same interests lie at the heart of today's global politics of sustainable development.

The constancy in the South's position at Stockholm and at Rio is striking and demonstrates that the original NIEO ideals of the South have not only survived but have resurfaced in these new rounds of global environmental negotiations. For example, Chris Mensah, himself a G-77 negotiator at UNCED, points out that the Southern leadership explicitly formulated its negotiation strategy around two key goals—first, to "ensure that the South has adequate environmental space for its future development," and, second, to "modify global economic relations in such a way that the South obtains the required resources, technology, and access to markets which would enable it to pursue a development process that is both environmentally sound and rapid enough to meet [its] needs and aspirations."[27] In short, developing countries have consistently contextualized environmental issues as being part of the larger complex of North-South concerns, particularly concerns about an iniquitous international order and their desire to bring about structural change in that order.

The experience in global environmental politics in the last decade seems to suggest that polarizations across North-South lines are unlikely to disappear either by ignoring them or wishing them away.[28] The resilience that the South has shown in pursuing what it considers its legitimate agenda of economic justice and international systemic change suggests that international environmental negotiations will continue to be influenced by a Southern agenda that looks very much like a call for a New International *Environmental* Order. As Gareth Porter and Janet Brown note, "Many developing countries, particularly the more radical members of the Group of 77, have viewed global environmental negotiations as the best, if not the only, opportunity to advance a broader agenda of change in the structure of North-South economic relationships."[29] Marc Williams elaborates, "The possibility of linking negotiations on global environmental change with demands for change in other areas of North-South relations is one crucial reason for the continued participation of developing countries in negotiations of environmental problems."[30] He adds, "It is not . . . a question of environment being co-opted into the North-South debate. It already exists in this debate and is conceived in North-South terms."[31]

If the new vulnerabilities brought forth by the end of the cold war were what motivated the developing countries to reinvigorate the collective South, and the concurrent onset of global environmental negotiations what provided forums in which to engage the North, it is the all-encompassing rubric of sustainable development that has enabled them to pursue the new North-South dialogue without having (yet) lost the North's attention. For some, the global politics of sustainable development, loosely defined as it is—and, in fact, because it is so loosely defined—provides a broad framework within which to build a global compact to address both the North's concern for environmental sustainability and the South's desire for economic and social development. For others, including many G-77 negotiators, this new politics encompasses "a struggle between the developing and developed countries to define sustainable development in a way that fits their own agendas. The developed countries, most of which are relatively rich, put environment first. By contrast, the developing countries, most of which are poor and still struggling to meet basic human needs, put development first."[32]

Around the time of the Rio Earth Summit, many in the North and South argued that sustainable development might be the trump card that the South had been seeking all along. The North's new concern for global environmental problems, it was argued, provided the South with considerable leverage and bargaining power because without the participation of the developing countries many such problems cannot be addressed effectively.[33]

For example, a Caribbean official suggested that "for the first time in more than a decade, the developing countries have an issue [the environment] where they have some real leverage," while India's environment minister went even further to proclaim that "the begging bowl is [now] really in the hands of the Western world."[34]

In retrospect, such Southern enthusiasm proved decidedly exaggerated, and with time it has certainly mellowed.[35] Although the South enjoyed influence in the Rio process, it soon found that its leverage lay less in influencing what went into the treaties than in what was kept out of them. Evidence since Rio confirms that while the South may have some leverage in the global politics of sustainable development, its extent is limited, its application is largely to avoid defeat, and its use is conditioned by the existence of a high level of concern, even alarm, in the North for the environmental issue under discussion. For example, Marian Miller's research on global regimes relating to the ozone layer, hazardous waste, and biodiversity found that "when there is a shared perception of environmental vulnerability, the Third World is able to gain a modest bargaining advantage."[36]

From the South's perspective, such assessments are sobering but not melancholy. Although the desire for systemic change endures in many quarters, it has been tempered by more realistic assessments. Moreover, part of the defining essence of the collective South is a desire to minimize risk rather than to maximize gain. From this standpoint, the Southern collective has been able to do exactly what it set out to do: minimize the risk of being bulldozed by a Northern environmental agenda, maintain a North-South focus on the global environmental dialogue, and eke out little victories (in terms of global transfers) whenever possible. Importantly, Southern hopes persist for a new North-South bargain constructed around the global politics of sustainable development. This potential emanates from two important differences between the first generation of North-South dialogue and its current incarnation.

First, unlike its predecessor, this new generation of North-South interaction is characterized by both sides wanting to establish a global dialogue, albeit with differing interests and agendas. For the South, such a dialogue is itself a long-standing goal. For the North, it is necessitated by the realization that global action on the environment cannot be successful without the active participation of the developing countries. This is a major sea change from the 1970s, when the South was calling for a dialogue and the North actively resisted. Furthermore, there is a certain sense of urgency on both sides, since the effects of both environmental devastation and abject poverty compound visibly over time.

Second, by their very nature, it is often difficult to conceive of global environmental problems in terms of victory and defeat, especially in the long run. Although the jury is still out on whether and how the global environment might become a win-win issue, all indications suggest that it can very easily be transformed into a lose-lose proposition. This, too, marks a difference from aspects of earlier North-South dialogues, such as the oil or debt crises of the 1970s, which failed partly because the issues were perceived as zero-sum games.

At the heart of North-South politics of sustainable development are debates about the costs to be borne, the ability to bear these costs, the responsibility for causing the problem, and the ability to influence future decisions. These can be reduced to contentions about past responsibility, present ability, and future priorities. Serious differences persist between North and South on all three. Bridging the deep differences is not an easy task and would require, at a minimum, innovative strategies from both North and South. One proposed strategy for the South would build upon the lessons of negotiation theory and the experiences of the South. The eight-point strategy can be paraphrased as: Stop feeling angry at the North and sorry for yourself.[37] It recommends that the South focus on interests, not positions; cultivate its own power; be hard on issues, not on people; redefine the international environmental agenda; organize itself; develop its constituency; clean up its own act; and remember that good agreements are more important than "winning." Such a strategy would also lead to a more productive international negotiation process.

Given the deeply felt interests that the South has resiliently pursued for so long, it is unlikely that it will voluntarily forsake its demands or be argued out of them. Given a realistic assessment of the South's bargaining leverage, it is equally unlikely that the South will be able to browbeat the North into simply accepting its positions. If meaningful headway is to be made, it will have to come through some mechanism that allows the interests of both sides to be met. In this regard, sustainable development can be a potentially fortuitous term in that it can (given the right conditions) allow efficient packaging of issues of concern to North and South—issues that they might otherwise be hesitant to deal with individually. However, issue linkage can be fraught with both dangers and opportunities. Some such as Christopher Stone fear that "adding cards to the deck raises the risk that the environment will get lost in the shuffle."[38] However, Lawrence Susskind reminds us that issue linkage can be "crucial to the success of negotiation[s]" that involve complex, multi-party, multi-issue bargaining.[39] While there is certainly the danger of issue linkage turning into blackmail—either by the North arm-twisting the South to follow its environmental dictates or by the South threatening environmental inaction in the absence of a restructured international system—there is a strong case for both to seek issue linkages in their pursuit of meaningful dialogue. After all, the very term "sustainable development" is the embodiment of creative issue linkage.

Southern Views on Global Environmental Politics since Rio

The 1992 UNCED conference is widely viewed as one of the high points of the last thirty years of global environmental politics. Rio's legacy probably owes as much to the many disappointments since that conference as it does to its actual achievements. For example, in a recent survey of 252 scholars and practitioners from 71 countries, nearly 70 percent of the respondents viewed the Rio Earth Summit as having been "very significant" or "monumental," even though only 6 percent believed that significant progress had been made toward implementing Rio goals. The survey suggests that Rio's greatest impact came from its indirect outputs: its success in giving a higher global profile to issues of environment and development; spurring the growth of national and international institutions, policies, projects, and multilateral agreements for environment and development; and giving more prominence to the views of developing countries on global environmental policy.[40]

For developing countries, a key manifestation of these indirect outputs was the so-called Rio Bargain. Although difficult to define with precision—and embraced with varying degrees of conviction by various parties—the Rio Bargain is generally understood to be an attempt to bridge lingering North-South differences through two key mechanisms: the concept of sustainable development and a set of design principles for global environmental agreements that addressed key concerns of the South.[41]

More than a decade after Rio, it is easy to forget that the notion of sustainable development—which has since become somewhat of a Southern mantra—was not the South's idea but rather a conceptual device used to appease developing countries apprehensive, since before the 1972 Stockholm conference, that environment protection would be used as a reason to stall their economic development. Indeed, the official name of the Rio Earth Summit—the United Nations Conference on Environment and Development—was crafted, after some debate, to signify that environment and development were complementary rather than contradictory categories.

Still, many in the South came to UNCED and viewed the notion of sustainable development with doubt and in some cases outright trepidation.[42] Eventually, however, developing country negotiations came to see this concept and the broader Rio process as good opportunities to reopen the North-South dialogue, which had languished through the 1980s, and to move toward a grand North-South bargain for which the South had been striving since the 1970s.[43]

Thus, for the G-77 (but perhaps not for many in the North), the most important legacy of the Rio process was a global commitment to sustainable development, which the South sees as providing an emphasis on development equal to environmental protection, and to three critical, subsidiary principles: additionality, common but differentiated responsibilities, and polluter pays.[44] Embodied in the frameworks of various Rio documents, these principles arose out of Southern fears that even though they had not been historically responsible for creating the major global environmental problems, the cost of global environmental action would somehow be transferred to them either in terms of forgone developmental opportunities or actual remediation and adaptation costs. This section reviews the impact of the last ten years on Rio's North-South bargain from the perspective of the South.[45]

Sustainable Development

Sustainable development was never a clear concept.[46] Indeed, it was never meant to be clear. It was a political compromise, and a rather good one at that. Its greatest strength was constructive ambiguity; actors that might otherwise not talk to one another could accept the concept for very different reasons and agree to talk.

The World Commission on Environment and Development had gravitated toward the concept of sustainable development in a conscious attempt to resolve developing country apprehension about the environmental agenda. The Earth Summit found the concept useful in getting the North and the South to sit at the same table. As a result, use of the concept began to evolve. By the time Rio ended, many saw sustainable development not as a nebulous ideal or vague goal but as a policy prescription, a desired if not mandatory pathway for future national and international policy.[47]

In practical terms, the good news is that many in the South have now totally internalized the concept of sustainable development and have become staunch advocates. This denotes a significant evolution. Many government as well as citizen organizations in developing countries have adopted sustainable development as a guiding principle for implementation and action. A variety of organizations, ranging from community groups to government agencies to international organizations, are experimenting with the concept, trying to give it practical and policy meaning on the ground. As a result, at the local level the concept of sustainable development is far more real today than it was a decade ago.[48]

The bad news is that at the level of intergovernmental debates, the concept has become more, rather than less, murky since Rio. Through repeated and often irrelevant inclusion in diplomatic rhetoric, the term stands in danger of being reduced from an innovative framework for negotiation to an empty declaratory aspiration—a label that diplomats can place on just about anything. Thus, while sustainable development was once seen in some quarters as a potentially powerful and even threatening concept—because it suggested the possibility of change in the status quo—it is today on the verge of becoming ineffectual and divorced from its initial action orientation. For those in the South who had come to accept and even embrace the term because of its embedded promise of systemic change, this dilution of the concept has been particularly disturbing.[49]

Additionality

The principle of additionality arose out of the Southern concern that environmental issues would divert international aid from traditional developmental matters. Developing countries feared that instead of raising new funds for dealing with global environmental issues, the North and international institutions would simply transfer to the environment resources that had been previously targeted for development. The principle of additionality sought to ensure that new monies would be made available to deal with global environmental issues.

Despite assurances given to the South, however, this principle was abandoned soon after UNCED, during negotiation of the Desertification Convention (UNCCD). Early in these negotiations it became clear that few if any new funds would be made available for implementation of the treaty. This dismayed developing countries, particularly those in Africa, and became a major source of contention in the negotiations. Ultimately, a Global Mechanism was established under the CCD whose role was essentially to use existing resources more efficiently in order to meet the action needs of the Convention.[50] Even though the Global Environment Facility (GEF) eventually decided to include desertification activities in its funding, the CCD negotiations severely damaged the principle of additionality. Since then, negotiations on several other multilateral environmental agreements (MEAs)—including, for example, those addressing climate change and toxic chemicals—have also seen arguments from Northern nations that utilizing market forces and better management of existing resources are adequate substitutes for at least some portion of the original promise of additionality.

Common but Differentiated Responsibility

This principle acknowledges that some nations have a greater and more direct responsibility for having created and, therefore, addressing global environmental problems. Although these problems are the concern of all nations, and all nations should work toward their solution, responsibility for action should be differentiated in proportion to the responsibility for creating the problem and the available financial and technical resources to take effective action.

While this principle places the primary responsibility for action on industrialized countries, it was actually a concession of sorts made by the developing countries. Placing responsibility for action on the North had been a major argument of the South since before the 1972 Stockholm conference.[51] In accepting this principle, the South agreed that it, too, would address global environment issues—provided that the primary burden of action, investment, and implementation was not shifted to the very countries that are least responsible for creating the problem and least able to resolve it.

The principle of common but differentiated responsibilities enjoys generally broad support and has been explicitly acknowledged in nearly all international environmental agreements since Rio. At the same time, one could argue that it faces an important assault in the context of the Climate Convention. The United States has taken the position that it cannot accept mandatory targets for greenhouse gas (GHG) emissions unless some type of restrictions are also placed on major developing countries such as China and India. Industrialized countries account for the vast majority of historical GHG emissions. In addition, although aggregate national GHG emissions are growing significantly in many developing countries, the per capita emissions of citizens in these countries will remain significantly smaller than those in the North for decades to come. Many in the South worry that the U.S. position constitutes a shift from past responsibility as a yardstick for future action—a change that would, from their perspective, make global environmental regimes even less equitable.[52]

Polluter Pays Principle

This principle has deep roots in domestic environmental policy in the North, particularly in the United States. It seeks to ensure that the costs of environmental action, economic and other, will be borne by those who created the need for that action. As with the principle of common but differentiated responsibility, the Polluter Pays principle is rooted in concerns about fairness and constitutes a key component of the Rio Bargain.

Along with other aspects of the Rio Bargain, many in the South believe that the Polluter Pays principle has been steadily diluted in the last ten years. They point to an increasing pattern of pushing MEA implementation steadily southward, including in the climate, desertification, and biodiversity regimes, by seeking relatively fewer changes in behavior patterns in the North and relatively more in the South—even though it was Northern behavior that gave rise to many problems in the first place.[53]

Consider, for example, the Clean Development Mechanism (CDM), a provision of the Kyoto climate agreement that allows industrialized countries to meet some of their responsibilities for greenhouse gas reduction by investing in projects in the South. In the name of efficiency, the CDM moves a great deal of climate action to developing countries where emission reductions are likely to be cheaper rather than imposing greater costs in the countries responsible for past GHG emissions. Although the logic of economic efficiency is potentially compelling, the CDM arguably threatens the core moral element of the Polluter Pays principle, in that it allows industrialized countries to avoid taking more significant and expensive action domestically—essentially allowing the polluters to buy their way out of their responsibility. In addition, while capturing efficiencies in the South may be enticing in the short term, it leaves subsequent generations in the developing countries with potentially ever more arduous tasks in the future, as they would have already sold away their rights to cheaper solutions.

Southern Frustrations in Global Environmental Politics

Thirty years of global environmental politics have left the Southern collective with rather mixed results. On the positive side, one could argue that the South, which had largely rejected the global environmental agenda at Stockholm in 1972, has today internalized and accepted much, if not most, of that agenda. The concept of sustainable development has allowed developing countries to incorporate long-standing concerns about economic development and social justice into the emerging environmental agenda, and by doing so they have influenced the nature of global environmental discourse. More broadly, global environmental politics has afforded the South a new arena in which to advance its persistent demand for radical, structural reform of the international system.

Yet the dominant feeling within the South remains one of frustration with global environmental politics. There are few tangible benefits to show for its continuing and increasing involvement and investment in this issue. The South has been no more successful in crafting a New International *Environmental* Order than it had been in building a New International *Economic* Order. Most of the concessions the South thought it had negotiated from the North have proved largely illusionary, and the so-called Rio Bargain seems to be unraveling. Much of the attention in terms of North-South environmental relations since UNCED is focused on what the South sees as the failure of the North to deliver what had been promised or implied at Rio, such as additional resources, technology transfers, and capacity building. The inability of the North to fulfill these commitments is a major contributor to the South's current sense of frustration. As the concept of sustainable development loses clarity and purpose at the global level, and as the key principles of additionality, common but differentiated responsibility, and polluter pays are steadily eroded (at least from the South's standpoint), developing countries have a diminishing interest in staying engaged in these processes. These issues defined the *raison d'être* for the South's engagement in global environmental negotiations. While Southern disenchantment may not turn into total disengagement, it is certainly not conducive to meaningful North-South partnerships for what still remain very pressing global environmental challenges.

Parallel to this unraveling of the Rio Bargain is the negotiation overload that has characterized the world of global environmental policy since the Rio Earth Summit. It is not without irony that the less we are able to implement existing MEAs, the more frantic we seem to become in trying to create new ones. MEA proliferation has led to a severe case of negotiation fatigue among all countries, particularly developing countries. The limited and already stretched human resources available to these countries are further thinned by increasing demands of even more, and more complex and demanding, MEA negotiations. While major Northern countries have responded to the negotiation proliferation by deploying more human and knowledge resources, most developing countries are unable to do so, compounding the systemic disadvantage they already face in the negotiations.[54]

As we move through the first decade of the twenty-first century, developing country negotiators often consider themselves disenchanted, disadvantaged, and disempowered in global environmental politics.[55] For the South, the sense of frustration stems directly from having seen the North-South bargain, a cherished legacy of the Rio Earth Summit, unravel over the last ten years. The failure of the 2002 World Summit on Sustainable Development in Johannesburg to revive the Rio Bargain in any meaningful way is likely to deepen Southern frustration and the sense that global environmental politics is in a disquieting state of malaise.[56] Yet the key assumption that had led to the forging of the original bargain is still valid: meaningful progress on the great environmental challenges of our times is unlikely, if not impossible, without the full and active participation of the developing countries. The view from the South is not without hope, but it contains many challenges that cannot be wished away.

Notes

1. For a more elaborate treatment of the argument made in this section, see Adil Najam, "The Collective South in Multinational Environmental Politics" in *Policymaking and Prosperity: A Multinational Anthology*, ed. Stuart Nagel (Lanham, Md.: Lexington Books, 2003), 197–240.
2. For discussion, see Craig Murphy, *The Emergence of the NIEO Ideology* (Boulder, Colo.: Westview Press, 1984).
3. Emile Van Lennep, "North-South Relations in the 80s: A Constructive Approach to New Realities," in *Global Development: Issues and Choices*, ed. K. Haq (Washington, D.C.: North-South Roundtable, 1983), 15.
4. See Stephen D. Krasner, *Structural Conflict: The Third World Against Global Liberalism* (Berkeley: University of California Press, 1985); and Caroline Thomas, *In Search of Security: The Third World in International Relations* (Boulder, Colo.: Lynne Rienner, 1987).
5. South Commission, *The Challenge to the South: The Report of the South Commission* (Oxford: Oxford University Press, 1990), 1.
6. See B. P. Menon, *Global Dialogue: The New International Order* (London: Pergamon Press, 1977); Murphy, *The Emergence of the NIEO Ideology.*
7. Barbara Crossette, "The 'Third World' Is Dead, but Spirits Linger," *New York Times*, November 13, 1994, A1.
8. Examples include A. Oxley, "North/South Dimensions of a New World Order," in *Whose New World Order?*, ed. Mara Bustelo and Philip Alston (Annandale, Va.: Federation Press, 1991).
9. Roger Hansen, *Beyond the North-South Stalemate* (New York: McGraw-Hill, 1979), 2. See also Marc Williams, "Re-articulating the Third World Coalition: The Role of the Environmental Agenda," *Third World Quarterly* 14, no. 1 (1993): 7–29; Cedric Grant, "Equity in International Relations: A Third World Perspective," *International Affairs* 71, no. 3 (1995): 567–587.
10. James K. Sebenius, "Negotiating a Regime to Control Global Warming," in *Greenhouse Warming: Negotiating a Global Regime*, ed. Jessica Tuchman Mathews (Washington, D.C.: World Resources Institute, 1991), 87.
11. South Commission, *The Challenge to the South;* Mohammed Ayoob, "The New-Old Disorder in the Third World," *Global Governance* 1, no.1 (1995): 59–77; Adil Najam, "An Environmental Negotiation Strategy for the South," *International Environmental Affairs* 7, no. 3 (1995): 249–287.
12. Dennis Pirages, *Global Ecopolitics: The New Context for International Relations* (North Scituate, Mass.: Duxbury Press, 1978); Hayward R. Alker Jr., and Peter M. Haas, "The Rise of Global Ecopolitics," in *Global Accord: Environmental Challenges and International Responses*, ed. Nazli Choucri (Cambridge: MIT Press, 1993), 133–171; Najam, "An Environmental Negotiation Strategy for the South."
13. William R. Moomaw, "International Environmental Policy and the Softening of Sovereignty," *Fletcher Forum of World Affairs* 21 (summer/fall 1997): 7–15.
14. Aaron Cosbey and S. Burgiel, *The Cartagena Protocol on Biosafety: An Analysis of Results*, IISD Briefing Note (Winnipeg, Canada: International Institute for Sustainable Development, 2000).
15. Anil Agarwal, Sunita Narain, and Anju Sharma, *Green Politics* (New Delhi: Centre for Science and Environment, 1999); Elisabeth Corell, *The Negotiable Desert: Expert*

Knowledge in the Negotiations of the Convention to Combat Desertification, Linkoping Studies in Arts and Sciences, no. 191 (1999), Linkoping University, Linkoping, Sweden.

16. Gareth Porter, Janet W. Brown, and Pamela S. Chasek, *Global Environmental Politics,* 3d ed. (Boulder, Colo.: Westview Press, 2000), 179.

17. K.–P. Sauvant, *The Group of 77: Evolution, Structure, Organization* (New York: Oceana Publications, 1981), 5.

18. Julius K. Nyerere, "Unity for a New Order," in *Dialogue for a New Order,* ed. K. Haq (New York: Pergamon Press, 1980), 3–10, 7.

19. *Principles and Objectives of the Group of 77 for the Year 2000 and Beyond* (New York: Office of the Chairman of the Group of 77, 1994), 1.

20. See Najam, "An Environmental Negotiation Strategy for the South"; Adil Najam, "A Developing Countries' Perspective on Population, Environment and Development," *Population Research and Policy Review* 15, no. 1 (1996): 1–19; Tariq Banuri, *Noah's Ark or Jesus's Cross?* Working Paper WP/UNCED/1992/1 (Islamabad, Pakistan: Sustainable Development Policy Institute, 1992); Makhund G. Rajan, "Bargaining with the Environment: A New Weapon for the South?" *South Asia Research* 12, no. 2 (1992): 135–147; and Agarwal, Narain, and Sharma, *Green Politics.*

21. See Banuri, *Noah's Ark or Jesus's Cross?;* Najam, "An Environmental Negotiation Strategy for the South"; Adil Najam, *The Case for a South Secretariat in International Environmental Negotiation,* Program on Negotiation Working Paper 94-8 (Cambridge: Program on Negotiation at Harvard Law School, 1994); Richard Sandbrook, "UNGASS Has Run Out of Steam," *International Affairs* 73, no. 4 (1997): 641–654.

22. Najam, "An Environmental Negotiation Strategy for the South."

23. Hansen, *Beyond the North-South Stalemate,* vii.

24. Mahbub-ul-Haq, "North-South Dialogue: Is there a Future?" in Hag, *Dialogue for a New Order,* 270–287, 270.

25. See Wade Rowland, *The Plot to Save the World* (Toronto: Clarke, Irwin & Co., 1973).

26. *Development and Environment,* Report and Working Papers of Experts Convened by the Secretary General of the United Nations Conference on the Human Environment, Founex, Switzerland, June 4–12, 1971 (Paris: Mouton, 1971).

27. Chris Mensah, "The Role of Developing Countries," in *The Environment After Rio: International Law and Economics,* ed. L. Campigio, L. Pineschi, D. Siniscalco, and T. Treves (London: Graham and Trotman, 1994), 33–53 (p. 38).

28. Banuri, *Noah's Ark or Jesus's Cross?;* Caroline Thomas, *The Environment in International Relations* (London: Royal Institute of International Affairs, 1992); Williams, "Re-articulating the Third World Coalition"; Tariq Osman Hyder, "Looking Back to See Forward," in *Negotiating Climate Change: The Inside Story of the Rio Convention,* ed. I. M. Mintzer and J. A. Leonard (Cambridge: Cambridge University Press, 1994), 201–226; Agarwal, Narain, and Sharma, *Green Politics;* Adil Najam, "Trade and Environment After Seattle: A Negotiation Agenda for the South," in *Journal of Environment and Development* 9, no. 4 (2000): 405–425.

29. Gareth Porter and Janet Brown, *Global Environmental Politics* (Boulder, Colo.: Westview Press, 1991), 129.

30. Williams, "Re-articulating the Third World Coalition," 19.

31. Ibid., 25.

32. Hyder, "Looking Back to See Forward," 205.

33. For example, G. J. MacDonald predicted that "the views of the developing nations will determine the direction, and probably the ultimate significance, of UNCED" ("Brazil 1992: Who Needs This Meeting?" *Issues in Science and Technology* 7, no. 4 [1992]: 41–44). The *New York Times* (March 17, 1992) noted that "for the first time . . . the developing countries have an issue where they have some real leverage." Oran Young argued that the South has "substantial bargaining leverage" and that "Northerners will ignore the demands of the South regarding climate change at their peril." Oran Young, "Negotiating an International Climate Regime: The Institutional Bargaining

for Environmental Governance," in *Global Accord: Environmental Challenges and International Responses*, ed. N. Choucri (Cambridge: MIT Press, 1993), 447.

34. Both statements quoted in Rajan, "Bargaining with the Environment," 135–136.

35. Ibid., 147.

36. Marian A. L. Miller, *The Third World in Global Environmental Politics* (Boulder, Colo.: Lynne Rienner, 1995), 141. Others have reached similar conclusions, including Susan Sell, who examined North-South environmental bargaining on ozone depletion, climate change, and biodiversity, and V. de Campos Mello, who analyzed the forestry negotiations at UNCED. See Susan Sell, "North-South Environmental Bargaining: Ozone, Climate Change, and Biodiversity," *Global Governance* 2, no. 1 (1996): 97–118; V. de Campos Mello, *North-South Conflicts and Power Distribution in UNCED Negotiations: The Case of Forestry*, IIASA Working Paper WP-93-26 (Laxenburg, Austria: International Institute for Applied Systems Analysis, 1993).

37. Najam, "An Environmental Negotiation Strategy for the South," 249–287.

38. Christopher D. Stone, *The Gnat Is Older than Man: Global Environment and Human Agenda* (Princeton: Princeton University Press, 1993), 115.

39. Lawrence E. Susskind, *Environmental Diplomacy: Negotiating More Effective Global Agreements* (New York: Oxford University Press, 1994).

40. Adil Najam, Janice M. Poling, Naoyuki Yamagishi, Daniel G. Straub, Jillian Sarno, Sara M. DeRitter, and Eonjeong M. Kim, "From Rio to Johannesburg: Progress and Prospects," *Environment* 4, no. 7 (September 2002): 26–38.

41. See, for example, Martin Khor K. Peng, *The Future of North-South Relations: Conflict or Cooperation?* (Penang: Third World Network, 1992).

42. Edward Kufour, "G-77: We Won't Negotiate Away Our Sovereignty," *Third World Resurgence* 14–15 (1991): 17; South Centre, *Environment and Development: Towards a Common Strategy of the South in UNCED Negotiations and Beyond* (Geneva: South Centre, 1991); Banuri, *Noah's Ark or Jesus's Cross?*; Najam, "An Environmental Negotiation Strategy for the South."

43. A. O. Adede, "International Environmental Law from Stockholm to Rio," *Environmental Policy and Law* 22, no. 2 (1992): 88–105; Williams, "Re-articulating the Third World Coalition"; Najam, "An Environmental Negotiation Strategy for the South."

44. For more on each, see chap. 3 above and David Hunter, James Salzman, and Durwood Zaelke, *International Environmental Law and Policy* (New York: Foundation Press, 1998).

45. This section builds upon the discussion in Adil Najam, "The Unraveling of the Rio Bargain," *Politics and the Life Sciences* 21, no. 2 (2002): 46–50.

46. Sharachchandra M. Lélé, "Sustainable Development: A critical review," *World Development* 19, no. 6 (1991): 607–621.

47. See Adil Najam and Cutler Cleveland, "Energy and Sustainable Development at Global Environmental Summits: An Evolving Agenda," *Environment, Development and Sustainability* 5, no. 2 (2003): 117–138.

48. Tariq Banuri and Adil Najam, *Civic Entrepreneurship: A Civil Society Perspective on Sustainable Development*, vol. 1: *Global Synthesis* (Islamabad: Gandhara Academy Press, 2002).

49. Banuri and Najam, *Civic Entrepreneurship*; Wolfgang Sachs, H. Acselrad, F. Akhter, A. Amon, T. B. G. Egziabher, Hilary French, P. Haavisto, Paul Hawken, H. Henderson, Ashok Khosla, S. Larrain, R. Loske, Anita Roddick, V. Taylor, Christine von Weizsäcker, and S. Zabelin, *The Jo'burg Memo: Fairness in a Fragile World* (Berlin: Heinrich Böll Foundation, 2002).

50. Pamela S. Chasek, "The Convention to Combat Desertification: Lessons Learned for Sustainable Development," *Journal of Environment and Development* 6, no. 2 (1997): 147–169; Corell, *The Negotiable Desert*.

51. United Nations Conference on The Human Environment, *Development and Environment*.

52. See Adil Najam and Ambuj Sagar, "Avoiding a COP-out: Moving Towards Systematic Decision-Making Under the Climate Convention," *Climatic Change* 39, no. 4

(1998): iii–ix; Adil Najam and Thomas Page, "The Climate Convention: Deciphering the Kyoto Convention," *Environmental Conservation* 25, no. 3 (1998): 187–194; Adil Najam, Saleemul Huq, and Youba Sokona, "Moving Beyond Kyoto: Developing Countries, Climate Change, and Sustainable Development," *Climate Policy* 3 (2003): 221–231.

53. See, for example, Anil Agarwal and Sunita Narain, *Global Warming in an Unequal World: A Case of Environmental Colonialism* (New Delhi: Centre for Science and Environment, 1991); Agarwal, Narain, and Sharma, *Green Politics.*

54. Adil Najam, *Knowledge Needs for Better Multilateral Environmental Agreements,* WSSD Opinion Paper (London: International Institute for Environment and Development, 2002).

55. Najam et al., "From Rio to Johannesburg."

56. This description comes from David Victor, in a presentation at a conference organized by the Centre for Global Studies, University of Victoria, at the Rockefeller Study and Conference Center, Bellagio, Italy, April 2002.

13

Debating the Dam:
Is China's Three Gorges Project Sustainable?

Lawrence R. Sullivan

June 1, 2003: The closure of the sluice gate at the Three Gorges dam on the Yangtze River has been completed successfully. . . . According to plan, the water level of the reservoir will be raised to 135 meters by June 15 and the 6.4 km-long ship lock will begin trials from June 16 for an unspecified period. Two power generating units, each with a capacity of 700,000 kilowatts, will be put in operation in August. . . . The whole project is expected to be completed in 2009.[1]

Ten years after its inauguration and six years following the successful damming of the Yangtze River, the Three Gorges Dam—the world's largest—is on the fast track to completion in central China's Hubei Province. With engineering specifications that call for a concrete and steel structure 185 meters high and stretching almost two kilometers across, the dam is slated to provide flood control, electrical power generation (17,680 megawatts of installed capacity), and improved navigability for ships traversing the dam's 600-kilometer reservoir, which will extend on the Yangtze River from the city of Yichang to Chongqing (currently China's largest city, with a population of 15 million, located in Sichuan Province). It is the largest engineering project undertaken in China since construction of the Great Wall 2,000 years ago.

The project's many supporters in the Chinese government, especially the bureaucratically powerful Ministry of Water Resources, and the business community view the dam as bolstering their varied interests. Completion of the project will fulfill long-standing goals of taming the Yangtze River for the benefit of millions of denizens of the river valley, which has endured centuries of massive flooding and economic backwardness. But for opponents of the dam in China—from the outspoken and renowned investigative journalist Dai Qing (author of two books on the project, both now banned in China) to the untold number of largely voiceless "reservoir refugees" who see their homes and ancestral lands being inundated by the vast reservoir—the giant project represents an engineering catastrophe for the environment, the economy, and the future of China's political reform.[2]

Although diametrically opposed to each other, the Chinese government and fledging dam opponents have often conducted their "dialogue" on the dam and its likely effects in largely the same terms and jargon associated with the concept of "sustainable development" (in Chinese *kechixu fajan*).[3] Opponents view the dam, and the decision to construct it rendered by the unelected elite of the Chinese Communist Party, as a gross violation of the sustainable development guidelines for dam construction, especially the one that calls for "introducing participatory processes that influence decision-making by recognizing the rights of all stakeholders including beneficiaries and affected communities."[4] Yet rather than ignore or denounce such objections in Marxist-Leninist terms or invoke a philosophy of economic growth *über alles*, the Chinese government has deftly embraced the principles and even some of the practices of sustainable development in a variety of policy areas, employing the very same concepts and terminology to defend the dam and paint the entire project "green." From the dam's impact on the environment, the economy, and the affected communities to the knotty and highly charged issue of the dam's structural integrity, the often very open clash between dam proponents and opponents has been fought on the basis of the sustainable development model—but for radically different ends. The contours of this ongoing debate over whether the massive project is, in fact, viable, despite its apparently successful inauguration, are examined here in its various environmental, economic, political, and structural terms.

China Goes "Green": 1998–2003

March 2002: China's strategy of sustainable development has now run through all aspects of the country's economic and social development efforts, which effectively promoted a sustained and harmonious development of the economy, population, resources, and environment and delivered remarkable successes.

—Chinese Premier Zhu Rongji [5]

Flashback to 1992—the year China's nominal parliament, the National People's Congress, approved construction of the Three Gorges Dam—and the contrast in policy line between then and now could not be greater. Song Jian, who was then the minister of science and technology, effectively degraded environmental protection as a "'luxury' that should not threaten the basic survival of the nation."[6] The question naturally arises: Why the Chinese government's sudden change in both terminology and, at times, real policies?

1998: A "Wake-up Call"

The reasons for China's sudden embrace of "sustainable development" as its official developmental model are, like any major political shift, multifaceted. But certainly the events of 1998 were a major factor, specifically that summer's massive flooding in both the Yangtze River valley in central China and the Songhua River valley in the industrial northeast. The Chinese government publicly admitted that the flooding was in large part due to man-made causes, namely the unchecked deforestation in the rivers' upper reaches.[7] While the loss of life in these two coterminous floods was, by historical standards in China, relatively small, the enormous economic impact, estimated at losses in the billions of dollars, combined with other high-profile ecological disasters to put the environmental issue on the front-burner of the policy agenda in China.

Sustainable development has become something of a cause célèbre in official China in the last half-decade, producing both symbolic and substantial policy initiatives. Among the most important are China's decisions to sign on to the Kyoto Protocol, scale back dramatically its massive logging enterprises, and undertake efforts to address other destructive environmental practices.[8] The government has also established a host of domestic and international organizations committed to pursuing its policy guidelines. These include the recently established China-U.S. Center for Sustainable Development, which on the Chinese side includes the Administrative Center for China's Agenda 21, and the Ecology and Sustainable Development Institute, which will be run jointly by Shanghai's Tongji University and the United Nations and will include among its many functions monitoring the environmental impact of the Three Gorges Dam.[9] A flurry of books, monographs, and officially sanctioned Web sites on sustainable development and environment have appeared.[10] The Hubei provincial government and the World Wide Fund for Nature (the first international environmental protection organization allowed to operate in China) initiated a joint effort for wetland protection in central China.[11] And there has been a dramatic increase in the real power of environmental bureaucracies and officials at the central and local governmental levels in China. As these and other developments testify, it is not surprising that when it comes to discussing the Three Gorges Dam, the government's defense of the controversial project is consistently wrapped in the environmental, economic, and social principles of sustainable development.[12]

This has made criticizing the project's impact on the environment more difficult, as its opponents constantly find themselves responding to government assertions that are couched in the mutually shared principles of sustainable development. However, by accepting the relevance of sustainable development, the government has, perhaps unwittingly, opened the door just a bit to legitimate criticism of the dam by the still heavily controlled media in China, as well as by scientists and nascent environmental and social-economic interest groups who are playing an increasingly assertive role as a result of the government's new policy line.[13] In this sense, the continuing controversy over the environmental, economic and financial, and social and political impact of the Three Gorges Dam provides a unique insight into the emergence in China of a more open and combative political system.

Environmental "Sustainability" of the
Three Gorges Dam and Reservoir

November 2002: After [the reservoir] is filled, the world's largest man-made lake [sic] will act as the greatest natural air-conditioner on the planet.

—Li Yongan, vice manager,
Three Gorges Project Development Corporation[14]

The environmental impact on the Yangtze River valley and its ecological environs has been perhaps the most controversial aspect of the Three Gorges project. Ever since it was approved in 1992, the dam has been consistently cited by the Chinese government for its positive, though largely indirect, environmental benefits, especially the potential reduction of China's enormous dependence on coal burning as a source of electricity. Critics of the dam, meanwhile, have focused on its possible negative impact on wildlife, water quality, downstream river regime, and ocean fisheries off the river's outlet to the East China Sea.[15]

By far the most contentious issue—one that in the last few years has elicited increasingly bold statements by the press and by groups of scientists and researchers—has to do with the possibility that the giant 600-kilometer reservoir will emerge not as the planet's "greatest natural air-conditioner" but as the world's largest cesspool. As the self-cleaning capacity of the river above the dam is dramatically weakened by the impounding of water and slower water flow, the fear is that the 200-meter-deep reservoir will become choked with billons of tons of untreated industrial, human, and animal wastes dumped into the Yangtze above Yichang annually.[16] "I have never seen such an astonishing sight," wrote the leader of the Chongqing Green Volunteers Union, describing massive belts of white foam floating on the Yangtze around Wu Gorge—the most spectacular of the Three Gorges—and the countless "sewage outlets along the river disgorging torrents of untreated wastewater."[17] Composed of trained biologists and ecologists who have openly expressed deep concerns about water quality in the reservoir without significant preventive measures, the Chongqing Green Volunteers exemplify how, in its haste to embrace sustainable development, the Chinese government has opened up something of a Pandora's box. In an effort to paint state policies "green," the government has sanctioned such groups, only to see them, frequently backed by a more assertive local press, question the real impact of these policies.

Not surprisingly, the Chinese government has responded to these and other concerns about water quality in the future reservoir with its own studies, which suggest that the environmental impact of the reservoir will be minimal. Substantial monies have been promised to help cities along the river build treatment plants to reduce the amount of potentially infectious and/or toxic waste dumped into the river.[18] Nevertheless, the formation of relatively independent research teams, along with a more assertive press, especially in the affected communities, means that the Chinese state no longer exercises a monopoly on the story line concerning the dam and related issues.

Nowhere is this process more evident than on the issue of whether the Chinese government, in its haste to approve the project and follow a break-neck construction schedule to get an early start on electricity generation, overlooked or underestimated the crucial problem of cleaning up the vast area before inundation.[19] Approximately 300,000 square meters of public toilets, more than 40,000 grave sites (some containing anthrax), innumerable hospitals, factories, slaughterhouses, and gigantic garbage dumps (sometimes called garbage mountains by local residents), as well as other sites containing toxic materials (including radioactive waste and deadly bacteria), will be submerged by the reservoir. Critics fear that this could create an interminable and irremediable source of contamination and degradation of water quality.[20] Poisonous materials left buried under the bed of the future reservoir could, one scientist publicly argued, become hidden "time bombs"; this would have profound public health implications in such a heavily populated area, according to a high-level public health official.[21] An extensive report published in *Southern Weekend*—one of China's more outspoken and relatively independent newspapers—warned that research on the water quality of the river prior to the filling of the reservoir had already indicated increased levels of deadly E-coli bacteria during the flood season. The report openly questioned whether the government had committed the resources and adequate time to carry out the vast cleanup that must precede inundation as opposed to merely "giving the impression of doing it."[22] And while the government broadcast with much fanfare the demolition of buildings and factories to make way for the reservoir as the centerpiece of its cleanup campaign, officials from government environmental protection departments, especially at the local levels, along with reports from state-run CCTV, have raised serious doubts about the efficacy and relatively short time devoted to the cleanup effort prior to the submersion of these potentially damaging sites.[23]

From the project's inception, the core position of Chinese government policy has been that the dam will have minimal environmental effects. The government has also touted numerous net benefits, such as a reduction in soil erosion through a scaling back of small-scale agriculture and reductions in pollution as inefficient factories are shuttered in the towns and cities slated for submersion.[24] Thus, even before the SARS crisis in 2003 punctured the legitimizing aura of positive reporting in China's state-run press, the Chinese government was quick to rebut all suggestions that it had ignored or underestimated the potential environmental problems created by the reservoir. For example, no sooner had the comment been published that the reservoir would become the world's "greatest air-conditioner"—suggesting that the dam's climatic impact in the valley would, contrary to the official policy line, be substantial—than the *Three Gorges Project Daily* (the project's official publication) vehemently denied that any such "scientific" conclusion had been reached. Indeed, the paper even offered an unprecedented apology, saying it had "learned a lesson" in publishing the original story without first "double-checking the facts."[25] On a more serious note, when the highly regarded hydrologist Lu Qinkan and fifty-three specialists petitioned the leaders of the Chinese Communist Party in 2000, expressing opposition to the apparent plan to speed up the impoundment of water behind the reservoir, the Central Committee responded with a public letter assuring the petitioners that all problems associated with filling the reservoir, especially the possibility of rapid buildup of silt, would ultimately be solved in a manner that would "protect the region's environment."[26]

It remains to be seen whether the impact of the SARS crisis—in which initial government statements downplaying the epidemic were quickly followed by a 180-degree reversal and the dismissals of the health officials and mayor of Beijing, who had participated in the cover-up—has fundamentally undermined popular acceptance of such government reassurances in China.[27] But as one top engineer examining the dam commented, it will be the actual impact of the dam—including potential landslides, earthquakes, and other calamities that could possibly be engendered by the 39 billion cubic meters of water that will ultimately fill the reservoir—rather than government reassurances that will be the "real examiners" of the project's ultimate environmental sustainability.[28]

Economic and Financial Boon or Bust?

The Three Gorges project has succeeded in staying within budget as "total investment will probably be cut 20 billion yuan ($2.4 billion) from the budget."

—Li Yongan, China Yangtze River Three Gorges Project Development Corporation[29]

When completed in 2009, the Three Gorges dam will cost 203.9 billion yuan ($24.5 billion), more than double the figure forecast in 1993.

—State Council Three Gorges Project Construction Authority[30]

Diametrically opposed as these two statements appear, and coming within one month of each other from official sources in China, they clearly denote the murky and often contradictory environment surrounding the economic and financial condition of China's largest public works project since the construction of the Great Wall. With its bustling economy, China at first seems well-positioned to handle the financing of the Three Gorges Dam as well as other planned megaprojects, such as the South-to-North Water Diversion Project already under way.[31] Yet significant economic uncertainties potentially plague the Three Gorges Dam project.

Much of the uncertainty stems from contradictory economic and financial policies of the central government and ancillary governing bodies. With only 40 billion out of the planned 203 billion yuan having been spent, the major costs of the project are still to be borne. At the same time, government attempts to commercialize the former state-run power industry will make raising the necessary capital much more difficult. In the early stages of the project major financing came from interest-free government grants, but future costs are now supposed to come from interest-bearing loans because the government has apparently decided to stop financing all dam projects. In the case of Three Gorges, this policy change has inflated the projected final cost by tens of billions of yuan.[32]

It is also unclear where private-sector financing can actually be obtained. Chinese power companies are currently confronting difficulties raising capital in foreign markets. At home, Chinese banks giving financial backing to the dam face an enormous number of nonperforming loans. Indeed, some estimates state that from 25 to 60 percent of the loans at such institutions are to obsolescent state-owned industries that have little hope of financial recovery.[33] Moreover, just as the government is cutting off its financial umbilical cord, it has also set the delivery price of the dam's electricity at a level below the national average—in an effort to make Three Gorges electricity affordable to consumers, especially in regions outside central China, who often prefer to purchase electricity from local tax-paying plants.[34] Taken together, these factors mean that, at a minimum, Three Gorges will provide small returns to investors, and, even worse, the project could confront a death spiral of bankruptcy and stranded investment costs even before its completion.[35]

Adding to the uncertainty is the fact that at the very time China is engaged in this and other massive power projects, the government is also pushing major institutional reforms of the power industry—albeit very slow-moving—the consequences of which are far from predictable. The plan is to break the long-held monopoly of the State Power Corporation by creating five regional generating companies, thereby effectively separating the generation and distribution of electricity. But the plan also raises the prospect of reinforcing the very regional protectionism that prevents the creation of a true national power grid in China—a development that would allow Three Gorges and other interior projects, such as the recently completed Ertan Dam, to sell their electricity to rich coastal areas.[36] The hasty creation at the end of 2002 of the Yangtze Power Corporation (with the Three Gorges Development Corporation as the major stakeholder) was intended to strengthen the ability to raise money directly from capital markets, even as pleas were being made to the government to absorb much of the project's growing debt.[37] In China's still very opaque transitional economy, with persistent and often arbitrary state intervention in markets at investor expense and with the country's own version of rent-seeking and crony capitalism increasingly widespread (for example, the Huaneng International Power Development Corporation is run by the son of Li Peng, former premier and Three Gorges Dam enthusiast), the prospect of the Three Gorges project being financially swept away by a collapsing financial bubble cannot be discounted.[38]

Even in the absence of a cataclysmic financial black hole, the economic and financial pressures on the Three Gorges Dam are already evident. According to one of its earliest proponents, the decision to maintain the accelerated construction schedule in order to begin generating electricity and repay the project's huge debts could be impacting quality control—cracks have already appeared in the dam's facade.[39] "I have seen the following scenario on many occasions," Qian Zhengying, former minister of water resources, recently warned. "Today a brand-new hydropower station starts generating electricity after a grand ceremony celebrating the completion of the project—and the next day the station has to cease operating for a lengthy period of inspection and repair."[40]

Cracks in the dam's facade are not the only problem that could shut down the project for long and costly repairs. Questions have also been raised about whether the twenty-nine giant turbines that will generate the power—currently undergoing construction by foreign and domestic firms using what some believe is an excessive number of subcontractors—are "ideally suited" to the lower water-level conditions of the Yangtze River. This concern has only been heightened by recent revelations that similar turbines produced for the Xiaolangdi Dam on the Yellow River by the same company contracted for Three Gorges—Voit Hydro of Germany—developed severe cracks in their operating blades.[41] There is also the still largely untested five-stage ship lock designed for Three Gorges; despite government assurances that it has passed all preliminary tests, if it malfunctions, navigation on the Yangtze river would be shut down for weeks, if not months. This would add to the significant economic costs that shipping companies have already borne during the massive project's long period of construction.[42]

All these issues, combined with skyrocketing costs for the resettlement program and various and ingenious forms of embezzlement of funds (both discussed below), continue to be a drain on the project's financing and make the economic and financial sustainability of Three Gorges more and more suspect.[43] In the end, the high priority of the project, as well as the complete, consistent, and public blessings given it by the Chinese Communist Party, probably ensures that the government will come up with whatever funding is necessary to complete the dam on schedule in 2009. However, as financing hurdles, construction difficulties, local governments, resettlement petitioners, and a variety of opportunists up and down the Yangtze tap into the central government's financial spigot, the total amount of money that must be raised in China's increasingly investor-conscious society may be of such a magnitude that it could be capitalist economics, rather than environmental activism, that ends up significantly slowing, altering, or perhaps even halting the project.

Social and Political Stability or Turmoil?

All the land is already occupied. There is nowhere for us to go.
—peasant in Hong Miao Village, Gaoyang Township[44]

[T]he resettlement work is going in order according to plan.
—Guo Zhenhua, Three Gorges Resettlement Office, Beijing[45]

Resettling almost 2 million people from the slated reservoir area was considered by both dam supporters and critics the most daunting task facing the project, one with potentially enormous social and political consequences for the region and perhaps the nation. More people, more corruption, less land, and fewer jobs than even the pessimists had imagined have created a huge tug of war between the Chinese state and local society. Petitions and lawsuits charging local officials with corruption have been brought from the Chongqing municipal courts to the highest levels of government in Beijing. Outright protests by farmers in places like Gaoyang Township have brought a harsh government crackdown and threats to rely on the rising reservoir waters to oust reluctant migrants, commonly referred to as "nail households" because of their holding tight to houses or land they have claimed for generations.[46] In the end, the Chinese state, with its enormous coercive and economic capacity, will undoubtedly prevail over local opposition, but at what cost to stability in the region remains to be seen.

The prospect that this will become a long-term and irremediable struggle between state and society in the region stems from the multifaceted nature of the conflict. For local farmers, there is the issue of land, which throughout the history of China and other predominantly rural societies has been a primordial root of sustained social upheaval. In addition to valley dwellers' natural resistance to giving up fertile farmland, enriched by periodic floods, in return for often minuscule plots on rock-infested mountainsides, the government exacerbated the problem by grossly underestimating the number of people to be resettled and overestimating the available land to which these people could be moved.[47] In an effort to ameliorate the situation, in 1999 Premier Zhu Rongji announced that 125,000 migrants would be relocated in different parts of the country, including the remote western province of Xinjiang. But this measure produced a host of new problems between resettlers and the often hostile communities to which they had moved, leading migrants to attempt to slip back home—the phenomenon of "reverse flow"—where they manage to live off the entrails of the valley economy, such as scavenging abandoned buildings and becoming in the process a potentially explosive force.[48]

As for urban residents in the reservoir area, conventional wisdom has held that their anxiety and potential opposition to resettlement would be mitigated by the greater amenities available in the newly constructed towns and cities; in particular, compensation levels generally favored urban over rural dwellers by granting city residences a higher valuation. The resettled residents of 2,300-year-old Fengjie (Poet's Town), Fengdu (Ghost City), and other towns and cities facing full or partial inundation are not likely to constitute direct threats to local stability, even though their traditional social fabric is being frayed. However, they have not been exactly quiet in the face of widespread corruption and mismanagement by officials who have engaged in everything from outright embezzlement of funds to excessive charges and "fees" leveled on urban resettlers for infrastructure costs and giving higher priority to construction of new office buildings and hotels than to residential apartments.[49] Along with the substantially higher costs for new housing that resettlement monies, when allocated, are inadequate to cover, new jobs have also been slow in coming. The government's promises to invest heavily in the region have been hampered by the diversion of funds to other ends, such as giving bonuses to local officials for reaching their quotas of resettled people.[50] "We would have had a better life without the dam," one urban resident is quoted as saying soon after the reservoir began to fill on June 1, 2003. "But now everything has gone with the dam." [51]

The government has, not surprisingly, tried to counter such attitudes by wrapping the Three Gorges project in nationalistic and ideological appeals, such as calling on individuals "to make sacrifices for the sake of society and the nation," that are more reminiscent of the Maoist era of the 1960s than China's get-rich-quick mentality of the recent past.[52] However, these entreaties as well as government promises of swift action against corruption and mismanagement seem to be falling on deaf ears among valley residents, many of whom have become inured to the bureaucratic inertia and brazen self-enrichment of local government officials.[53]

In the past, China's top leadership could count on an essentially pliant populace that would follow its dicta and descriptions of its beneficent effects. Now, however, in the midst of the transformation from a collective to a more market-oriented economy, an apparent sea change is on display among resettlers, who appear much more concerned with their individualistic interests and rights than with grand matters of state and economic benefits that will largely accrue to people outside the affected communities.[54] To the extent that this undermines the authority of local officials whom the locals seem increasingly inclined to criticize, condemn, and challenge, the social and political order in the Three Gorges region could be in for a change. At a minimum, this means more attempts by affected parties to seek redress through the courts, to expose corruption via the media, and to demand more accountability by governing authorities—activities largely in line with the sustainable development guidelines the Chinese government now says it embraces.[55] But to the extent that the Chinese state relies on a traditional iron fist to deal with petitioning and other legally acceptable actions, the clash between state and society in the Three Gorges region could become surprisingly sharp.

Protecting Structural Integrity

The dam will never collapse and the reservoir will never flood the cities downstream.

—Lu Youmei, director, Three Gorges Project[56]

One certainly hopes that these assurances given by the Three Gorges project director to a Beijing University student audience are correct. The collapse of a 1.4-mile-long, 40-story-high concrete and steel structure impounding upward of 39 billion cubic meters of water sitting in the middle of a very heavily populated region would produce a cataclysm that would dwarf China's horrific 1975 dam disaster, in which 275,000 people died as a result of the successive collapse of several dams in Henan Province.[57] Whereas the 1975 catastrophe was effectively covered up with little political consequence during what were the final years of the tightly controlled society of Maoist China, the much larger disaster produced by a collapse of the Three Gorges Dam would occur in a far more open society. This would undoubtedly produce enormous political consequences, especially after officials such as Lu Youmei have constantly reassured the public of the dam's safety.

Concern over such a possibility undoubtedly explains the very quick official reactions to the appearance—and reappearance—of cracks in the dam's facade.[58] The fact that the dam is located in a seismically active area that is already prone to landslides and other subterranean gyrations that may intensify with the impounding of so much water in the reservoir makes a possible rupture in the giant edifice more than just an exciting script for a megadisaster movie.[59]

This also probably explains the attention given to the most unlikely scenario involving the dam's collapse—that it would become the target for attack, with devastating consequences for people living downstream, during a military confrontation with Taiwan.[60] Dams are traditional military targets, and some of this commentary from China can, of course, be dismissed as part of the on-and-off-again barbs tossed by Beijing at Taiwan.[61] At the same time, China's defense establishment and elements of the press and public have revealed concern that the development of precision weapons by the United States could result in their eventual arrival in Taiwan's arsenal. The prospect of the dam becoming a target has compelled the Chinese government to issue repeated assurances that any assault on the structure could be deterred by defensive measures.

Conclusion

> *The administration of a country's national affairs becomes easier when its rivers are tamed.*
> —Classical Chinese saying

> *It's more dangerous to silence the people than to dam a river.*
> —Classical Chinese saying[62]

First proposed more than seventy years ago, the giant Three Gorges Dam is on track toward completion. If the dam proves to be relatively benign in terms of its environmental impact and does not generate severe economic, social, and political turmoil or suffer from major structural problems, the Chinese government can indeed claim the Three Gorges project as a model of sustainable development.[63] This, in turn, would likely lead the government to commit resources in the future for similarly massive projects to address China's growing need for fresh water, electrical power, and flood control. These include the South-to-North Water Diversion Project, mentioned above, and additional megadam projects, such as the immense structure—larger than Three Gorges—contemplated for construction on Tibet's Yarlung Zangbo River in the Himalaya Mountains.

However, should one of the many potential problems discussed here become a reality—significant environmental degradation, economic and financial turmoil, social and political upheaval, and/or loss of structural integrity—it would be difficult for the Chinese government to claim that the dam met the sustainable development goals. In this scenario, the political and economic momentum behind such large projects, which the Chinese state has sponsored throughout its long history, imperial and communist, could be challenged. The government might then embrace more small-scale models of development that dam critics, such as the environmental journalist Dai Qing, have long advocated for China. Time and events will determine which of these two diametrically opposed paths an increasingly wealthy China will pursue.

Notes

1. Xinhua (China's official news agency), May 21 and June 1, 2003. The forty-seven-member expert panel gave its approval to fill the reservoir after inspecting the project for eight days.
2. Dai Qing, *Yangtze! Yangtze!: Debate Over the Three Gorges Project*, ed. Patricia Adams and John Thibodeau (Toronto and London: Probe International and Earthscan, 1994), originally published in China as *Chiangjiang sanxia kongcheng fouxing qian* (Guizhou Province People's Publishing House, 1989); and Dai Qing, *The River Dragon Has Come! The Three Gorges Dam and the Fate of China's Yangtze River and Its People*, ed. John G. Thibodeau and Philip B. Williams, trans. Yi Ming (Armonk, N.Y.: M. E. Sharpe, 1998).
3. Also translatable into English as "continued" or "keeping up," the term *kechixu* was also employed in phrases from the period of the Soviet-style planned economy in China (1953–1978), such as "continued leap forward in production" and "keeping up a steady increase in the output of crude oil," indicating, perhaps, a connotation stressing gross production that does not exist in English.
4. "Third World Water Forum—Theme Summary for Ministerial Conference, Dams and Sustainable Development, 20–21 March 2003"; see the Web site http://www.uneps-dams.org/document.php?doc_id=258.
5. Speech delivered to the World Summit on Sustainable Development, March 9, 2002, cited in *Alexander's Gas & Oil Connections* 7, no. 18, September 19, 2002.
6. Stanley Leung, "Environment Considered 'Secondary' to Development," *Hong Kong Standard*, June 12, 1992, cited in Lawrence R. Sullivan, ed., *China Since Tiananmen: Political, Economic, and Social Conflicts* (Armonk, N.Y.: M. E. Sharpe, 1995), 243–44. "Sustainable development" was included in Song's comments to the United Nations Conference on Environment and Development in Rio, but with economic growth and development given overwhelming priority.
7. These events and the Chinese government's response are vividly documented in Ma (Michael) Jun, *China's Water Crisis (Zhongguo shui weiji)* (Beijing: China Environmental Science Publishing House, 1999; English ed., Armonk, N.Y.: EastBridge Press, 2003).
8. China announced a national ban on logging soon after the floods, but it has apparently been widely ignored in remote areas, especially by newly formed private companies. *South China Morning Post*, October 16, 2001. For a full description of the floods and their impact, see Ma Jun, *China's Water Crisis*.
9. The recently established China-U.S. Center for Sustainable Development (see the Web site http://www.chinauscenter.org) is described as "a new type of international organization, focused on achieving results to accelerate sustainable development in China, the United States, and the world."

10. See the Web site http://www.chinauscenter.org/purpose/default.asp for innumerable articles on the Three Gorges Dam as a "model" of "sustainable development." Among the many recently published volumes on the topic of sustainable development is *Report on the Research on Sustainable Water Resources Strategy in China,* ed. Qian Zhengying (former minister of water resources and a major advocate of the Three Gorges Dam) and Zhang Guangdou (Beijing: China Water Publishing House, 2001).

11. For the announcement of the joint program involving Hubei Province and the WWF, see *People's Daily* Online, September 4, 2002. Many factories, especially local town- and village-owned enterprises (TVEs) that wantonly violate pollution rules, have been summarily shut down, though many manage to reopen under new auspices.

12. See, for instance, the many articles on China's official sustainable development Web site. Most of these articles laud the project, though some, especially highly technical studies by scientists, raise significant concerns about the project's impact on the local environment, especially rainfall patterns and flood levels, and, hence, its overall "sustainability."

13. Green Earth Volunteers, an informal group of environmental enthusiasts based in Beijing, is but one of many examples of new, semi-independent groups that have been allowed to emerge in "environmentally friendly" China.

14. China News Service (Zhongguo xinwen she), November 19, 2002. This story was quickly picked up by major regional media, including *Hubei Daily, Changjiang (Yangtze) Daily, Yangcheng Evening News,* and the ever-popular Sina.com Web site.

15. The negative impact on fisheries comes from reduced water levels in the lower Yangtze River valley as a result of the impounding of water in the reservoir. *United Daily* (Taiwan), September 2, 2002. The same phenomenon is likely to have a deleterious effect on downstream wetlands, such as Poyang Lake, that serve as major breeding grounds for a rich variety of birds. *Jiangnan City Post,* August 30, 2002. River regime effects include possible severe "scouring" of the riverbed below the dam and radical changes in water chemistry that could dramatically reduce rice yields in areas that employ irrigated Yangtze River water.

16. Discharging more than a billion tons of industrial waste water and 300 million tons of sewage annually into the Yangtze, the city of Chongqing, located above the dam, was ranked last in an environmental-quality survey of China's forty-six largest cities. *Chongqing Morning Post* (n.d.), cited in Three Gorges Probe, February 4, 2002; see the Web site http://www.Probeinternational@e-p-r-f.org.

17. *Chongqing Daily,* February 14, 2003. For another example of a semi-independent "survey" of the Three Gorges area that often contradicted official government statements, see the report by the Chongqing Southwest Normal University students investigative team, who cited 100 papermaking, chemical, and glass factories discharging untreated wastewater into the Yangtze River. Agence France-Presse, November 13, 2000.

18. All cities and towns are to have their own rubbish disposal facilities by 2009, with two water treatment plants for Chongqing to be built with assistance from the World Bank. However, some media reports indicate that operators run the new treatment plants only when government inspectors come and immediately shut them down after they leave. Agence France-Presse, November 18, 2002, and Three Gorges Probe, March 7, 2003.

19. Critics charge that this understating or ignoring potential problems with the dam occurred from the very beginning, with the 1988 feasibility study on the project (which they claim was hastily prepared and largely reflected the views of dam supporters), through the period of construction, which began in 1992.

20. Agence France-Presse, November 18, 2002. China's official news agency, Xinhua, has also reported that the reservoir water will inundate at least "178 garbage dumps containing 2.87 million tons of garbage, [as well as] 15 million tons of discarded solid objects." Three Gorges Probe, January 23, 2002.

21. See the comments made by Ma Xiaowei, vice minister of public health, to the *Three Gorges Project Daily,* May 15, 2002. Known for its bold reporting that has led to reprimands and dismissal of its editorial staff by the government, *Southern Weekend (Nanfang zhoumou)* was, nevertheless, instrumental in revealing the existence of anthrax in grave sites of 1937–1945-vintage scheduled to be inundated by the reservoir. Three Gorges Probe, April 25, 2002.

22. *Southern Weekend,* January 31, 2002. A mere eighteen months were devoted to cleaning up the entire area slated for submersion by the gigantic reservoir.

23. Three Gorges Probe, April 25, 2002, and January 23, 2002. Infestation of the reservoir area by rats fleeing the floodwaters is also a matter of grave concern, especially after millions of them died from being poisoned and blanketed the soon-to-be-inundated area. *Three Gorges Project Daily,* May 15, 2002.

24. Xinhua, January 20, 2003.

25. China News Service, November 19, 2002.

26. "Official Response to Experts' Three Gorges Dam Petition," April 17, 2000, Three Gorges Probe, May 27, 2003.

27. Desperate to prevent a local outbreak of SARS at the Three Gorges construction site, all officials from the Beijing area visiting the area were virtually quarantined, and the gigantic celebration planned for the June 1 start-up was canceled. Three Gorges Probe, May 16, 2003, and June 2, 2003.

28. Comments by Pan Jiazheng, a senior member of the inspection team monitoring construction of the Three Gorges Dam, who warned his fellow scientists not to play up the positive aspects of such gigantic projects while ignoring the down sides. Three Gorges Probe, February 28, 2003.

29. Xinhua, November 6, 2002. Li attributed these felicitous results to "scientific management and profit orientation."

30. Agence France-Presse, September 10, 2002.

31. The water diversion scheme will draw on waters, possibly heavily polluted, from the Three Gorges reservoir, further reducing water flow in the river.

32. See the statement by project director Lu Youmei cited in Three Gorges Probe, March 19, 2002. Unofficial estimates put the total final cost at 280 billion yuan, or $35 billion, because of cost overruns discussed below, though some predict a final cost as high as $70 billion.

33. According to the *Wall Street Journal* (May 30, 2003), China admits to a 24 percent rate of nonperforming loans that have little if any prospect of being paid back by the state-owned firms that continue to be the recipients of the government's financial largess through its four state banks. Informal estimates put the figure as high as 40 to 50 percent of nonperforming loans to total bank capitalization.

34. Xinhua, November 7, 2002. Underpricing in the energy sector in China is a remnant of the urban bias endemic to the country's former Soviet-style planned economy, which has yet to be eliminated by market forces.

35. For the 1999 Probe International study, see *Inter Press Service,* July 25, 2000. Even as China plans to create a more "foreign investor-friendly power regime," Three Gorges project vice manager Li Yongan has said that "the era of 15 percent guaranteed rate of return for power projects in China is gone forever." Indeed, China's State Development Planning Commission has reportedly capped returns on investment capital in the power sector at "slightly above" cost—an example of state intervention in the market that sours investors, both domestic and foreign. The Huaneng International Power Development Corporation—China's largest independent power company—has taken a mere 3 percent stake in Three Gorges, with the expectation that it will lose money but, in return, hopes to gain government "goodwill." In all, 100 billion yuan for the project will be sought from the domestic capital market in China over the next several years, while anti-dam groups pressure international investment firms such as Morgan Stanley to stay out of such environmentally destructive infrastructure projects. Financially, the central government is chipping in by approving a favorable tax

policy for Three Gorges and ordering regions outside the Yangtze valley that they must give preference to Three Gorges power over local sources. Three Gorges Probe, March 19, 2002, May 23, 2002, and December 5, 2002; *Financial Times* (London), April 11, 2002, and *Guardian*, March 20, 2002.

36. Three Gorges Probe, May 23, 2002.
37. Three Gorges Probe, March 19, 2002.
38. For extensive documentation on the pervasive "rent seeking" and attendant corruption in the entire Chinese economy, see He Qinglian, "China's Descent into a Quagmire (Zhongguo de xianjing)," in *The Chinese Economy: Translations and Studies*, parts 1–4 , published in four issues May–June 2000 to January–February 2002 (Armonk, N.Y.: M. E. Sharpe). As an example of state intervention undermining investment returns, the Guangdong government recently forced electric prices down despite being in the midst of a power shortage in order to ensure profits for provincially owned transmission companies. *South China Morning Post*, April 28, 2003.
39. *China Economic Review*, May 23, 2002 (which also noted cracks in the ship lock and ship lift), and *Three Gorges Project Daily*, April 11, 2002, cited in Three Gorges Probe, April 18, 2002. Another example of the role a more "independent" media is playing in China, *South Wind Window (Nanfeng chuang)*, a popular Canton magazine, also reported the existence of cracks and quoted dam officials as downplaying the cracks' importance. Three Gorges Probe, April 3, 2002.
40. *China Economic Review*, May 23, 2002, and *Three Gorges Project Daily*, April 11, 2002, cited in Three Gorges Probe, April 18, 2002. Qian Zhengying went on to blame the poor construction on "'formalism,' where the quality of the project is totally ignored" by officials who blindly follow orders.
41. *Big River News (Dahe bao)*, Henan Province, March 20, 2003, reported in Three Gorges Probe, March 28, 2003. "We won't know the truth about the quality of the turbines until they are actually put in operation," one project engineer also stated.
42. Shipping firms have already complained about lost revenue from river shutdowns during crucial stages of dam construction. *Chongqing Morning Post (Chongqing chenbao)*, April 14, 2003, cited in Three Gorges Probe, April 16, 2003. Also undermining the local economy, at least in the short term, are layoffs from shuttered factories and declining incomes for farmers. Agence France-Presse, September 23, 2002.
43. Despite cases of embezzlements in the tens of millions of dollars, official media in China still tout the project as largely "free of graft and embezzlement." A flurry of stories demonstrates how local authorities have conjured up, often with the assistance of migrants and migrant wannabes, all sorts of methods for squeezing more money, legitimately and illegitimately, out of the central government—from inflating the amount of farmland to be lost and the number of resettlers ("fake migrants") to be compensated to pleas for investment to create jobs, while the peasants themselves often demand cash instead of land. Xinhua, November 5, 2002; *South China Morning Post*, October 26, 2000; *Inter Press Service*, July 25, 2000; *Times of India*, October 5, 2000; Channel News Asia, January 21, 2003; and Three Gorges Probe, November 11, 2001.
44. *South China Morning Post* , February 14, 1999.
45. *Toronto Star*, May 16, 1999.
46. *Independent*, December 31, 2002, and Three Gorges Probe, September 25, 2002. "They will have to take us away in handcuffs," one old wizened peasant is quoted as saying; he also claimed his family had received virtually no compensation for new housing that is considerably more expensive than current residences. Gaoyang Township has been the epicenter of outright protests that led to the arrest and imprisonment of individuals who traveled to Beijing to submit their complaints and to migrant attacks on local officials for alleged corruption. By linking petitioners to such outlaw groups as the Falun Gong, the government was able to claim that the Gaoyang petitioners were not being prosecuted for their actions vis-à-vis the dam

project. *Times of India*, October 5, 2000, and Three Gorges Probe, March 12, 2002. Also see *Toronto Star*, May 16, 1999, and *Financial Times*, February 15, 1999.

47. According to the former deputy mayor of Chongqing Municipality, with farmers being given only half as much land as they had prior to resettlement and being expected to eke out a living on inferior, steeply sloped land after resettlement, the problems surrounding rural resettlement will be "enormous," with the prospect of social unrest. Three Gorges Probe, March 14, 2003.

48. A 2002 Chinese Academy of Sciences' survey of migrants resettled outside the Three Gorges area indicated that they were significantly less well off than they had been prior to the move and that the average landholdings of migrants and existing residents in the host community had shrunk substantially; the survey noted intense competition for farmland and job opportunities, creating the prospect of unrest that has already reportedly broken out among migrants and their "hosts" in Shandong Province. Three Gorges Probe, March 1, 2002, and *Age* (Melbourne), July 23, 2002. Migrants displaced to other, richer areas have complained about high prices, discrimination in employment, and tell other stories of woe that often lead them to engage in "reverse flow." *South China Morning Post*, December 7, 2002, and *Christian Science Monitor*, December 4, 2002.

49. *Toronto Star*, May 16, 1999, and *South China Morning Post*, February 14, 1999.

50. Three Gorges Probe, January 10, 2002, which also notes the high rate of turnover among resettlement cadres who feel squeezed between two equally hostile camps—the resettlers and a government pressing for more resettlement. The Chinese government has promised to invest heavily in promoting the region as the world's largest center of orange juice production. *Independent*, December 31, 2002.

51. Three Gorges Probe, June 2, 2003.

52. Three Gorges Probe, April 16, 2003. The official press in China has "loyally hailed the dam as a triumph for the [Communist] party's leadership." *Guardian*, November 7, 2002. Such numbing statements as those by Vice Premier Wu Bangguo exalting the "spirit of being highly responsible to the party, the people, and future generations" and "demonstrating a strong sense of history and mission" must sound to the economically tuned valley residents as something out of the distant past. BBC Monitoring International Reports, October 29, 2002.

53. The fact that resettlement funds were dispersed in a top-down bureaucratic fashion from the central level to the province, then to the county, township, and village left the system ripe for corruption and skim-offs, especially by local cadres who were free from any independent grievance mechanism. One government official in Chongqing reportedly gambled away 1.2 million yuan in resettlement funds. Three Gorges Probe, "Reservoirs of Repression," April 16, 2003; International Rivers Network, January 20, 2003; *South China Morning Post*, May 3, 2000; and Agence France-Presse, April 30, 1999. Whenever officials were caught in embezzlement schemes, the government produced high-profile stories. Agence France-Presse, November 20, 1998.

54. "Reservoirs of Repression, Part Two," Three Gorges Probe, April 16, 2003.

55. One delegate to China's NPC has proposed that rules governing dam-related development schemes in China should be given the force of law, thereby protecting migrants' interests and rights. *Three Gorges Project Daily* (n.d.), cited in Three Gorges Probe, March 13, 2002.

56. *Three Gorges Project Daily*, December 31, 2002, cited in Three Gorges Probe, December 24, 2003.

57. Yi Si, "The World's Most Catastrophic Dam Failures: The August 1975 Collapse of the Banqiao and Shimantan Dams," in Dai Qing, *The River Dragon Has Come!* 25–38.

58. Three Gorges Probe, May 30, 2003.

59. In December 2001 a major earthquake occurred in Hubei (4.1 on the Richter scale), producing massive landslides in the area. *Three Gorges Project Daily*, cited in Three

Gorges Probe, December 6, 2001, and January 4, 2002. It is even possible that the reservoir could increase the likelihood or exacerbate the impact of earthquakes in the area.

60. Xinhua, November 6, 2002, and China Radio International Web site, Beijing, August 29, 2002, cited by BBC Monitoring Asia Pacific, September 2, 2002.

61. Especially as Taiwan's new president, Chen Shui-bian, and his Democratic Progressive Party once advocated independence for the island.

62. First quotation: *Financial Times,* November 6, 2002; second quotation: "Reservoirs of Repression, Part Two," April 16, 2003.

63. In addition to the controversy over whether the dam would have halted the massive flooding of 1998—with supporters saying it would have and opponents rejecting that claim—several academics and officials have suggested that the existence of the dam "will not completely solve the Yangtze River flood problem." See comments by Cai Qihua, director of the Changjiang Water Resources Commission, who reaffirmed the role of "traditional" flood-control measures, such as adequate dike reinforcement and larger diversion areas, especially in light of alterations in the river's hydraulics brought about by the dam, such as downriver scouring and dike collapses. Three Gorges Probe, December 20, 2001; Agence France-Presse, June 5, 2003; Xinhua, August 30, 1998; and AAP Information Services Pty. Ltd., AAP News Feed, August 6, 1998.

14

Democracy and Nuclear Power in the Czech Republic

Regina S. Axelrod

How could it have happened that we let ourselves be led too far by the old totalitarian megalomania? Why with Temelin did we proceed on a steep slope at whose foot everything is different, not only the relationship with the environment, but also the relationship between the citizen and the state? How could we miss the juncture from which a road led to savings, sustainable development and to an uninhabitable country?

Petr Pithart, former prime minister, Czech Republic, and current chair of the Czech Senate, translated from *Listy,* 5 1994, by Mirka Jehlickova

Private property, rational prices and individual responsibility are more important for environmental protection than the activities of governments, legislators and of environmental organizations.

Vaclav Klaus, former prime minister, Czech Republic, "Quality of Life, Environment and Systemic Changes," Address to the International Geographic Union Congress, Prague, August 22, 1994

This chapter explores the construction of the 1,000-megawatt Temelin nuclear power plant in the Czech Republic. It examines the extent to which sustainable development policy is being addressed in a country still undergoing political transformation and also offers insights into the problems of building democratic institutions. In 1989 the Iron Curtain fell and communism as it was known ended in central and eastern Europe, but the transition to democracy and a market economy has been more complex than most westerners anticipated. This chapter begins by examining energy policy and then discusses, more specifically, nuclear policy in central and eastern Europe (CEE). The European Union (EU) has played an increasingly important role in these policies, as CEE states applied for membership. The chapter then addresses sustainable energy/environmental policy in the Czech Republic, utilizing the Temelin controversy as a model for analysis.

The Czech Republic was in the first group of candidates in central and eastern Europe to join both the European Union (EU) and the North

Atlantic Treaty Organization (NATO). In December 1997 the Czech Republic, Estonia, Hungary, Poland, and Slovenia were invited to begin negotiations for EU accession. The Czech Republic harmonized its environmental and energy legislation with the EU as a prerequisite for membership. The country's ability to develop the necessary democratic attributes familiar to western Europe was also a prerequisite. The adoption of the *acquis communautaire*—the body of European Community law—presented financial difficulties for the nations of central and eastern Europe joining the EU because of the huge financial investment necessary to meet EU standards.

Austria, a nonnuclear state, has consistently and aggressively opposed construction of the Temelin nuclear power plant. As Temelin is approximately fifty miles from its border, the Austrians have made this proximity an issue in the Czech accession proceedings. Other states such as Germany, which closed its Russian-made nuclear plants in the eastern part of the country, also have a stake in the future of Temelin.

The Czech experience with nuclear power is a test case that will affect the viability and future marketability of nuclear power in central and eastern Europe. Upgrading Temelin was part of a G-7 (Canada, France, Germany, Italy, Japan, the United Kingdom, and the United States) commitment to take action in response to the legacy of unsafe Russian-built nuclear power plants. The Chernobyl accident in the Ukraine is a constant reminder of the danger to human life and the environment. The European Bank for Reconstruction and Development (EBRD) refused to fund the completion of two nuclear power plants in the Ukraine until it shut down the remaining units at Chernobyl. Countries such as Bulgaria, Hungary, and Slovakia must now decide if they wish to have a nuclear future.[1] However, those decisions are influenced by EU policy. The international nuclear community also has a stake in the outcome, as there is intense competition among American and European nuclear engineering companies for contracts to upgrade and complete nuclear plants in the region.

Of the ten candidate states joining the EU in 2004, eight are nuclear. The EU does not have a policy regarding nuclear power reactor safety because of the divergent policies of nuclear and nonnuclear states. Austria, Greece, Ireland, Denmark, Portugal, and Luxembourg have no nuclear plants. Some member states, for example, Belgium, Spain, Germany, Sweden, and the Netherlands, have declared a phasing out of nuclear power. It remains to be seen whether the current 15 percent of energy derived from nuclear power in the older EU states will decline or increase in the next few years. However, the nuclear industry is lobbying heavily to expand the nuclear sector.

Because CEE states never planned to prematurely close their nuclear plants as a precondition for joining the EU, they are unprepared for the decommissioning, including costs and procedures.

However, as a condition for EU accession, CEE states have pledged to decommission their Russian-designed nuclear plants or upgrade the more modern ones with aid and loans from the EU through Euratom loans and Phare and Tacis programs. Without the prospect of joining the EU, these actions would never have been taken. For example, in October 2002 Lithuania's parliament voted to close the first two units as a precondition for beginning EU negotiations. Bulgaria, because of extensive modifications, is contesting the closing of Kozloduy 3 and 4 but did close units 1 and 2 on December 31, 2002. The upgrading of units 5 and 6 is covered by a loan from the European Bank for Reconstruction and Development. In neighboring Ukraine (which will border on the enlarged EU), the population is demanding the reopening of Chenobyl to provide jobs and electricity.[2] They want the G-7 states to provide promised funds to cover the social impact of Chernobyl. Western states and the EU pledged over $700 million to replace the sarcophagus, which is leaking, but only a small portion has been spent. Local protesters advocated restarting the closed plant if funds were not forthcoming.

The proposed timetable for closing nuclear plants is:

Bulgaria–Kozloduy units 1 and 2 by 2003 and units 3 and 4 no later than 2006

Lithuania–Ignalina 1 by 2005 and Ignalina 2 by 2009

Slovakia–Bohunice VI, unit 1 by 2006 and unit 2 by 2008

Other plants in the Czech Republic, Hungary, Slovakia, and Bulgaria need to be upgraded.

EU Energy Commissioner Loyola de Palacio was more supportive of nuclear power as one of a mix of energy sources to meet Kyoto Protocol goals than is Environment Commissioner Margot Wallstom. That the nuclear energy portfolio has been moved from the environment to the energy commissioner may influence commission policy.

In addition to safety, another concern is that these Russian-designed plants that produce and export electricity to the West will be abandoned just when the demand for electricity will be increasing. Bulgaria and Lithuania could fear their economies would suffer from the closure of these plants.

Energy Policy in Central and Eastern Europe

Building large nuclear power plants to produce electricity was consistent with the former Soviet Union's communist vision of progress. Throughout central and eastern Europe, energy-intensive industries were supported by cheap energy: the higher the energy intensity, the greater the inefficiency in the use of energy, and the higher the energy demand for a given level of output. According to 1996 statistics from the Ministry of Environment, Czech energy intensity was much higher than that in western countries that were members of the Organization for Economic Cooperation and Development (OECD) and one-third higher than that in the United States. The Stalinist model required maximum production levels, and economic incentives encouraged increased energy consumption.[3] The energy sector used from 30 to 50 percent of total industrial investment.[4] The results were distorted economies and overdependence on low energy prices.

Central and eastern European countries paid a high price to the former Soviet Union for their energy. They needed oil and natural gas, for which they paid less than the market price, but in return these nations sold goods to the former Soviet Union at less than market prices. The former Soviet Union controlled the natural gas and oil pipelines and could close them without notice. This power was a type of blackmail, and the regimes in central and eastern Europe took the threat seriously. They could not risk the political instability that could result from a cutoff of oil. Since 1990 these states have actively sought ways to free themselves from energy sources in the former Soviet Union.

The soft brown coal with high sulfur content used in many countries of central and eastern Europe is a source of severe air pollution. The crude mining practices, larger plant size, and absence of desulfurization equipment have led to a catastrophic situation in northern Bohemia in the Czech Republic, an area termed the Black Triangle that extends to the German and Polish borders. Children have been forced to stay home from school because the air is too dangerous to breathe, and cars have been banned from city centers. In the winter, there is permanent smog. Some have argued that it would be beneficial to the environment to substitute nuclear power for coal, thereby reducing harmful air emissions.

The Eastern Movement of Nuclear Power

Nuclear power advocates saw the opportunity and accepted the challenge. The former Soviet Union, with compliance or agreement from the states of central and eastern Europe, had planned dozens of nuclear power plants for the region. Skoda, a Czech company, was named the prime contractor. The success of the Temelin project would now give the Czech electric utility Ceske energeticke zavody (CEZ) and Skoda a future in the modernization of these partially completed plants throughout the area.

The former Soviet Union's monopoly over nuclear reactors in central and eastern Europe has left enormous problems. The reactors are considered to be poorly engineered, lacking many of the safety features mandatory in the West. To restore public confidence in the safety and reliability of nuclear power, foreign assistance was sought to improve safety through the upgrading or closing of these plants located in Bulgaria, the Czech Republic, Hungary, Lithuania, Slovakia, and the Ukraine.

A G-7 summit held in July 1992 focused on the safety of these plants, especially in view of the 1986 Chernobyl disaster. The industrialized states wanted many of them closed, and an emergency plan was developed. "A longer term goal of the assistance program is to shut down the most dangerous nuclear power reactors and replace them with alternative energy sources."[5] Almost $1 billion was pledged by the EU, the International Atomic Energy Agency (IAEA), the OECD, the ERBD, and individual states to develop alternative energy sources and energy efficiency programs. The EU earmarked 4.5 million ECU (European currency units*) in 1990, 3.5 million ECU in 1991, and 20 million ECU in 1992 to update regulations and improve safety and off-site preparedness. Since these funds promised new life to the nuclear industry in the form of orders for new equipment, instrumentation, control systems, and nuclear waste storage facilities, the focus shifted to temporarily increasing the safety of the plants instead of closing them. Indeed, although a few plants have been taken off-line since the collapse of communism, a vast new market benefiting suppliers of nuclear technology has emerged.[6]

One of the major problems encountered by the nuclear industry is grafting western technology onto Russian-designed reactors. Temelin was to be the first such redesign project on a Russian VVER 1,000-megawatt plant. Skeptics were concerned that Russian reactor containment designs cannot be properly retrofitted. A 1993 IAEA study of the VVER 440 and 230 reactor models concluded that the containment structure could not withstand a primary circuit pipe breach.[7] The cooling systems are also inadequate, and the reactors are prone to metal fatigue. Even more recent versions, for example, the 213 model, did not meet western safety standards.

The nuclear industry consulted with Russian nuclear engineers to facilitate western financing of new projects. The irony is that the nuclear industry in the West found itself in the awkward position of supporting the use in eastern Europe of a technology it had criticized only a few years earlier. Plant designs considered too dangerous for the West are still in use in central and eastern Europe. However, Germany closed a former East German VVER 440/213 plant and canceled upgrading a VVER 1000 plant because the government considered them too expensive and problematic to upgrade safely.

The nuclear industry has nevertheless taken steps to move eastward in Europe and to Asia. Nathaniel Woodson, president of Westinghouse, said, "We believe we bring solutions to Central and Eastern Europe and will continue to try to grow our service business outside the U.S. and set new standards in the U.S."[8] Originally, the anticipated market in central and eastern Europe was not new plant construction but upgrading existing Russian-designed plants. But the strategy changed, and the nuclear industry is now poised to develop a new generation of nuclear power reactors if financing can be found.

Sustainable Development and the Environment in the CEE

The most widely used definition of sustainable development is "development that meets the needs of the present without compromising the ability of future generations to meet their own needs."[9] It was popularized by the 1987 UN Brundtland Commission report, *Our Common Future* (see Chapter 1).

---

* At the time, 1 ECU equaled approximately U.S. $1.30.

From Communism to a Free Market

In central and eastern Europe the transition from a centralized economy run by an economic and technocratic elite to one based on free market principles and pluralism has been swift as well as often painful and marked by uncertain policy. The demise of central planning left a vacuum in policy direction. Decisions about energy production, supply, and consumption were made in the absence of environmental criteria. "The application of Marxist ideology in practice led to environmental devastation in all Communist countries but its low point was probably reached in the Czech Republic."[10]

Under communism, environmentalists were labeled right wing because they were accused of trying to destroy socialist dreams by imposing costly demands on the government. After 1992, they were branded left-wing extremists trying to ruin the free market economy by advocating a role for the state in protecting the environment.

One major difference between western democracies and communist systems and states undergoing political transformation is that in the West the public has more opportunities to influence policymaking. Greater public participation encourages problems to surface and solutions to be considered early in the decision-making process. A sustainable development program that includes the environmental impact of energy usage could call on the expertise of interest groups, nongovernmental organizations (NGOs), and the general public, resulting in not only better decisions but also popular support for them.

Embracing Sustainable Development in the Czech Republic

The first postcommunist government of Czechoslovakia (which split into the Czech Republic and Slovakia in 1993) enthusiastically developed policies consistent with principles of sustainable development. Environmental issues had been part of the pre-1989 opposition, and some of the dissidents held government positions. Bedrich Moldan, the Czech environment minister—the Czech and Slovak republics had their own environment ministers—instituted a Green Parliament, which was a forum for environmental interest groups to discuss and recommend proposals. The period was full of optimism and a sense of mission. Influenced by the Brundtland Commission, the new government issued a report, "Concept of State Ecological Policy" (also known as the Rainbow Program), which called for the integration of the environment into all policy sectors. Air and water pollution, solid waste disposal, and the cleanup of highly contaminated areas were given priority.[11]

During that period an environmental code of ethics for business was proposed and endorsed by many. It called for the rational use of natural resources, the internalization of environmental costs, and the establishment of a Czech environmental protection agency. A proposed eco-tax on fossil fuels would provide funds to clean up contaminated areas such as northern Bohemia.[12] The overall strategy was to use economic and financial instruments to change the behavior of the polluters rather than relying on end-of-the-pipe solutions. The national-level Federal Committee for the Environment wanted to make environmental recovery a central concern in the shift to a market economy. Its chair, Josef Vavrousek, raised his committee's activity to the international arena by hosting a pan-European EU-sponsored conference on the environment at Dobris Castle in 1991. The conference produced a notable EU report on the state of Europe's environment, called the "Dobris Assessment," in 1995. Additional conferences followed.

All of this changed following the elections of 1992, which brought to power a new Czech government headed by Vaclav Klaus. The Federal Committee was dismantled, and the Czech Environment Ministry became demoralized while losing political clout. The ministry's dedicated environmentalists were replaced by party stalwarts. There were no monitoring systems or inspection programs to follow up and enforce legislation. Other issues such as crime, inflation, and the Czech-Slovak split replaced the environment on the government agenda, although a majority of people still believed environmental problems were urgent.[13]

The Klaus government ignored the work of the earlier government, focusing instead on free market rationalizations for ignoring the environment. During the preparation of the State Environmental Policy document in 1995, Prime Minister Klaus refused to allow the term "sustainable development" to be used. A ministry official explained that the term was dropped for domestic political reasons, because support of the concept could be perceived as a way for socialists to return to greater state-directed activity.[14] But Klaus wanted to limit any government responsibility for environmental matters. The document stated, "The Czech Republic's environmental policy is conceived as a dynamic approach which will facilitate identifying ecologically, economically, socially and politically optimal policies as opposed to establishing an inflexible system which could hamper economic development and lead to State control."[15] The government's perspective was that environmental problems would be solved in the marketplace and that it was the environmentalists who were the problem.[16] The optimal level of pollution was proclaimed to be whatever was socially acceptable, although few mechanisms existed for determining what that was.

The 1995 State Environmental Policy document referred to the Temelin nuclear facility as a remedy for the air pollution caused by coal-burning units. It also projected that the Czech Republic would achieve a level of environmental quality comparable to that in the countries of western Europe by the year 2005—an unrealistic expectation given the state of the environment and the level of administrative infrastructure, resources, and expertise necessary to realize that goal.

After 1992, NGOs no longer had access to the Environment Ministry, and relations became strained. Some environmental groups discovered they were on a list of extremist NGOs (which included skinheads and anarchists) compiled by the Security Information Services, presumably to discredit them and deny them the opportunity to address the public. According to the government, it was an unofficial list, but environmentalists insisted that their names be removed. In June 1997 the list was given to the police, who apologized and said that the responsible person would be punished. Many of these environmental activists were pre-1989 dissidents but were now labeled enemies of the state.

Perhaps the diminished interest in environmental issues was due to a "lack of social basis for the pursuit of advanced environmental policies typical of the first two years of the 1990s."[17] Czech scholar Petr Jehlicka maintains that the lack of public involvement and information provided by the media and government, as well as the absence of an educated and economically secure middle class, strongly influenced the public perception that environmental concern meant no more than reducing pollution.[18]

Energy Policy in Transition

The government stated it would retire coal-burning plants when Temelin came on-line. However, these plants will still be needed as backup when Temelin is off-line for maintenance and repairs. The closing of coal-burning plants also has the unpopular prospect of increasing unemployment. The Ministry of Industry and Trade has not prepared an energy plan since 1992, although its public statements describe a free market orientation.[19] Its only policy has been to offer subsidies to encourage switching to home electric heating, which has the unfortunate consequence of increasing consumption of electricity.

The Road to Temelin

The Decision to Upgrade

The Temelin nuclear facility was approved in 1978, and in 1981 Czechoslovakia received the designs from the former Soviet Union. Construction started in 1986. It was part of a massive project to build at Temelin four 1,000-megawatt reactors designed in the former Soviet Union, with others to be located throughout Czechoslovakia. Because of the Chernobyl accident, construction was suspended in 1989 pending a review of the reactor design. The government was under pressure to take action due to general concern about the safety of Russian-designed reactors. The plan was scaled back in 1990 for several reasons: the Czech government wanted to use the opportunity to build ties to the West; the Russians could not deliver the designs on schedule; and environmental problems surfaced.

During this period Petr Pithart, the first postcommunist prime minister of the Czech Republic, complained about the lack of information essential to making a decision about the plant's future. He reduced the number of reactors from four to two and tried to initiate a public debate but left the final decision to the next government. In the spring of 1992 new data indicated that energy consumption would not increase substantially from 1989 to 2005. It could have been used to show that Temelin was unnecessary, but the Klaus government, led by the Ministry of Industry and Trade, favored the nuclear facility. Not even the parliament could initiate a public discussion of the issue.

A 1990 analysis by the International Atomic Energy Agency found design flaws in the VVER 1000 and recommended changes, for example, replacement of the instrumentation and control systems and fuel assembly. This provided the rationale for upgrading Temelin. In the fall of 1992 CEZ and Westinghouse signed letters of intent for supplying nuclear fuel and replacing the instrumentation and control systems subject to U.S. Export-Import Bank (Exim Bank) loan guarantees. Halliburton NUS, an American company, completed a probabilistic safety assessment that examined issues such as commercial policy and personnel issues.

In March 1993 CEZ awarded the contract to Westinghouse after two rounds of bidding. Controversy erupted over the bidding process in 1996, when it was revealed that information may have been leaked to Westinghouse about the bids of its competitors, allowing it to enter a second bid that was just under the next lowest bid.[20]

The U.S. Role

U.S. support for Westinghouse's bid to upgrade Temelin was critical. There was intense lobbying by Westinghouse to get the Exim Bank to approve the loan guarantees in support of a seventeen-bank consortium headed by Citibank. For Westinghouse, the goal was to replace Russia as the supplier of nuclear fuel and provide the instrumentation and control systems. CEZ and the Czech Ministry of Industry and Trade told the United States that the Temelin project could lead to additional upgrading contracts. According to U.S. officials, without the support of the Exim Bank, Westinghouse would not have won the contract because other bidders had the support of their governments. The United States told the Czech government that if Westinghouse won the contract, it would encourage increased cooperation between the United States and Czech firms in nuclear and other industries.[21] After the Exim Bank gave preliminary approval in September 1991, the U.S. embassy in Prague assured Czech officials that Westinghouse would have access to competitive financing through the bank for the instrumentation and control systems and the specially designed nuclear fuel assembly. It is clear that both the Czechs and the Americans were interested in making the deal.

At the request of the Exim Bank, the National Security Council began an interagency review of the reactor design and the technical ability of the Czech regulatory authorities to ascertain compliance with U.S. environmental policy. However, the unified procedures established for interagency review of projects were not triggered because the exports for Temelin did not include "the entire nuclear reactor or nuclear steam supply system."[22] An environmental impact assessment of the redesigned Temelin project was therefore never performed.

The Exim Bank's nuclear engineer reviewed the project to assess safety, environmental risks, and feasibility. To learn about Soviet reactors, he relied on U.S. Department of Energy (DOE) reports, IAEA analyses, Czech officials in Prague and Temelin, and a DOE study of VVER reactors. However, officials at IAEA and DOE deny that "any such assessment had actually been made."[23]

Although the Nuclear Regulatory Commission (NRC) did not perform its own evaluation of the reactor design, it lent its support. Temelin opponents alleged that the NRC's cautious report was rewritten to obtain the approval of Vice President Al Gore. Moreover, the Exim Bank consultations with Czech officials were frustrating because the information requested was not freely forthcoming. One bank official complained, "It is absolutely unacceptable to have a situation where we don't get a document or are not otherwise informed of something because we didn't ask exactly the 'right' question in the 'right way.'"[24]

Nevertheless, in March 1994 the Exim Bank's board of directors approved the loan.

Because of lobbying by American and Czech environmental NGOs, as well as by Austria, in both the U.S. Congress and the Czech Republic, Congress decided to investigate the project. By then, more than 1 million Austrians had signed a petition protesting the loan. The Austrian government had offered to pay the Czech government to switch from nuclear power to natural gas at Temelin. It had also called for an environmental impact assessment with public comment, or at least a preliminary safety review—the procedure that would be followed if the reactors were located in Cuba or Mexico. Thirty-two members of the U.S. Congress sent a letter to Kenneth Brody, the Exim Bank chairman, strongly recommending that Temelin be required to meet western health and safety standards as a condition for the loan guarantee.[25]

The House Energy and Commerce Committee began an investigation of the Exim Bank decision in March 1994. Congress expressed concern about potential liability in the event of a nuclear accident, as well as the potential costs of more projects to upgrade Russian plants with American tax dollars. Committee chairman John Dingell was concerned about an information gap, "because the Russians refused to relinquish the documentation with design specifications of the Temelin plant."[26] Dingell requested all communications between the Exim Bank, the Czech Republic, the DOE, the NRC, and Westinghouse concerning safety and cost. He wanted data on the entire project, not just Westinghouse's role; however, the Czech government was unwilling to produce any documents, for example, even about the internal organization of CEZ.[27]

A General Accounting Office (GAO) study was carried out at the request of Dingell's committee, but by the time the report was ready, a new

Republican-led Congress was in place and Dingell was no longer chairman of the Energy and Commerce Committee. The GAO report found the Exim Bank's analysis and actions in reviewing Temelin to be "reasonable." It stated, "U.S. officials strongly supported industry's participation in the Temelin project and worked with Westinghouse and the Czech government to help bring about the acceptance of a U.S. firm for the project."[28] The new committee chairman had no interest in pursuing the matter of safety at Temelin.

Exim Bank officials recommended that in the future "unified nuclear procedures"—which require extensive analysis and an environmental assessment—should be applied to the export of major parts of nuclear power plants, with the participation of relevant U.S. agencies. "The fact that there will be many more nuclear upgrades in the future supports the need for environmental review. . . . In Temelin, there was no procedure and we had to exert a lot of effort to push the other agencies to deal with the issue."[29] The bank said that it would change its internal procedures to address environmental concerns about the components of nuclear plants that do not fall under the State Department's unified nuclear procedures.

On December 3, 1996, the Exim loan guarantee for the consortium was signed at the U.S. embassy in Prague. Rep. Joseph Kennedy, D-Mass., had tried (unsuccessfully) to get a last-minute reversal from the Exim Bank.[30] However, the project had support in the United States—from former president George H. W. Bush, Vice President Gore, the NRC, the DOE, and the State Department—on the grounds that it benefited American competitiveness.

Problems at Temelin

The many delays in the construction of Temelin contributed to an escalation of costs. In 1992 the price tag was estimated at 68 billion Czech crowns (Kc), with half already spent. The projected cost rose to 98.5 billion Kc in 1998, exceeding the financial break-even point established by CEZ and potentially discouraging investors.

Westinghouse asked for increased compensation, claiming it underestimated its charges due to safety and design changes, salary increases, and prolonged labor contracts.[31] CEZ blamed Westinghouse for insisting on about 2,000 design changes—Temelin has gone though its its sixth major round of changes.

CEZ also blamed Skoda for raising prices, but it had no choice but to pay. Other delays had to do with coordinating suppliers and work schedules. CEZ admitted that experts had underestimated the work needed to upgrade the Russian design to meet western standards.[32] A summary of administrative, safety, and technical problems is given in the box in this chapter.

The opening of Temelin was continually postponed. In 1989 it was discovered that less construction than officially claimed had actually been completed. The start-up date was moved from 1992 to 1994, 1995, and 1997. The first unit finally came on-line in October 2000.

Even after the first unit opened, problems continued to plague Temelin, including leaks in the steam supply pipes. The Czech solution used restraints or covers for the pipes that would not meet American or German standards, which required separation by a wall. Other problems surfaced in the nonnuclear system, including improperly fitted safety valves (Russian-designed) and improperly connected welded pipes. Technical problems caused unit 1 to be shut numerous times, and unit 2, launched in May 2002, also experienced many shutdowns for repairs, including replacement of its turboset rotors. Even as recently as May 2003, unit 1 was shut because of a faulty pump, and unit 2, which was in start-up mode since its launch, was in another trial run lasting eighteen months.[33]

Opposition to Temelin

There was little public discussion surrounding the decision to resume construction of Temelin. However, two groups, Hnuti Duha (Rainbow Movement) and the South Bohemian Mothers Against Temelin, developed a small but substantial presence. A newer group, Within Sight of the Temelin Nuclear Power Plant Civic Association, tried to arouse interest in the local community.

Numerous protests against the Temelin plant occurred in the 1990s, especially on the anniversary of the Chernobyl accident. In 1995 former prime minister Pithart was among the demonstrators, and in 1996 the deputy chair of the parliament, Petra Buzkova, joined the protest. Groups such as Children of the Earth, Citizens Against Temelin, and Greenpeace often cooperated. The Austrian Green Party, accompanied by citizens from Germany, Denmark, and Austria, also held demonstrations. Petitions were presented to the government, which made no official response.

Austria has a strong interest in the plant because of Temelin's close proximity to its border. Low-level radiation and the risk of major accidents make location of nuclear power plants a transboundary issue. Austria began lobbying Washington in the early 1990s. The Greens in Austria were vocal in their opposition, gaining political party support. They wanted Austrian government to make the decommissioning of Czech nuclear plants a condition for EU membership. The provincial governor (*Landeshauptmann*) of Upper Austria tried to arouse public awareness of the dangers of nuclear power and supports antinuclear groups.

In 1997 the Provincial Assembly of Upper Austria recommended that the Austrian government propose to the EU the conversion of Temelin to gas or steam, offering an Austrian loan to pay for it. It also established a fund to finance activities to stop Temelin construction, as well as studies on energy conservation and consumption forecasting. Austrians claim that it would be too expensive to bring Temelin into compliance with EU nuclear standards, making the plant unprofitable. Austria stationed a permanent representative in Prague to channel information about safety and cost to the Czech and Austrian governments.

Summary of Administrative, Safety, and Technical Problems at the Temelin Plant

1. Lack of adequate documentation from the Russians necessitating redrawing of designs.
2. Safety goals not well defined. Too many suggestions and insufficient standards to assess degree of change necessary.
3. CEZ underestimated magnitude and complexity of integrating western and Russian technology.
4. Westinghouse had no incentive for timely completion.
5. Inadequate communication and coordination of activities on site and with Westinghouse Pittsburgh headquarters.
6. Russian and American cables were incompatible, requiring total replacement.
7. Russian and American safety codes differed.
8. Russian and American assumptions about equipment capability differed.
9. Westinghouse designs lacked level of detail familiar to Czech workers.
10. Absence of plans for long-term storage of nuclear waste.
11. Westinghouse misplaced two nuclear fuel rods that were found in the airport.
12. State Office of Nuclear Safety inspections revealed some noncompliance with safety standards.
13. Tritium could be released in the Vltava River, which supplies drinking water to Prague.

The Tide Turns

An unusual opportunity to discuss and assess energy policy began in January 1998 following the defeat of the Klaus government in parliament. In a ministerial meeting of the interim government, appointed by President Vaclav Havel, questions were raised about the continued postponement of Temelin and its increasing cost. Martin Bursik, the environment minister, asked that an energy policy concept be prepared consistent with the law requiring an environmental impact assessment. The Ministry of Industry and Trade agreed to present two scenarios—one with increased coal mining and the other with limits to coal but increased energy imports. Environmentalists proposed a third option that included the closing of Temelin. Three public hearings were held, attended by the Czech Senate, environmental NGOs, business groups, CEZ, and the general public. Both the press and television increased coverage of Temelin, focusing on cost and continuing safety problems. Alternatives were debated publicly for the first time.

It is significant that an issue hidden from public scrutiny by prior governments finally emerged in the public arena. The Ministry of Industry and Trade report issued in June 1998, however, reaffirmed plans for the completion of Temelin and discounted the outside analysis it had commissioned, which was more favorable to conservation and renewable energy. It appears that the Social Democratic Party—which won the largest number of votes in the June 1998 elections—was just as committed to the completion of Temelin as the Klaus government was. Nevertheless, it formed a commission in October 1998 to study the situation further, chaired by Deputy Prime Minister Pavel Mertlick. While it examined only fiscal and contractual issues associated with Temelin, focusing on the competitiveness of Temelin, Milôs Kuzvart, the environment minister, hoped to introduce questions concerning reactor safety and the cost of the total nuclear fuel cycle. The report supported the government position to complete Temelin, which was reinforced by a vote of 11–8 in the Cabinet in the spring of 1999.

Government and Regulation

The Czech government has been under pressure to revise the way it has conducted business since 1989. The legacy of past practices lingers, especially when learning takes place "on the job." Many from the old communist elite found ways to stay on in local government and in managerial positions in the new privatized economy.

From 1992 to 1996, the government was preoccupied with the economy and other matters such as education, judicial reform, and privatization. The transformation to a market economy was supposed to be completed by 1996. Former prime minister Klaus convinced the public that the Czech Republic was well on its way to becoming a partner equal to its western neighbors. It joined the OECD in 1995 and was then first in line for EU and NATO membership. It was disappointing, when, in 1997, the currency lost value, banks failed, inflation increased, unemployment grew, and the International Monetary Fund asked that remedial measures be taken. Klaus was a firm believer in leaving the market alone and taking minimal action to intervene in environmental matters.

The Czech government is a coalition, and the leadership of ministries is assigned to political parties according to electoral results. Ministers are not necessarily expert in their area of responsibility, which makes reaching consensus on decisions difficult. The first Environment Ministry was enthusiastic about its mission, compared with later ministries, which produced few new initiatives. The Environment Ministry under Klaus had little influence, but since 1997 it has improved relations with NGOs, giving them more opportunities to present information and analyses.

Regulating industry, specifically the energy industry, is a new task for the Czech government. With little experience in promulgating and enforcing regulations and resistance by those being regulated, the record is poor. The Ministry of Industry and Trade oversees CEZ, but CEZ is primarily state-owned, and there is little incentive to exercise vigorous oversight. Under communism, the party/state was both owner and regulator. Checks and balances were absent because theoretically all parties had similar interests. The administration of the system of fines for environmental pollution prior to 1989 illustrates the lack of interest in enforcing government laws and rules. Penalties were most often waived, or, if not, they were so low that paying the fine was more cost-effective than correcting the problem. "National Committees" responsible for administering the fines were notorious for forgiving them. There was little incentive to observe laws and regulations.[34] The Environment Inspectorate established in 1992 to exercise oversight of potential polluters has had few resources and powers to do the job.

In February 1998 CEZ shareholders asked that the roles of managing director and chairman of the CEZ board be separated and that members of the supervisory and management boards be changed. The Ministry of Industry and Trade, which is the majority shareholder, now has a representative on the CEZ board, along with the CEZ director. The supervisory board members were reduced to six from eleven. The goal was to increase state control of CEZ and oversight over Temelin construction.

EU Membership as a Force for Change

The prospect of becoming a full partner in the EU has been a catalyst for change in the Czech Republic. As part of the accession process, the Czech Republic had to demonstrate that it adopted European Community legislation. Environmental and energy legislation presented the greatest challenges. Although there will be financial burdens, for which EU programs can cover only a small portion, there will also be advantages for the countries of central and eastern Europe, such as trade and business opportunities and greater political security and stability. A few specific areas are worth noting:

- Sustainable development has become an integral component of EU policy. The Czech Republic had to incorporate the concept into its environmental and energy programs and planning.
- Although the EU has been unable to agree on a nuclear energy policy, it has adopted standards for worker health and exposure to ionizing radiation. The nuclear plants at Temelin and Dukovany must be brought up to EU and international safety standards.
- Energy pricing must now be competitive, consistent with EU policy. Price subsidies, an obstacle to competitiveness and conservation of energy, must be eliminated. The Czech government must undertake legislative reform and encourage energy-saving technology. According to Deputy Energy Minister Miroslav Tvrznik, Czech policies are out of line with EU directives. "Only the expanded support of effective energy use and the development of alternative sources of energy in the Czech Republic can help us reach a comparable level of energy source utilization." [35]
- Access to documents and the transparency of decision making must be improved. The Free Access to Information Act proposed in 1992

was passed May 11, 1999. In June 1998 an environmental right-to-know act was passed. Access to environmental information is essential for public input into government policymaking.

• More than one hundred environmental regulations have been issued in the Czech Republic, half of them since 1989. However, most need better implementation. Existing legislation in the field of chemicals and water is inadequate.

By 2000, the conflict over Temelin switched from a domestic debate to the international arena in the context of EU enlargement. Protests from Germany and Austria increased when Temelin was launched in October 2000, with blockades of the Czech/Austrian border at various sites. Austrian protesters fueled by the Freedom Party, led by Jörg Haider, demanded that Austria veto the closing of the energy chapter of the *acquis communautaire*, thereby preventing the Czech Republic from joining the EU unless it closed Temelin.[36] The Austrian government said it would lobby the fifteen EU states' parliaments as well. The Austrians, as inhabitants of a nuclear free state, claimed they had the right to protect their citizens against a potential threat. Relations between Austria and the Czech Republic became strained. In December 2000 the EU enlargement commissioner volunteered to serve as a mediator, and a process began that included hearings in both countries, an EIA completed by the Czech government, and an expert trilateral mission to assess safety issues. The Czech Republic agreed to establish a hotline between the two countries to exchange information. On November 21, 2001, the heads of government of Austria and the Czech Republic signed an agreement, concluding the Melk process. (Melk is the city in which the document was signed.) The Czechs agreed to improve security at Temelin. The commission report stated that after examination of the environmental impacts on soil, water, minerals, climate, and health, damage was not probable. This was the only case in the EU where a finished project was assessed using an EIA.

The European Council directed that a Report on Nuclear Safety in the Context of Enlargement be undertaken on all candidate states. The report, issued in June 2001, assessed nuclear safety and made recommendations. Regarding Temelin, the report recommended greater protection against breakage of pipes and failures in steam and feed-water lines and also suggested improvements in safety and relief valve functioning.[37] This cleared the way (in late 2001) for Austria to cease its opposition to the closing of the energy chapter in the accession negotiations, although the far-right Freedom Party maintained its anti-Temelin stance.

Prior to the December 2002 Copenhagen summit that voted on EU enlargement, Austria wanted to attach a proposal regarding Temelin to the Czech Accession Treaty, making the Melk Protocol subject to the European Court of Law. Without an EU nuclear policy and with the influence of nuclear states, the attempt failed. One likely concern was that such a step might put other nuclear plants under European Court jurisdiction, with possible lawsuits by antinuclear groups. The right-wing Freedom Party and Social Democrats argued that without enforcement the Melk agreement was meaningless.

Austrian chancellor Wolfgang Scheussel and Czech prime minister Vladimir Spidla did agree on a declaration to be attached to the Treaty for Czech Accession pledging the fulfillment of the Melk agreement. It will remain a bilateral agreement, not part of international law. The situation of nuclear power in the EU remains unchanged; there are no EU-wide standards on nuclear power plant safety, and therefore standards continue to vary among states.

Building Democracy and Environmental Protection through Public Participation

When democratic attributes such as public participation are compared in the countries of central and eastern Europe, similar deficiencies may be traced to the influence of Soviet political and bureaucratic structures and patterns of interaction. Nevertheless, one must keep in mind that these states have distinctive histories and cultures that temper the Soviet influence. Much of the reluctance to participate directly in politics can be traced to the dearth of real opportunities for public involvement prior to 1989. While bodies such as the National Committees theoretically involved the public in local administration, there was also an absence of electoral competition and public input.[38] The "highly centralized structure of the state itself" was constraining.[39] In fact, individuals were punished if they challenged or questioned government decisions. The public was discouraged from making demands on their leaders because the state, in theory, provided for their needs. There were no means to link people to their leaders other than through the Communist Party.

The public therefore lacked experience in civic life, including membership in intermediary organizations such as NGOs and political parties. Information was the property of the technical elites, and criticism was denied to citizens. General apathy and passiveness were pervasive; people appeared content and remained withdrawn from public life.

Some experts on central and eastern Europe, such as scholars Keith Crawford and Piotr Sztompka, point out the difficulty of changing this political culture.[40] Since the political transformation of 1989, the average Czech has been preoccupied with economic issues. Membership in political parties or NGOs is still low; political parties are still considered a dirty business.[41] The problem is how to create political efficacy so that the public has the resources and motivation to play an active role in the policymaking process. Unfortunately, there is still a reluctance to seek information or challenge authorities.

Accountability

The hierarchical government structure originating in the Austro-Hungarian empire and reinforced under communist rule not only discouraged public participation but also influenced bureaucratic behavior. Bureaucrats were not regarded as public servants but as servants of the state. Bureaucratic accountability meant that no one took responsibility.[42] Administrators could be severely disciplined, even at the local level, for a small deviation, so a poor decision that did not have the intended result could be costly for the decision maker. Administrators disliked making decisions for which they might be blamed and held accountable. Therefore, most orders were passed orally, with no written record. The reluctance to take responsibility for actions was typical of the communist legacy and is a continuing problem.

Since 1989, people have been encouraged to take responsibility for themselves, yet the policymaking process does not provide sufficient opportunities to make decisions about their future. People hesitate to become involved in problems they do not believe they can solve or assess properly because of a lack of expertise, for example, the building of a nuclear plant. A poll by the Institute for Public Opinion Research in Prague in 1993 and 1995 indicated that a majority of people trusted the government to make the right decision on nuclear power.[43] (Those under twenty-nine and over sixty were more distrustful than the other age groups.) Ironically, 65 percent also agreed with demonstrators supporting environment protection! Because most information is still controlled by the government, it is difficult to make independent judgments without countervailing facts. Even some academic elites do not feel qualified to have an opinion about nuclear power because it is outside their particular expertise.

Accessibility of Information

Another study of attitudes in central Europe reported that the Czech people are dissatisfied with the amount and quality of information, which lacks policy alternatives. These attitudes are consistent throughout Hungary, Poland, Russia, Slovakia, and Ukraine.[44] Without information, the public is precluded from playing a role in shaping issues and defining the government agenda. Authorities may be threatened by the potential creation of alternative centers of power that challenge bureaucratic decisions. Without an active political culture, bureaucratic expertise remains a valuable tool for keeping the public at a distance.

The few avenues for public input to policymaking are inadequate. There is a legal requirement to conduct environmental impact assessments, but the period for public comment is very short. Citizens are excluded from participating in the critical early stages of decision making.[45] Permits for nuclear power plant construction are approved at the district level, but the central government appoints the head of the district, and the citizens cannot veto this official's decisions. From the government's perspective, public participation slows decision making. This attitude reinforces the reluctance of the public to learn about issues, especially technically complex issues such as nuclear power.

The media could have a role in providing public input but so far have proved timid. The implementation of freedom of information laws has been slow. Most newspapers give an account of events but do little investigative reporting. They cover government actions with little analysis, tending instead to present different ideological interpretations of the same events. Journalists may fear embarrassing the government. Television gives ample opportunity for political talk, but too often interviewers fail to ask probing questions, and government officials use the opportunity to address the public without debating each other on issues.

The Relationship between Czech Political Culture and Temelin

Political culture involves attitudes, values, and beliefs about political institutions and practices. The Czech political culture described in the previous section influenced policymaking at Temelin as follows:

- The low level of information about nuclear power contributed to the belief that it was safe. Some residents near the Dukovany nuclear power plant do not respond to alarms because they say they cannot see any pollution. The public has been unable to challenge government pronouncements about safety at the Temelin plant. The public is unaware of alternative energy resources that would be compatible with sustainable development while reducing air pollution in northern Bohemia. Information was not used to shape public opinion and encourage public interest and debate.
- The media often discredit NGOs and protest activity, giving minimum coverage to their activities. Television showed foreigners at a Temelin demonstration to raise questions about the power plant's legitimacy. The media have begun to challenge this complacency and increase public debate. In the spring of 1998, for example, the future of Temelin was finally explored on television with discussion from representatives of government ministries, CEZ, and other experts.
- The lack of public debate left decision making to special stakeholders such as bureaucrats. Public activity is considered an impediment to government decisions. Even the parliament never debated the decision to complete Temelin. The lack of communication among members of the parliament, NGOs, scientists, researchers, professional associations, and bureaucrats inhibits sharing of information and, consequently, the development of a civil society.
- Local governments were not involved in the licensing process for Temelin. Communities were denied an opportunity for public discussion even after requests were made to the central government. Local authorities' opinions were not considered. The decision to grant a construction license was approved by the state office, which evaluated only the building plans and not the environmental impact of the plant.

- The lack of individual responsibility within the organization's decision-making hierarchy contributed to delays at Temelin. Difficulties in obtaining clearance or approval on highly technical issues potentially can compromise safety levels if decisions are made under pressure and without proper oversight.
- Administrative practices and rules were loosely enforced. There is a poor history of monitoring and implementing environmental legislation. Nuclear energy technology requires a high level of safety and low levels of risk and uncertainty, with a decision structure that provides for extensive monitoring, oversight, and redundancy.
- Because discussion of the decision to continue construction of Temelin was suppressed, with government officials refusing to engage in open debate, the potential for latent conflict remains. "There existed no legitimate alternative political grouping able to offer a fresh approach to dealing with a particular problem such as the environment, and the leadership was thus trapped and prevented from seeking solutions to the worsening ecological situation."[46] The NGOs are weak, with low membership and few resources. Except for the Rainbow Movement, most have dropped Temelin from their agendas.
- Temelin was consistent with the practice of building grandiose projects, which symbolically reinforced loyalty to the state. However, if Temelin turns into an unprofitable financial and environmental liability, without public debate to legitimize the decision to continue construction, it could become the center of a future political conflict.
- The attitude that there is an objective nonpolitical solution to Temelin that is best made by experts ignores the political aspects of a conflict. It is as if the truth were waiting to be found by a divine expert. According to this view, the public should not have a role in decision making on a technical issue, and the government should not ask them. Some decision makers lack the understanding that participants in any conflict have particular biases and that any decision will reflect those biases as well as the objective analysis.

Despite all of this, it is also true that the Czech political culture is undergoing a transformation. Many Czechs want closer ties with western Europe. The adjustment will not be easy; beliefs and attitudes that worked well in the past are slow to change. According to eastern European scholar Klaus von Beyme, the peaceful revolution of 1989 led by "intellectuals and their followers" did not transform political systems.[47] There is still a lack of trust between authorities, accompanied by a low level of political efficacy. As people become more familiar with democratic forms of political activity, they will begin to challenge existing bureaucratic/technocratic elites.

Concepts such as "sustainability" are new to the Czech Republic. But the issue is not just the difference between a communist system or a free market system; serious environmental problems such as air pollution plague both economic systems, and both discount environmental criteria in their decision making. Sustainability requires group or collective action with a concern for the public interest; it is future oriented. Sustainable development can succeed only if public support emerges and Czechs participate more fully in civil society. Public participation transfers legitimacy to sustainability. But the discredited planning legacy of the past may also have to be revitalized to develop environmental policies consistent with the principle of sustainability. Planning and public input can be compatible, but this requires an educated and informed public willing to make the investment. The challenge for the Czech government is to develop an energy policy that is consistent with sustainable environmental goals in a democracy that includes a greater role for the public through a variety of participatory mechanisms.

A public debate finally began in 1998, providing an opportunity for citizens to engage in a political discussion of the problems associated with nuclear power as well as coal burning from a long-term perspective. Comprehensive review and planning could produce an energy policy with a diverse mix of sources, including renewable energy and conservation. However, the Social Democratic minister of industry and trade announced the continuation of construction of Temelin, rejecting further analysis of cost-effectiveness and safety, and in October 1998, without informing other ministers, he proposed building more nuclear plants. His threat to resign if Temelin was not completed on time was ignored by Prime Minister Milôs Zeman. As of 2004 the government was still floating proposals to expand Temelin and build more nuclear power plants. The development of an energy policy compatible with sustainable development is still in the future.

Former prime minister Pithart summarized the dilemma: "The construction of Temelin does not only change our attitude to energy saving, nature, and our health; it changes the whole social, economic, and political climate. With Temelin producing energy on a large scale, we are closer to a centralized, strong state and further away from regions, municipalities, and from citizens. . . . With Temelin, 'small is beautiful' is not valid, the statement which is valid says 'huge is also powerful.'"[48]

Notes

This chapter is based on work supported by the National Science Foundation under Grant No. SBR-9708180. Any opinions, findings, and conclusions or recommendations expressed in this chapter are the author's and do not reflect the views of the National Science Foundation. The author wishes to thank Petr Jehlicka for his helpful and insightful comments on this chapter and Stanislava Hybnerova for her enthusiastic support for the project.

1. *Financial Times*, February 27, 1997.
2. Associated Press, December 17, 2002.
3. For a discussion of energy policy in central and eastern Europe, see Peter Rutland, "Energy Rich, Energy Poor," *Transition* 3, no. 9 (1996): 5; and John M. Kramer, "Energy and the Environment in Eastern Europe," in *To Breathe Free*, ed. Joan DeBardeleben (Washington, D.C.: Woodrow Wilson Center, 1991), 57–79.

4. Janusz Cofala, "Energy Reform in Central and Eastern Europe," *Energy Policy* 22 (1994): 486.
5. "Nuclear Safety: International Assistance Efforts to Make Soviet Designed Nuclear Reactors Safer," General Accounting Office, *Report to Congressional Requesters,* GAO/RECD, 94–234, September 1994, 1.
6. Colin Woodard, "Western Vendors Move East," *Transition* 17 (November 1995): 24.
7. Ibid.
8. *Nucleonics Week,* December 14, 1995, 4.
9. World Commission on Environment and Development, *Our Common Future* (London and Oxford: Oxford University Press, 1987), 43.
10. Petr Jehlicka and Jan Kara, "Ups and Downs of Czech Environmental Awareness and Policy: Identifying Trends and Influences," in *Protecting the Periphery: Environmental Policy in Peripheral Regions of the European Union,* ed. Susan Baker, Kay Milton, and Steven Yearly (London: Frank Cass, 1994), 154. See also Barbara Jancar-Webster, "Environmental Politics in Eastern Europe in the 1980s," in DeBardeleben, *To Breathe Free,* 25–56; and Andrew Tickle and Ian Welsh, eds., *Environment and Society in Eastern Europe* (New York: Longman, 1998).
11. Richard Andrews, "Environmental Policy in the Czech and Slovak Republics," in *Environment and Democratic Transition: Policy and Politics in Central and Eastern Europe,* ed. Anna Vari and Pal Tamas (Dordrecht, Netherlands: Kluwer Academic Publishers, 1995), 28.
12. Ibid., 31.
13. "Status of National Environmental Action Programs in Central and Eastern Europe," *Country Reports* (Szentendre, Hungary: Regional Environmental Center, May 1995), 43.
14. Brian Slocock, "Paradoxes of Environmental Policy in Eastern Europe: The Dynamics of Policy-making in the Czech Republic," *Environmental Politics* 5 (autumn 1996): 513.
15. "State Environmental Policy." Document approved by the Government of the Czech Republic, Ministry of the Environment, August 23, 1995.
16. For an excellent discussion of environmental policy in the Czech Republic, see Bedrich Moldan, "Czech Republic," in *The Environmental Challenge for Central European Economies in Transition,* ed. Jurg Klarer and Bedrich Moldan (West Sussex, England: Wiley, 1998), 107–130.
17. Petr Jehlicka, "The Development of Czech Environmental Policy in the 1990s: A Sociological Account" (paper presented at the Summer Symposium of the University of Bologna, July 1997), 14.
18. Ibid., 12–14.
19. "Energy Policy of the Czech Republic," draft, Ministry of Industry and Trade, April 24, 1996, 2.
20. Czech News Agency (CTK), May 11, 1996; and *Prague Post,* June 5, 1996.
21. "Nuclear Safety: U.S. Assistance to Upgrade Soviet-Designed Nuclear Reactors in the Czech Republic," Report to the Ranking Minority Member, Committee on Commerce, House of Representatives, GAO, June 1995, 4–5.
22. Ibid., 7.
23. S. Jacob Scherr and David Schwarzbach, "Turning Points," *Amicus Journal* (winter 1995): 14.
24. "Nuclear Safety," 11.
25. *East European Reporter,* March 25, 1994.
26. *Energy Daily,* March 17, 1994.
27. *Nucleonics Week,* March 17, 1994, 3.
28. "Nuclear Safety," 1.
29. Ibid., 12.
30. *Prague Post,* December 18, 1996.
31. *Prague Post,* January 14, 1998.

32. *Nucleonics Week,* August 24, 1995.
33. CTK, May 20, 2003.
34. For an excellent description of environmental policy administration, see Andrews, "Environmental Policy in the Czech and Slovak Republics," 5–48.
35. "An Interview with M. Tvrznik, Deputy Minister at the Ministry of Industry and Trade," *Energy,* English Supplement, June 1997, 5.
36. For a comprehensive analysis of the Austrian opposition to the Temelin nuclear power plant, see Michael Getzner, *Nuclear Policies in Central Europe* (Frankfurt am Main: Peter Lang Gmbh, Europäischer Verlag der Wissenschaften, 2003).
37. Commission of the European Communities 2001 Regular Report on the Czech Republic's Progress toward Accession, SEC (2001) 1746, Brussels, 13.11.2001,73.
38. Kenneth Davy, "The Czech and Slovak Republics," in *Local Government in Eastern Europe: Democracy at the Grasssroots,* ed. Andrew Coulson (Lyme, N.H.: Edward Elgar, 1995), 41.
39. Adam Fagin and Petr Jehlicka, "Sustainable Development in the Czech Republic: A Doomed Process?" *Environmental Politics* 7 (spring 1998): 119.
40. Keith Crawford, *East Central European Politics Today* (New York: St. Martin's, 1996); and Piotr Sztompka, "The Intangibles of the Transition to Democracy," *Studies in Comparative Communism* 24, no. 3 (1991).
41. Z. Vajdova, "Politicka kultura lokalnich politickych elit: srovnani ceskeho a vychodonemeckeho mesta," (Political Culture of Local Political Elites: A Comparison of Czech and East German Cities), Working Papers, Institute of Sociology, Academy of Sciences of the Czech Republic, 97:3, 1997, 38.
42. Jehlicka and Kara, "Ups and Downs of Czech Environmental Awareness and Policy," 156.
43. CTK, November 29, 1995.
44. "Security for Europe Project," Final Report, Center for Foreign Policy Development, Thomas J. Watson Institute for International Studies, Brown University, December 1993.
45. Fagin and Jehlicka, "Sustainable Development in the Czech Republic," 120.
46. Adam Fagin, "Environment and Transition in the Czech Republic," *Environmental Politics* 3 (autumn 1994): 481.
47. Klaus von Beyme, *Transition to Democracy in Eastern Europe* (New York: St. Martin's, 1996), 41.
48. *Listy* 5 (1994).

Index